Write It Review
A Process Approach
to College Essays, with Readings

Revised Fifth Edition

Linda Strahan
Kathleen Moore

University of California, Riverside

Kendall Hunt
publishing company

Cover image © Shutterstock, Inc.

Kendall Hunt
publishing company

www.kendallhunt.com
Send all inquiries to:
4050 Westmark Drive
Dubuque, IA 52004-1840

Copyright © 2006, 2007, 2009, 2015, 2018 by Kendall Hunt Publishing Company

ISBN 979-8-7657-7733-6

Published in the United States of America

Contents

Part 2 WRITING ASSIGNMENTS   85

Assignment #6: "The Protestant Work Ethic: Just Another 'Urban Legend'?" by Jonathan Klemens 385

Assignment #7: "The American Paradox" by Michael Pollan 439

Assignment #8: Arguments in Literature: "The Nightingale and the Rose" by Oscar Wilde 505

Part 3 CASE STUDIES 551

Acknowledgments

This text is in many ways a collaborative effort, so we wish first of all to thank the faculty of the University of California Writing Program for their inspiring ideas and contributions. For this edition we wish to acknowledge in particular Benedict Jones, for his commitment, tenacity, and perspicacity in producing the final version of the manuscript. We also want to recognize the Kendall Hunt people who worked on this project, especially the managerial and supervisory efforts of Natalie White and Katie Celarek for this reprinted edition. Their reliable and professional support has been indispensable and much appreciated. Our interaction with Kendall Hunt has been a great pleasure.

A Note on Writing

Some say writing is challenging. Others have used the word "hard." Very few have suggested that writing is easy. Sometimes people will romanticize the act of writing, saying that authors like William Shakespeare or Frederick Douglass simply sat down and watched the words form on the page in a fit of passion and intellectual energy. While that image is enchanting, it belies what is much more common and more likely in these great authors. Writing is hard. One must stare at the blank page. One is humbled in the moment, thinking about what message or idea that may be communicated if there is, indeed, a message to be communicated.

I know of no writer, regardless of how skilled or unskilled, who can sit in front of a computer screen and simply write. We all struggle to find the right words, the right grammar, and the right ideas. We may be at different skill levels, but we all have these struggles to endure, and that means we all share in this difficult process of writing. When we write, we belong to a community of writers. Sitting before a screen and typing out one's thoughts demands much in terms of courage, tenacity, and intellect.

Even in the midst of these many challenges writing presents, the act of writing is vitally important to each person. Survey after survey of CEOs reveals how critical the skill of writing is in getting and retaining a position in a company. Advancement is often tethered to writing, and companies in the Fortune 500 have even relied on writing tests and on demand writing to determine which candidates are to be recruited. To be sure, on demand writing in particular is a skill that serves those in companies well on a daily basis. Emails, reports, and memos regularly need to be drafted in the moment, and a reliance on others (or even Artificial Intelligence) cedes the authority over the document and may even result in consequential inaccuracies. Such professional writing is hard because it requires attention to detail, a keen eye for organization, and a strong understanding of the language at the sentence level.

Writing is a means to a voice, and it enables you to have something represent you and you alone when you are not physically present. That seemingly simple act is radical and defies space, time, and even mortality. To use that voice, though, you need to access the language in ways that can be interpreted by others. That activity is hard and requires thoughtful attention, even recursive attention to the language.

Writing is hard. Joining a community of writers, *which you are doing*, is also worthy of your greatest efforts.

Preface

The goal of *Write It Review* is to reinforce the academic reading and writing skills you learned in *Write It*. Each section of *Write It Review*, just as in *Write It*, helps you develop a range of writing strategies. As you are guided through the writing process, you learn how to use each stage to maximize its benefits. Using the strategies this book teaches will help you strengthen the confidence and understanding you need to write effective academic essays. As you work through the assignments and exercises in *Write It Review*, be sure to complete all the activities, and give special attention to activities devoted to building reading comprehension and idea development skills. If you have already worked through *Write It*, you likely have adjusted some of the stages in the writing process to suit your own methods and approaches to writing assignments; however, it is important that you reassess the process you are using. In this way, you will focus on areas that need improvement and thereby maximize the potential of *Write It Review*.

As you work through the writing process for each assignment, remember the series of skills we introduced in *Write It* that are necessary for producing a successful essay: focused reading, critical thinking, careful analysis, marshaling of evidence, drafting and editing. *Write It Review*'s exercises will guide you through each stage in the production of an essay, and will encourage you to practice each skill, one stage at a time. As you go through the writing process step by step, remember that writing is always a recursive activity and when you begin a paper you may not always begin at step one with your topic and proceed in a linear way, one step at a time, to proofreading. As you move through the guiding exercises *Write It Review* provides, new ideas will come to you. Don't set these discoveries aside, but carry them forward into the remaining exercises. As you relate old and new information, you will explore each assignment's topic from several angles so that your ideas will build on one another. In this way the steps, though done in isolation, will come together in a unified perspective. The organization of this book is intended to help reinforce your understanding of essay-building as a process not a formula, the stages as necessary steps to internalize until each becomes an intuitive part of writing itself.

Write It Review's activities, exercises, and assignments will be familiar to those of you who have used *Write It*. The book is organized to guide you through each stage in the writing process, each unit beginning with a central reading and then moving through a sequence for essay development, from "Questions to Guide Your Reading," to "Questions to Guide Your Writing." A peer draft review form and a personal assessment form will help you revise and edit your essay. You will also find class discussion and homework activities that reinforce grammar, comprehension, and critical thinking skills. Following the assignment units is a section that contains student essays, and you will be able to read and evaluate the essays other students have written in response to similar essay topics. Like *Write It, Write It Review* is designed to encourage you not just to become a writer of college essays, but also to become a reader and writer in college. We hope that, as you become a proficient college writer, and exchange ideas with others in the academic community, you will both shape and be shaped by that community. Your experiences are unique to you, and your writing will reflect the knowledge you've accumulated from those experiences as you engage with others in defining the world in which we all live.

Here Is How to Use This Skill-Building Book

Write It Review is presented in three parts.

Part 1: BASIC INFORMATION AND DOCUMENTATION that presents information and guidance for completing reading and writing assignments in your English classes. Included in Part 1 are:

- A Step-by-Step Strategy for Reading Thoughtfully
- A Reminder of the Definitions of Plagiarism and Copyright Infringement
- A Review of the Resources in a Handbook
- A Review of the Argument Essay Structure and Two Alternative Structures
- A Strategy for Writing a Timed Essay
- A Review of the Elements of the Conventional Argument Essay.
- A Review of an Introduction in an Argument Essay
- A Review of the Guidelines for Writing a Directed Summary
- Strategies for Developing Your Ideas
- Writing Supporting Paragraphs for Your Thesis Statement
- A Review of Logical Fallacies
- Transitions
- Conclusions
- Strategies for Participating in a Rough Draft Workshop
- A Sample Scoring Rubric
- Finding and Using Arguments in Literature
- Proofreading Your Essay for Mistakes in Grammar, Punctuation, and Mechanics
- Grammar Diagnostic Tests and Self-Assessment Forms

Part 2: EIGHT ASSIGNMENT UNITS that contain a central essay to read and analyze and a writing assignment to respond to with your own essay. For each of these, the book will lead you through the writing process as you:

- read for comprehension and learn to recognize and evaluate a writer's argument.
- develop your own position and supporting evidence.
- organize your ideas into an effective essay structure.
- revise and edit for coherence and clarity.

- incorporate supplemental readings to expand and broaden the scope and complexity of your essay response.
- participate in class discussion activities at the end of each supplemental reading selection.

Part 3: CASE STUDIES that provide student writing examples to highlight strategies other students have used to construct essays. This section gives you an opportunity to practice applying criteria from the scoring rubric to evaluate others' essays. By evaluating the writing of others, you will become better at evaluating your own writing.

The step-by-step lessons in this skill-building workbook will provide you with a strong foundation for good writing. The book's techniques have been widely tested and proven successful. In a recent survey on our campus, students awarded first place in their success on an important writing exam to the lessons in this book. We are confident that this book will work for you, too.

Basic Information

Part 1 of *Write It Review* is designed to be used as a writing reference section. We advise you to work through it carefully. It contains many of the basic strategies and conventions for academic writing. As such, you can rely on many of its basic elements to complete academic writing assignments in any discipline. For your purposes in this course, however, the strategies and information in this section should be practiced as fundamental writing strategies that you will be asked to apply in completing Part 2's essay assignments. We urge you to turn back frequently to Part 1 as you work on the essays in Part 2; these pages will support your prewriting, drafting, and revising as you move through the writing process, and they will supplement and reinforce the writing support pages in each of the units in Part 2.

The information in Part 1 is organized around the stages of the writing process and includes guidance on building each of the conventional essay parts that come together to form the essay's overall structure.

Part 1 contains the following information:

A Review of Some Basic Guidelines

> A Step-by-Step Strategy for Reading Thoughtfully
> A Reminder of the Definitions of Plagiarism and Copyright Infringement
> A Review of the Resources in a Handbook
> A Review of the Argument Essay Structure and Two Alternatives
> A Review of Strategies for Writing a Timed Essay

A Review of the Elements of the Conventional Argument Essay

> A Review of an Introduction in an Argument Essay
> A Review of the Guidelines for Writing a Directed Summary
> Strategies for Developing Your Ideas
> Writing Supporting Paragraphs for Your Thesis Statement
> A Review of Logical Fallacies
> Transitions
> Conclusions
> Strategies for Participating in a Rough Draft Workshop
> A Sample Scoring Rubric

A Review of Basic Information

A Step-by-Step Strategy for Reading Thoughtfully

Students tell us that one of the most challenging aspects of working through this book and writing successful essays is the reading selections. Most of these readings are not particularly difficult to read, nor are they overly long. The difficulty lies in fully comprehending the arguments they contain. Because each of the writing topics in Part 2 asks you to respond to a particular reading selection, it will be important for you to spend some time with the reading. Work through it several times until you fully understand the writer's central argument and are able to identify the argument's supporting evidence. Until that understanding is reached, you will not be able to respond appropriately in your own essay.

We all read—on a daily basis and without much effort—common things such as signs, text messages, e-mails, and menus without thinking about them very much. In an academic setting, however, reading becomes an activity that requires effort and thought. Use the steps below to ensure that your reading is focused and productive.

1. **Consider the title given to the material you are to read.**
   It should suggest a particular topic or issue. Think about what you already know about the topic. Think about what else you need to know about the topic in order to have an informed opinion about it. Look at the title again and ask yourself what its wording suggests about the writer's opinion and perhaps his or her reason for writing about the topic.

2. **Learn about the author.**
   If biographical information about the writer is presented with the reading, look for biographical information that may have influenced the content and perspective of the reading. Sometimes you can better evaluate a writer's argument by taking into account his or her level of expertise or personal connection to the subject of the essay.

3. **Read through the material once quickly.**
   This first rapid reading gives you an overview of the subject, the writer's attitude toward the subject, and the nature of the supporting evidence that the reading contains.

4. **Read again to identify the thesis.**

For your second reading, you need a pen or highlighter and not just your eyes. Your first task on the second reading is to find and mark the thesis. The thesis states the writer's position on the topic. Often, it is contained in a single sentence, but, in some cases, it takes several sentences to make clear the point of the work. There are times when the writer does not state his or her thesis explicitly, but you should be able to state it after reading through the essay once. You might want to note the thesis in the margin.

5. **Read slowly and methodically through the rest of the material.**

Each paragraph has a topic sentence that expresses the main point of the paragraph. The topic sentence is usually found at the beginning of the paragraph, but it can be anywhere within the paragraph. You should note the point (or topic sentence) of each paragraph as you work through your second reading. The remainder of the paragraph contains evidence to support the topic sentence. While you read, your job is to evaluate this evidence for its logic and validity. For future reference, you may find it useful to make comments in the margins regarding the strength and weakness of the paragraph's evidence.

6. **Read again for review.**

Now that you have thought through the ideas and evidence supporting the ideas in your reading, read the whole thing again. Watch for any anomalies—statements or points that don't fit with your overall understanding of the material. If you find any, take time to determine whether the material is the writer's error or a misreading on your part. You may find that you need to go back to Step 4 and begin working through the reading again. Once you are certain that your reading is accurate, you are prepared to discuss, summarize, and respond to the reading with your own essay.

Look over the following essay and notice the way that one writer used *Write It Review*'s guidelines to underline main ideas and make notations in the margins. These notes help identify the essay's argument and supporting details.

An Example

Do Women in Politics Face a Glass Ceiling?

LIZ CHADDERDON POWELL

Liz Chadderdon Powell is vice president of political strategies with BatesNiemand, Inc., a Democratic consulting firm in Washington, DC. This reading selection originally appeared in Winning Campaigns Magazine.

From *Winning Campaigns*, March 19, 2007 by Liz Chadderdon. Copyright © 2007 by Liz Chadderdon. Reprinted by permission.

Is there a glass ceiling for women in the political consulting industry? (**This is a rhetorical question that the thesis statement will answer.**)

(**This is introductory material.**) Whenever an article is written about the professional glass ceiling for women, men get jumpy. They defensively point to articles written about women sportscasters interviewing male football players in the locker room, female soldiers fighting alongside their male counterparts, and wives outearning their husbands. They usually say this with a look on their face clearly saying, "C'mon, what more do you want?" (**The thesis statement has to be inferred: For women, there is a glass ceiling in politics. So the answer to the opening rhetorical question is "yes," in Powell's opinion.**)

(**Here is the Controlling Idea Sentence.**) There are plenty of examples of women succeeding in traditionally male-dominated professions. (**The next two sentences are Careful Description Statements defining "success" in terms of how the writer is using the term.**) But let's define success as actually running the company, the corporation, or even the country. You know—the good jobs with the power and sweet paychecks. (**The next five sentences are Corroborating Details.**) There are nineteen female CEOs running Fortune 500 companies. This sounds good until you remember there are 500 companies in the Fortune 500 (thus the name) and women only run nineteen of them. That is only 3.8%. And then there are the celebrated seventy-four women in Congress. Seventy-four seems applause-worthy unless you count all 535 seats in both the House and Senate. That means women hold only 13.8% of Congress while being 52% of the voting population of America. (**This final sentence is the Connection Sentence that ties back to and supports the thesis.**) We may have come a long way, baby, but we still have a very long way to go before we have an equal share of the real power in this country. (**This paragraph is compelling—probably because it uses all four of the 4Cs.**)

(**Here is the Controlling Idea, but "that" is a bit unclear. A noun would have been clearer, especially as the sentence is the first in a new paragraph and the referent is unclear.**) (**The rest of this paragraph, except for the last sentence, gives Corroborating Details in the form of examples.**) That is very true in the political consulting industry. Women are making inroads, but the victories are small. Mary Beth Cahill managed John Kerry's presidential campaign, but all-male consultants surrounded her. More disturbing, she was the only female in a visible, top-level role among the '04 Democratic presidential nominees. While Karen Hughes played an advisory role for President Bush, she was always second to Karl Rove, who definitely got all the credit for Bush's victory. Furthermore, there is not one female in a high level position on Bush's internal White House staff. (**The final sentence ties back to the thesis, but the too-informal tone of it detracts somewhat from the point it is trying to make.**) And while Secretary Rice's influence is impressive, let me know when she gets Rummy's job. (**Note: This paragraph would have been stronger if it had spent more time on Careful Explanation of Why the Details Are Significant. The writer gives the details and assumes that readers will interpret them in the way she has.**)

At the political committees, women are scattered through the organization, usually in fundraising positions. But there are no female Executive Directors or Political Directors at any of the four committees (DSCC, DCCC, RNCC, RSCC), and neither national party has a woman Executive Director or Party Chairperson. So women work there, but none have achieved the most visible, and most profitable, positions. Women are working for the cause. They are just not leading it. (**The 4Cs are here, but the ideas could be more fully developed.**)

(**Here is another observation about the Controlling Idea in the previous paragraph. The writer has many Corroborating Details and Careful Explanation of Why the Details Are Significant, so she extends the topic to a second paragraph.**) I see three primary causes of the political consulting industry's glass ceiling: (**These are Corroborating Details and Careful Explanation of Why the Details Are Significant presented together in a list of causes and a list of solutions.**) 1) women have children, which means they are not available to their clients 24/7/365 and lose that edge to their male competitors; 2) being a committee executive director or a partner in a firm requires a killer instinct, and some women shy away from being that aggressive; and 3) people in powerful positions (usually men) are loath to move out and give others a leg up. It is a societal issue, not just a political consulting issue, that children hurt mommies in the workplace more than daddies. The idea of men being able to work late nights with no adverse effects to their family because the wife will always handle it is archaic. Women in every professional industry will remain trapped beneath the glass until their male counterparts share equally in parenting. Men are no longer the sole breadwinners, so why should women be the sole caregivers? (**This is a good question, really—a good point to make.**) As to women not being aggressive enough, I know there are plenty of aggressive women in the political business. But there are plenty more who fear the label of "bitch" or "hard-ass," which prevents them from making the tough decisions and rising to the top positions. By now, we should be wise to this age-old male defense mechanism. Women need to move past this and see it for what it is—an intimidation tactic, not to mention a load of horse crap. (**Too informal!**) So the solutions to breaking the glass ceiling require effort on everyone's part. Women need to get over the stigma of being aggressive and close the deal. Men need to stay home and change a few diapers. And consultants who worked for George McGovern or Richard Nixon need to retire. This will immediately usher in many new women to top positions.

(**In this paragraph, the writer continues with the same topic and gives more solutions for the problem.**) Furthermore, women consultants need to work together to train and support the next generation of female campaign operatives. We all know how tough it is to get that first campaign job and to live "on the road" for a few years while building your résumé. Women tend to get off the road and take safe jobs far more often than men. I envision training seminars exclusively for female operatives given exclusively by female consultants. After the training, these operatives would receive mentoring support from a female consultant, giving them advice and encouraging them to stick it out, even when they want to take a "real" job. Then perhaps young women would stay on the road longer and get the experience they need to get the higher-level jobs. I would also encourage female candidates and female-oriented political action committees to work only with female consultants. If we don't help our own, we will never be successful at tearing down walls. Men have been hiring men exclusively for years, and I think it's high time we follow their lead. In 2001, a male staff member at the DSCC told me I could not run one of the top Senate races because I was female and none of his candidates would take orders from a woman. If that is true, then female candidates should stop "taking orders" from male managers and male consultants and start working with more women.

(Conclusion type: a Request for Action. This is an effective way to end—it assumes that change can happen.) I am not interested in sparking a "gender war" within this industry. I am interested in seeing the Campaigns and Elections "Rising Star" list have as many women as men. I am interested in seeing the C & E Political Pages list at least ten Democrat media firms with named female partners. I am interested in seeing 278 women in the Senate and House, to reflect the fifty-two percent of the voting population that women represent. I am interested in never being asked again whether there is a glass ceiling for women in the political consulting industry.

Application

1. After reading the selection on women in politics, write your own annotations in its margin. Then, compare your margin notes to the ones given in the parentheses within the reading. How similar are they? How do you account for any differences you notice?

2. Discuss with a classmate your responses to these questions: Have you used annotating in the past? If so, do you see a way to modify this strategy to improve its effectiveness? If you haven't been using this strategy, do you think that you might try it in the future to better aid your comprehension? Explain your responses.

3. Build an outline for "Do Women in Politics Face a Glass Ceiling?" Then, discuss with a classmate how effective the outline is in helping you to understand Powell's argument. Which strategy was most effective for you, annotating or outlining? Would you choose to use both strategies? Explain.

A Reminder of the Definitions of Plagiarism and Copyright Infringement

You may be aware of the requirement that all work you turn in for credit must be your own, but sometimes students inadvertently commit plagiarism because they are unclear about what constitutes plagiarism or infringement of copyright laws. Review the following definitions and rules, and check to see that your own paper meets all the requirements of intellectual and academic honesty.

Copyright refers to the legal ownership of published material. Any writing—a play, an essay, a pamphlet, a website—is the intellectual property of the person who wrote it. If, in your paper, you borrow that property by quoting, summarizing, or paraphrasing, you must give credit to the original author. The *fair use* laws allow you to borrow *brief passages* without infringing on copyright, but you must credit the source and document it properly. Your handbook will show you the correct form to use for each and every source.

Plagiarism can occur in different ways. For example, some students make poor choices and turn in another student's work as their own. Institutions of higher learning have strict policies regarding this type of plagiarism, and the consequences for this action can be significant. Plagiarism may also be committed by oversight; a student may have forgotten where he or she found the particular material or even that the material was not his or her own. It is important during your research that you include all the source information in your notes so that you will not accidentally commit plagiarism and be held accountable for it.

Remember to acknowledge the following:

> *Ideas*—any idea or concept that you learned elsewhere that is not common knowledge
> *Words and Phrases*—exact reproduction of another author's writing
> *Charts/Tables/Statistic/Other Visuals*—other forms of work done by an author
> *Your Own Work*—with permission from your instructor, work of your own done for a different assignment or purpose

Intellectual property is the result of work people do with their heads rather than their hands; nevertheless, the result of that work still belongs to the person who did it. If a carpenter made a chair, that chair is owned by its maker. You would consider taking that chair an act of theft. Try to think of printed material as a similar object, and show that property the same respect you would any other. By doing so, you will avoid plagiarism and copyright infringement.

A Review of the Resources in a Handbook

How to Use a Handbook

Many students have never bothered to buy a handbook, or they own one but never use it. This may be because they do not realize what a powerful tool a handbook is for writers. A good handbook contains a great deal of information. It presents the conventions for formatting an academic essay, it suggests some good prewriting activities to help you develop ideas, it includes a grammar and punctuation guide, and it shows you how to use and cite quotations and paraphrases in your essays. It is important to become familiar with the extensive resources available in a handbook, and to take the time and care to follow all the guidelines that govern academic writing. Many of these you already know; your handbook will be able to refresh your memory when you aren't sure of yourself, and it will give you information that you may meet for the first time.

A handbook helps at every stage of the writing process. It has sections that show you how to get started by defining your purpose and your audience. Your handbook has chapters that can aid you as you make a plan for your writing and chapters that can lead you through the drafting process. When your rough draft is completed, your handbook will give you ideas and techniques for improving and revising the work you have done. Most importantly, a handbook contains all the information and explanations of the conventions of written English. You will want to consult your handbook extensively as you correct and edit your final draft.

You need to familiarize yourself with two important features of your handbook: the **table of contents** and the **index.** Learning how to use them and training yourself to consult them will save you time and improve your writing.

The Table of Contents

The table of contents appears at the beginning of your handbook. It gives the title (topic) of each chapter and lists the subtopics covered in each of the chapters. A page number follows each listing for easy access to the information.

Example:

Your instructor has given a general assignment for your paper. You are to write a research paper on the novel *The Sun Also Rises* by Ernest Hemingway, but you are expected to come up with your own topic. You have no idea where to begin, so you look at your handbook's table of contents. You find a section devoted to Writing Topics. There are subheadings, such as:

> "Finding a Topic"
> "Selecting a Topic"
> "Narrowing the Topic"

Because you do not have any particular topic in mind, you follow the activities the handbook suggests to help you think about subjects for your paper. It suggests you first try some of the following activities to generate a topic that interests you:

freewriting
brainstorming
mapping
listing
browsing
questioning

You try them all, but the final technique, using the question words, produces the following:

Who? Jake Barnes
When? 1920s
Where? Paris
What? Expatriate
Why? Physical/mental wounds
How? World War I

The penultimate question, "Why?" produces a relevant and researchable, though still quite broad, topic. "Jake's wound." You can begin by thinking and researching more on that topic. Once you have gathered information from secondary sources and the primary text, you can then return to the section in the handbook for ideas on ways to narrow your subject and begin to refine and limit your topic.

Once you have decided on your topic, your handbook can also help you produce a thesis that is appropriate and manageable in terms of your assignment.

Index

The index appears at the very end of your handbook. It contains an alphabetical listing of every topic, concept, and problem addressed within the handbook's pages. A page number or a sequence of page numbers follows each listing. These numbers indicate pages where information on a particular listing can be found.

Example:

You are writing about your chemistry study group and want to discuss the commitment of all the members. You have written the following sentence:

My study group, named "Good Chemistry," brings their textbooks to each meeting.

You are unsure about your pronoun choice. Should it be "their" or "its"? You know that "group" is a collective noun. You use your handbook to find the answer. In the index, you find alphabetical listings for the following:

"Pronoun-antecedent agreement
        collective nouns and"
"Collective nouns
        pronoun agreement with"

Both listings direct you to the same page. On that page, you discover that collective nouns such as "group" can take both the singular and plural pronoun, depending on the content and meaning of the sentence. If the unit (collective noun) functions as a whole, or one, the singular pronoun is correct. If the members of the group act individually, the plural pronoun is needed. In your sentence, the group has members that must show commitment by each completing certain actions on their own Remembering to bring the book is an action completed separately by the individuals in the group. Which pronoun would be correct?

A Review of the Argument Essay Structure and Two Alternatives

The Conventional Argument Essay Structure

The most commonly used structure for a thesis-centered essay is established by convention. That is, the thesis essay format has an introduction that contains the thesis statement, followed by body paragraphs that support it, and ending with a conclusion that gives closure to the essay. The majority of college writing assignments anticipate this structure.

An Introduction That Contains

an **INTRODUCTORY SENTENCE** that introduces the reading selection's title, author, and subject.

a **DIRECTED SUMMARY** of the reading selection that includes an answer to the first part of the writing topic.

your thesis statement in response to the writing topic.

Body Paragraphs, Each of Which Includes

a **TOPIC SENTENCE** that gives the paragraph's ONE central point that supports your thesis statement.

CONCRETE EVIDENCE, EXPLAINED so that it supports the central point and ties that point to the thesis statement.

A Conclusion That Gives

a **RESTATEMENT** of the reading selection's argument and your argument.

a sense of **CLOSURE** for the essay

The conventional academic structure delivers its central, overarching point in the opening of the essay. Its direct and efficient presentation of the essay's main point is followed by the step-by-step logic and evidence that have led the writer to the conclusion he or she has reached, the insight or revelation that has determined the thesis statement of the essay. Writers might use this structure when they are writing for purposeful readers who are reading for intellectual insight, rather than for entertainment or for general, thoughtful commentary on current issues of social interest.

Example

You will meet the following reading selection in a different context in Part 2 of this book. For now, examine it as an essay written in the academic essay format.

The Ethics of Work-Life Balance

BRUCE WEINSTEIN

Bruce Weinstein received a BA from Swarthmore College and a PhD from Georgetown University. From 2006 to 2012, he contributed to Bloomberg Businessweek's *online edition, which also posted his twelve-episode series* Ask the Ethics Guy. *He is now a blogger at the* Huffington Post *and is a professional public speaker, lecturing on ethics and leadership. His latest book,* Ethical Intelligence, *was published in 2011. The essay below appeared on* Bloomberg Businessweek *in 2009.*

We are a nation in pain. According to a March 12 Gallup poll, the number of people in this country classified as "suffering" has increased by three million over the past year. Managers and business owners experienced the greatest loss of well-being; 60.8% of businesses were thriving in the first quarter of 2008, but this number decreased by almost 14% by the fourth quarter. Given the difficult economic climate and the number of jobs being lost daily, most of us are feeling the pressure to work harder than ever. But in spite of the increasing intensity of our economic crisis, it is not only unfortunate to give in to such pressure. It's unethical.

It's not too late to make a change for the better, though.

It may seem misplaced to discuss work-life balance in a column about ethics. But recall that one of five fundamental ethical principles is fairness, and that we demonstrate fairness in everyday life by how we allocate scarce resources. The most precious commodity you have is time, both in your professional and your personal life. It's also your most critical nonrenewable resource. As a manager, you must constantly ask yourself how you should allocate your time. You know it's wrong to spend so much time on one project at the expense of equally critical ones, or to spend so much time managing one employee that you're unable to manage others.

But a good manager should be, first and foremost, a good human being. Just as managing your career well means allocating your time wisely among the different projects and people you oversee, managing your life wisely means giving due time not just to work but to family, friends, community, self, and spirit. You wouldn't think of spending most of your work day talking with one client on the phone. Why, then, is it okay to devote so much time to your job when you don't give non-work-related things the attention they deserve?

Ethics isn't just about how you treat others. It's also about how you treat yourself—at work and beyond. You're not being fair to others and yourself if you haven't had a vacation in a long time, or if you force yourself to work when you've got the flu. You're also not being fair to others and yourself if you spend so much time being a good manager that you're not able to be a good parent, spouse, or friend. And let's face it: You can't do your job to the best of your ability if you're thoroughly exhausted, and that's not fair to your coworkers or your employer. But working to the exclusion of all else isn't just unfair (and thus unethical). It's also tragic, because the time you spend away from the other meaningful relationships in your life is time you can never get back.

Let's now look at some of the common excuses people give for working so much and how to get beyond them.

"I want to make sure I keep my job."

More than 2.5 million jobs were lost in 2008, and the losses continue to mount. What could be wrong with working all the time in such a climate if it will mean hanging onto your job? Speaking of ethics, isn't there an ethical obligation to keep your job? After all, what would be ethical about not paying bills, or your mortgage, or not being able to take care of your family?

Of course it's important to remain an employee in good standing. But you shouldn't assume that there is a direct correlation with the number of hours you work and the likelihood that you'll hold onto your job. Downsizing is largely a function of economics rather than of job performance; companies are letting people go to cut their losses and hit budget targets. (And yes, letting go of good employees raises other ethical issues, but that deserves its own column.) Working twelve-hour days six or seven days a week isn't going to guard against getting downsized.

In fact, it could even backfire. You might look like someone who can't manage his or her time or isn't up to the responsibilities of the job. And if you work without any letup, you will reach the point of diminishing returns. This isn't a time to be less than a stellar employee, but working overtime won't get you there.

"I need to work more to make what I did last year."

Many of the recently downsized are taking lower-paying jobs because that's all that is available. Some are even taking second jobs and still not making what they did a year ago. But how important is it now to live in the manner to which you have become accustomed? It's one thing to have to work seventy hours a week just to put food on the table and pay the rent or mortgage. It's another to work so much to be able to afford lavish trips, expensive clothes, or a certain lifestyle. Instead of working longer, couldn't you shift your priorities so that you're able to spend more time with family and friends, exercise more often, or even just read some of those books you've been thinking about?

"I have a demanding job."

Gone are the days when leaving your office meant leaving work behind. Many of us choose to use our BlackBerrys, iPhones, laptops, and social networking sites to remain constantly available to our bosses, clients, and colleagues, but this can get out of control. It's flattering to believe that you're indispensable to your company, and that only you can do the work you spend so much time doing. This is rarely true, however painful that may be to accept. Be honest with yourself: Are you spending so much time on the job because you must, or because of habit, ego, or some other reason? We owe it to ourselves and the people we care about (and who care about us) to work smarter, not harder.

"I just love to work."

It's a blessing to be able to say this, but all passions should have limits. A fully human life is a life in balance, and that means giving due time to all of the things that enrich us, fulfill us, and make our lives worth living. When Freud said that work and love were essential components of a happy life, he didn't mean that these were one and the same thing.

There is a time to work and a time to leave work behind. The good manager leaves time to do both.

Discussion Questions

1. Identify the thesis statement in Weinstein's article. Restate his claim in your own words. Discuss your initial response to it. What are some identifying labels (such as "provocative," "unexpected," "commonplace," etc.) you would attach to his thesis? Explain your answer.

2. Summarize in a few sentences the argument of "The Ethics of Work-Life Balance."

3. Why do you think Weinstein wrote this essay? How does the placement of the thesis in his essay help make his readers more open to the position he takes?

4. Weinstein uses the second person in his essay. Who do you think he imagines that he is addressing when he says "you"? Discuss what types of readers might be interested in reading this essay. Although the second person is not conventionally used in academic writing, why do you think this writer chooses to use it in this essay?

Two Alternative Structures

Although it is most common in an argumentative essay to place the thesis early—usually towards the end of the first paragraph—alternative structures can be used in an argument essay. Each of the two alternative essay structures in this section contains a clear thesis statement, but neither thesis can be found at the beginning of the essay. The first essay uses what we call the "hourglass structure," and the second uses what we call the "funnel structure." You might notice that several of the reading selections in this book use one of these alternative structures, in part because the articles were not written for an academic readership. In your own essays, however, we recommend that you use the conventional academic essay structure.

A First Alternative: The Hourglass Structure

One alternative structure for an essay places the thesis statement somewhere in the middle of the essay. Here is a diagram of this type of essay.

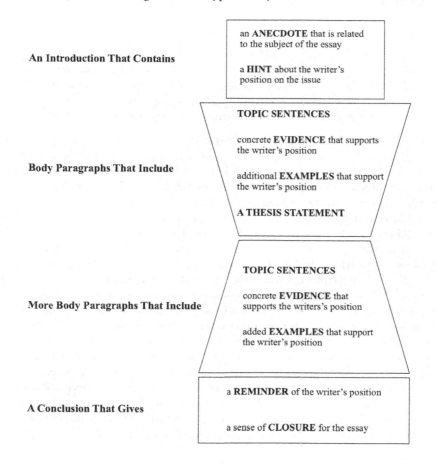

An Introduction That Contains

an **ANECDOTE** that is related to the subject of the essay

a **HINT** about the writer's position on the issue

Body Paragraphs That Include

TOPIC SENTENCES

concrete **EVIDENCE** that supports the writer's position

additional **EXAMPLES** that support the writer's position

A THESIS STATEMENT

More Body Paragraphs That Include

TOPIC SENTENCES

concrete **EVIDENCE** that supports the writers's position

added **EXAMPLES** that support the writer's position

A Conclusion That Gives

a **REMINDER** of the writer's position

a sense of **CLOSURE** for the essay

With the hourglass structure, writers ask readers to read a fair portion of the essay before they come to the essay's central point. Writers begin talking about a subject, offering assertions, anecdotes, and observations whose significance isn't yet clear. These assertions and observations are meant to create a path to the central point—stated in a thesis statement—followed by more corroborating assertions and observations.

Writers might use this structure when their thesis is controversial and they do not want to risk losing dissenting readers up front. To persuade readers who disagree, a writer tries to draw them in by offering material more widely agreed upon and accessible. You will want to notice when a writer uses an alternative essay structure because it will help you to identify the argument and the linking ideas that support it.

Example

Time to Cerebrate

BENEDICT JONES

Benedict Jones received a bachelor's degree with a double major from the University of California, San Diego, and earned an English MA at the University of California, Riverside, where he is now a lecturer in the University Writing Program. His scholarly work focuses on Victorian-era prehistoric fiction and evolutionary theories, but he has written articles, reviews, and conference papers on a variety of topics.

The race was on: My ten-page literature paper was due at noon the next day. I had been stewing about the essay for days, reading and rereading the poems to be analyzed and scribbling down random ideas. I often just stared off into space and simply thought about the project, afraid to commit and dreading to start. But I still hadn't typed a word, and I had under twenty-four hours left.

This type of delayed start was my *modus operandi*, and I therefore considered myself something of a failure as a college student. Sure, I was smart. No question of that. And I loved academics and especially literature, my area of focus; I spent hours and hours thinking about what I had read and what I planned to write. But when a due date loomed, I habitually procrastinated and agonized, waiting until the deadline was hard upon me before I could force myself to sit down and actually tap out a product.

I did not delay on purpose, nor was I indifferent about my grade. I truly wanted to do well. I longed to begin writing earlier and avoid the seemingly inevitable all-nighter, the day-long last-minute mad dash to both start and finish. If only I could be sensible, I thought. If I could bring myself to start writing a week earlier, I would produce a couple of pages a day and still have time left to revise and edit—and I would never again have to face the terrifying possibility of *not* finishing. Breaking up the project well before the due date would mean low stress, plenty of sleep, and my best work possible: the perfect combination. However, no amount of logic penetrated my dense skull, so I continued as I was, hating myself with a passion but always sliding under the wire at the eleventh hour. The system did work, even if it made me uncomfortable and ashamed. After all, I usually earned As and never got below a B.

After dropping out of school and taking several years off, I reentered the university as a working student—and still found that many of my essays were last-minute affairs completed in the wee, small hours of the morning they were due. Although my second attempt at academic life was certainly challenged by both the ten-week quarter system and a full-time job, it seemed that not much else had changed. Even in graduate school, I would spend weeks doing research, taking notes, and thinking, thinking, thinking about a project, but I would allow only a few days to actually write the essay.

Now I teach my own students, and many of them seem to be on the same path I was on. They make plans to see me in office hours for advice but often e-mail me to say that they cannot make it because they are still writing the first draft. They skitter into class ten minutes late with a paper they have just barely finished. Or they submit an assignment on time but note that their last-minute scheduling did not allow time for editing and proofreading, so "it might have a few mistakes." Perhaps nothing much *has* changed.

But I'm beginning to think it actually has. I am gradually coming to the conclusion that I was not as dramatic a procrastinator as I have always thought. After all, I spent hours, days, even weeks thinking about my projects, although the writing took only a short time. In contrast, the final product that my students now expect me to grade is often superficial, with indifferent organization, jumbled paragraphs, and discrete points that don't always add up to a cohesive whole. Most of these essays do not seem to have required much time to write and do not appear to have invited much thought. And that, I think, might be a key difference between me and my students: the time we take to think.

To prepare for my various writing assignments, I always allowed long periods of rumination, and I truly doubt that very many of my students do the same. Before writers ever get to the drafting stage, they should reserve a generous portion of the project's allotted time for focused reflection. Some students will require less time and some more; some will think more in the middle of the project than in the beginning. Some will think in the shower, and some on the bus. But careful, uninterrupted thought is still the absolute best guarantee of high-quality content.

I don't often see such results, so I wonder whether thinking has lately become an eccentric pursuit, the butt of jokes. Oddly enough, I see evidence of this trend on television—on *The Big Bang Theory*, a program devoted to the brainiac experience. For example, a sequence in an episode called "The Pirate Solution" shows Sheldon, a string-theory physicist, and Raj, an astrophysicist, comically practicing the manly art of mental exercise.

In his cluttered university office, Sheldon declares, "We're doing serious research which requires complete and utter focus."

"All right," agrees Raj, "let's buckle down and work."

And with that, audiences are treated to a rousing musical excerpt from "The Eye of the Tiger," accompanied by various shots of the two scientists standing, sitting, leaning, all while staring intently at equations on a dry erase board. The laugh track tells viewers that this sequence is very funny indeed.

In another episode, "The Pulled Groin Extrapolation," supergeek and social disaster Amy Farrah Fowler, a neurobiologist, sits on the couch in Sheldon and Leonard's apartment while Leonard works at his computer, his back to her. Amy sits erect, with her hands on her thighs, staring blankly at nothing in particular. Finally, the increasingly uncomfortable Leonard cannot help himself. "Amy?" he says tentatively.

"Yo," replies Amy, her concentration momentarily broken.

"You okay?"

"Oh, sure," she says with confidence, and goes back to staring.

Leonard persists: "I thought you were reading."

"I was," she replies, and adds with obvious satisfaction, "Now I'm *thinking* about what I read." Again the laugh track tells us to respond with hilarity. Is the number one comedy in America, supposedly a paean to geekdom, telling its audience that thinking is funny?

I laughed, and still do, because I can relate. What Raj and Sheldon and Amy do, I also do, minus the equations but probably with the same dorky, far-off look in my eyes. Busy as I am, I still take time to sit and think, to *percolate*. I contemplate what I have read, how I need to spend my day, what I want to cover in class, what I want my students to get out of an assignment. I ponder my writing projects, too, often for long periods of apparent inactivity. When a problem is particularly knotty, I get up and pace around while I exercise my little gray cells. While walking back and forth, I often talk out the problem: I am thinking out loud.

That's why I think the TV scenes are funny; they are a slice right out of my own nerdy life. But now I wonder exactly what everyone else is laughing about. Is mental reflection really so funny? Is it an alien occupation, something to poke fun at? Do people laugh because they see Raj and Sheldon's idea of labor as not worthy of the label "work" because "work" must refer to significant physical activity rather than intellectual exertion? I expect that for most viewers, the answer to all of these questions is a resounding "yes." I also suspect that fewer and fewer people simply sit and think; our young people, and even middle-aged geezers like me, are busy filling in their mental interstices with external stimulation from their technological gadgets. It seems that every spare minute is filled with texting, googling, facebooking, youtubing, browsing. While I have nothing against these pursuits in their proper place, they seem to have taken over, leaving no space for contemplation. In addition, writing on a computer seems to encourage sloppy products, since students are not obliged to think carefully about their essays before committing them to paper, as they would need to do when working on a typewriter. In short, I worry that lengthy rumination is becoming a thing of the past, especially among college students.

I'll admit that this loss might not be much of a tragedy for most people, but it is a travesty for our universities. I may come across as an elitist for believing as I do, but universities are geared primarily toward people who like to think, people whose ability to ruminate helps them to flourish in their disciplines. What will happen if that population is rapidly diminishing? I am concerned that by filling in every mental pause with rapid-fire gadget-centered interactions, my own students are robbing themselves of the ability to think deeply or for sustained periods of time. I believe I can say that in recent years, the overall quality of thinking-on-paper has diminished noticeably in my classes—and I worry about what that trend means for higher education, for good old American ingenuity or, indeed, for the world. It is still too early to be sure what long-term effects our technology will have on our thinking, but the preliminary conclusions of various recent studies do not inspire confidence.

Looking back on my past life as a student, I feel that the hours that I used to devote to simply thinking about my own undergraduate essays were well spent. I was engaged by interesting issues and problems. I learned how to make connections between ideas and how to organize my thoughts. I learned to reason effectively and, occasionally, write my way out of a corner. As a result, I became a strong critical thinker. I should also note that my essays generally did not read like the work of a single day—because they weren't. They tended to earn high grades because they were the product of hours, days, or weeks of careful introspection even if the execution was a little rushed. I procrastinated on the writing but not on the mental preparation that led up to the writing.

Consequently, I do wish that my writing students would manage their time a bit differently and fill their quiet moments with less browsing and more brooding. Not everyone has the same process, but thinking deeply about their writing projects should be an essential component of all students' creative process and will improve their mental acuity, the quality of their work, probably their grades, and perhaps even their future professions and personal lives.

Now that nerds are achieving a semi-mythic status in American culture, we ought to recognize the value of some of their strongest characteristics—among them the ability to simply ponder. Student writers in particular must take an occasional sustained break from gadget heaven and devote time to think more deeply about their writing projects before ever penning—or, more likely, typing—a draft. I'm not saying to ditch the devices; they are here to stay, and they are valuable tools and entertaining toys in twenty-first-century life. But if Raj and Sheldon and their friends can be heavily invested in their electronic devices and still allow time for sustained deep thinking, I am sure that my own students can do the same. Focused thinking should be included in every writer's toolbox. In the lingo of *The Big Bang Theory*, America's next episode should be "The Cerebration Celebration."

Works Cited

"The Pirate Solution." *The Big Bang Theory.* CBS. KFMB, San Diego, 12 Oct. 2009. Television.

"The Pulled Groin Extrapolation." *The Big Bang Theory.* CBS. KFMB, San Diego, 29 Sept. 2011. Television.

Discussion Questions

1. Identify the thesis statement in Jones's article. Restate his claim in your own words. Discuss your initial response to it. Do you think the position he takes is controversial? Explain.

2. Summarize in a few sentences the argument of "Time to Cerebrate."

3. Where, specifically, did Jones choose to place the thesis? How does the placement of the thesis in this particular position help make his readers more open to the position he takes in the article? Who are the readers Jones imagines he is writing to, in your opinion? Explain your answer.

A Second Alternative: The Funnel Structure

Another alternative structure for an argument essay is one that places its thesis somewhere within the conclusion of the essay. Here is a diagram of this type of essay structure.

An Introduction That Contains

> One of the following
> an **ANECDOTE**
> an **EXAMPLE**
> a **SUMMARY** of the topic
> **INFORMATION** related to the topic

Body Paragraphs That Include

> **TOPIC SENTENCES**
>
> other **ANECDOTES** that point toward a position on the subject
>
> facts, statistics, or other **INFORMATION** that points toward a particular position on the subject
>
> additional **EXAMPLES** that point toward a particular position on the subject
>
> concrete **EVIDENCE** that points toward a particular position on the subject

A Conclusion That Gives

> a clear statement of the author's **THESIS**
>
> a sense of **CLOSURE** for the essay

With the funnel structure, writers pile up the evidence piece by piece but do not draw the significance of this evidence until the end. Writers might use this structure to present the reasonableness of their argument to a hostile audience, to lead an uninformed audience to form the writer's desired conclusion on an issue, or simply to prepare readers to accept a surprising conclusion.

Example

Grammar Gets Real

JEROME WINTER

> *Jerome Winter completed his PhD in English at the University of California, Riverside. For the last few years, he has been involved in teaching entry-level writing at the college level in various capacities: in the University Writing Program and Writing Across the Curriculum Program at UCR, in instruction at writing laboratories, and in basic writing courses. His studies center on the intersection of globalization and contemporary speculative fiction (SF). In this regard, he is the editor of* Speculative Fiction *for the* Los Angeles Review of Books *and contributed a chapter on SF art and illustration to the* Oxford Handbook of Science Fiction *(2014). He has published articles, reviews, and interviews in* Science Fiction Studies, Extrapolation, *and* Journal of Fantastic in the Arts. *In 2015, the University of Wales Press published his book* Science Fiction, New Space Opera, *and* Neoliberal Globalism: Nostalgia for Infinity.

The story goes that Winston Churchill replied to an editor's insistence that one of his sentences should not end with a preposition with this genius one-liner: "This is the kind of tedious nonsense up with which I will not put." The comeback sticks in my mind probably because it reminds me that the best offense against Grammar Nazis is a good defense. For the sentence misattributed to Churchill is, on a purely technical level, grammatically correct. It fails, however, at achieving clarity and concision, our prime directive as far as the purpose of good writing goes. The tortured sentence clearly calls into question the rule of rearranging word order so as never to end sentences with a preposition.

Such questioning finds support in Dilin Liu's "Making Grammar Instruction More Empowering", published in the May 2011 issue of the journal *Research in the Teaching of English*. Liu is a so-called "descriptivist" who believes usage reflects a naturally evolving set of bottom-up norms that help writers communicate their meanings with the least amount of possible confusion. Liu therefore joins the academic fight against the overly nitpicky teaching of grammar still common in schools, which dates back at least to the nineteenth-century version of the Grammar Nazi archetype, the learned G. P. Quackenbos. This practice garnered support well into the late twentieth century with the writings of the eminent Henry Watson Fowler. The overly picky approach, so the complaint lodged against these so-called "prescriptivists" goes, has become widely enforced through a series of "Dos" and "Don'ts" scrawled on a whiteboard. These rules are then blandly memorized and regurgitated in the bubbled pencil lead of multiple-choice Scantrons. Liu therefore conducted research on the use of searchable databases of grammatical usage in the college classroom. Students who used these vast databases of acceptable usage to answer their grammatical queries reported their shock when real-world grammar frequently debunked the idea that certain usages are off-limits, for example, split infinitives, beginning sentences with "but" or "because," or placing commas before or after "therefore."

But the tendency to rigidly cling to such rules still exists; therefore, the grammar of sentences such as this one remains uncertain to a shrinking minority of readers. Other sources of pointless controversy on the subject of English and American lexicogrammatical rules are legendary. Should commas be placed after any prepositional phrases or only those prepositional phrases with five words or more? Does "begging the question" mean provoking follow-up questions, or does the phrase mean, in its more philosophically rigorous sense, conflating a proven conclusion with an assumed premise? To indicate a possessive, does one put an apostrophe after an "s" for a name that ends in "s," or does one add an apostrophe and another "s"? That is, is it Hopkins' or Hopkins's? Should "due to" be used only as an adjectival phrase in the mode of "attributable to," or can it also be used like the preposition "because of"? Can "hopefully" be used only as an adjective or adverb ("she asked hopefully"), or can it be used also as an initial position to modify an entire sentence—as in the phrase: "Hopefully, the grammar is not atrocious"? If you haven't answered this harangue with your own impatiently begged question—namely, "who cares?"—then you might want to do so now. A nagging doubt arises, then: "Is all attention to grammatical issues hairsplitting and nitpicky?" You don't have to be a Grammar Nazi to answer that question with a decisive negative.

Stephen King claims that the main rule he followed when he taught grammar in high school was a straightforward one, "Keep It Simple, Stupid." The writer surely means no disrespect to his or his students' high intelligence by these words that beginning college writers should live by. As readers, writers often absorb standard usage through immersion in reading. However, when certain grammatical issues fail to sink in, then major breakdowns in clarity can occur. The most severe problems are not the trivial peccadilloes discussed above at all. Major errors include the usual suspects every writer invested in being understood clearly should be vigilant in avoiding, including sentence fragments, run-on sentences, subject-verb disagreement, mixed construction, pronoun confusion, tense errors, and comma splices. When writers revise drafts with a handy checklist of major errors such as these, the final drafts will be not only significantly more polished but also more comprehensible.

It is small wonder, then, that contemporary researchers suggest that beginning writers should avoid learning grammar out of context. Make no mistake; no one is suggesting that an academic or professional writer should resort to casual textspeak of liberally applied "LOL"s sprinkled with emoticons. The correction of severe grammatical problems is not a petty concern, and when college instructors demand the elimination of such grammatical mistakes, they are not being arbitrary. Severe grammatical errors fatally impair the author's ability to communicate clearly and appropriately to readers. However, a fussy obsession with memorizing grammar rules can undermine the writer's goal of developing meaningful and complex insights. The writer runs the risk of recreating the Churchill anecdote. Clarity comes from the lengthy and involved process of drafting and revising language, while also exploring ideas, rather than from a strict and unwavering faithfulness to a set of grammar rules that have been studied and memorized by rote.

Discussion Questions

1. Identify the thesis statement in Winter's article. Restate his claim in your own words. Discuss your initial response to it; do you think the position he takes is controversial? Explain.

2. Summarize in a few sentences the argument of "Grammar Gets Real."

3. Where, specifically, did Winter choose to place the thesis? How does the placement of the thesis in this particular position help make his readers more open to the position he takes in the article?

Applications

1. Using a couple of the reading selections from this book, identify which of the three structures each one uses, and speculate on the possible reasons for each writer's choice.

2. As a class, list some possible reasons that the conventional argument essay structure is most often expected in college writing assignments.

A Strategy for Writing a Timed Essay

When writing an essay under time constraints, you need a clear and thoughtful strategy. Look over the following suggestions, and then write a plan of your own that takes into consideration your particular strengths and weaknesses.

1. **Read the questions in the writing topic.** Circle the interrogatives (question words: who, what, where, when, why, and how) in the first part of the writing topic.

2. **Read the essay** and underline the information that specifically answers the question(s). Make margin notes.

3. **Write your summary** in a manner that responds directly to the question(s) asked.

4. **Reread the writing topic.** Determine which point of the author's argument you are being asked to take a position on. Think about what you believe and why you believe the way you do. Write your thesis to express that position clearly.

5. **Write a series of paragraphs** that offer developed reasons and concrete examples that support your thesis. In each paragraph, be sure to show the connection between your reasons, your examples, and your thesis.

6. **Write a conclusion.** It should provide a sense of closure for your essay. It can be a restatement of your thesis or a recalling of certain important information in your summary. It must, however, leave no doubt as to your own position on the topic.

7. **Proofread your complete essay.** Then, double-check grammar and spelling by reading from the end of your essay to the beginning. Read your essay again to check that your ideas are fully developed and logically connected.

One Way You Might Budget Your Time

Here is one person's time plan for a timed final essay exam lasting two hours and forty-five minutes. You should arrange your own time plan in a way that works best for your particular skills and the time you have.

> **Step 1:** Reading the question—5 minutes
> **Step 2:** Reading/marking the reading selection—20 minutes
> **Step 3:** Writing the summary—15 minutes
> **Step 4:** Writing the thesis—10 minutes
> **Step 5:** Supporting the thesis—60 minutes
> **Step 6:** Writing the conclusion—10 minutes
> **Step 7:** Proofreading the essay—45 minutes

When creating your own time schedule, carefully consider your strengths and weaknesses. If you need more time for, say, understanding the reading selection, but are generally strong when it comes to writing clear, correct sentences, you might plan to spend thirty or more minutes examining and marking the reading selection, and thirty or less on proofreading your essay.

Once you create your time schedule, try to stick with it so that you take advantage of all of the stages of the writing process yet still finish on time. If you use your schedule, you won't run out of time, but neither will you waste some of the time you are given because you rushed through and neglected some important elements related to relevance, development, support, or sentence clarity and correctness. You may discover that you left something out, or that you made a mistake in the way you presented an idea or used a vocabulary word. We tend to hurry when doing timed writing, and often our hand struggles to keep up with our thoughts. It is too easy to make mistakes that will have an impact on how the essay is received by readers.

A Review of the Elements of the Conventional Argument Essay

A Review of an Introduction in an Argument Essay

Even if you are already familiar with the elements of a good introduction, review the guidelines below. Also, be sure to look back at these guidelines once your draft is completed. At that point in the writing process, you are more likely to understand your argument better than when you began to draft. For this reason, many writers draft their introduction after they have written their body paragraphs.

The introduction is often the most difficult part of an essay to draft. A paper's opening creates a first impression for readers, and deciding how to begin can be difficult. The introduction should do three things: capture readers' attention, set the stage for the paper's argument, and present the thesis statement. Length is also an important consideration: An introductory paragraph should be only as long as necessary to provide a context for the argument that the paper will develop. Too much detail or background information will bog down your introduction and leave readers feeling confused. Save the details for the paper's body.

Customarily, the last sentence of the introduction is the ***thesis statement***. A strong thesis statement is essential to developing, organizing, and writing a successful persuasive paper. An essay isn't successful simply because its grammar is correct or because it has an introduction, a set of body paragraphs, and a conclusion. These components must have a thesis statement to tie them together and give them significance. The thesis statement is an important part of the introduction because it unifies the essay and gives it a purpose. Including it at the end of the introduction ensures that readers clearly understand the paper's purpose at the outset.

The essays you are assigned to write in *Write It Review* will follow the same format, and the introduction for each essay assignment will be effective if you follow these steps:

1st: Introduce the reading selection by giving the author's first and last name and the selection's title.

2nd: Give a directed summary of the reading selection (see the next page).

3rd: Present your thesis statement (be sure it answers the question or questions in the writing topic).

Hints

- **Don't offer a flat explanation of what you will cover in the paper:**
  "This essay will discuss. . . ."
- **Avoid clichés:**
  "It is certainly true that love is blind."
- **Avoid meaningless platitudes:**
  "People often find it difficult to get along with others in this world."
- **Do not resort to overly broad statements:**
  "Since the beginning of time, humans have tried to live peacefully."

A Review of the Guidelines for Writing a Directed Summary

The summary guidelines we give here are based on a specific type of writing assignment, one that asks you to read a persuasive piece of writing and respond to its argument in an essay of your own. We have said that the techniques that you learn in this book can be used for any persuasive academic writing assignment, and that is true. However, you should always take into consideration the specific context of any assignment because you will have to adjust your response to satisfy the particular requirements of that assignment.

The writing topics in *Write It Review* have a common set of requirements, as you will see. One of these requirements is that, for each unit's assignment, you will asked to write a *focused* summary of a reading, meaning a summary of a particular aspect of a reading designated in the writing topic that follows it. In other words, while a general summary asks you to take an entire reading into account, each of the assignments in Part 2 asks for a *directed* summary of a specific aspect of a reading.

To write a directed summary that is complete and correct, follow the steps below:

Preparation

Step 1: Carefully read through the reading selection and the writing topic questions that follow it.
Step 2: Underline the key terms in the first question.
Step 3: Locate in the essay the specific sentences that provide information relevant to answering the first question.
Step 4: Decide on the answer to that question. Be sure you have read through the essay more than once and are ready to provide a thorough and correct response.

Writing

Step 1: In or near the opening sentence, include the title of the essay (in quotation marks) and the full name of the author (after the first mention, the author should be referred to by last name only).
Step 2: In your own words, fully answer the first question in the writing topic.
Step 3: Explain this answer using careful reasoning.
Step 4: Use direct quotation sparingly and only when appropriate, to emphasize the answer the author provides to the question.

Hints

- Do not include minor details or points.
- Do not insert your own opinions or ideas and attribute them to the author.
- Do not ordinarily include examples.

Applications

Examine the following student-written introductions, taken from a case study in Part 3 of this book. Using the two sets of guidelines given above, "A Review of an Introduction in an Argument Essay" and "A Review of the Guidelines for Writing a Directed Summary," discuss some of the strengths and weaknesses of these four introductions. If you wish, you can turn to Part 3 and familiarize yourself with the reading selections and the writing topics each of the students is responding to.

1. In "What Management Doesn't Know", Devon Hackelton writes about the communication breakdowns that occur because management doesn't understand their employee's jobs and associated stresses. The author believes that managers should have hands-on experience in a variety of jobs that are part of the business before holding supervisor positions. Managers need hands-on experience so they make correct judgments and decisions, because college degrees can't be substituted for years of experience.

2. In the essay "What Management Doesn't Know," the author describes the lack of communication between employers and employees and the lack of hands-on experience of many employers. He writes that if employers don't have any experience in the fields they're managing, there is a lack of communication with the employees. Managers do not know the kind of stress and dangers their employees go through every day. This problem occurs because managers and supervisors are hired straight out of college and do not know the workings of a company. Many are also hired straight out of college to create cost-cutting plans. They have no idea how the field works and do not create the most cost effective plans. Employees who have been in the field for a long time are the best for management because of the experience and the knowledge of the tasks involved in the field. Manager should understand and experience the work of their employees before taking the role of a supervisor. I agree with the author's argument because I have been employed in a case where the manager had no hands-on experience and in a case where he did.

Strategies for Developing Your Ideas

Students often say that they know *how* to write an essay—that is, they know it should have an introduction, thesis statement, supporting body paragraphs, and a conclusion—but they don't have anything to write *about*. They don't know what to say, and they can't think of any experiences they have had that they can use. Consider using the techniques below for exploring your thoughts and finding strategies that work whenever you are faced with a challenging writing assignment.

Time is the crucial element here. It takes time to think carefully and systematically about a subject. You will have to focus your thoughts and have patience in order for your mind to work, to develop insights that go beyond surface impressions and quick, easy judgments. You should do much of your thinking in writing—this aspect is very important. Writing your thoughts down will give them definition and clarity.

If you find yourself without good ideas about a subject, try these strategies. You might not use all of them for any given assignment. Instead, look them over and choose those that seem most promising for the particular piece of writing you are developing:

1. *Focus*: Write down the issue of the reading selection that you want to explore; a simple phrase might be enough.
2. *Response*: Look over the selection again (and the reading and summary questions you have answered) and list its ideas. Write down:
   a. any questions and/or doubts you have about these ideas, and list your reasons.
   b. any points the writer makes that you find persuasive, and the reasons you find them convincing.
   c. your thoughtful impression of the reading selection.
   d. a final conclusion about the selection's argument, its weaknesses, and its strengths.

Hint

Your responses here do not have to be polished. Allow yourself to write freely, putting down all ideas that come to you. You will sort them out later.

3. *Reflection*: Now you need some data, some basic observations from your own experience that you can examine and use to draw conclusions or insights. First, write down, in a rough list, any personal memories you have that seem to relate to the subject you are writing on. Do a few minutes of freewriting to explore these memories. Try some *focused freewriting*, whereby you keep the essay's general subject in mind but write down everything that you can, even things you roughly associate with the subject. Stay with it until you feel you have something substantial, something your readers will find thoughtful and compelling.

If you need more structure, try using these general guidelines for each incident:

a. Begin by simply recounting what you remember: Make it as brief as possible, but don't omit anything that seems important.

b. Now expand your thinking: Try to speculate about the importance of the memory and its relevance to the subject you are exploring.

c. Look over what you have written: Underline the ideas that you think are important. Think about the way they relate to the reading selection's ideas. How are your ideas like the selection's? How are they different?

d. Take note: Consider any judgment words in your freewriting, such as *sometimes, always, seems to, might mean, only when, but if.* These will help you formulate the position you want to take in your thesis statement.

4. *Expansion*: Keeping the subject in mind, write down any relevant experiences you can think of from the world at large. Do you know of any examples from books, the news, movies, and your cultural awareness in general? Freewrite for each example that comes to mind.

5. *A Reconsideration of Your Freewriting*

a. First, begin by simply recounting the event or text, summarizing its main elements as briefly as you can without omitting important elements.

b. Now move beyond the basic facts and try to explore the implications of each for the subject. What thoughts come to mind as you reflect on the event or text? What do those thoughts suggest about the subject? Take your freewriting as far as you can for each event or text you have listed.

c. Then, look over all that you have written. Underline the ideas that you think are important. Try to explain in writing how they relate to the reading selection's ideas. How are they like the reading selection's? How are they different?

d. Finally, look for the judgment words. These will help you formulate the position you want to take in your thesis statement. What seems to be your strongest feeling about the subject, the one most dominant in your freewriting?

6. *Shape*: Consider what you have underlined and the judgment words you found. What significance do they have once you consider them all together? What do they "add up to"?

a. Group parts of your freewriting together. Find some main ideas that you came back to two or three times using different experiences, examples, or texts. Try to identify all of the main ideas you find, and write out the connection between them and the underlined portions of your freewriting.

b. Explore the parts you underlined and the implications you noted by asking yourself the following questions:

• Which parts seem important, and why?

• How do the lists you made fit together, or what do they add up to?

• Do any parts of your freewriting contradict other parts, or do parts have similar ideas?

• What do either the contradictions or the similarities suggest?

c. Identify the ideas that you feel strongly about. Write about the reasons they are important and the way they relate to the subject you are exploring.

Hint

Sometimes it is too restrictive to think in terms of "for or against" the reading selection's issue. There are often more than two positions on a topic, and disagreeing with the position taken in the reading selection may mean that, while the selection's ideas may be sound, the conclusions drawn are not as convincing, in your mind, as the conclusions you want to draw.

Hint

Your goal is to uncover what you know and develop it so that you can show your readers how you arrived at your main ideas and how your ideas led to your thesis statement.

Once you've done some freewriting and located important topics and supporting details, you have the foundation pieces to create an outline.

When you are assigned an essay from a unit in Part 2, the writing support pages that are in the unit will guide you to develop your ideas on the relevant issue presented in the lead essay. But do not forget the strategies given here in Part 1. They may be useful to you as you work to complete any of the assignments in Part 2.

Writing Supporting Paragraphs for Your Thesis Statement

The body paragraphs make up the largest part of an essay, and each paragraph should develop one important point in support of the thesis statement. Paragraphs should be unified around a central point and should contain concrete evidence that clarifies and supports that central point. Readers need concrete evidence as examples that help them to understand your ideas. Therefore, body paragraphs usually open with a topic sentence, and include evidence, a discussion of the evidence, and an explanation of how the paragraph's subject matter connects to your thesis claim. Writing a well-developed paragraph can be easy once you understand the paragraph's conventional structure. Here is a useful memory device that will help you construct well-developed body paragraphs:

Remember the 4Cs:

Controlling idea sentence
Corroborating details
Careful explanation of why the details are significant
Connection to the thesis statement

Once you determine your thesis statement, you can develop your supporting paragraphs using the following guidelines:

Controlling idea sentence

First, write a topic sentence that announces the point you want to make in the paragraph.

Corroborating details

Then, think of one or more specific examples that will help you explain and prove the point.

Careful explanation of why the details are significant

Now, carefully explain how each example proves the point you are making in the paragraph.

Connection to the thesis statement

Be sure to connect your examples and explanation to the position you have taken in your thesis statement. Tell your reader what the paragraph's point and examples have to do with your argument.

Here's an example:

Thesis: The violence on television desensitizes viewers to violence and can ultimately lead to a thoughtless and uncaring society.

Controlling idea sentence for a paragraph supporting the thesis statement

Write a sentence stating the point you want to make in the paragraph:

After seeing casual violence repeatedly on television, viewers come to see real-life violence in terms of entertainment rather than real human tragedy.

Corroborating details

Think of some examples that will show that people see violence in terms of entertainment rather than real tragedy. Here are some sample sentences:

- A couple of weeks ago, there was a pause in the traffic flow because there was an accident on the freeway and people like to slow down and look.

- The last time I watched the evening news, reporters spent most of the time reporting on acts of violence in our society rather than on more positive events, I think because more people want to hear about violence.

Careful explanation of why the details are significant

Explain how these examples show that people see violence in terms of entertainment rather than real-life tragedy.

Connection to the thesis statement

Explain how we can understand this view of violence as an indication of society's growing lack of thought and care (paragraph's controlling idea), and how this is a direct result of television violence (tie to thesis statement).

Here is a sample body paragraph from a student paper on the issue of genetic cloning and its use. See if you can follow the 4Cs paragraph development.

Essay

> The paper's thesis statement: I agree with McMillan that, in spite of the excitement about cloning, it shouldn't be used right now because our limited knowledge makes it too dangerous.

(Controlling Idea Sentence) Although many experts are excited about pushing forward with the uses of cloning, the promise of cloning is still far on the horizon, and much more work must be done before it is widely used with confidence. (*Corroborating Details*) At a recent biotechnology conference, one expert said, "I am convinced that human cloning is going to play a critical role in the future of our species. We cannot afford to ignore the potential benefits of this science. It may well mean the ultimate survival of our species" (McDermott 29). Many people agree with him. In fact, scientists all over the world are experimenting with animals, and even humans, to gain some of the benefits that our early stages of knowledge allow, but cloning is still primarily a matter of trial and error, and successful attempts have been few. Methods of cloning are still very crude, and only a mere 3% of the successfully reconstructed embryos reach the birth stage (Doyle 69). The first attempt made to clone an animal, a sheep now named "Dolly," took 276 cloning attempts. (*Careful Explanation of Why the Details are Significant*) The chances of serious mistakes, with such a low success rate, suggest caution is

necessary. The responsibility attached to such a powerful tool is enormous, and scientists must be careful as they move forward, and wait to introduce such a significant ability to widespread social use. *(Connection to the Thesis Statement)* Hence, in spite of the excitement about genetic cloning, we must, for now, keep genetic cloning limited to laboratory experiment because our limited knowledge makes it too dangerous to use.

Remember that you should use the 4Cs with great flexibility, rather than rigidly as a set formula. Each paragraph in an argument essay requires its own stylized structure and application of these basic elements. The goal, after all, is to maximize the support of your thesis statement. You may find, for example, that you have more than one corroborating detail to add to support the topic of a paragraph and you may decide to include most or all of it to support your topic sentence. Sometimes, too, one sentence will be all you will need to show the paragraph's relevance to your thesis statement; other times, you may need several sentences. Think of the 4Cs as layers in a paragraph, elements that must be present, but that may intertwine and develop in creative and even necessary ways that are different each time you use them to build a supporting paragraph.

Application

1. Look over several of the supporting paragraphs in the essays in this book. Evaluate the strengths and weaknesses: Are the paragraphs fully developed? Are the topic sentences clear? Are the corroborating details convincing? Are there enough of them to support the writer's assertions? Is the writer able to tie the paragraphs to the overarching argument of the paper?

2. Rewrite one of the paragraphs you feel is weak, or restructure a set of short, incomplete paragraphs to make one strong one. Explain your revision.

A Review of Logical Fallacies

A writer's job is to provide as much evidence and support as possible for his or her thesis. However, the argument that a writer offers to defend that thesis must be sound. If some of the arguments the writer presents are illogical or unfair, the writer will undermine his or her own position and lose credibility with readers.

Arguments that lack reason or justice are called *fallacies*. Fallacies are simply false arguments. Often, writers are so enthusiastic about their own position that they make false claims, unethical arguments, or assertions that cannot be proven by the evidence at hand. The best way to guard against spurious arguments is to become familiar with some of the most common types of fallacies and learn to recognize them in your own writing and the writing of others.

Fallacies fall into two categories. The first category contains unethical arguments. These arguments attempt to manipulate the reader emotionally or attack the opposing position in some way that is unjust. Here are some examples of fallacies that are manipulative or unfair:

1. *Ad hominem*—attacking the person rather than the argument itself

    example: A well-known plant pathologist, Harold Weber, has written a book discussing the relationship between plant health and human disease, but his ideas should not be taken seriously because he gambles too much in Las Vegas.

    example: The members of the Glee Club are a bunch of prima donnas, so, of course, they would oppose spending money to charter a bus instead of using cars to go to Disneyland for Senior Ditch Day.

Hint

Check to see if your argument remains focused on ideas and reason rather than the character of an individual.

2. *Birds of a feather*—using guilt by association to blame the person for actions of friends or family

    example: Lupe Santiago belonged to a Girl Scout troop whose leader embezzled money from the cookie fund, so Lupe should not be the treasurer of our club.

    example: John Smith's sister has a drug problem, so even though he is a qualified nurse, he shouldn't be trusted in a job that requires him to administer prescribed narcotics to dying patients.

Hint

Check to see that your rejection of a point of view is based on its merit rather than its supporters.

3. *Sob story*—using a sad situation or dramatic case to manipulate the readers' emotions
   example: A wildfire set by an arsonist cost Kenji Yamamoto his house and his family, so you should agree to go with him to the prom.
   example: Santiago Cortez was the only member of his family to survive a horrific plane crash, so he is the best candidate for mayor of our town.

Hint

Check to see if you are appealing to the audience's reason rather than their pity.

The majority of fallacies are illogical because the thinking behind their arguments is flawed; the conclusions offered by these fallacies follow neither inductive nor deductive reasoning. Here are some examples of false reasoning:

1. *Circular reasoning*—restating the same argument in other words instead of giving evidence or proof
   example: *The Big Bang Theory* is my favorite television show, so it is the best show on television because I like it a lot.
   example: The president has thought a lot about health care, so his plan is the most well-thought-out plan available.

Hint

Check to see that you support your argument with evidence, not repetition.

2. *Post hoc, ergo propter hoc* (Latin for "after this, therefore because of this")—assuming because one event follows another, the first causes the second

    example: The night before the midterm, Karl Johnson played a game of baseball with his friends. The next day, he performed badly on his test. Karl failed the exam because he played baseball.

    example: On Saturday night, Eun Hee went to the movies with her girlfriends, and on Sunday her boyfriend Jun Ho broke up with her. Jun Ho ended his relationship with Eun Hee because she went out with her friends.

Hint

Check to see that the relationship between two occurrences is causal, not temporal.

3. *False dichotomy*—assuming an either/or choice so that the writer's position seems the only correct one

    example: Olmsted Hall is not earthquake safe. Either we tear it down, or students will die.

    example: Either we eradicate the Pit Bull breed altogether, or children playing outside will not be safe from dog attacks.

Hint

Check to see that there are no other alternatives to the two options you are asking the audience to choose between.

4. *Hasty generalization*—basing a conclusion on limited evidence

    example: The girls in my college dorm wrote their lab notes in green ink; therefore, green is the color of ink used by college girls in biology lab.

    example: My dog leaves the carrots in his bowl when I give him my leftover beef stew. Therefore, dogs do not eat vegetables.

Hint

Check to see that the sample you are using to draw your conclusion is not overly small.

5. *False authority*—citing a source that has no validity in terms of the subject

> example: Edmund Craft, the Pulitzer Prize-winning journalist, wears Brock loafers, so they must be comfortable.
>
> example: Li'l' Hound, a popular rapper, took his mother to Mexico for expensive cancer drug treatments unapproved by the FDA, so the medicine must really work.

Hint

Check to see that the source you use is recognized as having authority on the subject under discussion.

Transitions

Connect or Correct

Essays need transitions to link the ideas in individual sentences to each other and to tie paragraphs together. Transitions are the words or phrases that help relate thoughts and ideas to each other. Without transitions, sentences are merely lists, and paragraphs can seem disconnected from each other.

Transitions link concepts in one of two ways: They can signal that individual sentences or paragraphs extend a train of thought (***connect***), or they can predict for the reader that whatever follows will change the direction of thought (***correct***). Careful use of transitions improves the overall coherence of your essay.

There are a number of categories of transitional words that ***connect*** sentences and paragraphs. Here are some of the kinds of transitions and some examples of words and phrases that ***connect***:

Relationship	Transition Word
time	afterward, later, meanwhile, next, now, suddenly, then
continuation	also, finally, furthermore, in addition, secondly
reasons	for this reason, in order to, to that end
examples	for example, for instance, to illustrate, to show that
assertion	in fact, indeed, to tell the truth
repetition	as already noted, in other words
similarity	in the same way, likewise, similarly
space	here, near, opposite

Here are some kinds of transitions and some examples of words and phrases that ***correct***:

alternative	besides, not, or
contrast	however, in contrast, on the other hand, to the contrary

Smooth transitions between sentences and paragraphs can be achieved in other ways besides the use of particular transitional words and phrases. Here are some other ways to link ideas and thoughts.

repetition	repeating a word or phrase from the previous sentence or the previous paragraph in the new construction
parallelism	using a similar structure in consecutive sentences or paragraphs In other words, begin paragraphs with very similar sentences or with sentences noticeably similar in structure. Within a paragraph, repetition of sentence structure can be used for emphasis and to highlight the connection between ideas.

Hint

To check that you have provided transition words when necessary, identify the relationship you see between each sentence and the one that follows it, and between each paragraph and the one that follows it. Then, make sure you have provided a transition word when needed to help the reader see that relationship.

Application

Turn back to Weinstein's "The Ethics of Work-Life Balance" and find three good places to insert transition words. Rewrite the sentences in the space below, including the transition words; then, compare the new version to the original version. Discuss with a classmate the changes each of you made. Consider, based on your discussion, how transitions may be used to smooth out the flow of your sentences, and how they can also be overused so that your sentences become wordy or too long. You will want to develop a good sense of when to use transition words, and when to let your sentences stand more independently from one another.

Conclusions

The conclusion's primary purpose is to provide closure for your essay, but there are several effective ways to accomplish that goal. Consider the strategies below so that you can call on the most appropriate one for every essay you write.

Any essay that includes discussion of more than one point, idea, or example requires a conclusion. Without a conclusion, the reader has no sense of closure, no certainty that you have come to the end of your argument. It is important that you let the reader know that your essay is complete, not because you have run out of things to say or time to say them, but because you have fully explored and supported your thesis. The conclusion of the essay is also the place for you to impress upon the reader the importance of considering your ideas.

A good conclusion accomplishes two tasks:

1. It makes the reader aware of the finality of your argument.

2. It leaves the reader with an understanding of the significance of your argument.

Hint

Check to see that the conclusion of your essay fulfills the promise suggested by your introduction.

Writing the conclusion of your essay will offer you many choices and many challenges. You may choose a simple, formal ending, or you may choose to be somewhat creative and less conventional. Familiarize yourself with the possibilities below, and then decide which works best for your particular essay:

Types of Conclusions

Brief Summary	"In conclusion. . . ."
	"To summarize briefly. . . ."
Significance of Subject	"All these matters need to be understood because. . . ."
Most Important Point	"Lastly, remember that. . . ."
Request for Action or Opinion	X must be changed. . . ."
Useful Quotation	"In the words of Y. . . ."

Emotional Statement	an outcry, appeal, or plea such as "Let's all move to. . . ." or "Please. . . ."
Interesting Anecdote	a short relevant story, or a reference to a story mentioned in the introduction
Directive	"In the future. . . ." or "From now on. . . ."

Application

1. Look at the conclusions of the student essays in one of the case studies of Part 3 of this book, and identify which type of conclusion each one uses (a call to action, a summary, and so on).

2. Choose the one conclusion you feel is most effective and share your choice, and the reasons for that choice, with your classmates.

Strategies for Participating in a Rough Draft Workshop

After you have completed the first draft of your essay, your instructor may ask you to bring that rough draft to class for a workshop. Giving and receiving feedback is an important part of the writing process. While it is helpful to have friends and relatives who are not in your class read and comment on what you have written, other members of the class can better evaluate your writing in ways that are focused on the material and assignments for your particular course.

The process of reading and evaluating your classmates' papers provides you with a valuable learning experience and requires you to think again about the assignment as you read responses to it by your peers. You will be able to bring the insight you gained from this activity to your own work.

While you are reading papers written by members of your class, they will be reading and commenting on your paper. It is important that you seriously consider the critique you receive, and use it to improve your essay. If you disagree with a suggested change, you must make sure that you can give a good reason for not taking your reader's suggestion. You have to remember that the reader is judging your response to the assignment solely by the words on the printed page. Something that may seem clear to you in your own head but is confusing to the reader requires more thought on your part. Remember that the reader's remarks are intended to help you improve your work and are not meant as criticism of your writing ability.

How to Get the Most out of Your Rough Draft Workshop

As a Reader:

- Come prepared with your textbook, the assignment sheet, and writing apparatus.
- Listen to and carefully follow the directions given by your instructor.
- Do a quick first read through the essay you are reviewing without writing on either the draft itself or a review sheet.
- Then, carefully consider the questions or issues you have been instructed to evaluate one by one. As you consider each question, issue, section, or paragraph, make notes on your observations about the things that are working and the things that need more attention.
- The more specific the comment, the more helpful it will be to the writer. Ask what the writer intended in a particular sentence or passage, if it isn't clear; try to identify *why* a sentence or passage isn't clear or doesn't logically work; praise something that works and say why it does; avoid overused and unhelpful words such as "good," "nice," or "okay."
- Finally, think about the work as a whole and provide a written summary that clarifies the successes and problems you see in the draft as it is.

As a Writer:

- Bring a complete and readable draft of your own essay.
- When you get your paper back from your reader, if there are comments that are not clear to you, ask for a verbal explanation from your reviewer.
- Consider the suggestions carefully, and try to understand what in your essay led your reader to react in that particular way to the words on your paper.
- When you begin to revise, go back to the written peer review you have been given. Start with the final overview of the paper. Then, ask yourself whether you need to begin by rethinking the whole concept of your essay or by simply working to improve individual sections.
- Finally, use your handbook to review any grammatical or technical errors in your essay that were obvious to the reader. Once you feel that you understand the rules, make any necessary corrections.

Scoring Guide

Holistic reading requires scorers to assign essays to categories based on the dominant characteristics of the essay. As such, holistic scoring should avoid re-reading whole passages or marking student responses in any way. The categories below are used to identify scores of papers in six distinct groups.

A 6 paper (A, A-, B+) commands attention by engaging the material in an insightful and mature manner. The response is clear, logical, and convincing. Further, the response is fully developed, relying on well-chosen examples and persuasive reasoning. The 6 paper demonstrates a strong control of language, a fluid use of sophisticated sentences, and a notable understanding of the conventions of written English.

A 5 paper (B, B-) is clearly thoughtful and competent. The response consistently relies on effective examples that are carefully developed. All parts of a 5 paper will be on topic, though the overall response will not be as accomplished or elaborated upon as a 6 paper. A 5 paper often has a less fluent and complex style than a 6 paper, but it does show a clear control over word choice and sentence variety while coherently observing the conventions of written English.

A 4 paper (C+, C) is satisfactory, though uneven in its delivery. It demonstrates an understanding of the prompt and presentation of a thesis, though that thesis may not be logically positioned or clearly stated. Still, the thesis does have support in the form of examples, though the examples may not be fully developed, and some examples may not directly support or relate to the position and topic. The reasoning may be marginal in some parts of the response, and the response in general will be less developed and accomplished than a 5 paper. A 4 paper demonstrates adequate accuracy in sentence control and sentence construction. The 4 paper recognizes and adheres to the conventions of written English.

A 3 paper (C-) demonstrates that the student will benefit from additional instruction in reading, logic, and sentence construction. The response may indicate an unclear understanding of the text or topic, and the examples may benefit from additional development and analysis. A 3 paper may be characterized by any of the following: little sentence variety, word choice that could be more appropriate and concise, occasional misunderstandings of major concepts in grammar and usage, or frequent minor misunderstandings at the sentence level.

A 2 paper (D+, D) indicates a student is likely to receive significant benefits from instruction in reading, essay organization, and sentence generation. Typically, the response is basic in nature and often presents unclear logic or coherence throughout, and because of these qualities, the essay often diverges from the text or topic. Its prose is usually characterized by at least one of the following: simplistic or imprecise word choice; use of a single type of sentence construction; many repeated misunderstandings of grammar and syntax.

A 1 paper (D-, F) shows that a student would benefit from both intensive and extensive instruction in all aspects of reading and writing. The response may not engage the topic's demands, or there may not be a recognized response to the basic aspects of the prompt. The response may be very brief in nature. It often displays a pervasive struggle with word choice and coherence at the sentence level.

Finding and Using Arguments in Literature

One way to talk about fiction is to uncover the arguments it makes, arguments that are presented and supported through the elements of the story it tells. An argument is a kind of discussion in which reasons are advanced for (or against) some value or ethical position, often to influence or change people's ideas and actions. The first step to discussing fiction as argument is to understand the way fiction works *representationally*. In other words, readers are meant to see a fictional story and its characters as dramatizing general human experiences that all of its readers will recognize and understand. Authors hope to use the devices of fiction to capture a representation of life that is insightful and that rings true for readers.

For example, even though Shakespeare's *Romeo and Juliet* is a centuries-old story of two young lovers in a small town in Italy who cannot marry because of an old feud between their families, readers today understand that it is also about the experience of love and the ethical dilemmas we face when our individual desires conflict with the demands of those who have authority over us. We interpret the argument in *Romeo and Juliet* when we decide what the work is saying about this particular ethical dilemma. Those of you who know this play, what do you think it is arguing? That love is more important than duty? That love put over duty to others leads to tragedy? What details about the plot or characters in this play make you answer the way that you have? As you answer these questions, you begin to see *Romeo and Juliet* as a form of argument. Even though you and your classmates may have different answers, many of your answers may be equally compelling if each person can bring out the elements in the play that support her or his interpretation. One of the reasons that we continue to read works such as *Romeo and Juliet* is that they encourage us to discuss and question our experiences and our beliefs as individuals and as members of human society.

Works of literature contain one or more themes—in other words, ideas very similar to those in prose essays such as "The Benefits of 'Negative Visualization'" and "Competition and Happiness." Instead of stating arguments directly, however, as in prose essays, literary works take positions on human concerns indirectly, through the tools of literature. Sometimes authors will have a narrator present a "thesis statement" in a fairly straightforward manner, but more often the thesis will be implied through the events and characters of the story. Here is a set of strategies that you can use when analyzing the arguments in a work of literature:

1. Who are the main characters in the conflict? What is the subject or issue of the conflict?

2. Identify the two or more sides of the conflict. List the main characters and, by examining what they do and say, try to determine their role in the conflict. What contributions to the issue does each present through his or her words or actions? Look carefully at the evidence that each character presents and try to determine how the evidence is being linked to support a position.

3. Look over what you wrote for #2 and then try to state the argument that the story and its characters are representing. This time, try to state the argument in general

terms that readers can apply to their own lives. What more general issue is the story *representing* with this conflict?

4. Identify how the story resolves the conflict. The resolution sometimes carries an important perspective on the conflict it depicts. For example, think about how different Shakespeare's *Romeo and Juliet* would be if the two young lovers didn't die in the end.

Read the following excerpt taken from Dickens's "A Christmas Carol". Pay attention to the conflict between Scrooge's beliefs versus the beliefs of his nephew, two townsmen, and Scrooge's clerk Bob Cratchit. Then use these four steps to see the passage as an argument.

Essay ### A Christmas Carol

CHARLES DICKENS

an excerpt from Chapter 1—Marley's Ghost

Once upon a time—of all the good days in the year, on Christmas Eve—old Scrooge sat busy in his counting-house. It was cold, bleak, biting weather: foggy withal: and he could hear the people in the court outside, go wheezing up and down, beating their hands upon their breasts, and stamping their feet upon the pavement stones to warm them. The city clocks had only just gone three, but it was quite dark already: it had not been light all day: and candles were flaring in the windows of the neighbouring offices, like ruddy smears upon the palpable brown air. The fog came pouring in at every chink and keyhole, and was so dense without, that although the court was of the narrowest, the houses opposite were mere phantoms. To see the dingy cloud come drooping down, obscuring everything, one might have thought that Nature lived hard by, and was brewing on a large scale.

The door of Scrooge's counting-house was open that he might keep his eye upon his clerk, who in a dismal little cell beyond, a sort of tank, was copying letters. Scrooge had a very small fire, but the clerk's fire was so very much smaller that it looked like one coal. But he couldn't replenish it, for Scrooge kept the coal-box in his own room; and so surely as the clerk came in with the shovel, the master predicted that it would be necessary for them to part. Wherefore the clerk put on his white comforter, and tried to warm himself at the candle; in which effort, not being a man of a strong imagination, he failed.

"A merry Christmas, uncle! God save you!" cried a cheerful voice. It was the voice of Scrooge's nephew, who came upon him so quickly that this was the first intimation he had of his approach.

"Bah!" said Scrooge, "Humbug!"

He had so heated himself with rapid walking in the fog and frost, this nephew of Scrooge's, that he was all in a glow; his face was ruddy and handsome; his eyes sparkled, and his breath smoked again.

From *A Christmas Story* by Charles Dickens, 1843.

"Christmas a humbug, uncle!" said Scrooge's nephew. "You don't mean that, I am sure."

"I do," said Scrooge. "Merry Christmas! What right have you to be merry? What reason have you to be merry? You're poor enough."

"Come, then," returned the nephew gaily. "What right have you to be dismal? What reason have you to be morose? You're rich enough."

Scrooge having no better answer ready on the spur of the moment, said, "Bah!" again; and followed it up with "Humbug."

"Don't be cross, uncle," said the nephew.

"What else can I be," returned the uncle, "when I live in such a world of fools as this Merry Christmas! Out upon merry Christmas. What's Christmas time to you but a time for paying bills without money; a time for finding yourself a year older, but not an hour richer; a time for balancing your books and having every item in 'em through a round dozen of months presented dead against you? If I could work my will," said Scrooge indignantly, "every idiot who goes about with "Merry Christmas" on his lips, should be boiled with his own pudding, and buried with a stake of holly through his heart. He should!"

"Uncle!" pleaded the nephew.

"Nephew!" returned the uncle, sternly, "keep Christmas in your own way, and let me keep it in mine."

"Keep it!" repeated Scrooge's nephew. "But you don't keep it."

"Let me leave it alone, then," said Scrooge. "Much good may it do you! Much good it has ever done you!"

"There are many things from which I might have derived good, by which I have not profited, I dare say," returned the nephew: "Christmas among the rest. But I am sure I have always thought of Christmas time, when it has come round—apart from the veneration due to its sacred name and origin, if anything belonging to it can be apart from that—as a good time: a kind, forgiving, charitable, pleasant time: the only time I know of, in the long calendar of the year, when men and women seem by one consent to open their shut-up hearts freely, and to think of people below them as if they really were fellow-passengers to the grave, and not another race of creatures bound on other journeys. And therefore, uncle, though it has never put a scrap of gold or silver in my pocket, I believe that it **has** done me good, and **will** do me good; and I say, God bless it!"

The clerk in the tank involuntarily applauded. Becoming immediately sensible of the impropriety, he poked the fire, and extinguished the last frail spark for ever.

"Let me hear another sound from you," said Scrooge," and you'll keep your Christmas by losing your situation. You're quite a powerful speaker, sir," he added, turning to his nephew. "I wonder you don't go into Parliament."

"Don't be angry, uncle. Come! Dine with us to-morrow."

Scrooge said that he would see him—yes, indeed he did. He went the whole length of the expression, and said that he would see him in that extremity first.

"But why?" cried Scrooge's nephew. "Why?"

"Why did you get married?" said Scrooge.

"Because I fell in love."

"Because you fell in love!" growled Scrooge, as if that were the only one thing in the world more ridiculous than a merry Christmas. "Good afternoon!"

"Nay, uncle, but you never came to see me before that happened. Why give it as a reason for not coming now?"

"Good afternoon," said Scrooge.

"I want nothing from you; I ask nothing of you; why cannot we be friends?"

"Good afternoon," said Scrooge.

"I am sorry, with all my heart, to find you so resolute. We have never had any quarrel, to which I have been a party. But I have made the trial in homage to Christmas, and I'll keep my Christmas humour to the last. So A Merry Christmas, uncle!"

"Good afternoon!" said Scrooge.

"And A Happy New Year!"

"Good afternoon!" said Scrooge.

His nephew left the room without an angry word, notwithstanding. He stopped at the outer door to bestow the greeting of the season on the clerk, who, cold as he was, was warmer than Scrooge; for he returned them cordially.

"There's another fellow," muttered Scrooge; who overheard him: "my clerk, with fifteen shillings a week, and a wife and family, talking about a merry Christmas. I'll retire to Bedlam."

This lunatic, in letting Scrooge's nephew out, had let two other people in. They were portly gentlemen, pleasant to behold, and now stood, with their hats off, in Scrooge's office. They had books and papers in their hands, and bowed to him.

"Scrooge and Marley's, I believe," said one of the gentlemen, referring to his list. "Have I the pleasure of addressing Mr Scrooge, or Mr Marley?"

"Mr Marley has been dead these seven years," Scrooge replied. "He died seven years ago, this very night."

"We have no doubt his liberality is well represented by his surviving partner," said the gentleman, presenting his credentials.

It certainly was; for they had been two kindred spirits. At the ominous word "liberality", Scrooge frowned, and shook his head, and handed the credentials back.

"At this festive season of the year, Mr Scrooge," said the gentleman, taking up a pen, "it is more than usually desirable that we should make some slight provision for the Poor and destitute, who suffer greatly at the present time. Many thousands are in want of common necessaries; hundreds of thousands are in want of common comforts, sir."

"Are there no prisons?" asked Scrooge.

"Plenty of prisons," said the gentleman, laying down the pen again.

"And the Union workhouses?" demanded Scrooge. "Are they still in operation?"

"They are. Still," returned the gentleman, " I wish I could say they were not."

"The Treadmill and the Poor Law are in full vigour, then?" said Scrooge.

"Both very busy, sir."

"Oh! I was afraid, from what you said at first, that something had occurred to stop them in their useful course," said Scrooge. "I'm very glad to hear it."

"Under the impression that they scarcely furnish Christian cheer of mind or body to the multitude," returned the gentleman, "a few of us are endeavouring to raise a fund to buy the Poor some meat and drink, and means of warmth. We choose this time, because it is a time, of all others, when Want is keenly felt, and Abundance rejoices. What shall I put you down for?"

"Nothing!" Scrooge replied.

"You wish to be anonymous?"

"I wish to be left alone," said Scrooge. "Since you ask me what I wish, gentlemen, that is my answer. I don't make merry myself at Christmas and I can't afford to make idle people merry. I help to support the establishments I have mentioned: they cost enough: and those who are badly off must go there."

"Many can't go there; and many would rather die."

"If they would rather die," said Scrooge, "they had better do it, and decrease the surplus population. Besides—excuse me—I don't know that."

"But you might know it," observed the gentleman.

"It's not my business," Scrooge returned. "It's enough for a man to understand his own business, and not to interfere with other people's. Mine occupies me constantly. Good afternoon, gentlemen!"

Seeing clearly that it would be useless to pursue their point, the gentlemen withdrew. Scrooge resumed his labours with an improved opinion of himself, and in a more facetious temper than was usual with him.

Meanwhile the fog and darkness thickened so, that people ran about with flaring links, proffering their services to go before horses in carriages, and conduct them on their way. The ancient tower of a church, whose gruff old bell was always peeping slily down at Scrooge out of a gothic window in the wall, became invisible, and struck the hours and quarters in the clouds, with tremulous vibrations afterwards as if its teeth were chattering in its frozen head up there. The cold became intense. In the main street, at the corner of the court, some labourers were repairing the gas-pipes, and had lighted a great fire in a brazier, round which a party of ragged men and boys were gathered: warming their hands and winking their eyes before the blaze in rapture. The water-plug being left in solitude, its overflowings sullenly congealed, and turned to misanthropic ice. The brightness of the shops where holly sprigs and berries crackled in the lamp-heat of the windows, made pale faces ruddy as they passed. Poulterers' and grocers' trades became a splendid joke: a glorious pageant, with which it was next to impossible to believe that such dull principles as bargain and sale had anything to do. The Lord Mayor, in the stronghold of the might Mansion House, gave orders to his fifty cooks and butlers to keep Christmas as a Lord Mayor's household should; and even the little tailor, whom he had fined five shillings on the previous Monday for being drunk and bloodthirsty in the streets, stirred up tomorrow's pudding in his garret, while his lean wife and the baby sallied out to buy the beef.

Foggier yet, and colder! Piercing, searching, biting cold. If the good Saint Dunstan had but nipped the Evil Spirit's nose with a touch of such weather as that, instead of using his familiar weapons, then indeed he would have roared to lusty purpose. The owner of one scant young nose, gnawed and mumbled by the hungry cold as bones are gnawed by dogs, stooped down at Scrooge's keyhole to regale him with a Christmas carol: but at the first sound of God bless you, merry gentleman! May nothing you dismay! Scrooge seized the ruler with such energy of action that the singer fled in terror, leaving the keyhole to the fog and even more congenial frost.

At length the hour of shutting up the counting-house arrived. With an ill-will Scrooge dismounted from his stool, and tacitly admitted the fact to the expectant clerk in the Tank, who instantly snuffed his candle out, and put on his hat.

"You'll want all day tomorrow, I suppose?" said Scrooge.

"If quite convenient, Sir."

"It's not convenient," said Scrooge, "and it's not fair. If I was to stop half-a-crown for it, you'd think yourself ill-used, I 'll be bound?"

The clerk smiled faintly.

"And yet," said Scrooge, "you don't think me ill-used, when I pay a day's wages for no work."

The clerk observed that it was only once a year.

"A poor excuse for picking a man's pocket every twenty-fifth of December!" said Scrooge, buttoning his great-coat to the chin. "But I suppose you must have the whole day. Be here all the earlier next morning!"

The clerk promised that he would; and Scrooge walked out with a growl. The office was closed in a twinkling, and the clerk, with the long ends of his white comforter dangling below his waist (for he boasted no great-coat), went down a slide on Cornhill, at the end of a lane of boys, twenty times, in honour of its being Christmas Eve, and then ran home to Camden Town as hard as he could pelt, to play at blindman's buff.

Writing Topic

What is Scrooge's attitude toward earning money, and how does it differ from his nephew's? How valid do you find Scrooge's position as he explains it to the various characters in this passage of the novel? Be sure to support your position with evidence taken from your experience, your observation of others, the media, and your reading.

In the following activity pages, potential responses are offered for you to consider. As you read through these activities, imagine that you are preparing to write this essay and think about how you might formulate your thesis statement and what supporting material you might use.

Prewriting for a Directed Summary

As in earlier chapters of *Write It Review*, you will use the answers you fill in here when you write a directed summary in response to the first part of the prompt question for this assignment:

> *Prompt Question:* What is Scrooge's attitude toward earning money, and how does it differ from his nephew's?

This question asks you to look at this chapter from two particular points of view: that of the character Scrooge and that of his nephew. It asks you to determine, by these characters' words and actions, their beliefs regarding work and money. To answer this first part of the writing assignment, you will have to look carefully at the conversation between Scrooge and his nephew to understand how each man weighs the importance of these aspects of life. In addition to their discussion, look carefully at the story so as to draw conclusions about the type of life each leads and how their lifestyles underscore their beliefs about work and money.

You will remember from working on the prose essays in the previous chapters that argument works by putting together and linking evidence to support a conclusion. Rather than having a writer's views presented directly, as in "The Monsters in My Head" or "Competition and Happiness," for this assignment you will have to identify the evidence as the writer presents it through the plot and characters in the story. What position does Scrooge represent? What evidence can you gather from his words and actions and how will this evidence support your interpretation of his beliefs? What position on work and money does Scrooge's nephew represent? What evidence do you find in his words and actions that illustrates his position? Here are the four steps you can use to isolate and identify the two sides of the argument.

1. **Who are the main characters in the conflict? What is the subject or issue of the conflict?** Scrooge believes that people should accumulate as much money as they can by working as much as possible. His nephew believes that being with people and giving and receiving kindness are as important, or more important, than work and money. Their disagreement applies to people in general and how they choose to spend their time. This story makes us think about our own relationship to work and to how important we rate money and earning money versus being with family and friends.

2. **Identify the two or more sides of the conflict. List the main characters and, by examining what they do and say, try to determine their role in the conflict. What contributions to the issue does each present through his or her words or actions? Look carefully at the evidence that each character presents and try to determine how the evidence is being linked to support a position.**

Here is part of their conversation:

Scrooge: "Merry Christmas! What right have you to be merry? What reason have you to be merry? You're poor enough."

The Nephew: "Come, then," returned the nephew gaily. "What right have you to be dismal? What reason have you to be morose? You're rich enough."

Scrooge: What's Christmas time to you but a time for paying bills without money; a time for finding yourself a year older, but not an hour richer; a time for balancing your books and having every item in 'em through a round dozen of months presented dead against you?

The Nephew: "There are many things from which I might have derived good, by which I have not profited, I dare say," returned the nephew: "Christmas among the rest. But I am sure I have always thought of Christmas time, when it has come round— apart from the veneration due to its sacred name and origin, if anything belonging to it can be apart from that—as a good time: a kind, forgiving, charitable, pleasant time: the only time I know of, in the long calendar of the year, when men and women seem by one consent to open their shut-up hearts freely, and to think of people below them as if they really were fellow-passengers to the grave, and not another race of creatures bound on other journeys. And therefore, uncle, though it has never put a scrap of gold or silver in my pocket, I believe that it **has** done me good, and **will** do me good

Scrooge thinks that, because the nephew is poor, he should be unhappy. The nephew points out that, though Scrooge has plenty of money, he is miserable, so there is no connection between money and happiness. Scrooge answers that money is necessary to pay bills, and that without it, we will not be able to live a comfortable life because we'll always be dodging our creditors. Scrooge feels that Christmas is a waste of time because much money is spent and no work is done. The nephew, however, feels that he gets good from taking time away from thoughts of money and work in order to connect with others and form warm human relationships.

Scrooge appears to be in a bad mood through this part of the story. He is frustrated because, even though he doesn't want to change his lifestyle because of the Christmas holiday, those around him won't allow him to ignore it. The nephew seems cheerful and has a family, and he is able to reach out to his uncle to try and get him to join the holiday celebrations. Yet we learn that the celebration may be costing him money he doesn't have.

We can also look at Scrooge's discussion with the two men collecting money for the poor, and his comments to Bob Cratchit, his clerk. In both cases, Scrooge argues that people should concentrate on earning their living and supporting themselves, rather than taking time away from work to socialize.

3. **Look over what you wrote for #2 and then try to state the argument that the story and its characters are representing. This time, try to state the argument in general terms that readers can apply to their own lives. What more general issue is the story *representing* with this conflict?**

   The disagreement between Scrooge and his nephew makes us think about how much of our life and attention should be given to working and earning money. Should the human relationships in our life be placed above work, or should we think first and foremost about working to earn as much money as we can? Does happiness come more from our relationships with people or from our economic accomplishments?

4. **Identify how the story resolves the conflict. This resolution leads directly to the thesis statement, or the story's position in the argument.**

   We are working with an excerpt of the story, and there is not a resolution. Both characters are convinced that their position is the valid one.

   Notice that you can use the responses to these four questions to answer the first part of the writing topic: "What is Scrooge's attitude toward earning money and how does it differ from his nephew's?" If you were writing this essay, you could easily answer this question by rephrasing these answers in a way that answered this question directly.

Hint

Notice that, when writing about fiction, the convention is to use present tense verbs.

Opinion and Thesis Statement

The second question in the writing prompt that follows the selection from "A Christmas Carol" asks you to take a position of your own:

Prompt Question: How valid do you find Scrooge's position as he explains it to the various characters in this passage of the story?

Do you agree with the position on work and money that Scrooge represents in the story? To answer this, you would simply use the thesis frame (which you should recognize from previous chapters of this book) to formulate a thesis statement. As you may have done in previous chapters of *Write It Review*, if you're not sure what position you want to take, do some prewriting to develop your ideas, and then come back to writing a working thesis statement.

a. What is the subject of the prompt essay that the prompt question asks you to consider? In other words, what is the main topic the essay is about?

Our lives should focus on earning money and that should always be our priority.

b. What is the character Scrooge's opinion about that subject?

He believes that earning money comes first and that nothing should distract us from that concern.

c. What is your opinion about the subject, i.e., will you agree or disagree with him?

In this chapter of Dickens's "Christmas Carol," Scrooge believes that earning money is the most important priority in life, (add your position on the issue).

The last part of the prompt asks you to support the argument you put forward in your thesis statement:

Prompt Question: Be sure to support your position with evidence taken from your experience, your observation of others, the media, and your reading.

If you had to write this essay, the majority of it would be devoted to supporting the position you take in your thesis statement. You would do some prewriting to explore your ideas and develop your supporting topics, then use an outline to plan and draft your essay. As you can see, even though finding arguments in literature requires you to read with a somewhat different perspective, you can use the same steps of the writing process that you have worked with throughout the writing assignments in *Write It Review*.

A Closer Look at Your Control at the Sentence Level

Proofreading Your Essay for Mistakes in Grammar, Punctuation, and Mechanics

Students often feel that their work is completed once they have revised their rough draft by honing the content and arguments it contains, but they should still carefully examine their sentences to eliminate any errors. Frequently, errors in the rough draft are overlooked during the revision process because writers are focused on idea development and structure. Any writer should review her or his work several times to omit grammatical, mechanical, and spelling errors. While word processing programs can be helpful in finding some mistakes, computers are limited in this area. It is, therefore, the writer's responsibility to proofread and edit before printing out a final draft.

Here are a few strategies to focus your editing:

- Read your essay aloud, word for word, being careful to say exactly what you wrote, and not what you meant to write.
- Let the draft sit for a while after it is drafted; getting away from it will allow you to return to it with more objectivity.
- Be sure to edit using a paper copy; mistakes will be easier to find.
- For the errors you know you often make, read your draft several times, each time focusing on one error at a time.

Examine the following ten errors commonly made by writers.

Becoming familiar with these errors will help you to avoid them.

1. Verb Errors
   Underline the verbs and then
- check to see that they agree with their subjects. (For help, consult a handbook.)
- make sure you have used the correct verb tense. (For help, consult a handbook.)
- when possible, change "to be" verbs (is, are, was, etc.) to action words.
     Flat: Gloria Watkins is a good writer.
     Active: Gloria Watkins writes brilliantly.
2. Use of Inappropriate or Informal Language
   Mark sentences that contain informal language or slang. Rewrite them using more formal language.
     No: Kids' fairy tales are, like, really great to hear when you're a kid.
     Yes: We all enjoyed listening to fairy tales when we were young.
3. Pronoun Agreement or Reference Errors
   Circle all the pronouns in your draft and then
- check to be sure that the nouns they refer to are clear; if they aren't, change the unclear pronouns to nouns.
- be sure that each pronoun agrees with its referent.
     No: Even though a person may witness an accident, <u>they</u> will not be able to remember exactly what happened.
     Yes: Even though a person may witness an accident, he or she will not be able to remember exactly what happened.

4. Unwanted Repetition

   Identify sentences close to one another in the paper that use the same word two or more times (ignoring common words such as "the" or "to"). Eliminate the repetition by

   - looking for synonyms to replace repeated words.
   - seeing if you can combine two sentences into one and eliminate repetition that way.

5. Overuse of Sentences Similar in Construction

   To vary the pace of your sentences, try changing the construction of three or four of your sentences. For example, you can reorder the wording or turn sentences into phrases or dependent clauses.

   > Every culture has its own celebrations and rituals to mark special days.
   > Celebrations and rituals mark special days in every culture.
   > A writer might revise a paper several times before he or she submits it for a class.
   > Before submitting a paper for a class, a writer might revise it several times.

6. Comma Splice Errors

   Be sure there are no commas joining two complete sentences. For each comma splice, use one of the following methods to correct the error:

   > *comma splice error:*   Barbara decided to run for public office, however, she knew that the odds were against her winning.

   - Change the comma to a semicolon.
     > Barbara decided to run for public office; however, she knew that the odds were against her winning.
   - Change the comma to a period and a capital letter.
     > Barbara decided to run for public office. However, she knew that the odds were against her winning.
   - Link the sentences with a coordinating conjunction (for, and, nor, but, or, yet, so)
     > Barbara decided to run for public office, but she knew that the odds were against her winning.
   - Turn the second sentence into a dependent clause or phrase.
     > Although she knew that the odds were against her winning, Barbara decided to run for public office.

7. Unwanted Use of "You"

   Rewrite any sentence where "you" is used; eliminate "you" by replacing it with "I," "we," or another noun or pronoun.

   > *No:*   You can always identify a person who is wearing a uniform.
   > *Yes:*   We can always identify a person that is wearing a uniform.
   > *Yes:*   Everyone can identify a person that is wearing a uniform.

8. Word Choice Errors

   Use a dictionary to look up words you are unsure of and to make sure you've used them correctly.

9. Spelling Errors

   Use spell check to eliminate misspelled words.

10. Punctuation Errors

    Be sure all sentences begin with a capital letter and have the appropriate punctuation mark at the end.

Assessing Your Grammar Awareness

Below are two diagnostic tests that check grammar mastery. Take Test #1. Next, check your answers with an answer key (your instructor will supply one) and mark those you got wrong. Then, fill in the assessment sheet to identify your grammar weaknesses. The assessment sheet will give you a focus for further study. You might, for example, use the index in your handbook to find out why you made the errors you made and how to correct them.

Identify each item as correct or incorrect. If it is correct, then simply write "OK" on the lines below. If a sentence is incorrect, then rewrite the whole sentence and make it correct.

Verb Tense and Form

1. Homer was a blind poet of ancient Greece whose works are passing down in the oral tradition.

   _____

   _____

   _____

2. It may be that his epics are the compilations of stories by many authors.

   _____

   _____

   _____

3. Many works of art inspired by Homer's subject matter are hanged in museums all over the world.

   _____

   _____

   _____

4. The Trojan War had an economic basis even though the excuse the Greeks used was that Paris had stealed Helen.

   _____

   _____

   _____

5. In Homer's version, the Greeks say that Paris has kidnapped Helen, but the truth is that Helen loves the handsome, charming Paris.

_____

_____

_____

Subject-Verb Agreement

6. *The Iliad* begins when the flotilla of Greek ships are ready to leave for Troy, but the ships are becalmed.

_____

_____

_____

7. Agamemnon consults the priest, who tells him that he must sacrifice his sixteen-year-old daughter, Iphigenia, to bring the winds.

_____

_____

_____

8. When Iphigenia dies, the winds come; the Greeks reach Troy and camps on the beach.

_____

_____

_____

9. The battles in *The Iliad* often involves one-on-one combat between Greek and Trojan heroes.

_____

_____

_____

10. The residents of Troy are able to watch the bloody battles from the walls of the city.

Pronoun Agreement

11. Everyone in Troy is able to watch their loved ones die on the battlefield.

12. The Trojans reinforce when they see the Greeks getting ready to leave.

13. Some soldiers build a great wooden horse and conceal soldiers in them.

14. The Greek army pretends to leave after they roll the horse up to the city gates.

15. Someone in the crowd of soldiers says they think it might be a trick, but no one listens.

_____

_____

_____

Pronoun Reference

16. The Trojans bring the horse, a gift from the Greeks, into their city.

_____

_____

_____

17. The Trojans party when they see the Greek ships leave and know they are safe.

_____

_____

_____

18. In the middle of the night, the Greek soldiers come out of the great horse and attack the Trojans, and they are killed.

_____

_____

_____

19. As the Greek soldiers find reinforcements, many Trojan soldiers are killed or enslaved, and their anger further ignites the war.

_____

_____

_____

20. Since Homer wrote this story, something is called a "Trojan horse" because it is a ruse.

   _____

   _____

   _____

Dangling and Misplaced Modifiers

21. Having defeated the Trojans, the Greek ships depart after the war.

   _____

   _____

   _____

22. Odysseus has angered the Gods, throwing them off course.

   _____

   _____

   _____

23. Enduring many hardships and adventures, Odysseus wanders for ten years.

   _____

   _____

   _____

24. The English word "odyssey" is derived from Odysseus's name meaning a long wandering.

   _____

   _____

   _____

25. Often seeming crafty or sly, Homer describes Odysseus using the adjective "wily" in the epic poem.

_____

_____

_____

Parallelism

26. Odysseus and his men face great dangers on their journey and dependent on the wind.

_____

_____

_____

27. Imprisoned in Polyphemus's cave, they watch their comrades being eaten, realize they will soon share the same fate because they have no weapons of defense.

_____

_____

_____

28. Odysseus blinds the Cyclops, devises his escape by tucking himself under the sheep in the cave, and finds freedom when the sheep go out to graze.

_____

_____

_____

29. Next, Odysseus and his ship reach the Aeolian Isles, whose inhabitants are hospitable and entertain them.

_____

_____

_____

30. To help Odysseus on his way and speeding his return to Ithaca, Aeolus, Keeper of the Wind, gives Odysseus a west wind.

_____

_____

_____

Fused (Run-On) Sentences

31. Storms blow Odysseus's ships past Ithaca, and in ten days they reach the land where the lotus-eaters live the men go ashore and eat the magic lotus that induces memory loss.

_____

_____

_____

32. Odysseus orders other sailors to shore they have to drag the original search party back to the ship.

_____

_____

_____

33. When they come to an island inhabited by aggressive, fierce, one-eyed giants known as Cyclopes, one of the giants, Polyphemus, imprisons Odysseus and his twelve men in a cave.

_____

_____

_____

34. While Polyphemus is sleeping, Odysseus steals a piece of the giant's staff and sharpens it he makes the point red hot in the fire.

_____

_____

_____

35. Using the hot point, Odysseus burns out the giant's eye, and now Polyphemus is blind.

_____

_____

_____

Comma Splices

36. Back at the palace in Ithaca, Odysseus's wife Penelope has her own problems, her many suitors are pressing her to pick one of them as a husband.

_____

_____

_____

37. Many of the suitors stay at the palace, and they squander Odysseus's wealth on riotous living and sumptuous banquets.

_____

_____

_____

38. Penelope, as wily as Odysseus, staves off the suitors by declaring that first she must weave a shroud for Odysseus's father, every night she unravels what she has woven that day.

    _____

    _____

    _____

39. Some servants betray Penelope to the suitors, who angrily force Penelope to make a decision.

    _____

    _____

    _____

40. Penelope is smart and has a secret strategy, she says she will marry the man who can pull Odysseus's bow and send the arrow flying through the holes of twelve aligned ox blades.

    _____

    _____

    _____

Sentence Skills Assessment for Diagnostic Test #1

Problem	Needs Review	Needs Study	Completed
Verb Tense and Form			
Subject-Verb Agreement			
Pronoun Agreement			
Pronoun Reference			
Dangling and Misplaced Modifiers			
Parallelism			
Fused (Run-On) Sentences			
Comma Splices			

Identify each sentence as correct or incorrect. If a sentence is correct, write **"OK"** on the line below. If the sentence is incorrect, then rewrite the whole sentence and make it correct.

Verb Tense

1. Charles Dickens, the famous novelist, was born in Kent on February 7, 1812, but he moves to London when he is nine.

   _____

   _____

   _____

2. Dickens's father spent more than he made, so the whole family had been sent to debtors' prison in 1824.

   _____

   _____

   _____

3. For a short time while his family was living in prison, young Dickens is working in a blacking warehouse.

   _____

   _____

   _____

4. Many young children in Dickens's novels share a similar fate; for example, Oliver Twist is raised in a workhouse, and he later joins a gang of pickpockets.

   _____

   _____

   _____

Subject-Verb Agreement

5. *Great Expectations*, one of Dickens's autobiographical novels, tell the story of Pip, a poor, rural orphan boy with a job he hates.

   _____

   _____

   _____

6. Visiting his parents' grave, Pip meets Magwitch, an escaped convict.

   _____

   _____

   _____

7. Neither trust the other, but Pip steals food and a file as Magwitch orders.

   _____

   _____

   _____

8. When Magwitch is caught, he protects Pip and take the blame for the theft.

   _____

   _____

   _____

Pronoun Agreement

9. Since Pip is an orphan, he lives with his older sister and their husband Joe, a blacksmith who apprentices Pip.

   _____

   _____

   _____

10. Joe is a good man, but nobody can seriously claim that his wife, known as Mrs. Joe, is a nice woman, for she is mean and abusive.

    _____

    _____

    _____

11. Someone viciously attacks Mrs. Joe; perhaps they meant to kill her, but she survives and becomes a mute invalid.

    _____

    _____

    _____

12. Orlick, a journeyman who works for Joe, is responsible for attacking Mrs. Joe, threatening Pip, and planning to kill Pip; besides these, he does many other evil deeds.

    _____

    _____

    _____

Pronoun Reference

13. Pip is invited to play at Satis House, a place much different from his country home, which makes him feel special.

    _____

    _____

    _____

14. Miss Havisham lives there with her ward, Estella, and she always wears a wedding dress and keeps the clocks stopped at a certain hour.

    _____

    _____

    _____

15. Miss Havisham is unusual, and Estella is beautiful; Pip dreams of their wedding.

_____

_____

_____

16. Miss Havisham does not believe that Estella and Pip will ever marry, and, indeed, she says that she does not love Pip.

_____

_____

_____

Dangling and Misplaced Modifiers

17. Expecting to be a blacksmith for the rest of his life, a lawyer tells Pip that a secret benefactor has paid for the boy to be educated in London as a gentleman.

_____

_____

_____

18. After moving from Joe's home to London, Herbert Pocket becomes Pip's best friend.

_____

_____

_____

19. To live the life of a gentleman, former friends and relations are ignored by Pip.

_____

_____

_____

20. Using his newly acquired fortune, Pip helps Herbert buy a business.

_____

_____

_____

Parallelism

21. Herbert and Pip lead a life of drinking, gambling, and run up debts.

_____

_____

_____

22. Mrs. Joe dies, and Pip returns home for the funeral, overcome by grief, remorse, and by shame.

_____

_____

_____

23. One night, Magwitch breaks into Pip's room, announces that he, not Miss Havisham, is the benefactor, and again wants Pip's help.

_____

_____

_____

24. Magwitch needs a safe place to hide, for he is pursued by his former partner Compeyson, the police, and will be put to death for returning to England.

_____

_____

_____

Comma Splices

25. Estella marries an upper-class fellow, Bentley Drummle, he treats her badly.

_____

_____

_____

26. Miss Havisham bends over her fireplace, her clothing catches on fire, causing her, too, to go up in flames.

_____

_____

_____

27. She survives, and she spends her remaining days feeling sorry for her past misdeeds.

_____

_____

_____

28. Caught by the police, Magwitch is again sentenced to death, Pip loses his fortune.

_____

_____

_____

Fused (Run–On) Sentences

29. Pip chooses to go abroad with Herbert they will work in the mercantile trade.

_____

_____

_____

30. Many years later, Pip returns, and he encounters Estella in the garden of Satis House.

_____

_____

_____

31. Drummle is dead Estella is now free.

_____

_____

_____

32. Dickens originally wrote a different outcome this ending is a revision.

_____

_____

_____

Sentence Skills Assessment for Diagnostic Test #2

Problem	Needs Review	Needs Study	Completed
Verb Tense			
Subject-Verb Agreement			
Pronoun Agreement			
Pronoun Reference			
Dangling and Misplaced Modifiers			
Parallelism			
Comma Splices			
Fused (Run-On) Sentences			

Writing Assignments

Those of you who are familiar with *Write It* will recognize the writing process pages in each of the units in Part 2. We hope that you continue to use them in ways that work for you. Those of you new to these writing strategies will want to work carefully with the writing process pages in each of the assignment units because the writing process is crucial if you want to write successful essays. As you may already know, composition studies have identified four basic stages of the writing process—prewriting, drafting, revising, and editing. Successful writers use these stages either explicitly or implicitly whenever they write.

The writing support pages in this section of *Write It Review* will guide you to perfect your use of the writing process, or to develop a writing process of your own. The activities in each of the units will guide you to develop your ideas, formulate them into a conventional argument form, and present them to readers with clarity and effectiveness. You will find that, the more deliberate you become at making use of the writing process, the stronger your writing will become in both form and content. We encourage you to continue to practice your writing skills and to deepen your engagement with the critical reading and thinking that are so integral a part of successful academic writing.

A note on the organization of Part 2: If you have worked in the past with *Write It*'s format, you will already be familiar with the way each unit in *Write It Review* introduces you to a new topic using a lead reading selection followed by a writing assignment in the form of a writing topic based on that reading. For those of you who have not worked with *Write It* before, each writing topic is followed by worksheets that guide you through the writing process and help you to 1) clarify and deepen your understanding of the lead essay, 2) develop your own ideas about the issue contained in the lead essay, 3) focus your ideas and formulate a clear and well-developed thesis statement that responds to the writing assignment, 4) find specific and compelling support for your thesis statement, and 5) build concrete plans for drafting and revising your essay. For each unit's writing assignment, additional reading material is provided in the "Extending the Discussion" section. These supplemental readings are meant to provide a context for the argument in the main reading selection and help you explore the subject of that selection in greater depth.

A note on the importance of careful reading:

In general, college students today read less than ever before. Yet reading is the primary way that knowledge is communicated in an academic setting. Hence, we are hearing that college students report, on graduating, that they have learned very little in their four or five years spent in college. We urge you to be a tenacious and careful reader. For many of you, this will take some self-discipline and practice, but, as with anything difficult, your increasing proficiency as a reader will bring you not only intrinsic rewards but also a sense of success, increased learning, and ultimately higher grades. As with any challenging skill, reading sometimes-difficult college-level material will get easier with determined practice. Remember that it is unlikely that any reading selection, short or long, can be fully understood when read only once. Decide now to read everything you are assigned in this book two or three times initially, and then to go back to it frequently to refresh your memory and confirm your understanding of its ideas.

Assignment #1

"WHY WE CRAVE HORROR MOVIES"

For this assignment, you will write an essay responding to Stephen King's argument in a reading selection titled "Why We Crave Horror Movies." To complete the assignment successfully, be sure to read the essay and the writing topic carefully. Then carefully complete the assignments that follow. They will help you to understand the essay's ideas, think about the topic, and respond thoughtfully in your own essay.

The "Extending the Discussion" section for this assignment contains reading selections that explore King's subject from various points of view. Read these essays and compare their ideas to the ideas expressed in "Why We Crave Horror Movies." These supplementary readings will get you thinking about issues that relate to King's argument and that may be useful as you begin to develop your own essay in response to the writing topic.

WHY WE CRAVE HORROR MOVIES

STEPHEN KING

Stephen King is a best-selling writer, screenwriter, columnist, producer, and direc-
tor. He is best known as a writer of horror fiction, using the genre to confront some
of the basic concerns of modern society. He has sold over 350 million copies of his
books. Many of his stories have been adapted for movies, television series, and comic
books. King has also written under the pen names of Richard Bachman and John
Swithen. In 2003, he received The National Book Foundation's Medal for Distin-
guished Contribution to American Letters. He lives in Maine, the state of his birth.
The following well-known essay has appeared in a number of publications, includ-
ing several widely used composition textbooks.

I think that we're all mentally ill; those of us outside the asylums only hide it a little
better, after all. We've all known people who talk to themselves, people who sometimes
squinch their faces into horrible grimaces when they believe no one is watching, people
who have some hysterical fear—of snakes, the dark, the tight place, the long drop . . .
and, of course, those final worms and grubs that are waiting so patiently underground.

When we pay our four or five bucks and seat ourselves at tenth-row center in a theater
showing a horror movie, we are daring the nightmare. Why? Some of the reasons are simple and obvious. To show that we can, that we are not afraid, that we can ride this roller
coaster. Which is not to say that a really good horror movie may not surprise a scream out
of us at some point, the way we may scream when the roller coaster twists through a complete 360 or plows through a lake at the bottom of the drop. And horror movies, like roller
coasters, have always been the special province of the young; by the time one turns forty
or fifty, one's appetite for double twists or 360-degree loops may be considerably depleted.

We also go to reestablish our feelings of essential normality; the horror movie is
innately conservative, even reactionary. Freda Jackson as the horrible melting woman in
Die, Monster, Die! confirms for us that no matter how far we may be removed from the
beauty of a Robert Redford or a Diana Ross, we are still light-years from true ugliness.

And we go to have fun.

Ah, but this is where the ground starts to slope away, isn't it? Because this is a very
peculiar sort of fun, indeed. The fun comes from seeing others menaced—sometimes
killed. One critic has suggested that if pro football has become the voyeur's version of
combat, then the horror film has become the modern version of the public lynching.

It is true that the mythic, "fairy tale" horror film intends to take away the shades of
gray. . . . It urges us to put away our more civilized and adult penchant for analysis and
to become children again, seeing things in pure blacks and whites. It may be that horror
movies provide psychic relief on this level because this invitation to lapse into simplicity,
irrationality, and even outright madness is extended so rarely. We are told we may allow
our emotions a free rein . . . or no rein at all.

If we are all insane, then sanity becomes a matter of degree. If your insanity leads you to carve up women like Jack the Ripper or the Cleveland Torso Murderer, we clap you away in the funny farm (but neither of those two amateur-night surgeons was ever caught, heh-heh-heh); if, on the other hand, your insanity leads you only to talk to yourself when you're under stress or to pick your nose on your morning bus, then you are left alone to go about your business . . . though it is doubtful that you will ever be invited to the best parties.

The potential lyncher is in almost all of us (excluding saints, past and present; but then, most saints have been crazy in their own ways), and every now and then, he has to be let loose to scream and roll around in the grass. Our emotions and our fears form their own body, and we recognize that it demands its own exercise to maintain proper muscle tone. Certain of these emotional muscles are accepted—even exalted—in civilized society; they are, of course, the emotions that tend to maintain the status quo of civilization itself. Love, friendship, loyalty, kindness—these are all the emotions that we applaud, emotions that have been immortalized in the couplets of Hallmark cards and in the verses (I don't dare call it poetry) of Leonard Nimoy.

When we exhibit these emotions, society showers us with positive reinforcement; we learn this even before we get out of diapers. When, as children, we hug our rotten little puke of a sister and give her a kiss, all the aunts and uncles smile and twit and cry, "Isn't he the sweetest little thing?" Such coveted treats as chocolate-covered graham crackers often follow. But if we deliberately slam the rotten little puke of a sister's fingers in the door, sanctions follow—angry remonstrance from parents, aunts, and uncles; instead of a chocolate-covered graham cracker, a spanking.

But anticivilization emotions don't go away, and they demand periodic exercise. We have such "sick" jokes as "What's the difference between a truckload of bowling balls and a truckload of dead babies?" (You can't unload a truckload of bowling balls with a pitch-fork . . . a joke, by the way, that I heard originally from a ten-year-old.) Such a joke may surprise a laugh or a grin out of us even as we recoil, a possibility that confirms the thesis: If we share a brotherhood of man, then we also share an insanity of man. None of which is intended as a defense of either the sick joke or insanity but merely as an explanation of why the best horror films, like the best fairy tales, manage to be reactionary, anarchistic, and revolutionary all at the same time.

The mythic horror movie, like the sick joke, has a dirty job to do. It deliberately appeals to all that is worst in us. It is morbidity unchained, our most base instincts let free, our nastiest fantasies realized . . . and it all happens, fittingly enough, in the dark. For those reasons, good liberals often shy away from horror films. For myself, I like to see the most aggressive of them—*Dawn of the Dead*, for instance—as lifting a trap door in the civilized forebrain and throwing a basket of raw meat to the hungry alligators swimming around in that subterranean river beneath.

Why bother? Because it keeps them from getting out, man. It keeps them down there and me up here. It was Lennon and McCartney who said that all you need is love, and I would agree with that.

As long as you keep the gators fed.

Writing Topic

Explain the "dirty job" horror movies perform for us, according to King. Do you think horror movies potentially benefit all of us in the way he claims? Be sure to support your position with specific details taken from your own experiences, including the media, your observations of others, and your reading.

Vocabulary Check

Use a dictionary to find the meanings of the following words from King's essay. Choose the meaning or meanings that you think are useful in gaining a full understanding of King's ideas. Then, explain the way each of the definitions you wrote down is key to understanding his argument.

1. *province*

   definition: _____

   _____

   explanation: _____

   _____

   _____

   _____

2. *innately*

   definition: _____

   _____

   explanation: _____

   _____

   _____

   _____

3. *reactionary*

   definition: _____

   _____

   explanation: _____

   _____

   _____

   _____

4. *voyeur*

   definition: _____

   _____

   explanation: _____

   _____

   _____

   _____

5. *penchant*

   definition: _____

   _____

   explanation: _____

   _____

   _____

   _____

6. *exalted*

   definition: _____

   _____

   explanation: _____

   _____

   _____

   _____

7. *couplets*

   definition: _____

   _____

   explanation: _____

   _____

   _____

   _____

8. *covet*

definition: _____

_____

explanation: _____

_____

_____

_____

9. *remonstrance*

definition: _____

_____

explanation: _____

_____

_____

_____

10. *anarchistic*

definition: _____

_____

explanation: _____

_____

_____

_____

11. *subterranean*

definition: _____

_____

explanation: _____

_____

_____

_____

Questions to Guide Your Reading

Answer the following questions so you can gain a thorough understanding of "Why We Crave Horror Movies."

Paragraph 1

What are some of the behaviors that signal the hidden mental illness we all share, according to King? Have you noticed any other everyday behaviors that might fall into this category?

Paragraph 2

What does King claim is the obvious reason young people go to see a horror movie? Explain age as a factor defining the audience for this genre.

Paragraphs 3–4

According to King, what are some other reasons people watch horror movies? Can you think of any other reasons that he may have omitted?

Paragraph 5

Explain why King says it is "peculiar" to have "fun" watching a horror movie.

Paragraph 6

How do horror movies invite us to react in a childlike manner to their content, according to King?

Paragraphs 7–9

Explain the relationship King believes exists between degrees of sanity and emotions. How are humans in a civilized society taught to control their negative impulses?

Paragraph 10

What is another acceptable outlet for negative emotions, according to King? In what way can this outlet, along with horror movies, be seen as "reactionary, anarchistic, and revolutionary"?

Paragraph 11

Explain King's analogy of the hungry alligators.

Prewriting for a Directed Summary

It is always important to look carefully at a writing topic and spend some time ensuring that you understand what it is asking. Your essay must provide a thorough response that responds to all parts of the writing topic. The writing topic that follows "Why We Crave Horror Movies" contains three parts. The first part asks you about a central idea from the reading. To answer this part of the writing topic, you will have to summarize part of King's argument. In other words, you will write a *directed* summary, meaning one that responds specifically to the first question in the writing topic.

> first part of the writing topic:
>
> *Explain the "dirty job" horror movies perform for us, according to King.*

Do not stray too far from this question when writing your summary. Notice that it doesn't ask you to summarize the entire essay. Rather, it asks you to explain what particular job horror movies do for us. Use the questions below to help plan your response. They will guide you in identifying King's ideas.

Hint

It will be helpful to review Part 1's "A Review of the Guidelines for Writing a Directed Summary."

Focus Questions

1. According to King, is anyone completely mentally healthy?

2. How do civilized societies teach us to behave sanely and control, though not entirely eliminate, our negative emotions?

3. What is the relationship between the maintenance of sanity and the socially acceptable release of base instincts?

4. How do horror movies help with that process?

Developing an Opinion and Working Thesis Statement

The second question in the topic asks you to consider the author's position, think about the reasons he gives for taking this position, and decide if you are convinced that he is right.

second part of the writing topic:

Do you think horror movies potentially benefit all of us in the way he claims?

Make sure you answer this part of the question directly; your response to it will be your thesis statement. It is very important that you write a clear thesis statement, one that focuses on "anticivilization emotions" (as King calls them), their presence in our lives, and our strategies for dealing with them. In order to do this, you should take into account King's ideas about such emotions and the need to deal with our own "insanity."

1. Use the following thesis frame to formulate the basic elements of your thesis statement:
   a. What is the issue of "Why We Crave Horror Movies" that the writing topic asks you to consider?

   _____

   b. What is King's opinion about that issue?

   _____

   _____

   c. What is your opinion about the issue, and will you agree or disagree with King's opinion?

   _____

   _____

   _____

2. Now use the elements you isolated in 1a, b, and c to write a thesis statement. You likely will have to revise it several times until it captures your idea clearly.

   _____

   _____

Prewriting to Find Support for Your Thesis Statement

The last part of the essay topic asks you to develop and support the position you took in your thesis statement by drawing on your own experience and readings.

last part of the writing topic:

Be sure to support your position with specific details taken from your own experiences, including the media, your observations of others, and your reading.

Use the guiding questions below to develop your ideas and find concrete support for them. The proof or evidence you present is an important element in supporting your argument and a significant aspect of making your ideas persuasive for your readers.

1. As you begin to develop your own examples, think about your attraction to—or revulsion for—watching horror and violence in movies and in other forms of media. In the space below, make a list of personal experiences you or others have had with experiences such as the ones King discusses.

    How much fun have you had watching horror movies, reading horror novels, or telling/listening to what King calls "sick jokes"? List some of the horror movies you have seen. Which one would you say is your favorite? Why? Try to identify what you enjoy about these films.

    If you do not enjoy horror films, list some reasons you avoid them. Take into account some of the advertisements and trailers you have seen for these movies. What images, sounds, or language were used to entice people to see them? Then make a list of reasons others might enjoy them—based on your own observations of family or friends who like them.

    Any experience you have had that says something about this central idea can provide you with an example to support your thesis. List as many ideas as you can, and freewrite about the significance of each.

    Once you've written your ideas, look them over carefully. Try to group the ideas you've listed or developed in your freewriting into categories. Then, give each category a label. That is, cluster ideas that seem to have something in common and, for each cluster, identify that shared quality by giving it a name.

2. Now make another list, but this time focus on examples from your studies, the media, your reading (especially the supplemental readings in this section), and your knowledge of contemporary society. Do any of these examples affirm King's ideas? For example, do the plots of novels, films, or TV shows you are familiar with seem to be doing the "dirty job" that King claims they do? Do any of your examples challenge King's ideas and offer other ways of understanding fear and horror novels, and sick jokes.

What views do the supplemental essays in this section take? Review their arguments and supporting evidence, and compare them to King's. Are any of them especially convincing for you? If so, list them here. (If you refer to any of their ideas in your essay, remember to cite them.) List and/or freewrite about all the relevant ideas you can think of, even those about which you are hesitant.

Once you've written your ideas, look them over carefully. Try to group the ideas you've listed, or developed in your freewriting, into categories. Then give each category a label. That is, cluster ideas that seem to have something in common and, for each cluster, identify that shared quality by giving it a name.

3. Now that you've developed categories, look through them and select two or three to develop in your essay. Make sure they are relevant to your thesis and are important enough to persuade your readers. Then, in the space below, briefly summarize each item in your categories and explain how it supports your thesis statement.

The information and ideas you develop in this exercise will become useful when you turn to planning and drafting your essay.

Revising Your Thesis Statement

Now that you have spent some time working out your ideas more systematically and developing some supporting evidence for the position you want to take, look again at the working thesis statement you crafted earlier to see if it is still accurate. As your first step, look again at the writing topic, and then write your original working thesis on the lines that follow it.

writing topic:

Explain the "dirty job" horror movies perform for us, according to King. Do you think horror movies potentially benefit all of us in the way he claims? Be sure to support your position with specific details taken from your own experiences, including the media, your observations of others, and your reading.

working thesis statement:

_____

_____

Remember that your thesis statement must answer the second question in the writing topic while taking into consideration the writing topic as a whole. The first question in the topic identifies the issue that is up for debate, and the last question reminds you that, whatever position you take on the issue, you must be able to support it with specific examples.

Often, after extensive prewriting and focused thought, you will find that the working thesis statement is no longer an accurate reflection of what you plan to say in your essay. Sometimes, only a word or phrase must be added or deleted; other times, the thesis statement must be significantly rewritten. The subject or the claim portion may be unclear, vague, or even inaccurate. When we draft, we work out our thoughts as we write them down; consequently, draft writing is almost always wordy, unclear, or vague. Look at your working thesis statement through the eyes of your readers and see if it actually says what you want it to say.

After examining it and completing any necessary revisions, check it one more time by asking yourself the following questions:

a. Does the thesis statement directly identify King's argument?

b. Does it state your position on the issue?

c. Is your thesis well punctuated, grammatically correct, and precisely worded?

Write your polished thesis on the lines below and look at it again. Is it strong and interesting?

_____

_____

Planning and Drafting Your Essay

Now that you have examined King's argument and thought at length about your own views, draft an essay that responds to all parts of the writing topic. Use the material you developed in this section to compose your draft. Don't forget to turn back to Part 1, especially "The Conventional Argument Essay Structure," for further guidance.

Do take the time to develop an outline because it will give you a basic structure for incorporating all the ideas you have developed in the preceding pages. An outline will also give you a bird's-eye view of your essay and help you spot problems in development or logic. The form below is modeled on "The Conventional Argument Essay Structure" in Part 1, and it can guide you as you plan your essay.

Hint

This outline doesn't have to contain polished writing. You may want to fill in only the basic ideas in phrases or terms.

Creating an Outline for Your Draft

I. Introductory Paragraph

   A. An opening sentence that gives the reading selection's title and author and begins to answer the writing topic:

   _____

   B. Main points to include in the directed summary:

   1.

   2.

   3.

   4.

   C. Write out your thesis statement. (Look back to "Revising Your Thesis Statement," where you reexamined and improved your working thesis statement.) It should clearly agree or disagree with the argument in King's essay and state a clear position using your own words.

   _____

II. Body Paragraphs

    A. The paragraph's one main point that supports the thesis statement:

_____

       1. Controlling idea sentence:

_____

_____

       2. Corroborating details:

_____

_____

_____

_____

       3. Careful explanation of why the details are significant:

_____

_____

_____

_____

       4. Connection to the thesis statement:

_____

_____

_____

_____

    B. The paragraph's one main point that supports the thesis statement:

_____

       1. Controlling idea sentence:

_____

_____

2. Corroborating details:

_____

_____

_____

_____

3. Careful explanation of why the details are significant:

_____

_____

_____

_____

4. Connection to the thesis statement:

_____

_____

_____

_____

C. The paragraph's one main point that supports the thesis statement:

_____

1. Controlling idea sentence:

_____

_____

2. Corroborating details:

_____

_____

_____

_____

3. Careful explanation of why the details are significant:

_____

_____

_____

_____

4. Connection to the thesis statement:

_____

_____

_____

_____

D. The paragraph's one main point that supports the thesis statement:

_____

1. Controlling idea sentence:

_____

_____

2. Corroborating details:

_____

_____

_____

_____

3. Careful explanation of why the details are significant:

_____

_____

_____

_____

4. Connection to the thesis statement:

_____

_____

_____

_____

Repeat this form for any remaining body paragraphs.

III. Conclusion (Look back to "Conclusions" in Part 1. It will help you make some decisions here about what type of conclusion you will use.)

    A. Type of conclusion to be used:

    _____

    B. Suggestions, or key words or phrases to include:

    _____

Use the following guidelines to give a classmate feedback on his or her draft. Read the draft through first, and then answer each of the items below as specifically as you can.

Name of draft's author: _____

Name of draft's reader: _____

The Introduction

1. Within the opening sentences:
   a. King's first and last name are given.   yes   no
   b. the reading selection's title is given and placed within quotation marks.   yes   no
2. The opening contains a summary that:
   a. explains King's idea of human nature.   yes   no
   b. explains why he thinks we benefit from watching horror films.   yes   no
3. The opening provides a thesis that makes clear the draft writer's opinion regarding King's argument.   yes   no

If the answer to #3 above is yes, state the thesis below as it is written. If the answer is no, explain to the writer what information is needed to make the thesis complete.

_____

_____

_____

The Body

1. How many paragraphs are in the body of this essay? _____
2. To support the thesis, this number is   sufficient   not enough
3. Do paragraphs contain the 4Cs?

Paragraph 1	Controlling idea sentence	yes	no
	Corroborating details	yes	no
	Careful explanation of why the details are significant	yes	no
	Connection to the thesis statement	yes	no

Paragraph 2	Controlling idea sentence	yes	no
	Corroborating details	yes	no
	Careful explanation of why the details are significant	yes	no
	Connection to the thesis statement	yes	no
Paragraph 3	Controlling idea sentence	yes	no
	Corroborating details	yes	no
	Careful explanation of why the details are significant	yes	no
	Connection to the thesis statement	yes	no
Paragraph 4	Controlling idea sentence	yes	no
	Corroborating details	yes	no
	Careful explanation of why the details are significant	yes	no
	Connection to the thesis statement	yes	no
Paragraph 5	Controlling idea sentence	yes	no
	Corroborating details	yes	no
	Careful explanation of why the details are significant	yes	no
	Connection to the thesis statement	yes	no

(Continue as needed.)

4. Identify any of the above paragraphs that are underdeveloped (too short). _____

5. Identify any of the above paragraphs that fail to support the thesis. _____

6. Identify any of the above paragraphs that are redundant or repetitive. _____

7. Suggest any ideas for additional paragraphs that might improve this essay.

_____

_____

_____

The Conclusion

1. Does the final paragraph avoid introducing new ideas and examples that really belong in the body of the essay?   yes   no

2. Does the conclusion provide closure (let readers know that the end of the essay has been reached)?   yes   no

3. Does the conclusion leave readers with an understanding
   of the significance of the argument?   yes   no

4. State in your own words what the draft writer considers to be important about his
   or her argument.

   _____

   _____

   _____

5. Identify the type of conclusion used (see the guidelines for conclusions in Part 1).

   _____

Editing

1. During the editing process, the writer should pay attention to the following problems in sentence structure, punctuation, and mechanics:
       fragments
       misplaced and dangling modifiers
       fused (run-on) sentences
       comma splices
       misplaced, missing, and unnecessary commas
       misplaced, missing, and unnecessary apostrophes
       incorrect quotation mark use
       capitalization errors
       spelling errors

2. While editing, the writer should pay attention to the following areas of grammar:
       verb tense
       subject-verb agreement
       irregular verbs
       pronoun type
       pronoun reference
       pronoun agreement
       noun plurals
       prepositions

Final Draft Checklist

Content

_____ My essay has an appropriate title.

_____ I provide an accurate summary of King's position on the issue presented in "Why We Crave Horror Movies."

_____ My thesis states a clear position that can be supported by evidence.

_____ I have enough paragraphs and argument points to support my thesis.

_____ Each body paragraph is relevant to my thesis.

_____ Each body paragraph contains the 4Cs.

_____ I use transitions whenever necessary to connect ideas to each other.

_____ The final paragraph of my essay (the conclusion) provides readers with a sense of closure.

Grammar, Punctuation, and Mechanics

_____ I use the present tense to discuss King's argument and examples.

_____ I use verb tenses correctly to show the chronology of events.

_____ I have verb tense consistency throughout my sentences.

_____ I have checked for subject-verb agreement in all of my sentences.

_____ I have revised all fragments and mixed or garbled sentences.

_____ I have repaired all fused (run-on) sentences and comma splices.

_____ I have placed a comma after introductory elements (transitions and phrases) and all dependent clauses that open a sentence.

_____ If I present items in a series (nouns, verbs, prepositional phrases), they are parallel in form.

_____ If I include material spoken or written by someone other than myself, I have correctly punctuated it with quotation marks, using the MLA style guide's rules for citation.

Reviewing Your Graded Essay

After your instructor has returned your essay, you may have the opportunity to revise your paper and raise your grade. Many students, especially those whose essays receive nonpassing grades, feel that their instructors should be less "picky" about grammar and should pass the work on content alone. However, most students at this level have not yet acquired the ability to recognize quality writing, and they do not realize that content and writing actually cannot be separated in this way. Experienced instructors know that errors in sentence structure, grammar, punctuation, and word choice either interfere with content or distract readers so much that they lose track of content. In short, good ideas badly presented are no longer good ideas; to pass, an essay must have passable writing. So even if you are not submitting a revised version of this essay to your instructor, it is important that you review your work carefully in order to understand its strengths and weaknesses. This sheet will guide you through the evaluation process.

You will want to continue to use the techniques that worked well for you and to find strategies to overcome the problems that you identify in this sample of your writing. To recognize areas that might have been problematic for you, look back at the scoring rubric in this book. Match the numerical/verbal/letter grade received on your essay to the appropriate category. Study the explanation given on the rubric for your grade.

Write a few sentences below in which you identify your problems in each of the following areas. Then, suggest specific changes you could make that would improve your paper. Don't forget to use your handbook as a resource.

1. **Grammar/punctuation/mechanics**

   My problem:

   My strategy for change:

2. **Thesis/response to assignment**

   My problem:

   My strategy for change:

3. Organization

My problem:

My strategy for change:

4. Paragraph development/examples/reasoning

My problem:

My strategy for change:

5. Assessment

In the space below, assign a grade to your paper using a rubric other than the one used by your instructor. In other words, if your instructor assigned your essay a grade of *High Fail,* you might give it the letter grade you now feel the paper warrants. If your instructor used the traditional letter grade to evaluate the essay, choose a category from the rubric in this book, or any other grading scale that you are familiar with, to show your evaluation of your work. Then, write a short narrative explaining your evaluation of the essay and the reasons it received the grade you gave it.

Grade: _____

Narrative: _____

_____

_____

_____

_____

Extending the Discussion:
Considering Other Viewpoints

Reading Selections

"Fear" by Phil Barker
"A Peaceful Woman Explains Why She Carries a Gun" by Linda M. Hasselstrom
"Anxiety: Challenge by Another Name" by James Lincoln Collier
"The Solstice Blues" by Akiko Busch
"Inhibitions, Symptoms, and Anxiety" by Sigmund Freud
"The Tell-Tale Heart" by Edgar Allan Poe
"Peering Into the Darkness" by Joe Hill

FEAR

PHIL BARKER

In 2003, when this informative research article was published, Phil Barker was a graduate student in political science at the University of Colorado, Boulder, and was part of the research staff at the Conflict Research Consortium.

What Is Fear?

Fear is "an unpleasant and often strong emotion caused by anticipation or awareness of danger."[1] Fear is completely natural and helps people to recognize and respond to dangerous situations and threats. However, healthy fear—or fear which has a protective function—can evolve into unhealthy or pathological fear, which can lead to exaggerated and violent behavior.

Dr. Ivan Kos lays out several different stages of fear. The first is real fear, or fear based on a real situation. If someone or something hurts you, you have a reason to fear it in the future. Second is realistic, or possible fear. This is fear based in reality that causes a person to avoid a threat in the first place (i.e., waiting to cross a busy road for safety reasons). Next, exaggerated or emotional fear deals with an individual "recalling past fears or occurrences and injecting them into a current situation."[2] This type of fear is particularly relevant to conflict. Emotional fear affects the way people handle conflictual situations.

Causes of Fear

Conflict is often driven by unfulfilled needs and the fears related to these needs. The most common fear in intractable conflict is the fear of losing one's identity and/or security. Individuals and groups identify themselves in certain ways (based on culture, language, race, religion, and so on), and threats to those identities arouse very real fears—fears of extinction, fears of the future, fears of oppression, and so forth.

For many people, the world is changing rapidly, and their lives are being altered as a result. For some religious people, this change leads to the fear that young people will abandon the Church or Mosque, that the media will become more important and influential in the lives of their children, and that they are losing control of their own future. These threats to identity result in fear.[3]

Similarly, in many ethnic conflicts, a history of "humiliation, oppression, victimhood, feelings of inferiority, persecution of one's group, and other kinds of discrimination" lead to a fear of similar wrongdoing in the future.[4] These historical memories shape how groups and people see each other. As a result, historical violence between Israelis and Palestinians, Hutus and Tutsis, and Protestants and Catholics in Northern Ireland affects how these groups look at one another and often leads to fear of one

Barker, Phil. "Fear." *Beyond Intractability.* Eds. Guy Burgess and Heidi Burgess. Conflict Information Consortium, University of Colorado, Boulder. Posted: July 2003 <http://www.beyondintractability.org/essay/fear>

another. Group fears often translate into individual fears, as group extinction is often associated with individual extinction.

These examples illustrate the important role that history plays in the development of fear. Memories of past injustices lead individuals to anticipate future oppression or violence with a sense of anxiety and dread.

Why Fear Matters

Fear is a very important factor in intractable conflict. Emotions like fear can often cause extreme and seemingly irrational behavior in people, which can result in escalating conflict. According to James F. Mattil, the managing editor of *Flashpoints: Guide to World Conflicts,* "The common thread that weaves violent political movements together is fear. It is not the only motivating factor behind political violence, nor necessarily the most obvious, but it is virtually always there. Whenever we ask why people hate, or why they are willing to kill or die for a cause, the answer is invariably fear."[5]

People are social in nature, with shared values, religion, tradition, language, and so on. Whenever the basic characteristics that tie a group together are threatened, the group will fear for its survival. As a result, the group will also attempt to get rid of the threat, sometimes through distorted or violent means.

History plays an important role in this process. Historical experiences shape how groups view threats. If a group has been hurt or wounded in the past, it affects their outlook today. For example, historical tensions and wrongdoing affect the way Israelis and Palestinians see each other today. Oftentimes, history is exaggerated—meaning one group is portrayed as extremely heroic and another group is portrayed as barbarian or inhuman. This in turn leads to more mistreatment, as it is easier to abuse or hurt a group that has been dehumanized. A cycle develops—someone is hurt, resulting in fear and the demonization of the person or group that hurt them. This, in turn, makes it easier for future wrongdoing to occur.

It is also important to note the impact that elites, or leaders, have on fear and conflict. Oftentimes, leaders use fear to their political advantage. Leaders need support from those they lead, and one way to gain this support is by playing on the fears of the people. Leaders in Northern Ireland can use the fear of either the Protestants or the Catholics to their own political advantage. Many have asserted that George Bush used the fear of another 9/11 to support the second US war in Iraq. Leaders can even intentionally deepen these fears for their own purposes. Doing so can aggravate the already existing fears and lead to future difficulties.[6]

Dealing with Fear

Individuals: There are many ways of approaching fear in the context of conflict. However, since fear is such a personal issue, most approaches focus on the individual. There are various ways to deal with your own fear, including

- becoming aware of it,
- identifying the ways you express fear,

- recognizing the situations which trigger fear, and
- using behavioral techniques to reduce fear and stress.[7]

In order to overcome fears, individuals and groups must first come to terms with their own fears and understand just how destructive they can be. However, it is equally important to be aware of others' fears. Being aware of other people's fear allows you to deal with it appropriately. One of the most effective ways of handling the fear of others is through empathy, or seeing things from the other person's perspective. Once one does that, one can recognize actions of one's own that might be unnecessarily causing fear on the other side. By toning down one's language, or clarifying one's interests and needs, it is possible to dispel unwarranted fears, thereby helping the other side feel more secure. Empathy is also important in any attempt at reconciliation or mediation because it helps to foster a positive interaction between people.[8] It is also important to share your own fears so that others can empathize with you in return, and alter their behavior in ways that will lessen that fear as well.

Officials: Public support is essential for political leaders. One way leaders can gain this support is by addressing, playing off of, or even causing the fears of their people. As a result, leaders can play an important role in the creation and/or calming of fears, particularly in ethnic or intergroup conflicts. It is important that leaders be aware of the consequences of using fear as a motivational tool. Because fear is such a powerful emotion, leaders must be extremely cautious about playing on the fears of people. The former Yugoslavia is a perfect example of how the fears of the people can be used by leaders for power. Serb leaders often played on Serb fears in order to strengthen their power and to push people to do things they might otherwise have refused to do.[9] Contrast this with the very famous quotation of Franklin Roosevelt: "We have nothing to fear but fear itself." This is an overstatement; fear can be real and justified, but it is far too dangerous to exploit for other aims.

Third Parties: Mediators and third parties can play an important part in helping people to overcome their fears. By understanding the ways in which fear can create and escalate conflict, third parties can address these issues in a constructive manner. One way this can be accomplished is by assuring that people on both sides of a conflict feel that their individual needs and fears are being addressed. Oftentimes, this is done through no-fault discussions, wherein people are not allowed to discuss who is wrong in a situation, but only ways in which they may move toward a peaceful resolution. Neither side should have to sacrifice in areas that it considers to be an important need or fear. Solutions must always "satisfy fundamental needs and allay deepest fears."[10]

It is also important to remember that an issue such as identity and the fears associated with it are not zero-sum. In other words, the calming of one group's fear does not necessarily mean that another group has more reason to fear. Usually, quite the opposite is true. The more secure one group feels, the less it feels a need to attack other groups. Thus, security can actually be a win-win or positive-sum game: The more one side has, the more the other side has, too. This is true from the bully on the playground—who is usually an insecure child—to the bully in the international system.

Through empathy and understanding, groups in conflict can learn about the fears and needs of others and, in the process, overcome their own fears as well.

Endnotes

[1] "Merriam-Webster Online," book on-line (accessed 7 March 2003); available from http://www.webster.com; Internet.

[2] Paul Wahrhaftig, "Belgrade Combating Fear Project," article on-line (accessed 11 March 2003); available from http://www.conflictres.org/vol181/belgrade.html; Internet.

[3] James F. Mattil, "What in the Name of God?: Fundamentalism, Fear & Terrorism," article on-line (accessed 7 March 2003); available from http://www.flashpoints. info/issue_briefings/Analysis%20&%20Commentary/Analysis-Religion_main. htm; Internet.

[4] Steve Utterwulghe, "Rwanda's Protracted Social Conflict: Considering the Subjective Perspective in Conflict Resolution Strategies," article on-line (accessed 7 March 2003); available from http://www.trinstitute.org/ojpcr/2_3utter.htm; Internet.

[5] James F. Mattil, "What in the Name of God?: Fundamentalism, Fear & Terrorism," article on-line (accessed 7 March 2003); available from http://www.flashpoints. info/issue_briefings/Analysis%20&%20Commentary/Analysis-Religion_main.htm; Internet.

[6] Herbert Kelman, "Social-Psychological Dimensions of International Conflict," in *Peacemaking in International Conflict: Methods and Techniques,* eds. I. William Zartman and J. Lewis Rasmussen (Washington, D.C.: United States Institute of Peace Press, 1997), 197.

[7] **Endnote missing

[8] Herbert Kelman, "Social-Psychological Dimensions of International Conflict," in *Peacemaking in International Conflict: Methods and Techniques,* eds. I. William Zartman and J. Lewis Rasmussen (Washington, D.C.: United States Institute of Peace Press, 1997), 199.

[9] Anthony Oberschall, "The Manipulation of Ethnicity: From Ethnic Cooperation to Violence and War in Yugoslavia," article on-line (accessed 13 March 2003); available from http://www.unc.edu/courses/2002fall/soci/326/039/manipulation_of_ ethnicity.pdf; Internet.

[10] Herbert Kelman, "Social-Psychological Dimensions of International Conflict," in *Peacemaking in International Conflict: Methods and Techniques,* eds. I. William Zartman and J. Lewis Rasmussen (Washington, D.C.: United States Institute of Peace Press, 1997), 197.

Discussion Questions

1. What are the three categories of fear identified by Dr. Ivan Kos? Which category of fear does Barker feel accounts for many of the conflicts that result in war? Do you think his explanation is a reasonable way of understanding historical violence? Support your answer with a past and a current example.

2. How does Barker suggest we should deal with personal fears? Can you give an example of someone you know that may have benefited from following Barker's advice? If you don't think these strategies for dealing with fear would be helpful, explain your position.

3. Examine Barker's documentation style—the numbering system he uses to document his sources in the text of his essay, and the way he arranges his sources at the end. If you were giving him advice on documenting sources in MLA style, what would his citations and his works cited list look like? How might he have benefitted by using a formal style guide such as MLA or APA to cite his sources?

4. Which of King's reasons for watching horror movies relates to fear? Now consider the following list of synonyms for the word "fear": dread, anxiety, horror, distress, fright, panic, alarm, trepidation, apprehension. Choose words from this list that could be used to apply to fear as King uses it. Which of the words on the list apply to fear as discussed by Barker? Explain the difference between your two lists.

A PEACEFUL WOMAN EXPLAINS WHY SHE CARRIES A GUN

LINDA M. HASSELSTROM

Linda M. Hasselstrom is a rancher, an active environmentalist, and a writer of nonfiction and poetry. She writes about the Western landscape and environment and has said that she hopes her writing brings people to respect the life of the prairies and plains and live moderately so as to protect our resources. The following essay is taken from her book Land Circle: Writing Collected from the Land *(1991)*.

I am a peace-loving woman. But several events in the past ten years have convinced me I'm safer when I carry a pistol. This was a personal decision, but because handgun possession is a controversial subject, perhaps my reasoning will interest others.

I live in western South Dakota on a ranch twenty-five miles from the nearest town; for several years, I spent winters alone here. As a free-lance writer, I travel alone a lot—more than 100,000 miles by car in the last four years. With women freer than ever before to travel alone, the odds of our encountering trouble seem to have risen. Distances are great, roads are deserted, and the terrain is often too exposed to offer hiding places.

A woman who travels alone is advised, usually by men, to protect herself by avoiding bars and other "dangerous situations," by approaching her car like an Indian scout, by locking doors and windows. But these precautions aren't always enough. I spent years following them and still found myself in dangerous situations. I began to resent the idea that just because I am female, I have to be extra careful.

A few years ago, with another woman, I camped for several weeks in the West. We discussed self-defense, but neither of us had taken a course in it. She was against firearms, and local police told us Mace was illegal. So we armed ourselves with spray cans of deodorant tucked into our sleeping bags. We never used our improvised Mace because we were lucky enough to camp beside people who came to our aid when men harassed us. But on one occasion we visited a national park where our assigned space was less than fifteen feet from other campers. When we returned from a walk, we found our closest neighbors were two young men. As we gathered our cooking gear, they drank beer and loudly discussed what they would do to us after dark. Nearby campers, even families, ignored them; rangers strolled past, unconcerned. When we asked the rangers pointblank if they would protect us, one of them patted my shoulder and said, "Don't worry, girls. They're just kidding." At dusk, we drove out of the park and hid our camp in the woods a few miles away. The illegal spot was lovely, but our enjoyment of that park was ruined. I returned from the trip determined to reconsider the options available for protecting myself.

At that time, I lived alone on the ranch and taught night classes in town. Along a city street I often traveled, a woman had a flat tire, called for help on her CB radio, and got a rapist who left her beaten. She was afraid to call for help again and stayed in her car until morning. For that reason, as well as because CBs work best along line-of-sight, which wouldn't help much in the rolling hills where I live, I ruled out a CB.

As I drove home one night, a car followed me. It passed me on a narrow bridge while a passenger flashed a blinding spotlight in my face. I braked sharply. The car stopped, angled across the bridge, and four men jumped out. I realized the locked doors were useless if they broke the windows of my pickup. I started forward, hoping to knock their car aside so I could pass. Just then another car appeared, and the men hastily got back in their car. They continued to follow me, passing and repassing. I dared not go home because no one else was there. I passed no lighted houses. Finally, they pulled over to the roadside, and I decided to use their tactic: fear. Speeding, the pickup horn blaring, I swerved as close to them as I dared as I roared past. It worked; they turned off the highway. But I was frightened and angry. Even in my vehicle, I was too vulnerable.

Other incidents occurred over the years. One day, I glanced out at a field below my house and saw a man with a shotgun walking toward a pond full of ducks. I drove down and explained that the land was posted. I politely asked him to leave. He stared at me, and the muzzle of the shotgun began to rise. In a moment of utter clarity I realized that I was alone on the ranch, and that he could shoot me and simply drive away. The moment passed; the man left.

One night, I returned home from teaching a class to find deep tire ruts in the wet ground of my yard, garbage in the driveway, and a large gas tank empty. A light shone in the house; I couldn't remember leaving it on. I was too embarrassed to drive to a neighboring ranch and wake someone up. An hour of cautious exploration convinced me the house was safe, but once inside, with the doors locked, I was still afraid. I kept thinking of how vulnerable I felt, prowling around my own house in the dark.

My first positive step was to take a kung fu class, which teaches evasive or protective action when someone enters your space without permission. I learned to move confidently, scanning for possible attackers. I learned how to assess danger and techniques for avoiding it without combat.

I also learned that one must practice several hours every day to be good at kung fu. By that time I had married George; when I practiced with him, I learned how *close* you must be to your attacker to use martial arts, and decided a 120-pound woman dare not let a six-foot, 220-pound attacker get that close unless she is very, very good at self-defense. I have since read articles by several women who were extremely well trained in the martial arts, but were raped and beaten anyway.

I thought back over the times in my life when I had been attacked or threatened and tried to be realistic about my own behavior, searching for anything that had allowed me to become a victim. Overall, I was convinced that I had not been at fault. I don't believe myself to be either paranoid or a risk taker, but I wanted more protection.

With some reluctance, I decided to try carrying a pistol. George had always carried one, despite his size and his training in martial arts. I practiced shooting until I was sure I could hit an attacker who moved close enough to endanger me. Then I bought a license from the county sheriff, making it legal for me to carry the gun concealed.

But I was not yet ready to defend myself. George taught me that the most important preparation was mental: convincing myself I could actually *shoot a person*. Few of us wish to hurt or kill another human being. But there is no point in having a gun—in fact, gun possession might increase your danger—unless you know you can use it. I got in the habit of rehearsing, as I drove or walked, the precise conditions that would be required before I would shoot someone.

People who have not grown up with the idea that they are capable of protecting themselves—in other words, most women—might have to work hard to convince themselves of their ability, and of the necessity. Handgun ownership need not turn us into gunslingers, but it can be part of believing in, and relying on, *ourselves* for protection.

To be useful, a pistol has to be available. In my car, it's within instant reach. When I enter a deserted rest stop at night, it's in my purse, with my hand on the grip. When I walk from a dark parking lot into a motel, it's in my hand, under a coat. At home, it's on the headboard. In short, I take it with me almost everywhere I go alone.

Just carrying a pistol is not protection; avoidance is still the best approach to trouble. Subconsciously watching for signs of danger, I believe I've become more alert. Handgun use, not unlike driving, becomes instinctive. Each time I've drawn my gun—I have never fired it at another human being—I've simply found it in my hand.

I was driving the half-mile to the highway mailbox one day when I saw a vehicle parked about midway down the road. Several men were standing in the ditch, relieving themselves. I have no objection to emergency urination, but I noticed they'd dumped several dozen beer cans in the road. Besides being ugly, cans can slash a cow's feet or stomach.

The men noticed me before they finished and made quite a performance out of zipping their trousers while walking toward me. All four of them gathered around my small foreign car, and one of them demanded what the hell I wanted.

"This is private land. I'd appreciate it if you'd pick up the beer cans."

"I don't see no beer cans. Why don't you get out of there and show them to me, honey?" said the belligerent one, reaching for the handle inside my door.

"Right over there," I said, still being polite, "—there, and over there." I pointed with the pistol, which I'd slipped under my thigh. Within one minute, the cans and the men were back in the car and headed down the road.

I believe this incident illustrates several important principles. The men were trespassing and knew it; their judgment may have been impaired by alcohol. Their response to the polite request of a woman alone was to use their size, numbers, and sex to inspire fear. The pistol was a response in the same language. Politeness didn't work; I couldn't match them in size or number. Out of the car, I'd have been more vulnerable. The pistol just changed the balance of power. It worked again recently when I was driving in a desolate part of Wyoming. A man played cat-and-mouse with me for thirty miles, ultimately trying to run me off the road. When his car passed mine with only two inches to spare, I showed him my pistol, and he disappeared.

When I got my pistol, I told my husband, revising the old Colt slogan, "God made men *and women*, but Sam Colt made them equal." Recently, I have seen a gunmaker's ad with a similar sentiment. Perhaps this is an idea whose time has come, though the pacifist inside me will be saddened if the only way women can achieve equality is by carrying weapons.

We must treat a firearm's power with caution. "Power tends to corrupt, and absolute power corrupts absolutely," as a man (Lord Acton) once said. A pistol is not the only way to avoid being raped or murdered in today's world, but intelligently wielded, it can shift the balance of power and provide a measure of safety.

Discussion Questions

1. What fears cause Hasselstrom to carry a gun? What do you think of her means for managing her fear?

2. What are some of the alternatives Hasselstrom uses to try to protect herself from the things she fears? Which of Barker's suggestions for managing fear is she adapting to her individual situation?

3. Taking into consideration the benefits King believes result from watching horror movies, what impact do you think that activity would have on Hasselstrom's decision to arm herself?

4. Hasselstrom's piece is autobiographical and recounts events that really happened. Do such real-life accounts have the same effects on readers as King says horror movies have? viewers?

ANXIETY: CHALLENGE BY ANOTHER NAME

JAMES LINCOLN COLLIER

James Lincoln Collier graduated from Hamilton College and is a journalist, author, and professional jazz musician.

Between my sophomore and junior years at college, a chance came up for me to spend the summer vacation working on a ranch in Argentina. My roommate's father was in the cattle business, and he wanted Ted to see something of it. Ted said he would go if he could take a friend, and he chose me.

The idea of spending two months on the fabled Argentine Pampas was exciting. Then I began having second thoughts. I had never been very far from New England, and I had been homesick my first few weeks at college. What would it be like in a strange country? What about the language? And besides, I had promised to teach my younger brother to sail that summer. The more I thought about it, the more the prospect daunted me. I began waking up nights in a sweat.

In the end, I turned down the proposition. As soon as Ted asked somebody else to go, I began kicking myself. A couple of weeks later I went home to my old summer job, unpacking cartons at the local supermarket, feeling very low. I had turned down something I wanted to do because I was scared, and had ended up feeling depressed. I stayed that way for a long time. And it didn't help when I went back to college in the fall to discover that Ted and his friend had had a terrific time.

In the long run, that unhappy summer taught me a valuable lesson out of which I developed a rule for myself: Do what makes you anxious; don't do what makes you depressed. I am not, of course, talking about severe states of anxiety or depression, which require medical attention. What I mean is that kind of anxiety we call stage fright, butterflies in the stomach, a case of nerves—the feelings we have at a job interview, when we're giving a big party, when we have to make an important presentation at the office. And the kind of depression I am referring to is that downhearted feeling of the blues, when we don't seem to be interested in anything, when we can't get going and seem to have no energy.

I was confronted by this sort of situation toward the end of my senior year. As graduation approached, I began to think about taking a crack at making my living as a writer. But one of my professors was urging me to apply to graduate school and aim at a teaching career. I wavered. The idea of trying to live by writing was scary—a lot more scary than spending a summer on the Pampas, I thought. Back and forth I went, making my decision, unmaking it. Suddenly, I realized that every time I gave up the idea of writing, that sinking feeling went through me; it gave me the blues. The thought of graduate school wasn't what depressed me. It was giving up on what deep in my gut I really wanted to do. Right then, I learned another lesson. To avoid that kind of depression meant, inevitably, having to endure a certain amount of worry and concern.

The great Danish philosopher Søren Kierkegaard believed that anxiety always arises when we confront the possibility of our own development. It seems to be a rule of life that you can't advance without getting that old, familiar, jittery feeling. Even as children, we discover this when we try to expand ourselves by, say, learning to ride a bike or going out for the school play. Later in life, we get butterflies when we think about having that first child, or uprooting the family from the old hometown to find a better opportunity halfway across the country. Any time, it seems, that we set out aggressively to get something we want, we meet up with anxiety. And it's going to be our traveling companion, at least part of the way, into any new venture.

When I first began writing magazine articles, I was frequently required to interview big names—people like Richard Burton, Joan Rivers, sex authority William Masters, baseball great Dizzy Dean. Before each interview, I would get butterflies, and my hands would shake. At the time, I was doing some writing about music. And one person I particularly admired was the great composer Duke Ellington. On stage and on television, he seemed the very model of the confident, sophisticated man of the world. Then I learned that Ellington still got stage fright. If the highly honored Duke Ellington, who had appeared on the bandstand some ten thousand times over thirty years, had anxiety attacks, who was I to think I could avoid them?

I went on doing those frightening interviews, and one day, as I was getting onto a plane for Washington to interview columnist Joseph Alsop, I suddenly realized to my astonishment that I was looking forward to the meeting. What had happened to those butterflies? Well, in truth, they were still there, but there were fewer of them. I had benefited, I discovered, from a process psychologists call "extinction." If you put an individual in an anxiety-provoking situation often enough, he will eventually learn that there isn't anything to be worried about. Which brings us to a corollary to my basic rule: You'll never eliminate anxiety by avoiding the things that caused it. I remember how my son Jeff was when I first began to teach him to swim at the lake cottage where we spent our summer vacations. He resisted, and when I got him into the water he sank and sputtered and wanted to quit. But I was insistent. And by summer's end he was splashing around like a puppy. He had "extinguished" his anxiety the only way he could—by confronting it.

The problem, of course, is that it is one thing to urge somebody else to take on those anxiety-producing challenges; it is quite another to get ourselves to do it. Some years ago, I was offered a writing assignment that would require three months of travel through Europe. I had been abroad a couple of times on the usual "If it's Tuesday, this must be Belgium" trips, but I hardly could claim to know my way around the continent. Moreover, my knowledge of foreign languages was limited to a little college French. I hesitated. How would I, unable to speak the language, totally unfamiliar with local geography or transportation systems, set up interviews and do research? It seemed impossible, and with considerable regret, I sat down to write a letter begging off. Halfway through, a thought—which I subsequently made into another corollary to my basic rule—ran through my mind: You can't learn if you don't try. So I accepted the assignment. There were some bad moments. But by the time I had finished the trip, I was an experienced traveler. And ever since, I have never hesitated to head for even the most exotic of places, without guides or even advanced bookings, confident that somehow I will manage.

The point is that the new, the different, is almost by definition scary. But each time you try something, you learn, and as the learning piles up, the world opens to you. I've made parachute jumps, learned to ski at forty, flown up the Rhine in a balloon. And I know I'm going to go on doing such things. It's not because I'm braver or more daring than others. I'm not. But I don't let the butterflies stop me from doing what I want. Accept anxiety as another name for challenge, and you can accomplish wonders.

Discussion Questions

1. Explain the time that James Lincoln Collier gave in to his fears. What was the result? What rule did he form because of this experience? Tell about a time when you made a decision based on your fear and anxiety. What was the result of your decision? With hindsight, did you make the right choice?

2. How did Collier use his rule to make a career choice? Describe the possible safe career, and possible anxiety-producing career, you are considering. After reading Collier, which career do you think you will choose? Explain the reason for your choice.

3. Explain the psychological term "extinction." How do you think King might use it to explain the value of horror movies?

THE SOLSTICE BLUES

Akiko Busch

Akiko Busch taught at the University of Hartford and Bennington College and is now a faculty member of the MFA program at the School of Visual Arts. She is a widely published writer in the field of design, culture, and nature. Among other things, she wrote a book of essays about science and stewardship, titled The Incidental Steward: Reflections on Citizen Science *(2013) that was published by Yale University Press. She is also the author of* Geography of Home: Writings on Where We Live *(1999),* Nine Ways to Cross a River *(2007), and* Patience: Taking Time in an Age of Acceleration *(2010).*

In mid-June, the twilight seems to go on forever, the sky awash with translucent shades of rose, pearl, gray. These are evenings of enchantment—but also of apprehension. The moment the sun reaches its farthest point north of the Equator today is the moment the light starts to fade, waning more each day for the following six months. If the summer solstice doesn't signal the arrival of winter, surely it heralds the gradual lessening of light, and with that, often, an incremental decline in disposition.

It is easy to associate sundown with melancholy, to believe that temper can be so closely tied to degrees of illumination. The more floodlit our nights, the more we seem to believe that a well-lit world is part of our well-being. But equating the setting of the sun with that of the spirit may be misguided, at variance with some essential need humans have for darkness and shadow.

In his book *The End of Night*, Paul Bogard notes that two-thirds of Americans "no longer experience real night" (9). "Most of us go into the dark armed not only with 'a light,'" he writes, "but with so much light that we never know that the dark, too, blooms and sings" (271).

Certainly, that is true where I live in a rural area of the Hudson Valley in New York. It may be the country, but the gas station and convenience store down the road emit a halo of orange light; across the street at Stop & Shop, high-intensity-discharge lighting casts a radiant glow across the parking lot and beyond. The garish gleam of illuminated signs and street lighting further drenches the crossroad. Illumination, albeit artificial, bathes my world.

It occurs to me now that such an extravagance of light can work to diminish our comfort with nightfall, encouraging us to link darkness to fear, brightness to security. But it is a flawed connection.

In his 1933 anthem to obscurity, *In Praise of Shadows*, the Japanese writer Junichiro Tanizaki cataloged the oppressiveness of the illuminated world. An advocate for opacity, he lamented the bright, shining sterility of hotels, hospitals, Western living rooms and bathrooms, the glitter of diamonds, the glare of silver, steel and nickel tableware. "Were it not for shadows," he wrote, "there would be no beauty" (Tanizaki 46).

Tanizaki's appreciation for the subtleties of the shadow world resonate all the more today, when we tend to equate light with clarity and transparency, and assume that brightness and exposure in the environment have some corollary lucidity in thought and behavior. But of course, that is not so. We have a need for the shadow world, those things that cannot be easily explained, those things we suspect or imagine but do not know. And all those other areas in our lives that are defined by their gradations of uncertainty. Such ambiguity has a place in human thought and perception.

Here, when the sun finally falls, is the time one hears more acutely the cry of the coyotes, the courtship call of the barred owls. And if I am far enough away from the crossroads, from the floodlights of the town park and the headlight beams of traffic, I can make out the distant pinpoints of Orion, the dim shadows the white pines make in the moonlight, the random flicker of fireflies. The water in the marsh catches just a bit of the star shine.

One can have a similar experience in a city. Linnaea Tillett, a lighting designer in New York, spoke to me of a nighttime walk in Central Park, of listening more keenly to bird calls, the screech owls, foxes. But most of all, she spoke of understanding more fully night as a place of life. All species have their own cycles, and nocturnal rhythms are part of that, she said. "Standing at the edge of the pond, I heard an animal plunge into the water, maybe a raccoon or badger, I don't know. It is still a mystery."

Such experiences, she said, are important at a time when many of us are looking for ways to reconnect with the complex ecologies around us. Light, and its absence, are essential parts of this, and of the weeks that lie ahead now, Ms. Tillett said. "It's not about going from light to dark, but of being more sensitive to this progression of light, looking more acutely at the degrees of twilight, being more attentive to the nuances of half light."

The summer solstice may be a good time to recalibrate the impulse we often have to equate dusk with depression. Perhaps it makes sense to use the coming months of declining light as an opportunity to recognize the value of nightfall, the blooming and singing of the dark, in an increasingly illuminated world.

Works Cited

Bogard, Paul. *The End of Night: Searching for Natural Darkness in an Age of Artificial Light.* New York: Little Brown, 2013. Print.

Tanizaki, Junichiro. *In Praise of Shadows.* 1933. New York: Vintage-Random, 2001. Print.

Discussion Questions

1. For the most part, what mental states and ways of thinking are associated with darkness? How does Akiko Busch feel about that connection?

2. Before reading "The Solstice Blues," how did you feel about being alone in the deep dark? How has your reading this article changed the way you perceive darkness? How would you explain any changes you may have in regard to your thinking/ behavior and darkness after reading this article? If it is unlikely that there will be any changes, explain the reason for the lack of change.

3. Notice the several ways that "darkness" has been used in this unit's readings to represent a part of the human psyche and hence of human life. The writers focus on different approaches and strategies for dealing with this dark side of life: King, choosing a light tone to present a serious subject, suggests going to horror films; Hasselstrom carries a firearm; Collier recommends facing it head-on and finds it educational; Balzar makes it a priority in raising his child. How would you summarize Busch's depiction of darkness and her strategy for dealing with it? Discuss the different perspectives in these readings, and contrast their various approaches.

INHIBITIONS, SYMPTOMS, AND ANXIETY

SIGMUND FREUD

Sigmund Freud (1856–1939) was an Austrian-born physician and founder of the psychoanalytic school of psychology. Psychoanalysis is a clinical practice that uses patient-psychoanalyst dialogue to cure various forms of psychological disturbance. He is particularly remembered for his influential theories of the unconscious mind and its use of repression as a defense mechanism. He also argued that sexual desire, displaced through a wide spectrum of objects, is a key motivator in human beings. The excerpt below is from Freud's essay originally published in 1926.

The biological factor is the long period of time during which the young of the human species is in a condition of helplessness and dependence. Its intra-uterine existence seems to be short in comparison with that of most animals, and it is sent into the world in a less finished state. As a result, the influence of the real external world upon it is intensified, and an early differentiation between the ego and the id is promoted. Moreover, the dangers of the external world have a greater importance for it, so that the value of the object which can alone protect it against them and take the place of its former intra-uterine life is enormously enhanced. The biological factor, then, establishes the earliest situations of danger and creates the need to be loved, which will accompany the child through the rest of its life.

The existence of the second, phylogenetic, factor is based only upon inference. We have been led to assume its existence by a remarkable feature in the development of the libido. We have found that the sexual life of man, unlike that of most of the animals nearly related to him, does not make a steady advance from birth to maturity, but that, after an early efflorescence up till the fifth year, it undergoes a very decided interruption; and that it then starts on its course once more at puberty, taking up again the beginnings broken off in early childhood. This has led us to suppose that something momentous must have occurred in the vicissitudes of the human species which has left behind this interruption in the sexual development of the individual as a historical precipitate. This factor owes its pathogenic significance to the fact that the majority of the instinctual demands of this infantile sexuality are treated by the ego as dangers and fended off as such, so that the later sexual impulses of puberty, which in the natural course of things would be ego-syntonic, run the risk of succumbing to the attraction of their infantile prototypes and following them into repression. It is here that we come upon the most direct etiology of the neuroses. It is a curious thing that early contact with the demands of sexuality should have a similar effect on the ego to that produced by premature contact with the external world.

The third, psychological, factor resides in a defect of our mental apparatus which has to do precisely with its differentiation into an id and an ego, and which is therefore also attributable ultimately to the influence of the external world. In view of the dangers of [external] reality, the ego is obliged to guard against certain instinctual impulses in the id and to treat them as dangers. But it cannot protect itself from internal instinctual dangers as effectively as it can from some piece of reality that is not part of itself. Intimately bound up with the id as it is, it can only fend off an instinctual danger by restricting its own organization and by acquiescing in the formation of symptoms in exchange for having impaired the instinct. If the rejected instinct renews its attack, the ego is overtaken by all those difficulties that are known to us as neurotic ailments.

Further than this, I believe, our knowledge of the nature and causes of neurosis has not as yet been able to go.

Discussion Questions

1. What is the biological factor that Freud uses to explain the human need for love? Give your own explanation for the desire to love and be loved.

2. Use Freud's account of the id and the ego guarding against the dangers of the external world to explain the somewhat ordinary behaviors King terms manifestations of insanity. In what ways do Freud and King seem to share an understanding of human nature?

3. What is the definition of repression? How do you think King would see horror movies as aiding in the process of repression?

THE TELL-TALE HEART

EDGAR ALLAN POE

Edgar Allan Poe (1809–1849) was an American poet, author, literary critic, and editor. Now revered as a master of the short story, he was among the first writers in America to use that form and believed that the finest stories should be readable in one sitting. He is now best known for his mysteries and tales of the macabre and is considered the inventor of the genre of detective fiction; his fictional detective C. Auguste Dupin predates even Sherlock Holmes. Poe was determined to make his living solely by writing and is the first well-known American writer to attempt it. As a result, his life was difficult, both financially and professionally.

TRUE! nervous, very, very dreadfully nervous I had been and am; but why WILL you say that I am mad? The disease had sharpened my senses, not destroyed, not dulled them. Above all was the sense of hearing acute. I heard all things in the heaven and in the earth. I heard many things in hell. How then am I mad? Hearken! and observe how healthily, how calmly, I can tell you the whole story.

It is impossible to say how first the idea entered my brain, but, once conceived, it haunted me day and night. Object there was none. Passion there was none. I loved the old man. He had never wronged me. He had never given me insult. For his gold I had no desire. I think it was his eye! Yes, it was this! One of his eyes resembled that of a vulture—a pale blue eye with a film over it. Whenever it fell upon me my blood ran cold, and so by degrees, very gradually, I made up my mind to take the life of the old man, and thus rid myself of the eye for ever.

Now this is the point. You fancy me mad. Madmen know nothing. But you should have seen me. You should have seen how wisely I proceeded—with what caution—with what foresight, with what dissimulation, I went to work! I was never kinder to the old man than during the whole week before I killed him. And every night about midnight I turned the latch of his door and opened it oh, so gently! And then, when I had made an opening sufficient for my head, I put in a dark lantern all closed, closed so that no light shone out, and then I thrust in my head. Oh, you would have laughed to see how cunningly I thrust it in! I moved it slowly, very, very slowly, so that I might not disturb the old man's sleep. It took me an hour to place my whole head within the opening so far that I could see him as he lay upon his bed. Ha! Would a madman have been so wise as this? And then when my head was well in the room I undid the lantern cautiously—oh, so cautiously—cautiously (for the hinges creaked), I undid it just so much that a single thin ray fell upon the vulture eye. And this I did for seven long nights, every night just at midnight, but I found the eye always closed, and so it was impossible to do the work, for it was not the old man who vexed me but his Evil Eye. And every morning, when the day broke, I went boldly into the chamber and spoke courageously to him, calling him by name in a hearty tone, and inquiring how he had passed the night. So you see

"The Tell-Tale Heart" by Edgar Allan Poe, (1843).

he would have been a very profound old man, indeed, to suspect that every night, just at twelve, I looked in upon him while he slept.

Upon the eighth night I was more than usually cautious in opening the door. A watch's minute hand moves more quickly than did mine. Never before that night had I felt the extent of my own powers, of my sagacity. I could scarcely contain my feelings of triumph. To think that there I was opening the door little by little, and he not even to dream of my secret deeds or thoughts. I fairly chuckled at the idea, and perhaps he heard me, for he moved on the bed suddenly as if startled. Now you may think that I drew back—but no. His room was as black as pitch with the thick darkness (for the shutters were close fastened through fear of robbers), and so I knew that he could not see the opening of the door, and I kept pushing it on steadily, steadily.

I had my head in, and was about to open the lantern, when my thumb slipped upon the tin fastening, and the old man sprang up in the bed, crying out, "Who's there?"

I kept quite still and said nothing. For a whole hour I did not move a muscle, and in the meantime I did not hear him lie down. He was still sitting up in the bed, listening; just as I have done night after night hearkening to the death watches in the wall.

Presently, I heard a slight groan, and I knew it was the groan of mortal terror. It was not a groan of pain or of grief—oh, no! It was the low stifled sound that arises from the bottom of the soul when overcharged with awe. I knew the sound well. Many a night, just at midnight, when all the world slept, it has welled up from my own bosom, deepening, with its dreadful echo, the terrors that distracted me. I say I knew it well. I knew what the old man felt, and pitied him although I chuckled at heart. I knew that he had been lying awake ever since the first slight noise when he had turned in the bed. His fears had been ever since growing upon him. He had been trying to fancy them causeless, but could not. He had been saying to himself, "It is nothing but the wind in the chimney, it is only a mouse crossing the floor," or, "It is merely a cricket which has made a single chirp." Yes, he has been trying to comfort himself with these suppositions; but he had found all in vain. ALL IN VAIN, because Death in approaching him had stalked with his black shadow before him and enveloped the victim. And it was the mournful influence of the unperceived shadow that caused him to feel, although he neither saw nor heard, to feel the presence of my head within the room.

When I had waited a long time very patiently without hearing him lie down, I resolved to open a little—a very, very little crevice in the lantern. So I opened it—you cannot imagine how stealthily, stealthily—until at length a single dim ray like the thread of the spider shot out from the crevice and fell upon the vulture eye.

It was open, wide, wide open, and I grew furious as I gazed upon it. I saw it with perfect distinctness—all a dull blue with a hideous veil over it that chilled the very marrow in my bones, but I could see nothing else of the old man's face or person, for I had directed the ray as if by instinct precisely upon the damned spot.

And now have I not told you that what you mistake for madness is but over-acuteness of the senses? Now, I say, there came to my ears a low, dull, quick sound, such as a watch makes when enveloped in cotton. I knew that sound well, too. It was the beating of the old man's heart. It increased my fury as the beating of a drum stimulates the soldier into courage.

But even yet I refrained and kept still. I scarcely breathed. I held the lantern motionless. I tried how steadily I could maintain the ray upon the eye. Meantime the hellish tattoo of the heart increased. It grew quicker and quicker, and louder and louder, every instant. The old man's terror must have been extreme! It grew louder, I say, louder every moment!—do you mark me well? I have told you that I am nervous: So I am. And now at the dead hour of the night, amid the dreadful silence of that old house, so strange a noise as this excited me to uncontrollable terror. Yet, for some minutes longer I refrained and stood still. But the beating grew louder, louder! I thought the heart must burst. And now a new anxiety seized me—the sound would be heard by a neighbor! The old man's hour had come! With a loud yell, I threw open the lantern and leaped into the room. He shrieked once—once only. In an instant I dragged him to the floor, and pulled the heavy bed over him. I then smiled gaily, to find the deed so far done. But for many minutes the heart beat on with a muffled sound. This, however, did not vex me; it would not be heard through the wall. At length it ceased. The old man was dead. I removed the bed and examined the corpse. Yes, he was stone, stone dead. I placed my hand upon the heart and held it there many minutes. There was no pulsation. He was stone dead. His eye would trouble me no more.

If still you think me mad, you will think so no longer when I describe the wise precautions I took for the concealment of the body. The night waned, and I worked hastily, but in silence.

I took up three planks from the flooring of the chamber, and deposited all between the scantlings. I then replaced the boards so cleverly, so cunningly, that no human eye—not even his—could have detected anything wrong. There was nothing to wash out—no stain of any kind—no blood-spot whatever. I had been too wary for that.

When I had made an end of these labors, it was four o'clock—still dark as midnight. As the bell sounded the hour, there came a knocking at the street door. I went down to open it with a light heart, —for what had I now to fear? There entered three men, who introduced themselves, with perfect suavity, as officers of the police. A shriek had been heard by a neighbor during the night; suspicion of foul play had been aroused; information had been lodged at the police office, and they (the officers) had been deputed to search the premises.

I smiled, —for what had I to fear? I bade the gentlemen welcome. The shriek, I said, was my own in a dream. The old man, I mentioned, was absent in the country. I took my visitors all over the house. I bade them search—search well. I led them, at length, to his chamber. I showed them his treasures, secure, undisturbed. In the enthusiasm of my confidence, I brought chairs into the room, and desired them here to rest from their fatigues, while I myself, in the wild audacity of my perfect triumph, placed my own seat upon the very spot beneath which reposed the corpse of the victim.

The officers were satisfied. My MANNER had convinced them. I was singularly at ease. They sat and while I answered cheerily, they chatted of familiar things. But, ere long, I felt myself getting pale and wished them gone. My head ached, and I fancied a ringing in my ears; but still they sat, and still chatted. The ringing became more distinct: I talked more freely to get rid of the feeling: but it continued and gained definitiveness— until, at length, I found that the noise was NOT within my ears.

No doubt I now grew VERY pale; but I talked more fluently, and with a heightened voice. Yet the sound increased—and what could I do? It was A LOW, DULL, QUICK SOUND—MUCH SUCH A SOUND AS A WATCH MAKES WHEN ENVELOPED IN COTTON. I gasped for breath, and yet the officers heard it not. I talked more quickly, more vehemently but the noise steadily increased. I arose and argued about trifles, in a high key and with violent gesticulations; but the noise steadily increased. Why WOULD they not be gone? I paced the floor to and fro with heavy strides, as if excited to fury by the observations of the men, but the noise steadily increased. O God! what COULD I do? I foamed—I raved—I swore! I swung the chair upon which I had been sitting, and grated it upon the boards, but the noise arose over all and continually increased. It grew louder—louder—louder! And still the men chatted pleasantly, and smiled. Was it possible they heard not? Almighty God! —no, no? They heard! —they suspected! —they KNEW! —they were making a mockery of my horror! —this I thought, and this I think. But anything was better than this agony! Anything was more tolerable than this derision! I could bear those hypocritical smiles no longer! I felt that I must scream or die! —and now—again—hark! louder! louder! louder! LOUDER! —

"Villains!" I shrieked, "dissemble no more! I admit the deed! —tear up the planks! —here, here! —it is the beating of his hideous heart!"

Discussion Questions

1. Discuss the ways the narrator of the story attempts to convince the readers of his sanity. What impressions do readers form as a result of his attempts?

2. Discuss the fear—and the fearlessness—exhibited by the narrator through the course of the story. Consider the way the narrator's different experiences relating to fear illustrate Phil Barker's discussion of fear in the opening paragraph of his essay "Fear."

3. Explain the benefits you think King would attribute to reading "The Tell-Tale Heart." Suggest a reason of your own that might explain the time-honored popularity of Poe's horror stories.

PEERING INTO THE DARKNESS

JOE HILL

It was warm for October, so I went for a long ride to nowhere on my motorcycle, a seven-year-old Triumph Bonneville. I turned back for home when the sky was the color of marigolds, dead leaves whisking across the road in my wake, and in the peaceful light of dusk, I had a perfectly natural thought: What if a bat hit me in the face right now? What if my visor dropped, trapping it inside my helmet, shrilling and biting? What if I went off the road and snapped my back and was left paralyzed, out of sight down the embankment, with a dying bat in my helmet, its wings shattered, its claws scrabbling, the little white staples of its teeth sinking into me?

I wasn't kidding when I said this was a perfectly natural thought. It is. For me.

As the author of three unsettling fantasy novels and one collection of ghost stories, I work in the business of grotesque possibilities, and to quote Lt. Aldo Raine of *Inglourious Basterds*, business is a-boomin'! And not just for me. In entertainment, nothing gets you in the black faster than wading into the red.

On television, the zombies have lurched all the way to the top of the Nielsen ratings. A recent Newbery-Medal-winning novel follows the adventures of a boy who spends his entire childhood in a cemetery, where he is looked after by ghosts, ghouls, and a vampire. This is after his birth parents are knifed to death in chapter one. Just a little light entertainment for the kiddies.

At the movies, modestly budgeted pictures like *Oculus*, *The Purge*, and *Sinister* have been (blood) money in the bank. *Gone Girl*, a $60 million thriller with Oscar ambitions, almost suffered a humiliating upset at the box office in its opening weekend, when it nearly finished second to a bargain-basement screamer about a possessed doll, *Annabelle*.

But our preference for nightmares over daydreams is nothing new. You will recall that *Hamlet* is a ghost story, and that the hero muses about death while looking at a human skull.

I suggest to you that the compulsion to peer into the darkness, and wonder about what's there, is a distinctly useful and adaptive trait. And as it happens, the fiction of the horrific is unusually well tuned to address the most frightening and fascinating unknowns.

It is, for example, unlikely that any of us will ever have to worry about a real life zombie apocalypse. Yet we are, in truth, wildly outnumbered by the dead, and all of us will, in due course, be joining their ever-swelling ranks. The heroes of all those zombie stories, faced with diminishing resources and time, make final choices about what they need to say and do in their last hours. Someday you may well have to make the same choices, if only from a hospital bed or the wheelchair in the retirement home.

Ghost stories consider how much any of us are able to escape the horrors of the past. History casts a long shadow on the present, and sometimes this shadow is dark indeed. Ask the folks in Ferguson, Missouri, if the past is ever past.

Tales of the wolfman inevitably explore what it means to be an animal, which we are. We slaughter the living, we rend the dead flesh with our teeth, and we like it. The juice in your juicy steak is not juice.

And let's not even get started with His Infernal Majesty, who has trip-trapped on his goaty little hooves to visit every corner of the pop culture landscape. Stories of the devil are the lead-lined gloves we use to handle the radioactive material of our own ugliest, darkest compulsions—and hell but a stand-in for the bleakest corner of our souls.

The imagination is our final advantage as a species, a place to safely (and happily) explore experiences that are far from safe and far from happy. *Dracula* and *The Fly* may delight and appall in equal measure, but they also gently prepare us, helping us to think about how we would respond if faced with a terrifying seduction, or a corrupted and infected body.

The best fiction—in the genre of horror and elsewhere—eschews pat solutions for useful possibilities. This person did *that* and it ended horribly, so maybe don't do *that*. Another person did *this* and made the best of things when she was confronted with a bleak situation. Perhaps her example has some merit. If the literature of the unnatural is a lamp that can guide you through your own eventual nighttime journeys, it's still up to you to decide in which direction to strike out into the shadows.

And while the vast catalog of horrific fantasies may not be able to offer us simple answers to our biggest questions, it does occasionally remind us of small yet undeniably useful truisms: always look in the back seat before you get in the car; don't insult hillbillies with more power tools than teeth; whatever was making that awful noise out in the woods, you can check it out in the morning. And, oh yeah—always ride with your visor down.

Discussion Questions

1. What does Joe Hill mean when he says in the field of "entertainment, nothing gets you in the black like wading into into the red"? What examples, in addition to movies, does he cite? Which of his examples show that the connection between horror literature and entertainment is not new? What other historical examples can you list that use the spectacle of horror as entertainment? Discuss an example of horror entertainment, one of Hill's or your own, that you have enjoyed. If you have never enjoyed or experienced this genre, explain your reason for disliking or avoiding it.

2. How, according to Hill, can zombie stories aid us in real life? What are some other means of preparation available for such situations? Discuss some situations when the consumption of horror fiction might be a problem or cause problems.

3. What does good horror fiction have in common with other great fiction? Tell about a book, from horror or some other genre, that has been a "lamp" in your life.

4. Discuss Joe Hill's understanding of the value and function of the horror genre in relation to Stephen King's claim that horror movies have a "dirty job" to do.

Assignment #2

"THE BENEFITS OF 'NEGATIVE VISUALIZATION'"

This assignment asks you to write an essay in response to a reading selection that a reading selection that considers a certain life philosophy and its effect on our happiness. Once again, there are several essays in the "Extending the Discussion" section that your instructor may assign or that you may read on your own. These readings will help you explore the subject of Burkeman's argument in greater depth and develop your own ideas on the controversy that he addresses.

Whether you are assigned to read the supplemental readings or not, we encourage you to continue using all of the prewriting activities provided. They will ensure that you develop your thoughts and organize them within an effective essay format.

THE BENEFITS OF "NEGATIVE VISUALIZATION"

Oliver Burkeman

Oliver Burkeman is a British journalist who was educated at the University of Cambridge. He writes for the Guardian, *a British newspaper based in New York. His weekly column is titled* This Column Will Change Your Life, *and it focuses on issues related to social psychology, the self-help culture, and what he calls the science of happiness. His books to date are* HELP! How to Become Slightly Happier and Get a Bit More Done *(2011) and* The Antidote: Happiness for People Who Can't Stand Positive Thinking *(2012). The following reading is an excerpt from that book.*

Behind many of the most popular approaches to happiness is the simple philosophy of focusing on things going right. In the world of self-help, the most overt expression of this outlook is the technique known as "positive visualization": if you mentally picture things turning out well, the reasoning goes, they're far more likely to do so. "There is a deep tendency in human nature to become precisely what you visualize yourself as being," said Norman Vincent Peale, the author of *The Power of Positive Thinking*, in a speech he gave to executives of the investment bank Merrill Lynch in the mid-1980s. Even most people who scoff at Peale's homilies, however, might find it hard to argue with the underlying outlook: that being optimistic about the future, when you can manage it, is generally for the best.

Yet there are problems with this outlook, aside from just feeling disappointed when things don't turn out well. These problems are particularly acute in the case of positive visualization. Over the last few years, the German-born psychologist Gabriele Oettingen and her colleagues have constructed a series of experiments designed to unearth the truth about "positive fantasies about the future." The results are striking: Spending time and energy thinking about how well things could go, it has emerged, actually reduces most people's motivation to achieve them. Experimental subjects who were encouraged to think about how they were going to have a particularly high-achieving week at work, for example, ended up achieving less than those who were invited to reflect on the coming week, but given no further guidelines on how to do so.

It doesn't necessarily follow, of course, that it would be a better idea to switch to "negative visualization" instead, and to start focusing on all the ways in which things could go wrong. Yet that is precisely one of the conclusions that emerges from Stoicism, a school of philosophy that originated in Athens a few years after the death of Aristotle and that came to dominate Western thinking about happiness for nearly five centuries. For the Stoics, the ideal state of mind was tranquility—not the excitable cheer that positive thinkers usually seem to mean when they use the word "happiness." And tranquility was to be achieved not by strenuously chasing after enjoyable experiences, but by cultivating a kind of calm indifference towards one's circumstances. One way to do this, the

Stoics argued, is by turning towards negative emotions and experiences—not shunning them, but examining them closely instead.

When it comes to beliefs about the future, the evangelists of optimism argue that you should cultivate as many positive expectations about the future as you can. But this is not the good idea that it may at first appear to be. For a start, as Gabriele Oettingen's experiments demonstrate, focusing on the outcome you desire may actually sabotage your efforts to achieve it. More generally, a Stoic would point out, it just isn't a particularly good technique for feeling happier. Ceaseless optimism about the future only makes for a greater shock when things go wrong; by fighting to maintain only positive beliefs about the future, the positive thinker ends up being *less* prepared, and *more* acutely distressed, when things eventually happen that he can't persuade himself to believe are good. (And such things will happen.) This is a problem underlying all approaches to happiness that set too great a store by optimism. Trying to see things in an exclusively positive light is an attitude that requires constant, effortful replenishment. Should your efforts falter or prove insufficient when confronted by some unexpected shock, you'll sink back down into—possibly deeper—gloom.

The Stoics propose a more elegant, sustainable, and calming way to deal with the possibility of things going wrong: Rather than struggling to avoid all thought of these worst-case scenarios, they counsel actively dwelling on them, staring them in the face. The first benefit of dwelling on how bad things might get is a straightforward one. Psychologists have long agreed that one of the greatest enemies of human happiness is "hedonic adaptation"—the predictable and frustrating way in which any new source of pleasure we obtain, whether it's as minor as a new piece of electronic gadgetry or as major as a marriage, swiftly gets relegated to the backdrop of our lives. We grow accustomed to it, and so it ceases to deliver so much joy. It follows, then, that regularly reminding yourself that you might lose any of the things you currently enjoy—indeed, that you will definitely lose them all, in the end, when death catches up with you— would reverse the adaptation effect. Thinking about the possibility of losing something you value shifts it from the backdrop of your life back to center stage, where it can deliver pleasure once more. The second subtler and arguably even more powerful benefit of the premeditation of evils is as an antidote to anxiety. Consider how we normally seek to assuage worries about the future: We seek reassurance, looking to persuade ourselves that everything will be all right. But reassurance is a double-edged sword. In the short term, it can be wonderful, but like all forms of optimism, it requires constant maintenance: If you offer reassurance to a friend who is in the grip of anxiety, you'll often find that a few days later, he'll be back for more. Worse, reassurance can actually exacerbate anxiety. When you reassure your friend that the worst-case scenario he fears probably won't occur, you inadvertently reinforce his belief that it would be catastrophic if it did. You are tightening the coil of his anxiety, not loosening it.

All too often, the Stoics point out, things will not turn out for the best. But it is also true that, when they do go wrong, they'll almost certainly go less wrong than you were fearing. Losing your job won't condemn you to starvation and death; losing a boyfriend or girlfriend won't condemn you to a life of unrelenting misery. Those fears are based on irrational judgments about the future. The premeditation of evils is the way to replace these irrational notions with more rational judgments; spend time vividly imagining exactly how wrong things could go in reality, and you will usually find that your fears were exaggerated. If you lost your job, there are specific steps you could take to find a new one; if you lost your relationship, you would probably manage to find some happiness in life despite being single. Confronting the worst-case scenario saps it of much of its anxiety-inducing power. Happiness reached via positive thinking can be fleeting and brittle; negative visualization generates a vastly more dependable calm.

Writing Topic

According to Burkeman, in what ways is "negative visualization" more likely to make people happier than "positive visualization"? What do you think of his views? To develop your own position, be sure to discuss specific examples; these examples can be drawn from anything you've read, as well as from your observations and experiences.

Vocabulary Check

Use a dictionary to find the meanings of the following words from Burkeman's essay. Choose the meaning or meanings that you think are useful in gaining a full understanding of Burkeman's ideas. Then, explain the way each of the definitions you wrote down is key to understanding his argument.

1. *overt*

   definition: _____

   _____

   explanation: _____

   _____

   _____

   _____

2. *optimistic*

   definition: _____

   _____

   explanation: _____

   _____

   _____

   _____

3. *dominate*

   definition: _____

   _____

   explanation: _____

   _____

   _____

   _____

4. *tranquility*

definition: _____

_____

explanation: _____

_____

_____

_____

5. *indifference*

definition: _____

_____

explanation: _____

_____

_____

_____

6. *shun*

definition: _____

_____

explanation: _____

_____

_____

_____

7. *hedonic*

definition: _____

_____

explanation: _____

_____

_____

_____

8. *relegate*

definition: _____

_____

explanation: _____

_____

_____

_____

9. *backdrop*

definition: _____

_____

explanation: _____

_____

_____

_____

10. *antidote*

definition: _____

_____

explanation: _____

_____

_____

_____

11. *assuage*

definition: _____

_____

explanation: _____

_____

_____

_____

12. *exacerbate*

    definition: _____

    _____

    explanation: _____

    _____

    _____

    _____

13. *unrelenting*

    definition: _____

    _____

    explanation: _____

    _____

    _____

    _____

Questions to Guide Your Reading

Answer the following questions so you can gain a thorough understanding of "The Benefits of 'Negative Visualization.'"

Paragraphs 1 and 2

Identify and explain Burkeman's presentation of two different and opposing philosophies for the achievement of happiness.

Paragraph 2

How does Burkeman use a study done by Gabriele Oettingen to identify a potential problem with positive visualization?

Paragraph 3

Explain the life philosophy that the Stoics adopt in the pursuit of happiness, according to Burkeman.

Paragraph 4

What pervasive problem, according to Burkeman, underlies an optimistic approach to life?

Paragraph 5

What are two benefits, according to Burkeman, of adopting a Stoic-like approach to life?

What is "hedonic adaptation," and how does it work against happiness?

According to Burkeman's logic, how can positive reassurance actually heighten anxiety?

Paragraph 6

How can imagining the ways that things could go wrong turn fear into something positive, in Burkeman's view?

Prewriting for a Directed Summary

It is always important to look carefully at a writing topic and spend some time ensuring that you understand what it is asking. Your essay must provide a thorough response that responds to all parts of the writing topic. The writing topic that follows "The Benefits of 'Negative Visualization'" contains three parts. The first part asks you about a central idea from the reading. To answer this part of the writing topic, you will have to summarize part of Burkeman's argument. In other words, you will write a *directed* summary, meaning one that responds specifically to the first question in the writing topic.

first question in the writing topic:

> *According to Burkeman, in what ways is "negative visualization" more likely to make people happier than "positive visualization"?*

Notice that the question doesn't ask you to summarize the entire essay or simply to explain Burkeman's definition of "negative visualization" and "positive visualization." Rather, it asks you to explain Burkeman's reason(s) for claiming that "positive visualization" undermines happiness, while "negative visualization" promotes it. The questions below will help you plan your response. They will guide you in identifying what you should include in your directed summary.

Focus Questions

1. What does Burkeman mean by "positive visualization," and what problems does he think can result from it?

2. According to Burkeman, what does a Stoic believe is the ideal state of mind, and how is it achieved?

3. What does Burkeman mean by "negative visualization," and how, in his opinion, does this kind of thinking reduce fear and anxiety?

Developing an Opinion and Working Thesis Statement

The second question in the writing topic asks you to respond to Burkeman's central claim by taking a position of your own:

> second part of the writing topic:
>
> *What do you think of his views?*

You will have to explore your ideas on negative visualization and happiness and decide what position you want to take in your essay. Do you agree with Burkeman that positive visualization undermines our happiness while negative visualization enhances it? Be sure to answer this part of the question directly because it will become the thesis statement for your essay. You will want to be as clear as possible.

It is likely that you aren't yet sure what position you want to take in your essay, but it will be helpful now to draft a working thesis statement. Use your initial thoughts to take a position that seems reasonable to you right now. There will be a chance later to revise or even change your thesis statement completely once you've used the writing process to develop your thoughts more.

1. Use the following thesis frame to formulate the basic elements of your thesis statement:
   a. What are the two approaches to life Burkeman discusses in "The Benefits of 'Negative Visualization'"?

   _____

   b. Which of the two approaches leads to a happier life, according to Burkeman?

   _____

   c. Which approach do you think leads to a happier life?

   _____

   _____

   _____

2. Now use the elements you isolated in 1a, b, and c to write a thesis statement. You likely will have to revise it several times until it captures your idea clearly.

   _____

   _____

Prewriting to Find Support for Your Thesis Statement

The last part of the writing topic asks you to develop and support the position you took in your thesis statement by drawing on your own experience and readings.

last part of the writing topic:

To develop your own position, be sure to discuss specific examples; these examples can be drawn from anything you've read, as well as from your observations and experiences.

Use the guiding questions below to develop your ideas and find concrete support for them. The proof or evidence you present is an important element in supporting your argument and making your ideas persuasive for your readers.

1. As you begin to develop your own examples, think about how happiness connects to your own life and the lives of those you know. In the space below, make a list of several of the most memorable events or situations in your life that you associate with being happy, and a list of several that you associate with being unhappy.

    Look over your lists. Do the events that you associate with being happy have something in common? Is there a common thread among those events that you associate with being unhappy? See if you can find some relationship between your feelings of happiness and unhappiness, and Burkeman's idea of positive and negative visualization. See if you can find some connection in your own life to Burkeman's concerns.

    Now think of your friends and family members. Can you find any examples of someone you know who may have benefited from Burkeman's philosophy? How useful do you think Burkeman's strategies might be to generate more happiness and contentment in the lives of those you know?

    Explore as many ideas as you can. Do some lengthy freewriting to develop your thoughts and capture them for use later, when you begin to draft your essay.

2. Now make another list, but this time broaden your focus to explore examples from your studies, the media, your reading (especially the supplemental readings in this section), and your knowledge of contemporary society. Do any of these examples affirm Burkeman's ideas? For example, do you recall any novels or films whose theme connects to positive thinking? Do these examples affirm Burkeman's views or challenge them? How convincing do you find these examples? For example, think about a couple of TV shows or films that you are familiar with, and see if they feature a character who reflects or challenges Burkeman's philosophy. Find several examples, if you can, and determine whether they challenge or support Burkeman. Do you find any of these examples especially convincing, and will any of them help you decide which position you want to take in your essay? Will they be convincing for your readers? Do some freewriting on those that you think may be useful.

Do any of the supplemental essays in this section relate to Burkeman? Review their arguments and supporting evidence, and compare them to Burkeman's. Are any of them especially convincing for you? If so, list them here. (Remember to cite any of their ideas you include in your essay.) List and/or freewrite about all the relevant ideas you can think of, even those about which you are hesitant.

3. Look back at the lists and freewriting you did in 1 and 2, and decide what you think will be useful to develop in your essay; look for examples and ideas that will enable you to develop your argument and convincingly and concretely support your thesis statement. In the space below, briefly summarize how each of the ideas and examples will support your thesis statement. You may decide to revise or significantly change the working thesis statement you first drafted. That is a good sign that you are finding insights and developing your thoughts in productive ways.

The information and ideas you develop in this exercise will be the core of your body paragraphs when you turn to planning and drafting your essay.

Revising Your Thesis Statement

Now that you have spent some time working out your ideas more systematically and developing some supporting evidence for the position you want to take, it is a good time look again at the working thesis statement you crafted earlier. Does it still present the position you want to take? Is the wording accurate? As your first step, look again at the writing topic, and then write your original working thesis on the lines that follow it

> writing topic:
>
> *According to Burkeman, in what ways is "negative visualization" more likely to make people happier than "positive visualization"? What do you think of his views? To develop your own position, be sure to discuss specific examples; these examples can be drawn from anything you've read, as well as from your observations and experiences.*

working thesis statement:

_____

_____

Remember that your thesis statement must answer the second question in the writing topic but take into consideration the writing topic as a whole. The first question in the topic identifies the issue that is up for debate, and the last question reminds you that, whatever position you take on the issue, you must be able to support it with specific examples.

Now that you have spent some time thinking about your life view and happiness, it is likely that you need to alter your draft thesis statement. Sometimes, only a word or phrase must be added or deleted; other times, the thesis statement must be significantly rewritten. The subject or the claim portion may be unclear, vague, or even inaccurate. Draft writing is almost always wordy, unclear, or vague. Look at your working thesis statement through the eyes of your readers; does it actually say what you want it to say?

After examining it and completing any necessary revisions, check it one more time:

a. Does the thesis statement directly identify Burkeman's argument?

b. Does your thesis state your position on the subject?

c. Is your thesis well punctuated, grammatically correct, and precisely worded?

Write your polished thesis on the lines below and look at it again. Is it strong and interesting?

_____

_____

Planning and Drafting Your Essay

Now that you have examined Burkeman's argument and thought at length about your own views, draft an essay that responds to all parts of the writing topic. Use the material you developed in this section to compose your draft. Don't forget to turn back to Part 1, especially "The Conventional Argument Essay Structure," for further guidance on the essay's conventional structure.

Do not skip this step in the process because drafting an outline will give you a basic structure for incorporating all the ideas you have developed in the preceding pages. An outline will also give you an overview of your essay and help you spot problems in development or logic. The form below is modeled on "The Conventional Argument Essay Structure" in Part 1, but you may want to use your own outline form. Be sure to plan the body paragraphs, including the examples that will provide the concrete evidence to support your assertions. Once you complete your outline, you will be set to construct your rough draft.

Hint

This outline doesn't have to contain polished writing. You may want to fill in only the basic ideas in phrases or terms.

I. **Introductory Paragraph**

   A. An opening sentence that gives the reading selection's title and author and begins to answer the writing topic:

   _____

   _____

   _____

   B. Main points to include in the directed summary:

      1.

      2.

      3.

      4.

C. Write out your thesis statement. (Look back to "Revising Your Thesis Statement," where you reexamined and refined your working thesis statement.) It should clearly agree or disagree with Burkeman's position, and it should state your position using your own words. Remember that your essay will have to develop and argue for a single point of view. You should not simply discuss happiness, offering both pro and con views in relation to Burkeman. Avoid writing an essay that is inconclusive, one that merely examines both sides of the issue.

_____

II. Body Paragraphs

A. The paragraph's one main point that supports the thesis statement:

_____

1. Controlling idea sentence:

_____

_____

2. Corroborating details:

_____

_____

_____

_____

3. Careful explanation of why the details are relevant:

_____

_____

_____

_____

4. Connection to the thesis statement:

_____

_____

_____

_____

B. The paragraph's one main point that supports the thesis statement:

_____

1. Controlling idea sentence:

_____

_____

2. Corroborating details:

_____

_____

_____

_____

3. Careful explanation of why the details are relevant:

_____

_____

_____

_____

4. Connection to the thesis statement:

_____

_____

_____

_____

C. The paragraph's one main point that supports the thesis statement:

_____

1. Controlling idea sentence:

_____

_____

2. Corroborating details:

_____

_____

_____

3. Careful explanation of why the details are relevant:

_____

_____

_____

_____

4. Connection to the thesis statement:

_____

_____

_____

_____

D. The paragraph's one main point that supports the thesis statement:

_____

1. Controlling idea sentence:

_____

_____

2. Corroborating details:

_____

_____

_____

_____

3. Careful explanation of why the details are relevant:

_____

_____

_____

_____

4. Connection to the thesis statement:

_____

_____

_____

_____

Repeat this form for any remaining body paragraphs.

III. Conclusion (For help, see "Conclusions" in Part 1.)

A. Type of conclusion to be used:

_____

B. Suggestions, or key words or phrases to include:

_____

Getting Feedback on Your Draft

Use the following guidelines to give a classmate feedback on his or her draft. Read the draft through first, and then answer each of the items below as specifically as you can.

Name of draft's author: _____

Name of draft's reader: _____

The Introduction

1. Within the opening sentences:
   a. Burkeman's entire name is given.   yes   no
   b. the reading selection's title is given and
      placed within quotation marks.   yes   no
2. The opening contains a summary that:
   a. explains Burkeman's view of positive and negative
      visualization and their impact on our lives   yes   no
   b. explains how Burkeman supports the position he takes   yes   no
3. The opening provides a thesis that makes clear
   the draft writer's opinion regarding Burkeman's argument.   yes   no

If the answer to #3 above is yes, state the thesis below as it is written. If the answer is no, explain to the writer what information is needed to make the thesis complete.

_____

_____

_____

The Body

1. How many paragraphs are in the body of this essay? _____
2. To support the thesis, this number is   sufficient   not enough
3. Do paragraphs contain the 4Cs?

Paragraph 1	Controlling idea sentence	yes	no
	Corroborating details	yes	no
	Careful explanation of why the details are relevant	yes	no
	Connection to the thesis statement	yes	no

165

Paragraph 2	Controlling idea sentence	yes	no
	Corroborating details	yes	no
	Careful explanation of why the details are relevant	yes	no
	Connection to the thesis statement	yes	no
Paragraph 3	Controlling idea sentence	yes	no
	Corroborating details	yes	no
	Careful explanation of why the details are relevant	yes	no
	Connection to the thesis statement	yes	no
Paragraph 4	Controlling idea sentence	yes	no
	Corroborating details	yes	no
	Careful explanation of why the details are relevant	yes	no
	Connection to the thesis statement	yes	no
Paragraph 5	Controlling idea sentence	yes	no
	Corroborating details	yes	no
	Careful explanation of why the details are relevant	yes	no
	Connection to the thesis statement	yes	no

(Continue as needed.)

4. Identify any of the above paragraphs that are underdeveloped (too short). _____

5. Identify any of the above paragraphs that fail to support the thesis. _____

6. Identify any of the above paragraphs that are redundant or repetitive. _____

7. Suggest any ideas for additional paragraphs that might improve this essay.

_____

_____

_____

The Conclusion

1. Does the final paragraph avoid introducing new ideas and examples that really belong in the body of the essay? yes no

2. Does the conclusion provide closure (let readers know that the end of the essay has been reached)? yes no

3. Does the conclusion leave readers with an understanding
   of the significance of the argument?   yes   no

4. State in your own words what the draft writer considers to be important about his
   or her argument.

   _____

   _____

   _____

5. Identify the type of conclusion used (see the guidelines for conclusions in Part 1).

   _____

Editing

1. During the editing process, the writer should pay attention to the following problems in sentence structure, punctuation, and mechanics:
   fragments
   misplaced and dangling modifiers
   fused (run-on) sentences
   comma splices
   misplaced, missing, and unnecessary commas
   misplaced, missing, and unnecessary apostrophes
   incorrect quotation mark use
   capitalization errors
   spelling errors

2. While editing, the writer should pay attention to the following areas of grammar:
   verb tense
   subject-verb agreement
   irregular verbs
   pronoun type
   pronoun reference
   pronoun agreement
   noun plurals
   prepositions

Final Draft Checklist

Content

_____ My essay has an appropriate title.

_____ I provide an accurate summary of Burkeman's position on the issue presented in "The Benefits of 'Negative Visualization.'"

_____ My thesis states a clear position that can be supported by evidence.

_____ I have enough paragraphs and argument points to support my thesis.

_____ Each body paragraph is relevant to my thesis.

_____ Each body paragraph contains the 4Cs.

_____ I use transitions whenever necessary to connect ideas to each other.

_____ The final paragraph of my essay (the conclusion) provides readers with a sense of closure.

Grammar, Punctuation, and Mechanics

_____ I use the present tense to discuss Burkeman's argument and examples.

_____ I use verb tenses correctly to show the chronology of events.

_____ I have verb tense consistency throughout my sentences.

_____ I have checked for subject-verb agreement in all of my sentences.

_____ I have revised all fragments and mixed or garbled sentences.

_____ I have repaired all fused (run-on) sentences and comma splices.

_____ I have placed a comma after introductory elements (transitions and phrases) and all dependent clauses that open a sentence.

_____ If I present items in a series (nouns, verbs, prepositional phrases), they are parallel in form.

_____ If I include material spoken or written by someone other than myself, I have correctly punctuated it with quotation marks, using the MLA style guide's rules for citation.

Reviewing Your Graded Essay

After your instructor has returned your essay, you may have the opportunity to revise your paper and raise your grade. Many students, especially those whose essays receive nonpassing grades, feel that their instructors should be less "picky" about grammar and should pass the work on content alone. However, most students at this level have not yet acquired the ability to recognize quality writing, and they do not realize that content and writing actually cannot be separated in this way. Experienced instructors know that errors in sentence structure, grammar, punctuation, and word choice either interfere with content or distract readers so much that they lose track of content. In short, good ideas badly presented are no longer good ideas; to pass, an essay must have passable writing. So even if you are not submitting a revised version of this essay to your instructor, it is important that you review your work carefully in order to understand its strengths and weaknesses. This sheet will guide you through the evaluation process.

You will want to continue to use the techniques that worked well for you and to find strategies to overcome the problems that you identify in this sample of your writing. To recognize areas that might have been problematic for you, look back at the scoring rubric in this book. Match the numerical/verbal/letter grade received on your essay to the appropriate category. Study the explanation given on the rubric for your grade.

Write a few sentences below in which you identify your problems in each of the following areas. Then, suggest specific changes you could make that would improve your paper. Don't forget to use your handbook as a resource.

1. **Grammar/punctuation/mechanics**
   My problem:

   My strategy for change:

2. **Thesis/response to assignment**
   My problem:

   My strategy for change:

3. Organization
My problem:

My strategy for change:

4. Paragraph development/examples/reasoning
My problem:

My strategy for change:

5. Assessment
In the space below, assign a grade to your paper using a rubric other than the one used by your instructor. In other words, if your instructor assigned your essay a grade of *High Fail*, you might give it the letter grade you now feel the paper warrants. If your instructor used the traditional letter grade to evaluate the essay, choose a category from the rubric in this book, or any other grading scale that you are familiar with, to show your evaluation of your work. Then, write a short narrative explaining your evaluation of the essay and the reasons it received the grade you gave it.

Grade: _____

Narrative: _____

_____

_____

_____

_____

Extending the Discussion:
Considering Other Viewpoints

Reading Selections

"How to Create Your Own Happiness" by Norman Vincent Peale

"How Money Actually Buys Happiness" by Elizabeth Dunn and Michael
    Norton

"Stumbling on Happiness" (an excerpt) by Daniel Gilbert

"How to Be Happy When Everything Goes Wrong" by James Clear

"Lectures IV & V: The Religion of Healthy-Mindedness" by William James

"The Value of Suffering" by Pico Iyer

"The Downside of Cohabiting before Marriage" by Meg Jay

HOW TO CREATE YOUR OWN HAPPINESS

NORMAN VINCENT PEALE

Norman Vincent Peale was an American minister, writer, and speaker whose views made him a famous controversial figure. He earned degrees from Ohio Wesleyan University and from Boston University School of Theology. He is considered by many to be one of the most well-known American speakers, and for more than fifty years had his own radio program called The Art of Living. *During his long ninety-year life, he published more than twenty books. Perhaps the most well-known one is* The Power of Positive Thinking *(1952), from which the following excerpt is taken. This book was on the* New York Times *bestseller list for more than 180 consecutive weeks and has been purchased by over five million readers.*

This book is written with deep concern for the pain, difficulty, and struggle of human existence. It teaches the cultivation of peace of mind, not as an escape from life into protected quiescence, but as a power center out of which comes driving energy for constructive personal and social living. It teaches positive thinking, not as a means to fame, riches, or power, but as the practical application of faith to overcome defeat and accomplish worthwhile creative values in life. It teaches a hard, disciplinary way of life, but one which offers great joy to the person who achieves victory over himself and the difficult circumstances of the world. This book is written to suggest techniques and to give examples that demonstrate that you do not need to be defeated by anything, that you can have peace of mind, improved health, and a never-ceasing flow of energy. In short, that your life can be full of joy and satisfaction. Of this I have no doubt at all, for I have watched countless persons learn and apply a system of simple procedures that has brought about the foregoing benefits in their lives. These assertions, which may appear extravagant, are based on *bona fide* demonstrations in actual human experience.

Altogether too many people are defeated by the everyday problems of life. They go struggling, perhaps even whining, through their days with a sense of dull resentment at what they consider the "bad breaks" life has given them. In a sense there may be such a thing as "the breaks" in this life, but there is also a spirit and method by which we can control and even determine those breaks. It is a pity that people should let themselves be defeated by the problems, cares, and difficulties of human existence, and it is also quite unnecessary.

In saying this, I certainly do not ignore or minimize the hardships and tragedies of the world, but neither do I allow them to dominate. You can permit obstacles to control your mind to the point where they are uppermost and thus become the dominating factors in your thought pattern. By learning how to cast them from the mind, by refusing to become mentally subservient to them, and by channeling spiritual power through your thoughts, you can rise above obstacles that ordinarily might defeat you.

By methods I shall outline, obstacles are simply not permitted to destroy your happiness and well-being. You need be defeated only if you are willing to be.

Believe in yourself! Have faith in your abilities! Without a humble but reasonable confidence in your own powers, you cannot be successful or happy. But with sound self-confidence, you can succeed. A sense of inferiority and inadequacy interferes with the attainment of your hopes, but self-confidence leads to self-realization and successful achievement. Because of the importance of this mental attitude, this book will help you believe in yourself and release your inner powers.

It is appalling to realize the number of pathetic people who are hampered and made miserable by the malady popularly called the inferiority complex. But you need not suffer from this trouble. When proper steps are taken, it can be overcome. You can develop creative faith in yourself—faith that is justified.

After speaking to a convention of businessmen in a city auditorium, I was on the stage greeting people when a man approached me and with a peculiar intensity of manner asked, "May I talk with you about a matter of desperate importance to me?" I asked him to remain until the others had gone; then, we went backstage and sat down.

"I'm in this town to handle the most important business deal of my life," he explained. "If I succeed, it means everything to me. If I fail, I'm done for."

I suggested that he relax a little, that nothing was quite that final. If he succeeded, that was fine. If he didn't, well, tomorrow was another day.

"I have a terrible disbelief in myself," he said dejectedly. "I have no confidence. I just don't believe I can put it over. I am very discouraged and depressed. In fact," he lamented, "I'm just about sunk. Here I am, forty years old. Why is it that all my life I have been tormented by inferiority feelings, by lack of confidence, by self-doubt? I listened to your speech tonight in which you talked about the power of positive thinking, and I want to ask how I can get some faith in myself."

"There are two steps to take," I replied. "First, it is important to discover why you have these feelings of no power. That requires analysis and will take time. We must approach the maladies of our emotional life as a physician probes to find something wrong physically. This cannot be done immediately, certainly not in our brief interview tonight, and it may require treatment to reach a permanent solution. But to pull you through this immediate problem, I shall give you a formula that will work if you use it.

"As you walk down the street tonight, I suggest that you repeat certain words that I shall give you. Say them over several times after you get into bed. When you awaken tomorrow, repeat them three times before arising. On the way to your important appointment, say them three additional times. Do this with an attitude of faith, and you will receive sufficient strength and ability to deal with this problem. Later, if you wish, we can go into an analysis of your basic problem, but whatever we come up with following that study, the formula that I am now going to give you can be a large factor in the eventual cure."

Following is the affirmation that I gave him: "I can do all things through Christ which strengtheneth me" (Philippeans 4:13). He was unfamiliar with these words, so I wrote them on a card and had him read them over three times aloud.

"Now, follow that prescription, and I am sure things will come out all right."

He pulled himself up, stood quietly for a moment, then said with considerable feeling, "Okay, Doctor, Okay."

I watched him square his shoulders and walk out into the night. He seemed a pathetic figure, and yet the way he carried himself as he disappeared showed that faith was already at work in his mind.

Subsequently, he reported that this simple formula "did wonders" for him, and added, "It seems incredible that a few words from the Bible could do so much for a person."

This man later had a study made of the reasons for his inferiority attitudes. They were cleared away by scientific counseling and by the application of religious faith. He was taught how to have faith; was given certain specific instructions to follow. Gradually, he attained a strong, steady, reasonable confidence. He never ceases to express amazement at the way in which things now flow toward rather than away from him. His personality has taken on a positive, not negative, character, so that he no longer repels success, but, on the contrary, draws it to him. He now has an authentic confidence in his own powers.

Lack of self-confidence apparently is one of the great problems besetting people today. In a university, a survey was made of six hundred students in psychology courses. The students were asked to state their most difficult personal problem. Seventy-five percent listed lack of confidence. It can safely be assumed that the same large proportion is true of the population generally. Everywhere, you encounter people who are inwardly afraid, who shrink from life, who suffer from a deep sense of inadequacy and insecurity, who doubt their own powers. Deep within themselves, they mistrust their ability to meet responsibilities or to grasp opportunities. Always, they are beset by the vague and sinister fear that something is not going to be quite right. They do not believe that they have it in them to be what they want to be, and so they try to make themselves content with something less than that of which they are capable. Thousands upon thousands go crawling through life on their hands and knees, defeated and afraid. And in most cases, such frustration of power is unnecessary.

The blows of life, the accumulation of difficulties, the multiplication of problems, tend to sap energy and leave you spent and discouraged. In such a condition, the true status of your power is often obscured, and a person yields to a discouragement that is not justified by the facts. It is vitally essential to reappraise your personality assets. When done in an attitude of reasonableness, this evaluation will convince you that you are less defeated than you think you are.

Learn to expect, not to doubt. In so doing, you bring everything into the realm of possibility. This does not mean that by believing, you are necessarily going to get everything you want or think you want. Perhaps that would not be good for you. When you put your trust in God, He guides your mind so that you do not want things that are not good for you or that are inharmonious with God's will. But it does definitely mean that when you learn to believe, then that which has seemingly been impossible moves into the area of the possible. Every great thing at last becomes for you a possibility.

William James, the famous psychologist, said, "Our belief at the beginning of a doubtful undertaking is the one thing [now get that—is the one thing] that insures the successful outcome of your venture." To learn to believe is of primary importance. It is the basic factor of succeeding in any undertaking. When you expect the best, you release a magnetic force in your mind that by a law of attraction tends to bring the best to you. But if you expect the worst, you release from your mind the power of repulsion that tends to force the best from you. It is amazing how a sustained expectation of the best sets in motion forces that cause the best to materialize.

I asked an outstanding newspaper editor, an inspiring personality, "How did you get to be the editor of this important paper?"

"I wanted to be," he replied simply.

"Is that all there is to it?" I asked. "You wanted to be and so there you are."

"Well, that may not be all of it, but that was a large part of the process," he explained. "I believe that if you want to get somewhere, you must decide definitely where you want to be or what you want to accomplish. Be sure it is a right objective, then photograph this objective on your mind and hold it there. Work hard, believe in it, and the thought will become so powerful that it will tend to assure success. There is a deep tendency," he declared, "to become what your mind pictures, provided you hold the mental picture strongly enough and if the objective is sound."

So saying, the editor pulled a well-worn card from his wallet and said, "I repeat this quotation every day of my life. It has become my dominating thought."

I copied it and am giving it to you: "A person who is self-reliant, positive, optimistic, and undertakes his work with the assurance of success magnetizes his condition. He draws to himself the creative powers of the universe."

It is indeed a fact that the person who thinks with positive self-reliance and optimism does magnetize his condition and releases power to attain his goal. So expect the best at all times. Never think of the worst. Drop it out of your thought, relegate it. Let there be no thought in your mind that the worst will happen. Avoid entertaining the concept of the worst, for whatever you take into your mind can grow there. Therefore, take the best into your mind and only that. Nurture it, concentrate on it, emphasize it, visualize, prayerize it, surround it with faith. Make it your obsession. Expect the best, and spiritually creative mind power, aided by God power, will produce the best.

Who decides whether you shall be happy or unhappy? The answer—you do!

A television celebrity had as a guest on his program an aged man. And he was a very rare old man indeed. His remarks were entirely unpremeditated and of course absolutely unrehearsed. They simply bubbled up out of a personality that was radiant and happy. And whenever he said anything, it was so naïve, so apt, that the audience roared with laughter. They loved him. The celebrity was impressed, and enjoyed it with the others.

Finally he asked the old man why he was so happy. "You must have a wonderful secret of happiness," he suggested. "No," replied the old man, "I haven't any great secret. It's just as plain as the nose on your face. When I get up in the morning," he explained, "I have two choices—either to be happy or to be unhappy, and what do you think I do? I just choose to be happy, and that's all there is to it."

That may seem an oversimplification, and it may appear that the old man was superficial, but I recall that Abraham Lincoln, whom nobody could accuse of being superficial, said that people were just about as happy as they made up their minds to be. You can be unhappy if you want to be. It is the easiest thing in the world to accomplish. Just choose unhappiness. Go around telling yourself that things aren't going well, that nothing is satisfactory, and you can be quite sure of being unhappy. But say to yourself, "Things are going nicely. Life is good. I choose happiness," and you can be quite certain of having your choice.

Many of us manufacture our own unhappiness. Of course, not all unhappiness is self-created, for social conditions are responsible for not a few of our woes. Yet it is a fact that to a large extent by our thoughts and attitudes we distill out of the ingredients of life either happiness or unhappiness for ourselves. In a railroad dining car, I sat across from a husband and wife, strangers to me. The lady was expensively dressed, as the furs, diamonds, and costume that she wore indicated. But she was having a most unpleasant time with herself. Rather loudly she proclaimed that the car was dingy and drafty, the service abominable, and the food most unpalatable. She complained and fretted about everything. Her husband, on the contrary, was a genial, affable, easygoing man who obviously had the capacity to take things as they came. I thought he seemed a bit embarrassed by his wife's critical attitude and somewhat disappointed, too, as he was taking her on this trip for pleasure. To change the conversation, he asked what business I was in, and then said that he was a lawyer. Then he made a big mistake, for with a grin he added, "My wife is in the manufacturing business." This was surprising, for she did not seem to be the industrial or executive type, so I asked, "What does she manufacture?" "Unhappiness," he replied. "She manufactures her own unhappiness." Despite the icy coolness that settled upon the table following this ill-advised observation, I was grateful for his remark, for it describes exactly what so many people do—they manufacture their own unhappiness.

It is a pity, too, for there are so many problems created by life itself that dilute our happiness that it is indeed most foolish to distill further unhappiness within your own mind. How foolish to manufacture personal unhappiness to add to all the other difficulties over which you have little or no control!

Rather than to emphasize the manner in which people manufacture their own unhappiness, let us proceed to the formula for putting an end to this misery-producing process. Suffice it to say that we manufacture our unhappiness by thinking unhappy thoughts, by the attitudes that we habitually take, such as the negative feeling that everything is going to turn out badly, or that other people are getting what they do not deserve and we are failing to get what we do deserve.

Our unhappiness is further distilled by saturating the consciousness with feelings of resentment, ill will, and hate. The unhappiness-producing process always makes important use of the ingredients of fear and worry. Each of these matters is dealt with elsewhere in this book. We merely want to make the point at the present time and stress it forcefully that a very large proportion of the unhappiness of the average individual is self-manufactured. How, then, may we proceed to produce not unhappiness but happiness?

An incident from one of my railroad journeys may suggest an answer. One morning in a Pullman sleeping car, approximately a half dozen of us were shaving in the men's lounge. As always in such close and crowded quarters after a night on the train, this group of strangers was not disposed to be gay, and there was little conversation and that little was mostly mumbled.

Then a man came in wearing on his face a broad smile. He greeted us all with a cheery good morning, but received rather unenthusiastic grunts in return. As he went about his shaving he was humming, probably quite unconsciously, a gay little tune. It got a bit on the nerves of some of the men. Finally one said rather sarcastically, "You certainly seem to be happy this morning! Why all the cheer?" "Yes," the man answered, "as a matter of fact, I am happy. I do feel cheerful." Then he added, "I make it a habit to be happy." That was all that was said, but I am sure that each man in that lounge left the train with those interesting words in mind, "I make it a habit to be happy."

The statement is really very profound, for our happiness or unhappiness depends to an important degree upon the habit of mind we cultivate. That collection of wise sayings, the book of Proverbs, tells us that "he that is of a merry heart hath a continual feast" (Proverbs 15:15). In other words, cultivate the merry heart; that is, develop the happiness habit, and life will become a continual feast, which is to say you can enjoy life every day. Out of the happiness habit comes a happy life. And because we can cultivate a habit, we therefore have the power to create our own happiness.

If you are thinking thoughts of defeat, I urge you to rid yourself of such thoughts, for as you think defeat you tend to get it. Adopt the "I don't believe in defeat" attitude.

Discussion Questions

1. What three strategies does Peale recommend to help people to "rise above obstacles that ordinarily might defeat" them? Evaluate from your own perspective the importance of each of these to the attainment of a happy life.

2. According to Peale, what keeps people from becoming self-actualized and successful? What percentage of the university students surveyed had this problem? Why do you find this figure surprising or unsurprising? Why does or doesn't this figure surprise you? How does he suggest that this problem can be cured?

3. List the anecdotes Peale uses to support his thesis. Why do you or don't you think all of them were equally convincing and/or necessary? If you found one in particular most compelling, explain why.

4. Construct a short conversational debate between Norman Vincent Peale and Oliver Burkeman on the issue of positive versus negative visualization.

HOW MONEY ACTUALLY BUYS HAPPINESS

ELIZABETH DUNN AND MICHAEL NORTON

Elizabeth Dunn is an associate professor of psychology at the University of British Columbia, and Michael Norton is an associate professor of marketing at the Harvard Business School. They are coauthors of a book titled Happy Money: The Science of Smarter Spending *(2013). The following selection was published in 2013 in the* Harvard Business Review.

Warren Buffett's advice about money has been scrutinized—and implemented—by savvy investors all over the world. But while most people know they can benefit from expert help to make money, they think they already know how to spend money to reap the most happiness. As a result, they follow their intuitions, using their money to buy things they *think* will make them happy, from televisions to cars to houses to second houses and beyond.

The problem with this approach is that a decade of research, conducted by us and our colleagues, demonstrates that our intuitions about how to turn money into happiness are misguided at best and dead-wrong at worst. Those televisions, cars, and houses? They have almost no impact on our happiness. The good news is that we now know what kind of spending does enhance our happiness, insight that's valuable to consumers and companies alike.

Buffett recently penned an op-ed titled "My Philanthropic Pledge"—but rather than offer financial advice about giving, he suggested we give as a way to enhance our emotional well-being. Of his decision to donate 99% of his wealth to charity, Buffett said that he "couldn't be happier."

But do we need to give away billions like Buffett in order to experience that warm glow? Luckily for us ordinary folks, even more modest forms of generosity can make us happy. In a series of experiments, we've found that asking people to spend money on others—from giving to charity to buying gifts for friends and family—reliably makes them happier than spending that same money on themselves.

And our research shows that even in very poor countries like India and Uganda—where many people are struggling to meet their basic needs—individuals who reflected on giving to others were happier than those who reflected on spending on themselves. What's more, spending even a few dollars on someone else can trigger a boost in happiness. In one study, we found that asking people to spend as little as $5 on someone else over the course of a day made them happier at the end of that day than people who spent the $5 on themselves.[1]

Smart managers are using the power of investing in others to increase the happiness of their employees. Google, for example, offers a compelling "bonus" plan for employees. The company maintains a fund whereby any employee can nominate another employee to receive a $150 bonus. Given the average salaries at Google, a $150 bonus is small change. But the nature of the bonus—one employee giving a bonus to another rather than demanding that bonus for himself—can have a large emotional payoff.[2]

Investing in others can also influence customers. Managers at an amusement park were unable to convince patrons to buy pictures of themselves on one of the park's many rides. Less than one percent purchased the photo at the usual $12.95 price. But researchers tried a clever variation. Other customers were allowed to pay whatever they wanted (including $0) for a photo, but were told that half of what they paid would be sent to charity. Now, buying the picture allows the customer not only to take home a souvenir, but also invest in others. Given this option, nearly 4.5% of customers purchased the photo, and paid an average of more than $5. As a result, the firm's profit-per-rider increased fourfold.[3]

Warren Buffett, happiness guru. Just as we have taken his advice on making money, research suggests we should now take his advice on making happiness. By rethinking how we spend our money—even as little as $5—we can reap more happiness for every dollar we spend. And Buffett's happiness advice comes with a financial payoff as well. By maximizing the happiness that employees and customers get from every dollar they receive in bonuses or spend on products, companies can increase employee and customer satisfaction—and benefit the bottom line.

Endnotes

[1] Dunn, Elizabeth, and Michael Norton. *Happy Money: The Science of Smarter Spending*. New York: Simon & Schuster, 2013.

[2] Dunn interview with Laszlo Bock, March 20, 2012.

[3] Dunn and Norton. *Happy Money*, 120–123.

Discussion Questions

1. According to Elizabeth Dunn and Michael Norton, what is wrong with our intuition about spending and happiness? Describe the one item you would buy to make yourself feel happy. In your own situation, why do you believe the research they cite does or does not apply?

2. For Dunn and Norton, what is the relationship between giving and happiness? Describe the examples in this essay that show an understanding of this relationship being applied in a practical way. Give an example of a way, in your future career, that you might perform or institute an action based on your understanding of the benefit of giving.

3. Describe the tone in this article when the authors refer to Buffett as the "happiness guru." Do you think the authors agree with him, respect him, or are suspicious of him? Explain.

4. Explain the reason(s) you are more likely to take the advice of Buffett, Peale, or Burkeman in your own quest for success and happiness.

STUMBLING ON HAPPINESS

Daniel Gilbert

Daniel Gilbert is an American psychologist, writer, and speaker. He earned an MA from the University of Colorado, Denver, and a PhD from Princeton University. He now is the Edgar Pierce Professor of Psychology at Harvard University. Gilbert's articles have appeared in a number of prestigious publications, such as the New York Times, *the* Los Angeles Times, Forbes, *and* Time. *His book* Stumbling on Happiness (2006) was a New York Times *bestseller. The following selection is an excerpt from that book.*

Some of our cultural wisdom about happiness looks suspiciously like a super-replicating false belief. Consider money. If you've ever tried to sell anything, then you probably tried to sell it for as much as you possibly could, and other people probably tried to buy it for as little as they possibly could. All the parties involved in the transaction assumed that they would be better off if they ended up with more money rather than less, and this assumption is the bedrock of our economic behavior. Yet, it has far fewer scientific facts to substantiate it than you might expect. Economists and psychologists have spent decades studying the relation between wealth and happiness, and they have generally concluded that wealth increases human happiness when it lifts people out of abject poverty and into the middle class but that it does little to increase happiness thereafter.[1] Americans who earn $50,000 per year are much happier than those who earn $10,000 per year, but Americans who earn $5 million per year are not much happier than those who earn $100,000 per year. People who live in poor nations are much less happy than people who live in moderately wealthy nations, but people who live in moderately wealthy nations are not much less happy than people who live in extremely wealthy nations. Economists explain that wealth has "declining marginal utility," which is a fancy way of saying that it hurts to be hungry, cold, sick, tired, and scared, but once you've bought your way out of these burdens, the rest of your money is an increasingly useless pile of paper.[2]

So once we've earned as much money as we can actually enjoy, we quit working and enjoy it, right? Wrong. People in wealthy countries generally work long and hard to earn more money than they can ever derive pleasure from.[3] This fact puzzles us less than it should. After all, a rat can be motivated to run through a maze that has a cheesy reward at its end, but once the little guy is all topped up, then even the finest Stilton won't get him off his haunches. Once we've eaten our fill of pancakes, more pancakes are not rewarding; hence, we stop trying to procure and consume them. But not so, it seems, with money. As Adam Smith, the father of modern economics, wrote in 1776: "The desire for food is limited in every man by the narrow capacity of the human stomach; but the desire of the conveniences and ornaments of building, dress, equipage, and household furniture, seems to have no limit or certain boundary."[4]

If food and money both stop pleasing us once we've had enough of them, then why do we continue to stuff our pockets when we would not continue to stuff our faces? Adam Smith had an answer. He began by acknowledging what most of us suspect anyway, which is that the production of wealth is not necessarily a source of personal happiness: "In what constitutes the real happiness of human life, [the poor] are in no respect inferior to those who would seem so much above them. In ease of body and peace of mind, all the different ranks of life are nearly upon a level, and the beggar, who suns himself by the side of the highway, possesses that security that kings are fighting for."[5] That sounds lovely, but if it's true, then we're all in big trouble. If rich kings are no happier than poor beggars, then why should poor beggars stop sunning themselves by the roadside and work to become rich kings? If no one wants to be rich, then we have a significant economic problem because flourishing economies require that people continually procure and consume one another's goods and services. Market economies require that we all have an insatiable hunger for *stuff*, and if everyone were content with the stuff they had, then the economy would grind to a halt. But if this is a significant *economic* problem, it is not a significant *personal* problem. The chair of the Federal Reserve may wake up one morning with a desire to do what the economy wants, but most of us get up with a desire to do what *we* want, which is to say that the fundamental needs of a vibrant economy and the fundamental needs of a happy individual are not necessarily the same. So what motivates people to work hard every day to do things that will satisfy the economy's needs but not their own? Like so many thinkers, Smith believed that people want just one thing—happiness—hence, economies can blossom and grow only if people are deluded into believing that the production of wealth will make them happy.[6] If and only if people hold this false belief will they do enough producing, procuring, and consuming to sustain their economies:

> The pleasures of wealth and greatness. . . strike the imagination as something grand and beautiful and noble, of which the attainment is well worth all the toil and anxiety which we are so apt to bestow upon it. . . . It is this deception which rouses and keeps in continual motion the industry of mankind. It is this which first prompted them to cultivate the ground, to build houses, to found cities and commonwealths, and to invent and improve all the sciences and arts, which ennoble and embellish human life; which have entirely changed the whole face of the globe, have turned the rude forests of nature into agreeable and fertile plains, and made the trackless and barren ocean a new fund of subsistence, and the great high road of communication to the different nations of the earth.[7]

In short, the production of wealth does not necessarily make individuals happy, but it does serve the needs of an economy, which serves the needs of a stable society, which serves as a network for the propagation of delusional beliefs about happiness and wealth. Economies thrive when individuals strive, but because individuals will strive only for their own happiness, it is essential that they mistakenly believe that producing and consuming are routes to personal well-being. Although words such as *delusional* may seem to suggest some sort of shadowy conspiracy orchestrated by a small group of men in dark suits, the belief-transmission game teaches us that the propagation of false beliefs does not require that anyone be trying to perpetrate a magnificent fraud on an innocent populace. There is no cabal at the top, no star chamber, no master manipulator whose clever program of indoctrination and propaganda has duped us all into believing that money can buy us love. Rather, this particular false belief is a super-replicator because holding it causes us to engage in the very activities that perpetuate it.[8]

Most of us make at least three important decisions in our lives; where to live, what to do, and with whom to do it. We choose our towns and our neighborhoods, we choose our jobs and our hobbies, we choose our spouses and our friends. Making these decisions is such a natural part of adulthood that it is easy to forget that we are among the first human beings to make them. For most of recorded history, people lived where they were born, did what their parents had done, and associated with those who were doing the same. Millers milled, Smiths smithed, and little Smiths and little Millers married whom and when they were told. Social structures (such as religions and castes) and physical structures (such as mountains and oceans) were the great dictators that determined how, where, and with whom people would spend their lives, leaving most folks with little to decide for themselves. But the agricultural, industrial, and technological revolutions changed all that, and the resulting explosion of personal liberty has created a bewildering array of options, alternatives, choices, and decisions that our ancestors never faced. For the very first time, our happiness is in our hands.

How are we to make these choices? In 1738, a Dutch polymath named Daniel Bernoulli claimed he had the answer. He suggested that the wisdom of any decision could be calculated by multiplying the *probability* that the decision will give us what we want by the *utility* of getting what we want. By *utility*, Bernoulli meant something like *goodness* or *pleasure*.[9] The first part of Bernoulli's prescription is fairly easy to follow because in most circumstances we can roughly estimate the odds that our choices will get us where we want to be. How likely is it that you'll be promoted to general manager if you take the job at IBM? How likely is it that you'll spend your weekends at the beach if you move to St. Petersburg? How likely is it that you'll have to sell your motorcycle if you marry Eloise? Calculating such odds is relatively straightforward stuff, which is why insurance companies get rich by doing little more than estimating the likelihood that your house will burn down, your car will be stolen, and your life will end early. With a little detective work, a pencil, and a good eraser, we can usually estimate—at least roughly—the probability that a choice will give us what we desire.

The problem is that we cannot easily estimate how we'll feel when we get it. Bernoulli's brilliance lay not in his mathematics but in his psychology—in his realization that what we objectively get (*wealth*) is not the same as what we subjectively *experience* when we get it (*utility*). Wealth may be measured by counting dollars, but utility must be measured by counting how much goodness those dollars buy.[10] Wealth doesn't matter; utility does. We don't care about money or promotions or beach vacations per se; we care about the goodness or pleasure that these forms of wealth may (or may not) induce. Wise choices are those that maximize our pleasure, not our dollars, and if we are to have any hope of choosing wisely, then we must correctly anticipate how much pleasure those dollars will buy us. Bernoulli knew that it was much easier to predict how much wealth a choice might produce than how much utility a choice might produce, so he devised a simple conversion formula that he hoped would allow anyone to translate estimates of the former into estimates of the latter. He suggested that each successive dollar provides a little less pleasure than the one before it, and that people can therefore calculate the pleasure they will derive from a dollar simply by correcting for the number of dollars they already have:

> The determination of the value of an item must not be based on its price, but rather on the utility it yields. The price of the item is dependent only on the thing itself and is equal for everyone; the utility, however, is dependent on the particular circumstances of the person making the estimate. Thus, there is no doubt that a gain of one thousand ducats is more significant to a pauper than to a rich man though both gain the same amount.[11]

Bernoulli correctly realized that people are sensitive to relative rather than absolute magnitudes, and his formula was meant to take this basic psychological truth into account. But he also knew that translating wealth into utility was not as simple as he'd made it out to be, and that there were other psychological truths that his formula ignored.

> Although a poor man generally obtains more utility than does a rich man from an equal gain, it is nevertheless conceivable, for example, that a rich prisoner who possesses two thousand ducats but needs two thousand ducats more to repurchase his freedom, will place a higher value on a gain of two thousand ducats than does another man who has less money than he. Though innumerable examples of this kind may be constructed, they represent exceedingly rare exceptions.[12]

It was a good try. Bernoulli was right in thinking that the hundredth dollar (or kiss or doughnut or romp in the meadow) generally does not make us as happy as the first one did, but he was wrong in thinking that this was the *only* thing that distinguished wealth from utility and hence the only thing one must correct for when predicting utility from wealth. As it turns out, the "innumerable exceptions" that Bernoulli swept under the rug are *not* exceedingly rare. There are *many* things other than the size of a person's bank account that influence how much utility he or she derives from the next dollar. For instance, people often value things more after they own them than before, they often value things more when they are imminent than distant, they are often hurt more by small losses than by large ones, they often imagine that the pain of losing something is greater than the pleasure of getting it, and so on—and on and on and on. The myriad phenomena with which this book has been concerned are just some of the not-so-rare exceptions that make Bernoulli's principle a beautiful, useless abstraction. Yes, we *should* make choices by multiplying probabilities and utilities, but how can we possibly do this if we can't estimate those utilities beforehand? The same objective circumstances give rise to a remarkably wide variety of subjective experiences, and thus it is very difficult to predict our subjective experiences from foreknowledge of our objective circumstances. The sad fact is that converting wealth to utility—that is, predicting how we will feel from knowledge of what we will get—isn't very much like converting meters to yards or German to Japanese. The simple, lawful relationships that bind numbers to numbers and words to words do not bind objective events to emotional experiences.

So what's a chooser to do? Without a formula for predicting utility, we tend to do what only our species does: imagine. Our brains have a unique structure that allows us to mentally transport ourselves into future circumstances and then ask ourselves how it feels to be there. Rather than calculating utilities with mathematical precision, we simply step into tomorrow's shoes and see how well they fit. Our ability to project ourselves forward in time and to experience events before they happen enables us to learn from mistakes without making them and to evaluate actions without taking them. If nature has given us a greater gift, no one has named it. And yet, as impressive as it is, our ability to simulate future selves and future circumstances is by no means perfect. When we imagine future circumstances, we fill in details that won't really come to pass and leave out details that will. When we imagine future feelings, we find it impossible to ignore what we are feeling now and impossible to recognize how we will think about the things that happen later. Daniel Bernoulli dreamed of a world in which a simple formula would allow us all to determine our futures with perspicacity and foresight. But foresight is a fragile talent that often leaves us squinting, straining to see what it would be like to have this, go there, or do that. There is no simple formula for finding happiness. But if our great big brains do not allow us to go surefootedly into our futures, they at least allow us to understand what makes us stumble.

Endnotes

[1] R. Layard, *Happiness: Lessons from a New Science* (New York: Penguin, 2005); E. Diener and M. E. P. Seligman, "Beyond Money: Toward an Economy of Well-Being," *Psychological Science in the Public Interest* 5: 1-31 (2004); B. S. Frey and A. Stutzer, *Happiness and Economics: How the Economy and Institutions Affect Human Well-Being* (Princeton, N.J.: Princeton University Press, 2002); R. A. Easterlin, "Income and Happiness: Towards a Unified Theory," *Economic Journal* III: 465-84 (2001); and D. G. Blanchflower and A. J. Oswald, "Well-Being over Time in Britain and the USA," *Journal of Public Economics* 88: 1359-86 (2004).

[2] The effect of declining marginal utility is slowed when we spend our money on the things to which we are least likely to adapt. See T. Scitovsky, *The Joyless Economy: The Psychology of Human Satisfaction* (Oxford: Oxford University Press, 1976); L. Van Boven and T. Gilovich, "To Do or to Have? That Is the Question," *Journal of Personality and Social Psychology* 85: 1193-202 (2003); and R. H. Frank, "How Not to Buy Happiness," *Daedalus: Journal of the American Academy of Arts and Sciences* 133: 69-79 (2004). Not all economists believe in decreasing marginal utility: R. A. Easterlin, "Diminishing Marginal Utility of Income? Caveat Emptor," *Social Indicators Research* 70: 243-326 (2005).

[3] J. D. Graaf et al., *Affluenza: The All-Consuming Epidemic* (New York: Berrett-Koehler, 2002); D. Myers, *The American Paradox: Spiritual Hunger in an Age*

of Plenty (New Haven: Yale University Press, 2000); R. H. Frank, *Luxury Fever* (Princeton, N. J.: Princeton University Press, 2000); J. B. Schor, *The Overspent American: Why We Want What We Don't Need* (New York: Perennial, 1999); and P. L. Wachtel, *Poverty of Affluence: A Psychological Portrait of the American Way of Life* (New York: Free Press, 1983).

[4]   Adam Smith, *An Inquiry into the Nature and Causes of Wealth of Nations* (1776), book I (New York: Modern Library, 1994).

[5]   Adam Smith, *The Theory of Moral Sentiments* (1759); Cambridge: Cambridge University Press, 2002).

[6]   N. Ashraf, C. Camerer, and G. Loewenstein, "Adam Smith, Behavioral Economist," *Journal of Economic Perspectives* 19: 131-45 (2005).

[7]   Smith, *The Theory of Moral Sentiments*.

[8]   Some theorists have argued that societies exhibit a cyclic pattern in which people do come to realize that money doesn't buy happiness but then forget this lesson a generation later. See A. O. Hirschman, *Shifting Involvements: Private Interest and Public Action* (Princeton, N. J.: Princeton University Press, 1982).

[9]   Actually, it is a bit unclear just what Bernoulli meant by *utility* because he didn't define it, and the meaning of this concept has been debated for three and a half centuries.

[10] Most modern economists would disagree with this statement because economics is currently committed to an assumption that psychology abandoned a half-century ago, namely, that a science of human behavior can ignore what people feel and say and rely solely on what people do.

[11] D. Bernoulli, "Exposition of a New Theory on the Measurement of Risk," *Econometrica* 22: 23-36 (1954) (originally published as "*Speciment theoriae novae de mensural sortis*" in *Commentarii Academiae Scientiarum Imperialis Petropolitanae*, vol. 5 [1738], 175-92).

[12] Ibid., 25.

Discussion Questions

1. Explain the "declining marginal utility" of money. Are you surprised by this concept? Why?

2. How can what is good for the economy be opposed to what is good for people overall? What then motivates people to work hard when it does not make them happy? Consider your own or your family's situation: explain any behaviors that demonstrate the likelihood that you or a member of your family is doing work as a result of a delusion.

3. Why does Daniel Gilbert believe that Daniel Bernoulli's principle is "useless"? What circumstances might help you make this decision? Explain.

4. In making an important financial decision regarding your future, would you be more likely to use positive visualization, negative visualization, Bernoulli's formula regarding utility and probability, or some combination of the three? Why?

HOW TO BE HAPPY WHEN EVERYTHING GOES WRONG

JAMES CLEAR

James Clear is an American writer and travel photographer. His views on behavioral psychology, habit formation, and performance improvement can be found on the Internet at JamesClear.com.

In the summer of 2010, Rachelle Friedman was preparing for one of the best periods of her life. She was recently engaged, surrounded by her best friends, and enjoying her bachelorette party. Friedman and her friends were spending the day at the pool when one of them playfully pushed her into the shallow end of the water. Friedman floated slowly to the top of the pool until her face emerged. It was immediately obvious that something was wrong. "This isn't a joke," she said. Her head had struck the bottom of the pool and shattered two vertebrae. In particular, the fracture of her C6 vertebra severed her spinal cord and left her permanently paralyzed from the chest down. She would never walk again.

One year later, Rachelle Friedman became Rachelle Chapman as she married her new husband. She decided to share some of her own thoughts on the whole experience during an online question-and-answer session in 2013. She started by discussing some of the challenges you might expect. It was hard to find a job that could accommodate her physical disabilities. It could be frustrating and uncomfortable to deal with the nerve pain. But she also shared a variety of surprisingly positive answers. For example, when asked if things had changed for the worse, she said, "Well things did change, but I can't say in a bad way at all." Then, when asked about her relationship with her husband, she said, "I think we are just so happy because my injury could have been worse." How is it possible to be happy when everything in life seems to go wrong? As it turns out, Rachelle's situation can reveal a lot about how our brains respond to traumatic events and what actually makes us happy.

There is a social psychologist at Harvard University by the name of Dan Gilbert. Gilbert's best-selling book, *Stumbling on Happiness*, discusses the many ways in which we miscalculate how situations will make us happy or sad, and reveals some counterintuitive insights about what actually does make us happy.[1] One of the primary discoveries from researchers like Gilbert is that extreme inescapable situations often trigger a response from our brain that increases positivity and happiness. For example, imagine your house is destroyed in an earthquake or you suffer a serious injury in a car accident and lose the use of your legs. When asked to describe the impact of such an event, most people talk about how devastating it would be. Some people even say they would rather be dead than never be able to walk again. But what researchers find is that when people actually suffer a traumatic event like living through an earthquake or becoming a paraplegic, their happiness levels are nearly identical six months after the event as they were the day before the event. How can this be?

Traumatic events tend to trigger what Gilbert refers to as our "psychological immune systems." Our psychological immune systems promote our brain's ability to deliver a positive outlook and happiness from an inescapable situation. This is the opposite of what we would expect when we imagine such an event. As Gilbert says, "People are not aware of the fact that their defenses are more likely to be triggered by intense rather than mild suffering. Thus, they mis-predict their own emotional reactions to misfortunes of different sizes."[2]

This effect works in a similar way for extremely positive events. For example, consider how it would feel to win the lottery. Many people assume that winning the lottery would immediately deliver long-lasting happiness, but research has found the opposite. In a very famous study published by researchers at Northwestern University in 1978[3] it was discovered that the happiness levels of paraplegics and lottery winners were essentially *the same* within a year after the event occurred. You read that correctly. One person won a life-changing sum of money and another person lost the use of their limbs and within one year the two people were equally happy. It is important to note that this particular study has not been replicated in the years since it came out, but the general trend has been supported again and again. We have a strong tendency to overestimate the impact that extreme events will have on our lives. Extreme positive and extreme negative events don't actually influence our long-term levels of happiness nearly as much as we think they would.

Researchers refer to this as The Impact Bias because we tend to overestimate the length or intensity of happiness that major events will create. The Impact Bias is one example of affective forecasting, which is a social psychology phenomenon that refers to our generally terrible ability as humans to predict our future emotional states.

There are two primary takeaways I have from The Impact Bias. First, we have a tendency to focus on the thing that changes and forget about the things that don't change. When thinking about winning the lottery, we imagine that event and all of the money that it will bring in. But we forget about the other 99 percent of life and how it will remain more or less the same.

We'll still feel grumpy if we don't get enough sleep. We still have to wait in rush hour traffic. We still have to work out if we want to stay in shape. We still have to send in our taxes each year. It will still hurt when we lose a loved one. It will still feel nice to relax on the porch and watch the sunset. We imagine the change, but we forget the things that stay the same.

Second, a challenge is an impediment to a particular thing, not to you as a person. In the words of Greek philosopher Epictetus, "Going lame is an impediment to your leg, but not to your will." We overestimate how much negative events will harm our lives for precisely the same reason that we overvalue how much positive events will help our lives. We focus on the thing that occurs (like losing a leg), but forget about all of the other experiences of life. Writing thank you notes to friends, watching football games on the weekend, reading a good book, eating a tasty meal. These are all pieces of the good life you can enjoy with or without a leg. Mobility issues represent but a small fraction of the experiences available to you. Negative events can create task-specific challenges, but the human experience is broad and varied. There is plenty of room for happiness in a life that may seem very foreign or undesirable to your current imagination.

Endnotes

[1] D. Gilbert, *Stumbling on Happiness*. New York: Vintage Books (2006).

[2] Ibid., 201.

[3] P. Brickman, D. Coates, and R. Janoff-Bulman, "Lottery Winners and Accident Victims: Is Happiness Relative?," *Journal of Personality and Social Psychology*, 1978, Vol. 36, No. 8, 917-927.

Discussion Questions

1. How did Rachelle Friedman's life change after the summer of 2010? What challenges did she face? Do you find her response to the changes and challenges unexpected? Explain. Compare her attitude with your own negative visualization of such a catastrophic event in your own life. Do you think she is being honest or brave, or do you think she is in complete denial?

2. What does the research of Harvard social psychologist Dan Gilbert reveal about people's level of happiness before and after a traumatic event? What does the research at Northwestern University reveal about the impact of highly positive events in levels of happiness? How does this information influence your own fears and wishes?

3. What term do researchers use to explain human beings' inability to predict their own future emotional states? Explain the "takeaways" James Clear gains from learning about this phenomenon. Tell the most important insight you took away from this article.

4. Discuss some ways that Oliver Burkeman could have used Clear's example of Rachelle and some of the research into the brain and happiness levels to support his argument about the benefits of negative visualization.

LECTURES IV AND V: THE RELIGION OF HEALTHY-MINDEDNESS

WILLIAM JAMES

William James, the brother of renowned American writer Henry James, was an American philosopher, psychologist, and writer who was also trained as a physician. James spent most of his academic career at Harvard, becoming emeritus professor of philosophy in 1907. James was one of the leading thinkers of the late nineteenth century, and many consider him to be one of the most important and widely-read philosophers of the United States. History has labeled him as a "father of American psychology," but many of his well-known works are concerned with philosophy, and he is known as one of the founders of the school of pragmatism. His list of publications is long and various, and includes such books as Human Immortality: Two Supposed Objections to the Doctrine *(1898) and* Pragmatism: A New Name for Some Old Ways of Thinking *(1907). The following is an excerpt from James's important work* The Varieties of Religious Experience: A Study in Human Nature *(1902). The lectures are part of a set, delivered by James in Edinburgh in 1901 and 1902, and ultimately published in 1902 with immediate success and wide popularity.*

If we were to ask the question: "What is human life's chief concern?" one of the answers we should receive would be: "It is happiness." How to gain, how to keep, how to recover happiness, is in fact for most men at all times the secret motive of all they do, and of all they are willing to endure. The hedonistic school in ethics deduces the moral life wholly from the experiences of happiness and unhappiness which different kinds of conduct bring; and, even more in the religious life than in the moral life, happiness and unhappiness seem to be the poles round which the interest revolves. We need not go so far as to say with the author whom I lately quoted that any persistent enthusiasm is, as such, religion, nor need we call mere laughter a religious exercise; but we must admit that any persistent enjoyment may *produce* the sort of religion which consists in a grateful admiration of the gift of so happy an existence; and we must also acknowledge that the more complex ways of experiencing religion are new manners of producing happiness, wonderful inner paths to a supernatural kind of happiness, when the first gift of natural existence is unhappy, as it so often proves itself to be.

With such relations between religion and happiness, it is perhaps not surprising that men come to regard the happiness which a religious belief affords as a proof of its truth. If a creed makes a man feel happy, he almost inevitably adopts it. Such a belief ought to be true; therefore it is true—such, rightly or wrongly, is one of the "immediate inferences" of the religious logic used by ordinary men. "The near presence of God's spirit,"

From *The Varieties of Religious Experience: A Study in Human Nature*, Being the Gifford Lectures on Natural Religion Delivered at Edinburgh in 1901-1902 by William James. Longmans, Green and Company: New York, London, Bombay, Calcutta and Madras, 1917.

says a German writer, "may be experienced in its reality—indeed *only* experienced. And the mark by which the spirit's existence and nearness are made irrefutably clear to those who have ever had the experience is the utterly incomparable *feeling of happiness* which is connected with the nearness, and which is therefore not only a possible and altogether proper feeling for us to have here below, but is the best and most indispensable proof of God's reality. No other proof is equally convincing, and therefore happiness is the point from which every efficacious new theology should start."

In the hour immediately before us, I shall invite you to consider the simpler kinds of religious happiness, leaving the more complex sorts to be treated on a later day.

In many persons, happiness is congenital and irreclaimable. "Cosmic emotion" inevitably takes in them the form of enthusiasm and freedom. I speak not only of those who are animally happy. I mean those who, when unhappiness is offered or proposed to them, positively refuse to feel it, as if it were something mean and wrong. We find such persons in every age, passionately flinging themselves upon their sense of the goodness of life, in spite of the hardships of their own condition, and in spite of the sinister theologies into which they may be born. From the outset their religion is one of union with the divine. The heretics who went before the Reformation are lavishly accused by the church writers of antinomian practices, just as the first Christians were accused of indulgence in orgies by the Romans. It is probable that there never has been a century in which the deliberate refusal to think ill of life has not been idealized by a sufficient number of persons to form sects, open or secret, who claimed all natural things to be permitted. Saint Augustine's maxim, *Dilige et quod vis fac,*—if you but love [God], you may do as you incline,—is morally one of the profoundest of observations, yet it is pregnant, for such persons, with passports beyond the bounds of conventional morality. According to their characters they have been refined or gross; but their belief has been at all times systematic enough to constitute a definite religious attitude. God was for them a giver of freedom, and the sting of evil was overcome. Saint Francis and his immediate disciples were, on the whole, of this company of spirits, of which there are of course infinite varieties. Rousseau in the earlier years of his writing, Diderot, B. de Saint Pierre, and many of the leaders of the eighteenth century anti-Christian movement were of this optimistic type. They owed their influence to a certain authoritativeness in their feeling that Nature, if you will only trust her sufficiently, is absolutely good.

It is to be hoped that we all have some friend, perhaps more often feminine than masculine, and young than old, whose soul is of this sky-blue tint, whose affinities are rather with flowers and birds and all enchanting innocencies than with dark human passions, who can think no ill of man or God, and in whom religious gladness, being in possession from the outset, needs no deliverance from any antecedent burden.

. . .

If, then, we give the name of healthy-mindedness to the tendency which looks on all things and sees that they are good, we find that we must distinguish between a more involuntary and a more voluntary or systematic way of being healthy-minded. In its involuntary variety, healthy-mindedness is a way of feeling happy about things immediately. In its systematical variety, it is an abstract way of conceiving things as good. Every abstract way of conceiving things selects some one aspect of them as their essence for the time being, and disregards the other aspects. Systematic healthy-mindedness, conceiving good as the essential and universal aspect of being, deliberately excludes evil from its field of vision; and although, when thus nakedly stated, this might seem a difficult feat to perform for one who is intellectually sincere with himself and honest about facts, a little reflection shows that the situation is too complex to lie open to so simple a criticism.

In the first place, happiness, like every other emotional state, has blindness and insensibility to opposing facts given it as its instinctive weapon for self-protection against disturbance. When happiness is actually in possession, the thought of evil can no more acquire the feeling of reality than the thought of good can gain reality when melancholy rules. To the man actively happy, from whatever cause, evil simply cannot then and there be believed in. He must ignore it; and to the bystander he may then seem perversely to shut his eyes to it and hush it up.

But more than this: the hushing of it up may, in a perfectly candid and honest mind, grow into a deliberate religious policy, or *parti pris*. Much of what we call evil is due entirely to the way men take the phenomenon. It can so often be converted into a bracing and tonic good by a simple change of the sufferer's inner attitude from one of fear to one of fight; its sting so often departs and turns into a relish when, after vainly seeking to shun it, we agree to face about and bear it cheerfully, that a man is simply bound in honor, with reference to many of the facts that seem at first to disconcert his peace, to adopt this way of escape. Refuse to admit their badness; despise their power; ignore their presence; turn your attention the other way; and so far as you yourself are concerned at any rate, though the facts may still exist, their evil character exists no longer. Since you make them evil or good by your own thoughts about them, it is the ruling of your thoughts which proves to be your principal concern.

The deliberate adoption of an optimistic turn of mind thus makes its entrance into philosophy. And once in, it is hard to trace its lawful bounds. Not only does the human instinct for happiness, bent on self-protection by ignoring, keep working in its favor, but higher inner ideals have weighty words to say. The attitude of unhappiness is not only painful, it is mean and ugly. What can be more base and unworthy than the pining, puling, mumping mood, no matter by what outward ills it may have been engendered? What is more injurious to others? What is less helpful as a way out of the difficulty? It but fastens and perpetuates the trouble which occasioned it, and increases the total evil of the situation. At all costs, then, we ought to reduce the sway of that mood; we ought to scout it in ourselves and others, and never show it tolerance. But it is impossible to carry on this discipline in the subjective sphere without zealously emphasizing the brighter and minimizing the darker aspects of the objective sphere of things at the same time. And thus our resolution not to indulge in misery, beginning at a comparatively small point within ourselves, may not stop until it has brought the entire frame of reality under a systematic conception optimistic enough to be congenial with its needs.

In all this I say nothing of any mystical insight or persuasion that the total frame of things absolutely must be good. Such mystical persuasion plays an enormous part in the history of the religious consciousness, and we must look at it later with some care. But we need not go so far at present. More ordinary non-mystical conditions of rapture suffice for my immediate contention. All invasive moral states and passionate enthusiasms make one feelingless to evil in some direction. The common penalties cease to deter the patriot, the usual prudences are flung by the lover to the winds. When the passion is extreme, suffering may actually be gloried in, provided it be for the ideal cause, death may lose its sting, the grave its victory. In these states, the ordinary contrast of good and ill seems to be swallowed up in a higher denomination, an omnipotent excitement which engulfs the evil, and which the human being welcomes as the crowning experience of his life. This, he says, is truly to live, and I exult in the heroic opportunity and adventure.

The systematic cultivation of healthy-mindedness as a religious attitude is therefore consonant with important currents in human nature, and is anything but absurd. In fact, we all do cultivate it more or less, even when our professed theology should in consistency forbid it. We divert our attention from disease and death as much as we can; and the slaughter-houses and indecencies without end on which our life is founded are huddled out of sight and never mentioned, so that the world we recognize officially in literature and in society is a poetic fiction far handsomer and cleaner and better than the world that really is.

Discussion Questions

1. What, according to William James, is all men's secret motive? How might this chief concern of mankind manifest itself in a religious philosophy? Why do you or do you not think this feeling can be understood in another way?

2. Explain James's use of the term "healthy-mindedness." How can something that is healthy be "blind" and "insensible" to facts? How do you think people's behaviors would change if they constantly considered the fact of death?

3. How does James say people escape from being made unhappy by negative things? What is wrong with having an unhappy attitude when things have gone wrong? Give an example of someone you know, saw in a movie, or read about in a book who remained in a constant state of unhappiness. How do you and others feel about that person?

4. Explain why you think healthy-mindedness can best be achieved through positive or negative visualization.

THE VALUE OF SUFFERING

Pico Iyer

Pico Iyer (actual name Siddharth Pico Raghavan Iyer) is a distinguished British academic, author, and essayist. He earned a Double First in English Literature at Oxford University, and a second MA in literature from Harvard University. He taught writing and literature at Harvard, and then joined Time *as an essayist. He is best known for his travel writing, is a frequent guest speaker around the world, and has published several novels, including* The Lady and the Monk: Four Seasons in Kyoto *(1991), and* The Global Soul: Jet Lag, Shopping Malls, and the Search for Home *(2000).*

Hundreds of Syrians are apparently killed by chemical weapons, and the attempt to protect others from that fate threatens to kill many more. A child perishes with her mother in a tornado in Oklahoma, the month after an 8-year-old is slain by a bomb in Boston. Runaway trains claim dozens of lives in otherwise placid Canada and Spain. At least 46 people are killed in a string of coordinated bombings aimed at an ice cream shop, bus station, and famous restaurant in Baghdad. Does the torrent of suffering ever abate—and can one possibly find any point in suffering?

Wise men in every tradition tell us that suffering brings clarity, illumination; for the Buddha, suffering is the first rule of life, and insofar as some of it arises from our own wrongheadedness—our cherishing of self—we have the cure for it within. Thus in certain cases, suffering may be an effect, as well as a cause, of taking ourselves too seriously. I once met a Zen-trained painter in Japan, in his 90s, who told me that suffering is a privilege, it moves us toward thinking about essential things and shakes us out of shortsighted complacency; when he was a boy, he said, it was believed you should pay for suffering, it proves such a hidden blessing.

Yet none of that begins to apply to a child gassed to death (or born with AIDS or hit by a "limited strike"). Philosophy cannot cure a toothache, and the person who starts going on about its long-term benefits may induce a headache, too. Anyone who's been close to a loved one suffering from depression knows that the vicious cycle behind her condition means that, by definition, she can't hear the logic or reassurances we extend to her; if she could, she wouldn't be suffering from depression.

Occasionally, it's true, I'll meet someone—call him myself—who makes the same mistake again and again, heedless of what friends and sense tell him, unable even to listen to himself. Then he crashes his car, or suffers a heart attack, and suddenly calamity works on him like an alarm clock; by packing a punch that no gentler means can summon, suffering breaks him open and moves him to change his ways.

Occasionally, too, I'll see that suffering can be in the eye of the beholder, our igno-rant projection. The quadriplegic asks you not to extend sympathy to her; she's happy, even if her form of pain is more visible than yours. The man on the street in Calcutta, India, or Port-au-Prince, Haiti, overturns all our simple notions about the relation of terrible conditions to cheerfulness and energy and asks whether we haven't just brought our ideas of poverty with us.

But does that change all the many times when suffering leaves us with no seeming benefit at all, and only a resentment of those who tell us to look on the bright side and count our blessings and recall that time heals all wounds (when we know it doesn't)? None of us expects life to be easy; Job merely wants an explanation for his constant unease. To live, as Nietzsche (and Roberta Flack) had it, is to suffer; to survive is to make sense of the suffering.

That's why survival is never guaranteed.

Or, put it as Kobayashi Issa, a haiku master in the 18th century, did: "This world of dew is a world of dew," he wrote in a short poem. "And yet, and yet. . . ." Known for his words of constant affirmation, Issa had seen his mother die when he was 2, his first son die, his father contract typhoid fever, his next son and a beloved daughter die. He knew that suffering was a fact of life, he might have been saying in his short verse; he knew that impermanence is our home and loss the law of the world. But how could he not wish, when his 1-year-old daughter contracted smallpox, and expired, that it be otherwise?

After his poem of reluctant grief, Issa saw another son die and his own body para-lyzed. His wife died, giving birth to another child, and that child died, maybe because of a careless nurse. He married again and was separated within weeks. He married a third time and his house was destroyed by fire. Finally, his third wife bore him a healthy daughter—but Issa himself died, at 64, before he could see the little girl born.

My friend Richard, one of my closest pals in high school, upon receiving a diagno-sis of prostate cancer three years ago, created a blog called "This world of dew." I sent him some information about Issa—whose poems, till his death, express almost nothing but gratitude for the beauties of life—but Richard died quickly and in pain, barely able to walk the last time I saw him.

My neighbors in Japan live in a culture that is based, at some invisible level, on the Buddhist precepts that Issa knew: that suffering is reality, even if unhappiness need not be our response to it. This makes for what comes across to us as uncomplaining hard work, stoicism and a constant sense of the ways difficulty binds us together—as Britain knew during the blitz, and other cultures at moments of stress, though doubly acute in a culture based on the idea of interdependence, whereby the suffering of one is the suf-fering of everyone.

"I'll do my best!" and "I'll stick it out!" and "It can't be helped" are the phrases you hear every hour in Japan; when a tsunami claimed thousands of lives north of Tokyo two years ago, I heard much more lamentation and panic in California than among the people I know around Kyoto. My neighbors aren't formal philosophers, but much in the texture of the lives they're used to—the national worship of things falling away in autumn, the blaze of cherry blossoms followed by their very quick departure, the

Issa-like poems on which they're schooled—speaks for an old culture's training in saying goodbye to things and putting delight and beauty within a frame. Death undoes us less, sometimes, than the hope that it will never come.

As a boy, I'd learned that it's the Latin, and maybe a Greek, word for "suffering" that gives rise to our word "passion." Etymologically, the opposite of "suffering" is, therefore, "apathy"; the Passion of the Christ, say, is a reminder, even a proof, that suffering is something that a few high souls embrace to try to lessen the pains of others. Passion with the plight of others makes for "compassion."

Almost eight months after the Japanese tsunami, I accompanied the Dalai Lama to a fishing village, Ishinomaki, that had been laid waste by the natural disaster. Gravestones lay tilted at crazy angles when they had not collapsed altogether. What once, a year before, had been a thriving network of schools and homes was now just rubble. Three orphans barely out of kindergarten stood in their blue school uniforms to greet him, outside of a temple that had miraculously survived the catastrophe. Inside the wooden building, by its altar, were dozens of colored boxes containing the remains of those who had no surviving relatives to claim them, all lined up perfectly in a row, behind framed photographs, of young and old.

As the Dalai Lama got out of his car, he saw hundreds of citizens who had gathered on the street, behind ropes, to greet him. He went over and asked them how they were doing. Many collapsed into sobs. "Please change your hearts, be brave," he said, while holding some and blessing others. "Please help everyone else and work hard; that is the best offering you can make to the dead." When he turned round, however, I saw him brush away a tear himself.

Then he went into the temple and spoke to the crowds assembled on seats there. He couldn't hope to give them anything other than his sympathy and presence, he said; as soon as he heard about the disaster, he knew he had to come here, if only to remind the people of Ishinomaki that they were not alone. He could understand a little of what they were feeling, he went on, because he, as a young man of 23 in his home in Lhasa had been told, one afternoon, to leave his homeland that evening, to try to prevent further fighting between Chinese troops and Tibetans around his palace.

He left his friends, his home, even one small dog, he said, and had never in 52 years been back. Two days after his departure, he heard that his friends were dead. He had tried to see loss as opportunity and to make many innovations in exile that would have been harder had he still been in old Tibet; for Buddhists like himself, he pointed out, inexplicable pains are the result of karma, sometimes incurred in previous lives, and for those who believe in God, everything is divinely ordained. And yet, his tear reminded me, we still live in Issa's world of "And yet."

The large Japanese audience listened silently and then turned, insofar as its members were able, to putting things back together again the next day. The only thing worse than assuming you could get the better of suffering, I began to think (though I'm no Buddhist), is imagining you could do nothing in its wake. And the tear I'd witnessed made me think that you could be strong enough to witness suffering, and yet human enough not to pretend to be master of it. Sometimes it's those things we least understand that deserve our deepest trust. Isn't that what love and wonder tell us, too?

Discussion Questions

1. According to wise men in all traditions, what is the benefit of suffering? Do you think this philosophy naturally leads to positive or negative visualization? Explain your answer.

2. What did the reaction of the Japanese after the tsunami have in common with the attitude of the British during the blitz? From what you have seen in the news, do you think this attitude was shared by the victims of recent hurricanes, like Katrina or Irma? Explain the similarities or differences.

3. When Pico Iyer talks about the "And yet" of the poet Kobayashi Issa, what do you think he means? Tell about something in your own life that you still think about in an "and yet" way.

4. What is the lesson that you think Pico Iyer would like you to learn from his discussion of suffering?

THE DOWNSIDE OF COHABITING BEFORE MARRIAGE

MEG JAY

Meg Jay earned a PhD from UC Berkeley, where she later taught psychology as a member of the adjunct faculty. She is currently a professor of clinical psychology at the University of Virginia. She also works in private practice, makes public speaking appearances, and has written many articles in newspapers and magazines. She is the author of The Defining Decade: Why Your Twenties Matter—and How to Make the Most of Them Now *(2012). The essay below appeared in the* New York Times *online in 2012.*

At thirty-two, one of my clients (I'll call her Jennifer) had a lavish wine-country wedding. By then, Jennifer and her boyfriend had lived together for more than four years. The event was attended by the couple's friends, families, and two dogs.

When Jennifer started therapy with me less than a year later, she was looking for a divorce lawyer. "I spent more time planning my wedding than I spent happily married," she sobbed. Most disheartening to Jennifer was that she'd tried to do everything right. "My parents got married young so, of course, they got divorced. We lived together! How did this happen?"

Cohabitation in the United States has increased by more than fifteen hundred percent in the past half century. In 1960, about 450,000 unmarried couples lived together. Now the number is more than 7.5 million. The majority of young adults in their twenties will live with a romantic partner at least once, and more than half of all marriages will be preceded by cohabitation. This shift has been attributed to the sexual revolution and the availability of birth control, and in our current economy, sharing the bills makes cohabiting appealing. But when you talk to people in their twenties, you also hear about something else: cohabitation as prophylaxis.

In a nationwide survey conducted in 2001 by the National Marriage Project, then at Rutgers and now at the University of Virginia, nearly half of twenty-somethings agreed with the statement, "You would only marry someone if he or she agreed to live together with you first, so that you could find out whether you really got along." About two-thirds said they believed that moving in together before marriage was a good way to avoid divorce.

But that belief is contradicted by experience. Couples who cohabit before marriage (and especially before an engagement or an otherwise clear commitment) tend to be less satisfied with their marriages—and more likely to divorce—than couples who do not. These negative outcomes are called the cohabitation effect.

Researchers originally attributed the cohabitation effect to selection, or the idea that cohabiters were less conventional about marriage and thus more open to divorce.

As cohabitation has become a norm, however, studies have shown that the effect is not entirely explained by individual characteristics like religion, education, or politics. Research suggests that at least some of the risks may lie in cohabitation itself.

As Jennifer and I worked to answer her question "How did this happen?" we talked about how she and her boyfriend went from dating to cohabiting. Her response was consistent with studies reporting that most couples say it "just happened." "We were sleeping over at each other's places all the time," she said. "We liked to be together, so it was cheaper and more convenient. It was a quick decision, but if it didn't work out, there was a quick exit."

She was talking about what researchers call "sliding, not deciding." Moving from dating to sleeping over to sleeping over a lot to cohabitation can be a gradual slope, one not marked by rings or ceremonies or sometimes even a conversation. Couples bypass talking about why they want to live together and what it will mean.

When researchers ask cohabiters these questions, partners often have different, unspoken—even unconscious—agendas. Women are more likely to view cohabitation as a step toward marriage, while men are more likely to see it as a way to test a relationship or postpone commitment, and this gender asymmetry is associated with negative interactions and lower levels of commitment even after the relationship progresses to marriage. One thing men and women do agree on, however, is that their standards for a live-in partner are lower than they are for a spouse.

Sliding into cohabitation wouldn't be a problem if sliding out were as easy. But it isn't. Too often, young adults enter into what they imagine will be low-cost, low-risk living situations only to find themselves unable to get out months, even years, later. It's like signing up for a credit card with zero percent interest. At the end of twelve months when the interest goes up to twenty-three percent, you feel stuck because your balance is too high to pay off. In fact, cohabitation can be exactly like that. In behavioral economics, it's called consumer lock-in.

Lock-in is the decreased likelihood to search for, or change to, another option once an investment in something has been made. The greater the setup costs, the less likely we are to move to another, even better, situation, especially when faced with switching costs, or the time, money, and effort it requires to make a change.

Cohabitation is loaded with setup and switching costs. Living together can be fun and economical, and the setup costs are subtly woven in. After years of living among roommates' junky old stuff, couples happily split the rent on a nice one-bedroom apartment. They share wireless and pets and enjoy shopping for new furniture together. Later, these setup and switching costs have an impact on how likely they are to leave.

Jennifer said she never really felt that her boyfriend was committed to her. "I felt like I was on this multiyear, never-ending audition to be his wife," she said. "We had all this furniture. We had our dogs and all the same friends. It just made it really, really difficult to break up. Then it was like we got married because we were living together once we got into our thirties."

I've had other clients who also wish they hadn't sunk years of their twenties into relationships that would have lasted only months had they not been living together. Others want to feel committed to their partners, yet they are confused about whether they have consciously chosen their mates. Founding relationships on convenience or ambiguity can interfere with the process of claiming the people we love. A life built on top of "maybe you'll do" simply may not feel as dedicated as a life built on top of the "we do" of commitment or marriage.

The unfavorable connection between cohabitation and divorce does seem to be lessening, however, according to a report released last month by the Department of Health and Human Services. More good news is that a 2010 survey by the Pew Research Center found that nearly two-thirds of Americans saw cohabitation as a step toward marriage.[1]

This shared and serious view of cohabitation may go a long way toward further attenuating the cohabitation effect because the most recent research suggests that serial cohabiters, couples with differing levels of commitment, and those who use cohabitation as a test are most at risk for poor relationship quality and eventual relationship dissolution.

Cohabitation is here to stay, and there are things young adults can do to protect their relationships from the cohabitation effect. It's important to discuss each person's motivation and commitment level beforehand and, even better, to view cohabitation as an intentional step toward, rather than a convenient test for, marriage or partnership. It also makes sense to anticipate and regularly evaluate constraints that may keep you from leaving.

I am not for or against living together, but I am for young adults knowing that, far from safeguarding against divorce and unhappiness, moving in with someone can increase your chances of making a mistake—or of spending too much time on a mistake. A mentor of mine used to say, "The best time to work on someone's marriage is before he or she has one," and in our era, that may mean before cohabitation.

Endnotes

[1] Pew Research Center, January 6, 2011. http://www.pewresearch.org/daily-number/cohabitation-a-step-toward-marriage/

Discussion Questions

1. What effect do you think being married has on an individual's happiness? What benefits do you think marriage can bring to a person's overall sense of well being? What ways can a marriage be detrimental to a person's sense of well being? Why do you think that you personally would, in the future, be happier married, single and unattached, or in a relationship and cohabiting?

2. According to Meg Jay, how do researchers describe the different agendas for men and women who choose to cohabitate? How might positive and/or negative visualization figure into these agendas?

3. How does Meg Jay suggest young couples "safeguard" against divorce and unhappiness? Why are you likely to take or ignore her advice?

4. How could Norman Vincent Peale's philosophy about creating your own happiness apply to marriage? Keeping in mind the Rachelle Friedman example in James Clear's essay, discuss the way negative visualization could contribute to a happy marriage. Describe a happily married couple you have observed and tell whether you think the couple is more likely to have used positive or negative visualization to deal with their problems.

Assignment #3

"COMPETITION AND HAPPINESS"

This assignment asks you to write an essay in response to a reading selection that takes up the topic of competition and its place in our lives. Once again, there are several essays in the "Extending the Discussion" section that your instructor may assign or that you may read on your own. These readings will help you explore the subject of Rubin's argument in greater depth and develop your own ideas on the controversy that he addresses.

Whether you are assigned to read the supplemental readings or not, we encourage you to continue using all of the prewriting activities provided. They will ensure that you develop your thoughts and organize them within an effective essay format.

COMPETITION AND HAPPINESS

THEODORE ISAAC RUBIN

Theodore Rubin is a writer of both fiction and nonfiction. He is a psychoanalyst and a former president of the American Institute of Psychoanalysis. The essay below is adapted from his book Reconciliations: Inner Peace in an Age of Anxiety *(1980).*

Our culture has come to believe that competition "brings out the best" in people. I believe that it brings out the worst. It is intimately linked to envy, jealousy, and paranoia, and blocks the evolution and development of self. It ultimately has a depleting and deadening effect on self as its unrelenting demands are met and self-realizing needs are ignored.

In competition, the focus of one's life is essentially outside one's self. The use of our time and energy is determined by our competitors rather than by ourselves and our own real needs. This weakens our own sense of identity, and to compensate for this ever-increasing feeling of emptiness and vulnerability, we compete still more, perpetuating a self-depleting cycle. When enough depletion takes place to preclude further "successful" competition, we feel hopeless and futile, and our lives seem purposeless. Despite talk about good sportsmanship, competition is totally incompatible with the kind of easy aliveness that is the aim of this book.

Competition is a residual of a primitive past, and it is *not* a genetic residual. It is passed on to us through training in our society from generation to generation. This training starts early and can usually be seen in very early sibling rivalry. I do not believe that rivalry among children of the same family is instinctual. I believe that it is engendered by parents who themselves are caught in the same trap: They spend enormous time and energy getting ahead of the Joneses. Small wonder so many children are pressured into Little League or equivalent competitive structures—all with the rationalization that these activities will promote their self-development, well-being, and health. Actually, these activities and organizations nearly always serve as vicarious vehicles designed to satisfy *parental* craving for competitive success.

People brought up in this way feel lost if they are suddenly thrust into a situation of low competitive tension. Because they exist to compete and they've lost their *raison d'être* in the new situation, they invent hierarchies and games to provide the stimulation they need to "keep the motor running," even if these inventions are ultimately destructive to inner peace and personal health.

I am reminded of my own medical school experience as part of a group of about eighty Americans studying at the university in Lausanne, Switzerland. The system was noncompetitive. People who received passing grades in the required premedical or foundation courses were accepted into the school. Two series of examinations—one in the basic sciences one and one half years after admission, and the other after studies were completed—determined qualification for graduation. Students were allowed to postpone these examinations as long as they felt was necessary. To pass, students were required to demonstrate adequate knowledge of the material. The atmosphere was totally benevolent, with no coercion or intimidation whatsoever. There was no "curve," and students were not graded relative to each other.

The Swiss students exhibited great camaraderie among themselves, helped each other, and for the most part demonstrated great proficiency in grasping and integrating the material. There were no "tricks" whatsoever, no surprise quizzes or exams. Indeed, there were no examinations at all, other than the two sets of standardized government exams. Requirements for passing the examinations were well defined for everyone. Instruction was superb.

We Americans arrived as graduates of a highly competitive system. Few of us could believe that medical school could be a straightforward, noncompetitive activity, and that we would be required to learn only the material we were told to learn. Stimulation addicts like ourselves found little motivation in the Swiss system—so we formed competitive cliques. Some people convinced themselves and others that the Swiss professors were tricky and that the two sets of exams could never be passed. People kept secret from each other the ready availability of course notebooks. Bets were made as to who would and who would not get through. People tried to convince other people that they would never get through and should return home. There was much gossip about absences from classes and who was and who wasn't dedicated to medical school and his chosen field. Former friends who came to Switzerland together stopped talking to each other because they now saw each other as competition. The Swiss went on as they always did. The Americans did also. They had re-created American competition in Switzerland.

Competition damages people other than students. It provides a stressful, isolating, and paranoid atmosphere that is the very antithesis of peace of mind. Competitive strivings are not always felt directly or blatantly. They do not occur solely when we are locked in antagonistic embrace with adversaries—we have, after all, come a considerable distance from the dinosaurs. But the subtle influence of competitive standards to be met and our consciousness of how the next guy is doing—in terms of earnings, position, accomplishments, notoriety, possessions, or whatever—work their subtle and not-so-subtle corrosive effects. They provide constant pressure and undermine our efforts to build a self-realizing value system. This means that we are more involved with how the next fellow is doing than with knowing what *we* really want to do. We are more concerned with how *they* feel about us than how we feel about ourselves.

Competition also makes it very difficult to accept and to feel the nourishing effects of give-and-take, and often makes much-needed help from others impossible to accept. Our culture in large measure has made this paranoid closure to nourishment from others a virtue, often rationalized by ideas about independence and self-reliance. Independence and self-reliance are indeed valuable assets, but often they are actually cover-ups for fear of other people and are functions of sick pride invested in rejection of other people's much-needed help.

Writing Topic

How does competition limit people's ability to lead happy and satisfying lives, according to Rubin? Do you agree with his views? Be sure to support your position with evidence taken from your own experience, your observations of others, and your reading, especially the reading from this course.

Vocabulary Check

Use a dictionary to find the meanings of the following words from Rubin's essay. Choose the meaning or meanings that you think are useful in gaining a full understanding of Rubin's ideas. Then, explain the way each of the definitions you wrote down is key to understanding his argument.

1. *depleting*

   definition: _____

   _____

   explanation: _____

   _____

   _____

   _____

2. *unrelenting*

   definition: _____

   _____

   explanation: _____

   _____

   _____

   _____

3. *compensate*

   definition: _____

   _____

   explanation: _____

   _____

   _____

   _____

4. *futile*

definition: _____

_____

explanation: _____

_____

_____

_____

5. *instinctual*

definition: _____

_____

explanation: _____

_____

_____

_____

6. *engender*

definition: _____

_____

explanation: _____

_____

_____

_____

7. *raison d'être*

definition: _____

_____

explanation: _____

_____

_____

_____

8. *hierarchy*

   definition: _____

   _____

   explanation: _____

   _____

   _____

   _____

9. *benevolent*

   definition: _____

   _____

   explanation: _____

   _____

   _____

   _____

10. *coercion*

    definition: _____

    _____

    explanation: _____

    _____

    _____

    _____

11. *intimidation*

    definition: _____

    _____

    explanation: _____

    _____

    _____

    _____

12. *camaraderie*

   definition: _____

   _____

   explanation: _____

   _____

   _____

   _____

13. *corrosive*

   definition: _____

   _____

   explanation: _____

   _____

   _____

   _____

Questions to Guide Your Reading

Answer the following questions so you can gain a thorough understanding of "Competition and Happiness."

Paragraph 1

What effect do most people believe that competition has on individuals? What does Rubin believe?

Paragraph 2

Why does Rubin think that competition is a destructive force in our lives?

Paragraph 3

What does Rubin see as the origin of competition in society, and what has enabled it to continue from generation to generation?

Paragraph 4

According to Rubin, what happens when people who are used to competing are placed in situations where there is no competition?

Paragraphs 5-7

Discuss the author's and the other Americans' medical school experience in Switzerland. Consider the ways that medical school there differs from medical school in the United States.

Paragraph 8

In what ways does the author feel competition damages people? Can you think of any other ill effects of competition?

Paragraph 9

What problems does the author think are created by privileging independence and self-reliance in our competitive society?

Prewriting for a Directed Summary

It is always important to look carefully at a writing topic and spend some time ensuring that you understand what it is asking. Your essay must provide a thorough response to all parts of the writing topic. The writing topic that follows "Competition and Happiness" contains three parts. The first part asks you about a central idea from the reading. To answer this part of the writing topic, you will have to summarize part of Rubin's argument. In other words, you will write a *directed* summary, meaning one that responds specifically to the first question in the writing topic.

first question in the writing topic:

How does competition limit people's ability to lead happy and satisfying lives, according to Rubin?

Notice that the question doesn't ask you to summarize the entire essay or simply explain Rubin's definition of competition. Rather, it asks you to explain Rubin's reason(s) for claiming that competition undermines happiness. The questions below will help you plan your response. They will guide you in identifying what you should include in your directed summary.

Focus Questions

1. What emotions does the author believe that competition evokes in people?

2. What are the effects of competition on people's personal lives, according to Rubin?

3. What group of Americans does the author especially point to as suffering from the competitive nature of our society?

4. In what way, according to Rubin, does a competitive society make interpersonal relationships difficult?

Developing an Opinion and Working Thesis Statement

The second question in the writing topic asks you to respond to Rubin's central claim by taking a position of your own:

> second part of the writing topic:
>
> *Do you agree with his views?*

You will have to explore your ideas about competition and decide what position you want to take in your essay. Do you agree with Rubin that competition undermines our happiness and diminishes our lives? Be sure to answer this part of the question directly because it will become the thesis statement for your essay. You will want to be as clear as possible.

It is likely that you aren't yet sure what position you want to take in your essay. If this is the case, it will be helpful to do your best to draft a working thesis statement now. There will be a chance later to revise or even change it completely once you've used the writing process to develop your thoughts a little more.

1. Use the following thesis frame to formulate the basic elements of your thesis statement:

   a. What is the issue of "Competition and Happiness" that the writing topic asks you to consider?

   _____

   b. What is Rubin's opinion about that issue?

   _____

   c. What is your opinion about the issue, and will you agree or disagree with Rubin's opinion?

   _____

   _____

   _____

2. Now use the elements you isolated in 1a, b, and c to write a thesis statement. You likely will have to revise it several times until it captures your idea clearly.

   _____

   _____

Prewriting to Find Support for Your Thesis Statement

The last part of the writing topic asks you to develop and support the position you took in your thesis statement by drawing on your own experience and readings.

last part of the writing topic:

Be sure to support your position with evidence taken from your own experience, your observations of others, and your reading, especially the reading from this course.

Use the guiding questions below to develop your ideas and find concrete support for them. The proof or evidence you present is an important element in supporting your argument and making your ideas persuasive for your readers.

1. As you begin to develop your own examples, think about how competition connects to your own life and the lives of those you know. In the space below, make a list of personal experiences you or others have had with competition. How significant are Rubin's concerns in your life and in the lives of those you know? What strategies have you or others used to deal with competition? List as many ideas as you can, and freewrite about the significance of each.

   Once you've written your ideas, look them over carefully and see if you can group them into categories. Then, give each category a label. In other words, cluster ideas that seem to have something in common and, for each cluster, identify that shared quality by giving the cluster a name.

2. Now make another list, but this time focus on examples from your studies, the media, your reading (especially the supplemental readings in this section), and your knowledge of contemporary society. Do any of these examples affirm Rubin's ideas? For example, do you recall any novels or films whose theme is the harmful effects of competition? Do you know of any examples that challenge Rubin's view and portray competition as positive? Explore a couple of TV shows that pit contestants against one another. What do they show about competition? What views do the supplemental essays in this section take? Review their arguments and supporting evidence, and compare them to Rubin's. Are any of them especially convincing for you? If so, list them here. (Remember to cite any of their ideas you include in your essay.) List and/or freewrite about all the relevant ideas you can think of, even those about which you are hesitant.

As you did in #1, examine your ideas and try to arrange them in groups. Then, title each group according to the ideas they have in common.

3. Look back at the categories you created in #1 and #2, and decide which of them to develop in your essay; look for ones that will enable you to develop your argument and convincingly and concretely support your thesis statement. In the space below, briefly summarize how each chosen category supports your thesis statement.

The information and ideas you develop in this exercise will be the core of your body paragraphs when you turn to planning and drafting your essay.

Revising Your Thesis Statement

Now that you have spent some time working out your ideas more systematically and developing some supporting evidence for the position you want to take, look again at the working thesis statement you crafted earlier to see if it is still accurate. As your first step, look again at the writing topic, and then write your original working thesis on the lines that follow it.

writing topic:

How does competition limit people's ability to lead happy and satisfying lives, according to Rubin? Do you agree with his views? Be sure to support your position with evidence taken from your own experience, your observations of others, and your reading, especially the reading from this course.

working thesis statement:

_____

_____

Remember that your thesis statement must answer the second question in the writing topic but take into consideration the writing topic as a whole. The first question in the topic identifies the issue that is up for debate, and the last question reminds you that, whatever position you take on the issue, you must be able to support it with specific examples.

Now that you have spent some time thinking about competition, your draft thesis statement may not represent the position you want to take in your essay. Sometimes, only a word or phrase must be added or deleted; other times, the thesis statement must be significantly rewritten. The subject or the claim portion may be unclear, vague, or even inaccurate. Draft writing is almost always wordy, unclear, or vague. Look at your working thesis statement through the eyes of your readers, and see if it actually says what you want it to say.

After examining it and completing any necessary revisions, check it one more time:

a. Does the thesis statement directly identify Rubin's argument?

b. Does your thesis state your position on the issue?

c. Is your thesis well punctuated, grammatically correct, and precisely worded?

Write your polished thesis on the lines below and look at it again. Is it strong and interesting?

_____

_____

Planning and Drafting Your Essay

Now that you have examined Rubin's argument and thought at length about your own views, draft an essay that responds to all parts of the writing topic. Use the material you developed in this section to compose your draft. Don't forget to turn back to Part 1, especially "The Conventional Argument Essay Structure," for further guidance on the essay's conventional structure.

Do not skip this step in the process because drafting an outline will give you a basic structure for incorporating all the ideas you have developed in the preceding pages. An outline will also give you an overview of your essay and help you spot problems in development or logic. The form below is modeled on "The Conventional Argument Essay Structure" in Part 1, but you may want to use your own outline form. Be sure to plan the body paragraphs, including the examples that will provide the concrete evidence to support your assertions. Once you complete your outline, you will be set to construct your rough draft.

Hint

This outline doesn't have to contain polished writing. You may want to fill in only the basic ideas in phrases or terms.

Creating an Outline for Your Draft

I. Introductory Paragraph

    A. An opening sentence that gives the reading selection's title and author and begins to answer the writing topic:

    _____

    B. Main points to include in the directed summary:

      1.

      2.

      3.

      4.

C. Write out your thesis statement. (Look back to "Revising Your Thesis Statement," where you reexamined and refined your working thesis statement.) It should clearly agree or disagree with Rubin's position, and it should state your position using your own words. Remember that your essay will have to develop and argue for a single point of view. You should not simply discuss competition offering both pro and con views in relation to Rubin. Avoid writing an essay that is inconclusive, one that merely examines both sides of the issue.

_____

II. Body Paragraphs

A. The paragraph's one main point that supports the thesis statement:

_____

_____

1. Controlling idea sentence:

_____

_____

2. Corroborating details:

_____

_____

_____

3. Careful explanation of why the details are significant:

_____

_____

_____

_____

4. Connection to the thesis statement:

_____

_____

_____

_____

B. The paragraph's one main point that supports the thesis statement:

_____

1. Controlling idea sentence:

_____

_____

2. Corroborating details:

_____

_____

_____

_____

3. Careful explanation of why the details are significant:

_____

_____

_____

_____

4. Connection to the thesis statement:

_____

_____

_____

_____

C. The paragraph's one main point that supports the thesis statement:

_____

1. Controlling idea sentence:

_____

_____

2. Corroborating details:

_____

_____

_____

_____

3. Careful explanation of why the details are significant:

_____

_____

_____

_____

4. Connection to the thesis statement:

_____

_____

_____

_____

D. The paragraph's one main point that supports the thesis statement:

_____

1. Controlling idea sentence:

_____

_____

2. Corroborating details:

_____

_____

_____

_____

3. Careful explanation of why the details are significant:

_____

_____

_____

_____

4. Connection to the thesis statement:

_____

_____

_____

_____

Repeat this form for any remaining body paragraphs.

III. Conclusion

    A. Type of conclusion to be used:

    _____

    B. Suggestions, or key words or phrases to include:

    _____

Getting Feedback on Your Draft

Use the following guidelines to give a classmate feedback on his or her draft. Read the draft through first, and then answer each of the items below as specifically as you can.

Name of draft's author: _____

Name of draft's reader: _____

The Introduction

1. Within the opening sentences:
   a. Rubin's entire name is given.   yes   no
   b. the reading selection's title is given and
      placed within quotation marks.   yes   no
2. The opening contains a summary that:
   a. explains Rubin's view of competition and of its negative
      impact on our lives   yes   no
   b. explains why Rubin supports this position   yes   no
3. The opening provides a thesis that makes clear the draft writer's
   opinion regarding Rubin's argument.   yes   no

If the answer to #3 above is yes, state the thesis below as it is written. If the answer is no, explain to the writer what information is needed to make the thesis complete.

_____

_____

_____

The Body

1. How many paragraphs are in the body of this essay? _____
2. To support the thesis, this number is   sufficient   not enough
3. Do paragraphs contain the 4Cs?

Paragraph 1	Controlling idea sentence	yes	no
	Corroborating details	yes	no
	Careful explanation of why the details		
	are significant	yes	no
	Connection to the thesis statement	yes	no
Paragraph 2	Controlling idea sentence	yes	no
	Corroborating details	yes	no
	Careful explanation of why		
	the details are significant	yes	no
	Connection to the thesis statement	yes	no

Paragraph 3	Controlling idea sentence	yes	no
	Corroborating details	yes	no
	Careful explanation of why the details are significant	yes	no
	Connection to the thesis statement	yes	no
Paragraph 4	Controlling idea sentence	yes	no
	Corroborating details	yes	no
	Careful explanation of why the details are significant	yes	no
	Connection to the thesis statement	yes	no
Paragraph 5	Controlling idea sentence	yes	no
	Corroborating details	yes	no
	Careful explanation of why the details are significant	yes	no
	Connection to the thesis statement	yes	no

(Continue as needed.)

4. Identify any of the above paragraphs that are underdeveloped (too short). _____

5. Identify any of the above paragraphs that fail to support the thesis. _____

6. Identify any of the above paragraphs that are redundant or repetitive. _____

7. Suggest any ideas for additional paragraphs that might improve this essay.

_____

_____

_____

The Conclusion

1. Does the final paragraph avoid introducing new ideas and examples that really belong in the body of the essay?   yes   no

2. Does the conclusion provide closure (let readers know that the end of the essay has been reached)?   yes   no

3. Does the conclusion leave readers with an understanding of the significance of the argument?   yes   no

4. State in your own words what the draft writer considers to be important about his or her argument.

_____

_____

_____

5. Identify the type of conclusion used (see the guidelines for conclusions in Part 1).

Editing

1. During the editing process, the writer should pay attention to the following problems in sentence structure, punctuation, and mechanics:
    fragments
    misplaced and dangling modifiers
    fused (run-on) sentences
    comma splices
    misplaced, missing, and unnecessary commas
    misplaced, missing, and unnecessary apostrophes
    incorrect quotation mark use
    capitalization errors
    spelling errors

2. While editing, the writer should pay attention to the following areas of grammar:
    verb tense
    subject-verb agreement
    irregular verbs
    pronoun type
    pronoun reference
    pronoun agreement
    noun plurals
    prepositions

Final Draft Checklist

Content

_____ My essay has an appropriate title.

_____ I provide an accurate summary of Rubin's position on the issue presented in "Competition and Happiness."

_____ My thesis states a clear position that can be supported by evidence.

_____ I have enough paragraphs and argument points to support my thesis.

_____ Each body paragraph is relevant to my thesis.

_____ Each body paragraph contains the 4Cs.

_____ I use transitions whenever necessary to connect ideas to each other.

_____ The final paragraph of my essay (the conclusion) provides readers with a sense of closure.

Grammar, Punctuation, and Mechanics

_____ I use the present tense to discuss Rubin's argument and examples.

_____ I use verb tenses correctly to show the chronology of events.

_____ I have verb tense consistency throughout my sentences.

_____ I have checked for subject-verb agreement in all of my sentences.

_____ I have revised all fragments and mixed or garbled sentences.

_____ I have repaired all fused (run-on) sentences and comma splices.

_____ I have placed a comma after introductory elements (transitions and phrases) and all dependent clauses that open a sentence.

_____ If I present items in a series (nouns, verbs, prepositional phrases), they are parallel in form.

_____ If I include material spoken or written by someone other than myself, I have correctly punctuated it with quotation marks, using the MLA style guide's rules for citation.

233

Reviewing Your Graded Essay

After your instructor has returned your essay, you may have the opportunity to revise your paper and raise your grade. Many students, especially those whose essays receive nonpassing grades, feel that their instructors should be less "picky" about grammar and should pass the work on content alone. However, most students at this level have not yet acquired the ability to recognize quality writing, and they do not realize that content and writing actually cannot be separated in this way. Experienced instructors know that errors in sentence structure, grammar, punctuation, and word choice either interfere with content or distract readers so much that they lose track of content. In short, good ideas badly presented are no longer good ideas; to pass, an essay must have passable writing. So even if you are not submitting a revised version of this essay to your instructor, it is important that you review your work carefully in order to understand its strengths and weaknesses. This sheet will guide you through the evaluation process.

You will want to continue to use the techniques that worked well for you and to find strategies to overcome the problems that you identify in this sample of your writing. To recognize areas that might have been problematic for you, look back at the scoring rubric in this book. Match the numerical/verbal/letter grade received on your essay to the appropriate category. Study the explanation given on the rubric for your grade.

Write a few sentences below in which you identify your problems in each of the following areas. Then, suggest specific changes you could make that would improve your paper. Don't forget to use your handbook as a resource.

1. **Grammar/punctuation/mechanics**
   My problem:

   My strategy for change:

2. **Thesis/response to assignment**
   My problem:

   My strategy for change:

3. Organization
My problem:

My strategy for change:

4. Paragraph development/examples/reasoning
My problem:

My strategy for change:

5. Assessment

In the space below, assign a grade to your paper using a rubric other than the one used by your instructor. In other words, if your instructor assigned your essay a grade of *High Fail*, you might give it the letter grade you now feel the paper warrants. If your instructor used the traditional letter grade to evaluate the essay, choose a category from the rubric in this book, or any other grading scale that you are familiar with, to show your evaluation of your work. Then, write a short narrative explaining your evaluation of the essay and the reasons it received the grade you gave it.

Grade: _____

Narrative: _____

_____

_____

_____

_____

Extending the Discussion: Considering Other Viewpoints

Reading Selections

"Two Hopi Traditions: Running and Winning" by John Branch
"Dating as Competition" by Beth Bailey
"The Art of Choosing What to Do With Your Life"
"The Cost of High Stakes on Little League Games" by C. W. Nevius
"The Power of Two" by Joshua Wolf Shenk
"Securing the Benefits of Global Competition" by R. Hewitt Pate
"An Objective Look at the Benefits of Competition in the Workplace"
    by Carmine Coyote

TWO HOPI TRADITIONS: RUNNING AND WINNING

John Branch

John Branch earned a Bachelor of Science degree in Business and a Master of Arts degree in journalism from the University of Colorado, Boulder. Since earning his degrees, he has worked in sports journalism for The Gazette *and later the* Fresno Bee. *Since 2005 he has worked as a sports reporter and journalist for* The New York Times. *He won the Pulitzer Prize for his story "Snow Fall: The Avalanche at Tunnel Creek" (2012). His book* Boy on Ice: The Life and Death of Derek Boogaard *(2014) won the PEN/ESPN Award for Literary Sports Writing. His book* The Last Cowboys: A Pioneer Family in the New West *(2018) tells of three generations of ranchers and their world renown as saddle bronc riders. He has also published a collection of his essays,* Sidecountry: Tales of Death and Life from the Back Roads of Sports *(2021). The following is based on an article that he wrote in 2015 for* The New York Times.

Above the creased high-desert landscape of northeastern Arizona, the Hopi village Oraibi, continuously inhabited for nearly 1,000 years, sits atop a blond mesa crumbling at the edges.

Each fall, during one of the Hopi calendar's dozen or so ceremonial races, a hundred or more Hopi men gather in a pack on the scrubby plain below, all muted tones of mustard yellows and sage greens. A woman in Hopi dress holds a woven basket in the distance. Onlookers shout, "Nahongvita" — loosely, "stay strong" or "dig deep" in Hopi. A signal is given.

To the Hopi, to run is to pray. And the men run, several miles, past the bean field, beyond the barely marked graves of ancestors, around the decayed façade of a Spanish church and up the precariously steep passages to the top of the mesa, where they are received by a chorus of thanks — "asqwali" from the women, "kwakwai" from the men.

Juwan Nuvayokva, a former all-American cross-country runner at Northern Arizona, has been the first to the top in dozens of Hopi races. And he would probably win the one scheduled for Saturday in Oraibi, where he was raised, if it did not fall on the day of Arizona's high school cross-country championships, in suburban Phoenix. Nuvayokva is an assistant coach for the boys' team at Hopi High, vying for its 26th Arizona state championship in a row. Its streak is the longest in the country for cross-country and the fourth-longest active run for any high school sport, boys' or girls', according to the National Federation of State High School Associations. "Hopi have that running blood in them," Nuvayokva said. "It's up to us to find it and use it."

Hopi High, as modern as any suburban school, has about 400 students in Grades 9 to 12. Before it opened in 1986, many Hopi teenagers, like those from other tribes, went to Indian boarding schools in faraway places.

Among them, more than a century ago, was Lewis Tewanima. Sent to Carlisle Indian Industrial School in Pennsylvania — where he was a classmate and track teammate of Jim Thorpe of the Sac and Fox Nation — Tewanima became a two-time Olympian. He finished ninth in the marathon at the 1908 London Games and won the silver medal in the 10,000 meters in Stockholm in 1912. He remains a Hopi hero, and an annual race is held on the reservation each year in Tewanima's honor.

Rick Baker, 56, grew up in the Hopi village Tewa and ran cross-country 80 miles away at Winslow High and then in college in Oklahoma. He was hired in 1987 as a Hopi High physical education teacher and coach and was asked to start a cross-country program. "A lot of schools with Hopi kids had won state championships," Baker said. "And I thought if we could get all the Hopis here, we should have a pretty good team." His first three boys' teams finished in the top 10 in one of Arizona's small-school divisions. His fourth, in 1990, won the state title. The team has won every one since.

The championships are a point of pride, but Hopi modesty inhibits boasting. The 25 state championship trophies are scattered in a small storage room, five of them on the floor, two on a plastic bin next to a bike tire, one of them broken. But the pressure to keep the streak intact is palpable. Boys on this year's team admitted to nerves, and Baker uses the streak as motivation — do not be the team that breaks the streak. "I don't want to be part of the team that doesn't win the 26th in a row," the freshman Jihad Nodman said. Darion Fredericks, a senior, said he knew that the team was watched, both by opponents around the state and by Hopi on the reservation. "They know what we're capable of," he said. "I definitely feel the eyes on me, even in the community. They say, 'Hey, you're the one that runs.'"

Success is built on endurance, not speed. While Hopi High has had its share of individual state champions (Nuvayokva did it twice), winning a team title requires depth. Courses are generally 5,000 meters, or 3.1 miles. Time is less important than order.

The finishing place of each team's top five finishers (out of seven starters) are added together for a team score — 1 point for the overall first-place runner, 2 points for the second, 10 points for the 10th, 100 for the 100th, and so on. The team with the lowest score wins. A perfect score is 15, if a team sweeps the first five places. The Hopi did that at state one year. "A lot of our kids don't have a lot of speed," Baker said. "If you timed them in the 400 meters, they probably wouldn't break 70 seconds. But they have endurance. They can run and run and run."

In early October, a Hopi High bus, painted in the school colors, blue and white, drove five hours to a night meet in Casa Grande, between Phoenix and Tucson. Members of the boys' cross-country team sat in the back half of the bus. The girls' team, the winner of 22 state championships in 28 seasons — a seven-year string was broken last year — sat in the front.

The teams sometimes travel together, but they have different coaches and do not practice together. At the Casa Grande meet, they got off the bus and headed different directions into the cool night. They were quickly absorbed into an athletic carnival, acres of uniformed teams wandering to and from the course and huddled around team tents. The course crossed soccer fields, a stretch of dirt, and a golf course, and then snaked back along several fairways to the finish. The air was filled with dust and the sound of generators powering temporary lights.

Baker was nervous. A quiet and poised man, with glasses and spiky black hair lightly freckled with gray, he felt that this year's team was vulnerable. The team was young. It had melted in the heat of a meet in Phoenix the week before. More broadly, Baker had found it increasingly difficult to find Hopi boys dedicated to running. Fewer committed to the summer running program. There were too many distractions these days. This could be the year that the streak ended. "People stop me and say, 'How's the team doing?'" Baker said. "They know we didn't start too well. But they say, 'You'll be ready at state.'"

Hopi High ran in the meet's final race, with many of the state's biggest schools. At the start, Baker crowded in with his seven boys, including his son Steven, a sophomore.

"Come on, guys," he shouted. "Be strong! Be a fighter!"

"Nahongvita!" they shouted together.

The starting gun sounded. Baker and Nuvayokva watched a colorful blur of 100 runners fade into the dark of the golf course. Because of the serpentine route, they could jog to a spot on the course to watch and then move to the next switchback to watch the runners pass again, repeating the pattern several times toward the finish. "Where are they, where are they, where are they?" Baker said to himself, scanning a string of passing runners. "They should be here somewhere."

He and Nuvayokva share an ability both to count runners ("You're in 70th! Move up!" Baker shouted to one of his athletes) and to tally rivals ("That's their fourth! Their fifth!" Nuvayokva shouted as boys from Sedona Red Rock High blurred past). With each Hopi runner, Baker's calm deportment gave way to full-throated screams and hand gestures. He sometimes ran alongside the runners for a few strides and shouted instructions into their serious faces.

"Two minutes hard! Two minutes hard!" he shouted to one. "Get that guy in the white! Beat him!"

Another Hopi was told in the final mile that his score was going to count.

"You're No. 5," Baker called, imploring him to sprint and pass as many opposing runners as he could. "Ten guys! You can catch 10 guys!"

Individual Hopi runners finished nowhere near the top, and because of a registration glitch, their efforts were not recorded. Still, Baker boarded the bus relaxed and relieved. He saw progress. The bus stopped at Little Caesars to pick up 16 pizzas and then unloaded the boys and girls at a nearby Holiday Inn Express at about 11 p.m. "Be glad; be happy you finished," Baker told the boys in the lobby. "But don't be satisfied. Because there's more in you somewhere."

He scheduled a five-mile run for 7 a.m. When the Hopi stayed at the same hotel last year, their morning run took them past a cotton field, and Baker grabbed some to use for a couple of Hopi ceremonies. The field was gone this year, plowed over for a strip mall.

The boys huddled before heading off to bed. "1-2-3 Hopi!" they shouted.

On the reservation, the low and distant edges of the sky are pierced by spires and plateaus. The 12 villages of the Hopi reservation, surrounded by Navajo land, are connected by the two-lane thread of Highway 264, which winds over and among three large mesas — helpfully named First Mesa, Second Mesa and Third Mesa — about 6,000 feet above sea level. To the southwest is the snow-tipped summit of Humphreys Peak, the highest point in Arizona, part of a mountain range sacred to the Hopi, who believe it is home to spirits known as kachinas.

Three Fridays after the Casa Grande meet, as the morning sun lit Oraibi, the smell of burning wood and coal came from some of the houses. Like the perch itself, they are built of stone and sit in various states of surrender to time and gravity. Some are patched together with cinder blocks and clay. The 150 or so residents of Oraibi choose to live with no electricity or running water, and there are 13 underground kivas used for village ceremonies. Each has a wood ladder poking through a hole in the top.

Nuvayokva, a 36-year-old who smiles his way through nearly everything, wore running shoes and jogged down through the broken edges of the mesa. Parts of the trail were sprinkled with pottery fragments. "When we were kids, we were told to never pick them up," Nuvayokva said. "Otherwise the people who owned them before will come back and get you." He ran onto the plain and shrunk into a speck, then looped up a trail and returned full-size a few minutes later. As a boy, he often ran to work in his clan's cornfields, one of them 16 miles away. Last year, training for a marathon, he often ran from the high school, 29 miles away.

Leigh Kuwanwisiwma, director of the Hopi Cultural Preservation Office, said that the tribe's tradition of running flowed from its scouts, men who directed tribal migrations and searches for water. (One of roughly three dozen remaining Hopi clans, the Lizard clan, supposedly got its name from such scouts, who were able to survive in the desert with little water, he said.)

Running was the method of sending messages between Hopi villages. It became part of ceremonies, too, which can last days. Photographs from the early 1900s show Hopi men lined up to run in ceremonial races like the women's basket dance race, most wearing loincloths and no shoes. "They are for the blessings of the cloud people, for the rain, for the harvest, so we have a good life, a long life," Kuwanwisiwma said. "That's what these ceremonial runners do. They bring this positiveness to the people." In some variations, the first to the top receives a gourd of water, which he then carries to his cornfield to bless the crops in all four directions. In other races, winners bury sacred tokens in the ground as offerings. "It might sound a little funny, but running in cultural races is a lot different than running in high school or college," said Devan Lomayaoma, 33, who won two individual state cross-country titles at Hopi High, ran at Northern Arizona, teaches at a Hopi elementary school and has won many Hopi races. "In cultural races, you never got recognition for it. They have a deeper meaning."

Nuvayokva said the same thing. "It's different than the Anglo culture, where you run and it's every man for himself," Nuvayokva said. "When I competed in the N.C.A.A., you're trying to beat others. Here, you do it for others." He had to cut his morning run short because the team had a meet in Holbrook, about 90 minutes south. On a room-temperature day under blue skies and cotton ball clouds, the Hopi boys finished second among 18 teams.

Among more than 100 varsity competitors, the top five Hopi boys finished 6th, 12th, 15th, 21st and 23rd.

The meet was won by Tuba City, a rival school on Navajo land that some Hopi on the western side of the reservation attend. Baker mentioned how much Hopi High had gained on its rivals in the past couple of meets. But Tuba City is a substantially bigger school, in a different classification, so Hopi High will not compete against it head-to-head at the state meet.

"I feel pretty good," Baker said. "Pretty good. We're pretty much on pace for the state meet."

But he also knew that plenty of other schools, including a handful with reasonable hopes of an upset, dreamed of ending the streak. "We're banquet talk," Baker said. "That's what I tell the boys. At the other teams' banquet, they'll say, 'We beat the Hopi,' or 'You outraced the Hopi kid.'" As the boys cooled down and put on their white warm-up suits for the awards presentation, a 70-year-old Hopi man named Lee Grover stood to the side. He still jogs a few miles in the mornings, to greet and pray to the sun, and hopes that his running motivates the younger generations. The team has helped "put the Hopi back on the map," Grover said, but he worries that even the strongest of traditions can fade.

"We're gifted with this talent of running," Grover said. "It's something we should never let die."

Discussion Questions

1. What is the connection between running and Hopi culture? How does the Hopi attitude toward running differ from the traditional Anglo attitude toward the sport?

2. Contrast the final destination and care of trophies in most high schools with the those of trophies at Hopi High. How could these differences be seen as a cultural metaphor?

3. Do you think that the behavior of the spectators at Hopi track meets is similar to the behavior of the Little League parents discussed by C. W. Nevius in his article "The Cost of High Stakes on Little League Games?" What are the reasons and evidence for your opinion?

4. Consider the attitude toward competition of some of the other essay writers in this unit, such as Joshua Wolf Shenk and R. Hewitt Pate, and explain ways their positions do or do not align with those of the Hopi runners.

DATING AS COMPETITION

BETH BAILEY

Beth Bailey was for several years a professor of American studies at the University of New Mexico. She is now a professor of history at Temple University. The following passage is from her book From Front Porch to Back Seat: Courtship in Twentieth-Century America *(1988).*

In the early twentieth century, the gloomiest critics of the new system of male/female socialization called "dating" feared only that it would make it harder for youth to negotiate the true business of courtship: marriage. They worried that poor but ambitious and worthy young men could not attract suitable partners without spending vast sums on entertainment and that every theater ticket and late supper meant less money set aside toward the minimum figure needed to marry and start a family.

The critics were right, but in some ways, their criticisms were irrelevant. During the 1920s and 1930s, for mainstream, middle-class young people, dating was not about marriage and families. It wasn't even about love—which is not to say that American youth didn't continue to fall in love, marry, and raise families. But before World War II, long-term commitments lay in the future for youth and were clearly demarcated from the dating system. In the public realm, in the shared culture that defined the conventions of dating and gave meaning and coherence to individual experience, dating was not about marriage. Dating was about competition.

Shortly after World War II ended, anthropologist Margaret Mead gave a series of lectures on American courtship rituals. Although the system she described was already disappearing, she captured the essence of what dating meant in the interwar years. Dating, Mead stressed, was not about sex or adulthood or marriage. Instead, it was a "competitive game," a way for girls and boys to "demonstrate their popularity." This was not a startling revelation to the American public. Americans knew that dating was centered on competition and popularity. These were the terms in which dating was discussed, the vocabulary in which one described a date.

In 1937, in the classic study of American dating, sociologist Willard Waller gave this competitive system a name: "the campus rating complex." His study of Penn State detailed a "dating and rating" system based on very clear standards of popularity. To be popular, men needed outward, material signs: an automobile, the right clothing, fraternity membership, money. Women's popularity depended on building and maintaining a reputation for popularity. They had to *be seen* with popular men in the "right" places, indignantly turn down requests for dates made at the "last minute" (which could be weeks in advance), and cultivate the impression that they were greatly in demand.

Although Waller did not see it, the technique of image building was not always limited to women. For men, too, nothing succeeded like success. *Guide Book for the Young Man about Town* advised: "It's money in the bank to have lots of girls on the knowing list and the date calendar. . . . It means more popularity for you." As proof, the author looked back on his own college days, recalling how a classmate won the title of "Most Popular Man" at a small coed college by systematically going through the college register and dating every girl in the school who wasn't engaged.

The concept of dating value had nothing to do with the interpersonal experience of a date—whether or not the boy (or girl, for that matter) was fun or charming or brilliant was irrelevant. Instead, the rating looked to others, to public perceptions of success in the popularity competition. Popularity was clearly the key—and popularity defined in a very specific way. It was not earned directly through talent, looks, personality, or importance in organizations, but by the way these attributes translated into dates. These dates had to be highly visible, and with many different people, or they didn't count.

The rating-dating system, and the definition of popularity on which it was based, did not remain exclusively on college campuses. High school students of the late 1930s and 1940s were raised on rating and dating. Not only did they imitate the conventions of older youth, they were advised by some young columnists, who spoke with distinctly nonparental voices, that these conventions were natural and right. *Senior Scholastic*, a magazine used in high schools all over the United States, began running an advice column in 1936. "Boy Dates Girl" quickly became the magazine's most popular feature.

The advice in "Boy Dates Girl" always took the competitive system as a given. Its writer assumed that girls would accept any *straightforward* offer of a date if not already "dated" for the evening, and that boys, in trying for the most popular girl imaginably possible, would occasionally overreach themselves. The author once warned girls never to brush off any boy, no matter how unappealing, in a rude way, since "he may come in handy for an off-night."

Discussion Questions

1. What problem did some of the critics of the early twentieth century's new system of dating predict? Whom did they think would be most adversely affected? Did future events show their concerns to be valid? Explain your answer.

2. What had dating been about before World War II? What was the purpose of dating during the interwar years? Do you think dating in the twenty-first century has more in common with the years before or after World War II? Explain your choice.

3. Explain "the campus rating complex." When people use such a scale, what characteristics earn a high rating? What attributes are valueless on this scale? If you were to devise your own dating-rating scale, what would it look like?

THE ART OF CHOOSING WHAT TO DO WITH YOUR LIFE

BENJAMIN STOREY AND JENNA SILBER STOREY

Benjamin Storey is an author and Professor of Politics and International Affairs at Furman University. He earned a BA from the University of North Carolina, and an MA and PhD from the University of Chicago. He is director of the Tocqueville Program at Furman University, a program dedicated to looking into the moral and philosophical questions that govern political life. He has won the Furman University Award for Meritorious Teaching, and serves as a Visiting Fellow at Princeton University.

Jenna Silber Storey is an author and Assistant Professor in Politics and International Affairs at Furman University. She received a BA from Boston University and a PhD from the University of Chicago. She is Executive Director of the Tocqueville Program at Furman, a program dedicated to looking into the moral and philosophical questions that govern political life. Her articles have appeared in scholarly edited volumes and publications such as The Washington Post, The Boston Globe, *and* The New Atlantis.

Jenna Silber Storey and Benjamin Story have coauthored a book titled Why We Are Restless: On the Modern Quest for Contentment *(2021), an exploration based on the thesis that the modern-day pursuit of happiness leads to unhappiness.*

Our star student walks up to the lunch table with what seems like good news. The fellowship is now hers; next fall she will be off to teach English on the other side of the globe. She has trained her energies on this goal for many months and wants to accept it in grateful triumph. But her eyes are red and tired. She is not sure she wants the prize she has worked so hard to win.

Her adviser has just reassured her that this experience will "open doors." She need not worry about where this is going—those who spend a few years in such fellowships emerge with plenty of choices. But that thought, which once compelled her, is beginning to leave her cold. What is the point of a life that is nothing more than an endless series of opportunities?

As her thoughts flit among the prospects to which this next step is supposed to lead, she seems less excited by the promise of so many adventures than exhausted by the thought of so many decisions. She wonders aloud whether she might just go back home and work in a coffee shop.

The thought is raised halfheartedly. It sounds more like a doubt about the step she is about to take than a choice she would seriously consider. It's as though a life that rejects striving altogether is the only alternative she can imagine to a life of striving without purpose.

Colleges today often operate as machines for putting ever-proliferating opportunities before already privileged people. Our educational system focuses obsessively on helping students take the next step. But it does not give them adequate assistance in thinking about the substance of the lives toward which they are advancing. Many institutions today have forgotten that liberal education itself was meant to teach the art of choosing, to train the young to use reason to decide which endeavors merit the investment of their lives.

We spent many years teaching on a college campus, trying during office hours to help students struggling with their confusion. Eventually, we sought to address this problem systematically, by designing a course intended to introduce the young to the art of choosing. The syllabus begins with Plato's *Gorgias*—a messy dialogue that turns on an argument between a browbeating Socrates and the ruffian Callicles over whether the pursuit of virtue or of pleasure is the way to a good life. The dialogue ends inconclusively; no one is satisfied. But with remarkable regularity, it awakens the kind of thinking that students need to better understand the choices that shape their lives.

Students' first reaction to the *Gorgias* is incredulity, sometimes even horror. It is the dialogue's premise that alarms them: the idea that we can seriously argue about what constitutes the human good. Everything in their education has led them to believe that such arguments cannot bear fruit. "But happiness is subjective!" someone will exclaim, expecting to win over the room. We decline to affirm such assertions, which reliably astonishes the class. Our reticence is intended, in part, to dislodge our students from the idea that life's purpose comes from some mysterious voice within. Once students are freed from this idea, they can consider the possibility that people can reason together about the best way to live.

Then we seek to create a conversation in our classroom that puts into practice this constructively countercultural way of thinking about happiness. We ask students to give reasons for their opinions on how best to live. With a bit of practice, one starts to hear the speech patterns of Socrates entering their conversations. They cease expecting their assertions to be showstoppers. They start asking one another questions. They begin lining up premises, making inferences, and drawing conclusions.

These patterns of academic thinking soon penetrate their personal lives. To be asked to give reasons for one's personal decisions is to entertain the possibility that such reasons exist. Thomas Aquinas, another author on our syllabus, calls the reason that is the orienting point of all your other reasons your "final end." Those who discover that they have such final ends, and learn to assess them, see their way to the exit from the fun house of arbitrary decisions in which the young so often find themselves trapped.

For the number of final ends is not infinite. Aquinas usefully suggests that the ultimate objects of human longing can be sorted into only eight enduring categories. If we want to understand where we're headed, we should ask ourselves these questions: Am I interested in this opportunity because it leads to wealth? Or am I aiming at praise and admiration? Do I want enduring glory? Or power—to "make an impact"? Is my goal to maximize my pleasures? Do I seek health? Do I seek some "good of the soul," such as knowledge or virtue? Or is my ultimate longing to come face-to-face with the divine?

Most students find, to their surprise, that they can locate their desires on this old map. This does not leave students feeling constrained, as they have often been led to fear. It leaves them feeling empowered, like wanderers suddenly recognizing the orienting features of a landscape. Like any good map, Aquinas's reasoned analysis of the human goods can tell us something about where we're going before we get there. We start down the path to wealth, for example, because it is a universal means to almost any end. But wealth cannot be the final goal of life, for it gives satisfaction only when traded for something else. Admiration signals that people think we're doing something well. But it is conferred by the often errant judgment of others and can lead you astray.

Most students are grateful to discover this art of choosing. Learning to reason about happiness awakens an "indwelling power in the soul," as Socrates puts it, which is as delightful as discovering that one's voice can be made to sing. Why, then, do liberal arts institutions rarely teach it? In some cases, faculty members are incentivized to emphasize specialized research rather than thinking about the good life. In others, they share the conviction that reason is merely an extension of the quest for dominance, or the Rousseauean belief that sentiment is a better guide to happiness than the mind.

Most fundamentally, though, the reigning model of liberal education—opening doors without helping us think about what lies beyond them—prevails because it reprises a successful modern formula. Agnosticism about human purposes, combined with the endless increase of means and opportunities, has proved to be a powerful organizing principle for our political and economic life. It has helped create the remarkable peace, prosperity, and liberty we have enjoyed for much of the modern age.

Modern liberty and modern anxiety are, however, two fruits of the same tree. As Alexis de Tocqueville noted long ago, people who have freedom and plenty but lack the art of choosing will be "restless in the midst of their prosperity." Anxiety, depression and suicide—all of which are woefully familiar on college campuses—are the unhappy companions of the mobility and freedom that modern societies prize.

This is why liberal democratic societies need universities to play the role of constructively countercultural institutions. At their best, such societies are aware of their own incompleteness and support institutions that push against their innate tendency toward moral agnosticism, and the disorientation and restless paralysis that it brings in its wake.

Colleges should self-consciously prioritize initiating students into a culture of rational reflection on how to live, and this intention should be evident in their mission statements, convocation addresses, faculty hiring and promotion, and curriculums. Doing so will hold them accountable for performing their proper work: helping young people learn to give reasons for the choices that shape their lives and to reflect about the ends they pursue. For that art of choosing is what their students most need—and what liberal education, rightly understood, was meant to impart.

Discussion Questions

1. Why was the "star student" mentioned in the article by Benjamin and Jenna Silber Storey less than elated by the good news she had just received? In what ways do you find her reaction both surprising and understandable? Tell about a time in your life when something you expected to make you happy had the opposite effect.

2. What do the authors see as the purpose of a liberal arts education? How do their course syllabi address this goal? Do you think that most students and/or their parents are paying tuition to learn what the Storeys' classes teach? Explain your answer.

3. List the "eight enduring categories" as defined by Thomas Aquinas. How do discussions of the questions posed by Aquinas's categories allow students control over their futures?

4. Consider some of the additional readings in this unit. How does the Storeys' "counterculture" approach to a college education address or relate to a concern raised by the author of at least one of the other articles in this unit?

THE COST OF HIGH STAKES ON LITTLE LEAGUE GAMES

C. W. NEVIUS

C. W. Nevius is a writer and journalist. His column appears regularly in the San Francisco Chronicle. *The following essay was published in 2000.*

When he was ten years old, Joseph Matteucci had a coach for his Castro Valley Little League team who was a "screamer." Joseph's mother, Alexandra, had concerns, but as a single parent, she wanted to encourage her son to meet and play with other kids, so she didn't complain. Another parent did not hold back, however. In the parking lot after a game, he confronted the coach about the yelling at his son. The coach got out of the car and began throwing punches. The father went down in the barrage, and when his wife rushed out to aid him, the coach slugged her, too.

Joseph Matteucci, sitting in the car, saw it all and burst into tears. He quit Little League the next day. Alexandra Matteucci was relieved. Thank God she'd gotten her son out of that violent environment. Six years later, Joseph was dead. An innocent bystander, he stopped by a spring Little League game for sixteen-year-old players to pick up a friend. A brawl broke out after the game, the result of excessive taunting from spectators. A player swung a bat at one of his tormentors, he ducked, and Matteucci was hit in the back of the head. He died in less than twenty-four hours.

Some might call that 1993 incident a fluke, but the reality is the tragedy on that Castro Valley playground had all the elements of what has become an ugly trend in youth sports. Violence has become commonplace on the fields of play in America, and the formula is simple, direct, and brutal. Taunting from the sidelines escalates, coaches and spectators fail to quell the rising tensions, umpires or referees cannot control the situation, and, finally, rage boils over. "Before it was coaches helping the kids who were having trouble controlling their emotions," says Jim Thompson, director of Stanford's Positive Coaching Alliance. "Now it is, 'Let's provide leadership to help the coaches control the parents.'"

The incidents of enraged parents are so out of proportion that they sound absurd. Orlando Lago, an assistant coach with the Hollywood, Florida, All-Stars, broke the jaw of umpire Tom Dziedzinski after a disputed call at third base in a Connie Mack game between high school teams. Last January, police were called to a gym in Kirkland, Washington, when a heated confrontation at a wrestling match became so violent that a coach head-butted a parent and broke his nose. The wrestlers were six years old. And the most shocking display took place in Reading, Massachusetts, last July when Thomas Junta, a parent, beat to death Michael Costin, a hockey coach, at an ice rink. Junta, who was furious because he felt that Costin was allowing rough play, beat the coach to unconsciousness as his children begged him to stop. Junta, forty-two, has pleaded not guilty to charges of manslaughter.

But those are just the headlines. Anyone who has been to a youth sports game lately knows the truth. Parents are out of control. They scream at their kids, yell at the officials, and, in more cases than anyone would like to admit, something troubling happens. Worse, every indicator shows it is becoming more common. Bob Still, spokesman for the National Association of Sports Officials, says his organization gets "between one and three" reports of physical assaults on an official each week. "These are what we would call assaults as defined by law," says Still, whose organization has been tracking the numbers for twenty-five years. "The verbal attacks have always been there. But people acting out, coming on the field, there is a definite trend to more violence."

Kill the ump? It isn't so funny. Still says it has reached the point that in 1998 his association began offering "assault insurance" to its nineteen thousand members. The policy pays medical bills, provides counseling, and offers legal advice about how to prosecute attackers. It doesn't take much imagination to project the short-term result. Would you want to be a referee in this climate? "Finding referees is the single most important thing we have to deal with right now," says Bob Maas, president of Pleasanton's highly competitive Ballistic United Soccer League. "You get out there, some parent yells at you, and you think, 'You know, I am missing the 49ers game right now.'"

But the referee shortage is the symptom, not the problem. Fueled by unrealistic expectations and an unhealthy obsession with winning, parents have gone from cheerleaders to taskmasters. Having invested large sums in clinics and private instruction for their kids, anything but success is unacceptable. Alexandra Matteucci, who now runs the Joseph Matteucci Foundation, was speaking to a group in Los Angeles when she heard a recent example. A mother, watching her son in a baseball game for twelve- to fifteen-year-olds, was furious when her son was taken out. "She went out and sat on second base and refused to move until they put her son back in," Matteucci said. "They didn't know what to do, so they put him back in the game."

That kind of acting out may have worked in that case, but how many kids want their parent to become a laughingstock? The yelling, the gestures, and the intense pressure can drive even avid athletes out of organized sports. "I can't tell you how many times I have heard kids say, 'Shut up, Dad!'" says Danville's John Wondolowski, whose under-eleven soccer team won the State Cup last spring. When dad won't pipe down, the next step is off the field. Many kids drop sports—an estimated seventy percent quit before they reach the age of twelve—but some also find another outlet. Skateboarders, mountain bikers, and surfers are just part of an emerging X Games generation. There are fewer rules, less structure, and—best of all—dad doesn't know the first thing about it. "That's the protection," says Positive Coaching Alliance's Thompson. "No adults. It is not hypercompetitive. Fifteen or twenty years ago, adults didn't know anything about soccer. Now you've got guys who think they know all about it. My son is into surfing, skating, and snowboarding. His point was: Do I want to stand in line, wait to bat, and have the coach yell at me? Or do I want to sit out in the ocean?"

A kinder, gentler approach was the idea behind "Silent Sunday" last October in a Cleveland suburb. Coaches and parents in the 217-team league were told not to yell at the players, not even to cheer good plays. Was it hard to break old habits? Well, some parents, afraid they couldn't resist the temptation, put duct tape over their mouths.

Another soccer coach turned the tables on his parents. He put them on the field for a practice and let the kids scream instructions at them as they scrambled to kick the ball. Reportedly, the parents were ready for the exercise to stop long before the kids.

Are those the only choices? Do kids either have to drop out of sports or duct tape their parents' mouths shut? Well no, there are options, proposed by groups like Thompson's PSA and the Matteucci Foundation. It begins with what groups like Ballistic Soccer call "zero tolerance" for attacks on officials, but more than anything, it involves changing perceptions for parents. "After all," says Thompson, "when you go to a spelling bee, nobody screams at the officials. It isn't done." "We turn our heads," says Still of the Association of Sports Officials. "We say, 'I'm going to let it go. It is no big deal. Bill is a good guy, he just lost it that one time.'" That, says facilitators like Matteucci, has to stop.

A clear ethics code must be established before the season begins, and the parents must go over it. Expecting them to read a handout isn't enough. Matteucci advocates reading the code aloud before every game. Second, parents who get out of control need to be told so, and in a way that makes it clear that they are out of step with the entire group. And if the coach, or some of the other parents, cannot calm the transgressor down, enforce the rules and call a forfeit. "Call the game," says Matteucci. "If we do, life goes on."

But most important, parents need to monitor their level of involvement with an eye toward scaling it down. Chances are, their son or daughter is not going to get a college scholarship, or appear on a Wheaties box. In ten years, the best you can hope is that the kids still enjoy staying physically active and look back fondly on their sports career.

What's fun about sports if you don't win? Thompson recommends changing the goal. He worked with a soccer team that was so outclassed that it lost every game. Instead of winning, or even scoring, the team decided to make its objective to get the ball over midfield five times in one game. When they finally did it, cheers rang up and down their sideline, puzzling the opposing parents. "They were asking, 'What are they so happy about?'" Thompson said. "Aren't we beating them by eight goals?" Yes, but they were playing a different game.

Discussion Questions

1. Describe the kinds of behavior of the Little League parents or the soccer parents that concern Nevius. How do the details of their behavior relate to the case Rubin is trying to make about competition?

2. Because of the emphasis on winning in organized children's sports, what choice do seventy percent of the players make, according to Nevius? What other activities does Nevius think these kids prefer? Why? When you were twelve, what were your favorite activities? Why?

3. What change does Thompson recommend for children's sports? Do you think Rubin would like to see this change? Why or why not?

THE POWER OF TWO

JOSHUA WOLF SHENK

Joshua Wolf Shenk is the author of Powers of Two: Finding the Essence of Innovation in Creative Pairs *(2014), published by Eamon Dolan Books/Houghton Mifflin Harcourt.*

In the fall of 1966, during a stretch of nine weeks away from the Beatles, John Lennon wrote a song. He was in rural Spain at the time, on the set of a movie called *How I Won the War,* but the lyrics cast back to an icon of his boyhood in Liverpool: the Strawberry Field children's home, whose sprawling grounds he'd often explored with his gang and visited with his Aunt Mimi. In late November, the Beatles began work on the song at EMI Studios, on Abbey Road in London. After four weeks and scores of session hours, the band had a final cut of "Strawberry Fields Forever." That was December 22.

On December 29, Paul McCartney brought in a song that took listeners back to another icon of Liverpool: Penny Lane, a traffic roundabout and popular meeting spot near his home. This sort of call-and-response was no anomaly. He and John, Paul said later, had a habit of "answering" each other's songs. "He'd write 'Strawberry Fields,'" Paul explained. "I'd go away and write 'Penny Lane' . . . to compete with each other. But it was very friendly competition."

It's a famous anecdote. Paul, of course, was stressing the collaborative nature of his partnership with John (he went on to note that their competition made them "better and better all the time"). But in this vignette, as in so many from the Beatles years, it's easy to get distracted by the idea of John and Paul composing independently. The notion that the two need to be understood as individual creators, in fact, has become the contemporary "smart" take on them. "Although most of the songs on any given Beatles album are usually credited to the Lennon-McCartney songwriting team," Wikipedia declares, "that description is often misleading." Entries on the site about individual Beatles songs take care to assert their "true" author. Even the superb rock critic Greg Kot once succumbed to this folly. John and Paul "shared songwriting credits but little else," he says, writing in 1990, "and their 'partnership' was more of a competition than a collaboration."

Kot makes that observation in a review of *Beatlesongs*, by William J. Dowlding—a high-water mark of absurdity in the analysis of Lennon-McCartney. Dowlding actually tries to quantify their distinct contributions, giving 84.55 credits to John—"the winner," he declares—and 73.65 to Paul. (His tally also includes 22.15 credits for George Harrison, 2.7 for Ringo Starr, and 0.45 for Yoko Ono. For a few lines in the song "Julia," Dowlding gives 0.05 credits to the Lebanese poet Kahlil Gibran.)

For centuries, the myth of the lone genius has towered over us, its shadow obscuring the way creative work really gets done. The attempts to pick apart the Lennon-McCartney partnership reveal just how misleading that myth can be, because John and Paul were so obviously more creative as a pair than as individuals, even if at times they appeared to work in opposition to each other. The lone-genius myth prevents us from grappling with a series of paradoxes about creative pairs: that distance doesn't impede intimacy, and is often a crucial ingredient of it; that competition and collaboration are often entwined. Only when we explore this terrain can we grasp how such pairs as Steve Jobs and Steve Wozniak, William and Dorothy Wordsworth, and Martin Luther King, Jr., and Ralph Abernathy all managed to do such creative work. The essence of their achievements, it turns out, was relational. If that seems far-fetched, it's because our cultural obsession with the individual has obscured the power of the creative pair.

John and Paul epitomize this power. Geoff Emerick—who served as the principal engineer for EMI on *Revolver, Sgt. Pepper's Lonely Hearts Club Band*, some of *The White Album*, and *Abbey Road*—recognized from the outset that the two formed a single creative being. "Even from the earliest days," he wrote in his memoir, *Here, There and Everywhere*, "I always felt that the artist was John Lennon and Paul McCartney, not the Beatles."

One reason it's so tempting to try to cleave John and Paul apart is that the distinctions between them were so stark. Observing the pair through the control-room glass at Abbey Road's Studio Two, Emerick was fascinated by their odd-couple quality:

> *Paul was meticulous and organized: He always carried a notebook around with him, in which he methodically wrote down lyrics and chord changes in his neat handwriting. In contrast, John seemed to live in chaos: He was constantly searching for scraps of paper that he'd hurriedly scribbled ideas on. Paul was a natural communicator; John couldn't articulate his ideas well. Paul was the diplomat; John was the agitator. Paul was soft-spoken and almost unfailingly polite; John could be a right loudmouth and quite rude. Paul was willing to put in long hours to get a part right; John was impatient, always ready to move on to the next thing. Paul usually knew exactly what he wanted and would often take offense at criticism; John was much more thick-skinned and was open to hearing what others had to say. In fact, unless he felt especially strongly about something, he was usually amenable to change.*

The diplomat and the agitator. The neatnik and the whirling dervish. Spending time with Paul and John, one couldn't help but be struck by these sorts of differences. "John needed Paul's attention to detail and persistence," Cynthia Lennon, John's first wife, said. "Paul needed John's anarchic, lateral thinking."

Paul and John seemed to be almost archetypal embodiments of order and disorder. The ancient Greeks gave form to these two sides of human nature in Apollo, who stood for the rational and the self-disciplined, and Dionysus, who represented the spontaneous and the emotional. Friedrich Nietzsche proposed that the interaction of the Apollonian and the Dionysian was the foundation of creative work, and modern creativity research has confirmed this insight, revealing the key relationship between breaking and making, challenging and refining, disrupting and organizing.

John was the iconoclast. In early live shows, he would fall into the background, let Paul charm the audience, and then twist up his face, adopt a hunchback pose, and play dissonant chords. Sometimes, he deliberately kept his guitar slightly out of tune, which contributed to what the composer Richard Danielpour calls "that raw, raunchy sound." He was difficult with the press, at times even impossible. In the studio, he clamored constantly to do things differently. He wanted to be hung from the ceiling and swung around the mic. He wanted to be recorded from *behind*.

While John broke form, Paul looked to make it. He was the band's *de facto* musical director in the studio and, outside, its relentless champion. "Anything you promote, there's a game that you either play or you don't play," he said. "I decided very early on that I was very ambitious and I wanted to play." Among the Beatles, he said, he was the one who would "sit the press down and say, 'Hello, how are you? Do you want a drink?,' and make them comfortable." Distinctions are a good way to introduce ourselves to a creative pair. But what matters is how the parts come together. So it's not right to focus on how John insulted reporters while Paul charmed them. John was able to insult reporters *because* Paul charmed them. Their music emerged in a similar way, with single strands twisting into a mutually strengthening double helix.

The work John initiated tended to be sour and weary, whereas Paul's tended to the bright and naive. The magic came from interaction. Consider the home demo for "Help!"— an emotionally raw, aggressively confessional song John wrote while in the throes of the sort of depression that he said made him want "to jump out the window, you know." The original had a slow, plain piano tune, and feels like the moan of the blues. When Paul heard it, he suggested a countermelody, a lighthearted harmony to be sung behind the principal lyric—and this fundamentally changed its nature. It's not incidental that in the lyrics John pleaded for "somebody . . . not just anybody." He knew he was at risk of floating away, and Paul helped put his feet back on the ground.

And John knocked Paul off his, snorting at his bromides (as with Paul's original "She was just seventeen / Never been a beauty queen") and batting against his sweet, optimistic lyrics, as in the song "Getting Better." "I was sitting there doing 'Getting better all the time,'" Paul remembered, "and John just said, in his laconic way, 'It couldn't get no worse.' And I thought, *Oh, brilliant! This is exactly why I love writing with John.*"

John lived most of his youth in his Aunt Mimi's house, a prim, stuffy place, protected—or so Mimi thought—from the wreckage of his charming but dissolute parents. Even as a boy, John was a mischief-maker, a gang leader. When he discovered music, he wanted to get his gang onstage. He insisted that his best friend, Pete Shotton, join his band, the Quarry Men, even though Pete protested that he could hardly play. John didn't mind. He could hardly play himself.

Paul, by contrast, came from a warm, close-knit family. Music occupied a central place in the McCartney home, in the form of the upright piano that dominated the tiny living room. Music for Paul was family sing-alongs and brass-band concerts with his dad. When he began to write songs, Paul wasn't thinking about rock and roll. He wanted to write for Sinatra.

John's rebellious impulse took him in dangerous directions. By the time he met Paul, his boyhood pranks had progressed to shoplifting. He said later that had he not wound up in a truly outstanding band—which is to say, had he not met Paul—he probably would have ended up like his father, a likable ne'er-do-well jostling between odd jobs and petty crime.

Paul, for his part, might have ended up teaching, or doing some other job for which he could rely on his smarts and still live inside his own mind. He was studied and careful. Even his moments of abandon (his imitations of Little Richard, say) were conducted more or less by the book. John was twenty months older—a world apart for a teenager. He was the badass older brother Paul never had. For John, Paul was a studious and charming sidekick who could do something rare: keep up with him.

Alongside their many differences, John and Paul shared uncannily similar musical tastes and drives to perform. The chemistry between them was immediate. A member of John's band who watched them on the day they met later recalled that they "circled each other like cats."

But distance doesn't necessarily hinder creativity; often, it drives a pair forward. We flourish with an ongoing stream of new influences, new ideas. It's also true that we're affected by not just what people explicitly say to us, or their overt contributions to our work, but also the way they get in our heads. One sure way this happens is through competition—or what's known in business as "co-opetition," whereby two entities at once oppose and support each other. George Martin, the Beatles's longtime producer, noticed this element in John and Paul's relationship. "Imagine two people pulling on a rope, smiling at each other and pulling all the time with all their might," he said. "The tension between the two of them made for the bond."

That tension took on varying forms during the course of the Lennon-McCartney partnership. The two spun, time and again, through the same cycle. As the alpha, John would establish his dominance, and then Paul, like a canny prime minister under a tempestuous king, would gradually assert himself and take charge—until John, often suddenly, struck back.

This dynamic helped give birth to the two albums that represent the best of John and Paul's work together: *Sgt. Pepper's Lonely Hearts Club Band* and *The White Album*. In popular lore, *Sgt. Pepper* represents the zenith of the partnership ("It was a peak," John said), while *The White Album* represents its nadir ("the tension album," Paul called it). But the truth is that the two albums were born of the same cycle, just at different points in it.

Despite the tension—*because of* the tension—the work was magnificent. Though the *White Album* recording sessions were often tense and unpleasant (Emerick disliked them so much that he flat-out quit), they yielded an album that is among the best in music history. The album is notable for a number of role-raiding songs, with John doing the sort of ballads associated with Paul ("Julia" and "Goodnight"), and Paul drenching himself in the noise and aggression usually associated with John ("Helter Skelter," "Why Don't We Do It in the Road"). No matter how thick the tension got, it kept serving a creative purpose.

Discussion Questions

1. According to Joshua Wolf Shenk, what role did competition play in the song writing partnership of John Lennon and Paul McCartney? Explain the way this type of partnership could be responsible for the writing of such songs as "Strawberry Fields" and "Penny Lane." Considering that these particular songs were written in the late 1960s, how effectively do these examples support Shenk's argument?

2. Discuss the different personalities of John and Paul. How can their differences be considered archetypal? What is the relationship between these differences and a competition that results in increased production? Do you agree with Shenk's conclusion that the differences in character of John and Paul explain, in part, their creative genius? Explain your answer.

3. By applying Theodore Rubin's argument that competition must have placed limits on John's and Paul's satisfaction and happiness, what conclusion would you be forced to assume about their contentment with their careers as Beatles? Explain why you think that Rubin's point is, or is not, applicable to creative endeavors.

SECURING THE BENEFITS OF GLOBAL COMPETITION

R. HEWITT PATE

The following is a talk given by R. Hewitt Pate, an Assistant Attorney General for the United States from 2003 to 2005. The talk was sponsored by the US Department of Justice and presented at the Tokyo American Center in Tokyo, Japan, in 2004.

Good afternoon, ladies and gentlemen. I am very pleased to be here today to talk with you about the globalization of competition law. This is my first visit to Japan, on the occasion of the 26th annual US-Japan antitrust consultations. Chairman Takeshima has been a gracious host, and we have had very fruitful discussions over the past two days.

Introduction

Just two weeks ago, the 28th Olympic Games came to a conclusion in Athens, Greece. It was a tremendous event, with more than 10,000 athletes from a record 202 jurisdictions competing. As you know, this year's Olympics were the first to be held in Greece since the modern Olympics Games began in Athens at the end of the nineteenth century. The modern Olympics started in 1896, only six years after the American Sherman Antitrust Act was enacted. Believe it or not, there are some important parallels between the modern Olympics and global competition law.

As for the most basic parallel, the Olympics are a microcosm of globalization and of competition. They are based on the principle that competition creates excellence by providing the incentive to bring out the best capabilities in the athletes. Through the constant challenge of new competitors and new training techniques, world records are made and shattered, and goals once thought impossible are reached and then exceeded. The Olympic Committee and other sports authorities, like antitrust enforcers, attempt to impose certain basic rules to ensure that the competitions are fair, and that cheating—such as fixing the outcome of events or taking banned substances—is not allowed to undermine competitive outcomes. (Like antitrust enforcers, the governing bodies face challenges, and can make no claim to be perfect.)

Participation in the Olympics started slowly. At the first Modern Olympic games in 1896, 241 athletes from 14 nations took part. All of the participants were from Western Europe and North America. One might even say that the early Olympic Games were a regional, rather than a global, market. In 1920, when Ichiya Kumagai won Japan's first Olympic medals—silver medals in singles and doubles men's tennis—the number of participating nations had doubled to 29. Just eight years later, at the 1928 Olympics in Amsterdam, 46 countries competed and Japan won its first gold medals, in the triple jump and in the men's 200 meter breast stroke. At the 1932 Olympics in

"Securing the Benefits of Global Competition" presented at the Tokyo American Center, September 10, 2004 by R. Hewitt Pate, Assistant Attorney General, Antitrust Division, United States Department of Justice.

Los Angeles, a Japanese 14-year-old "new-entrant"—Kusuo Kitamur —won the 1500 meter freestyle swimming competition, to become the youngest male ever to win a gold medal at the Olympics. By 1964, at the Tokyo Olympics, the number of participating nations had doubled again to 93, and Japan—foreshadowing its emergence as a major economic power—was third among all participating nations in the number of gold medals won by its athletes. By the time of the 26th Olympiad in Atlanta in 1996, a truly competitive global athletic market had been established: 10,318 athletes from 197 countries competed in 271 different events, and men and women from 79 different nations won medals.

The Globalization of Competition Law

The history of antitrust laws also started slowly. In the 1890s, only the United States and Canada had comprehensive antitrust laws. It took some time, even in the United States, before enforcement became active or vigorous. By 1950, you still could count on the fingers of both hands the number of countries that were enforcing antitrust laws. Even in the 1970s, by which time many developed countries had adopted comprehensive antitrust laws, efforts by the United States to use our antitrust laws against harmful international cartels were met by strong resistance from our trading partners. US approaches to antitrust law, including the criminalization of cartel behavior and the prosecution of corporate executives, were viewed with puzzlement and suspicion by other governments and their business communities. A number of countries even adopted blocking statutes aimed at thwarting the application of US antitrust laws in the international context. Most countries did not view a law aimed at protecting the competitive process as something that was compatible with their economic or social cultures. And countries that did enact antitrust laws were more concerned with using them to maintain stability in the marketplace than in promoting real competition. In Japan, as we all know, the Antimonopoly Act (AMA) was adopted by the Japanese Diet in 1947. But it was not well accepted by Japanese society, and it was soon subject to amendments that substantially weakened the impact of the AMA on the economy. It was not until the oil shocks of the 1970s that the AMA and the Japan Fair Trade Commission (JFTC) began to be invigorated.

Looking at the global situation today, we see a remarkable change in the global acceptance of antitrust law as a promoter of economic growth and prosperity. More than one hundred countries have adopted antitrust laws, and there is unprecedented cooperation among countries in acting against international cartels. We now have the International Competition Network, an organization composed of antitrust enforcement agencies from, at current count, nearly eighty nations, working to improve our understanding of how best to apply competition laws in an era of globalization.

What happened to cause this remarkable change in the global recognition of the importance of competition law? Probably the most important single event was the triumph of capitalism over the failed command and control model of the Soviet Union. With the dismantling of the Berlin Wall came the realization by many countries that the path to successful economic growth lay in fostering market-based competition, and that one of the building blocks of successful market economies was the protection of the competitive process through strong and well-focused antitrust laws. This was accompanied by a more sophisticated understanding of how markets operate and a greater appreciation of the harm caused to consumers, to the business community, and to our economies as a whole by anticompetitive practices.

In addition, the tensions over US application of its antitrust laws in international matters gradually gave way to increased dialogue and cooperation. This was demonstrated by the antitrust cooperation agreements entered into between the United States and a number of major antitrust enforcing countries in the 1980s and 1990s. Increased cooperation was bolstered by the recommendations of the OECD Council on Cooperation on Restrictive Business Practices affecting International Trade in 1986 and on Hard-Core Cartels in 1998. Around the same time, some highly visible and economically damaging international cartels were uncovered—notably the feed additives, graphite electrodes, and vitamins cartels—that gave concrete evidence of the need for governments to work together and protect their consumers from these harmful global conspiracies.

Antitrust Enforcement Priorities in the United States

For the United States, our reevaluation of the proper role of antitrust law occurred somewhat earlier, in response to advances in economic learning that established the foundation for the landmark Supreme Court decision in the GTE Sylvania case. This reevaluation was based upon the recognition of the importance of promoting business efficiency through market mechanisms. It led to a clarification of the appropriate analytical framework and antitrust enforcement hierarchy for different categories of business conduct, a hierarchy that remains valid today.

At the top of this hierarchy is enforcement against cartels, conduct that is devoid of any efficiency justification and that inflicts tremendous harm on our economy. Our Supreme Court, in its recent *Trinko* decision, described collusive behavior as "the supreme evil of antitrust." Obviously, this is our core priority at the Antitrust Division. Second, we review mergers using the best analytical tools available, and make judgments on whether the effects of the merger may be "substantially to lessen competition or to tend to create a monopoly." If so, we must back up that judgment with a suit in court to block the merger. Third, we analyze unilateral conduct, as well as agreements subject to rule of reason analysis, in a cautious and objective manner. We do this mindful that it is often difficult to tell the difference between good, hard competition and anticompetitive conduct, but knowing that we must be ready to challenge conduct that is harmful to competition.

We need only look at the Olympic gold-medal performances of Mizuki Noguchi (who won the women's marathon) and Kosuke Kitajima (who was victorious in the men's 100 meter and 200 meter breaststroke), to understand how competition produces excellence. To make sure that competition continues to produce excellence in our economies, antitrust enforcers need the most modern investigatory tools and sanctions. The proposals by the JFTC to increase surcharge levels, introduce a corporate amnesty program, and strengthen its investigatory powers are important steps that reflect sound global trends in the antitrust area. They deserve strong support. At the same time, our challenge as antitrust enforcers is to ensure that our antitrust laws are applied in a manner that does not hinder the competitive process. I look forward to working hand-in-hand with the JFTC and our other antitrust colleagues around the world in continuing to promote convergence in the antitrust area and in stoking the flame of competition for the benefit of all our citizens.

Discussion Questions

1. Why does R. Hewitt Pate believe that global competition law is similar to the Olympics?

2. Does the author think these parallels present a positive or negative argument for global competition? Explain the reasons for his evaluation.

3. What connection does Pate draw between capitalism and the global recognition of competition law? Who would be harmed if these laws were not in place? Create a hypothetical example of your own that demonstrates a harmful result you might personally experience without such laws.

4. How do you think Pate would respond to other authors in this section, such as Nevius, who is less convinced than Pate that competition is a positive force in our society?

AN OBJECTIVE LOOK AT THE BENEFITS OF COMPETITION IN THE WORKPLACE

CARMINE COYOTE

Carmine Coyote is the founder and editor of Slow Leadership, *a blog that he discontinued in 2009. Coyote has been an economist and an academic, and he has worked in both the public and private sector. When he retired, he was a partner in one firm and the CEO of another. The following essay appeared in 2008 on a blog.*

Is competition a universal motivator? Is it worth encouraging? Does it work to bring out the best in people?

In business, competition is everywhere: Organizations compete for customers, suppliers compete for orders, and employees compete for attention and promotion. In most organizations, this employee competition is encouraged—even required. But is *more* competition—competition brought about deliberately or enhanced by management efforts—really the best way to motivate people and bring out the best in them? Is it, as conventional management thinking contends, the universal motivator?

Business uses ideas from many sources, but the military and the sports arena are the origin of more business ideas (and downright myths) than anywhere else. Perhaps that's because of the domination of business by men. The military was, until very recently, a male preserve; and sport has long been a staple of male conversation, since the days when it consisted of kicking an enemy's head around a muddy field. Sport has influenced business as much as business has now come to dominate sport.

Competition is essential to sport, whether you play against your own past achievements or another team or individual. Take away the element of competition, and football becomes a group of hooligans in helmets knocking one another over. Golf becomes the stupidest way imaginable for putting a small, white ball into a series of holes in the grass—and why would you want to do that anyway? And tennis . . . why should one person hit a ball to another over a piece of netting, only to have the other person hit the ball right back again?

Business is not a game—though many people treat it as such. It has a purpose, and supposedly that purpose is beneficial. Competition between products or corporations may be essential to prevent monopolistic exploitation in a free market (if only because we accept that organizations will not restrain themselves otherwise—and regulation is often rejected as government interference or frustrated by special interests); but the assumption that putting people into competition against each other inevitably causes them to work harder or better is just that—an assumption.

Outside the sporting arena, most people find that competition increases their anxiety and level of fear. Do people do their best work when they're anxious, frightened, and stressed? Do *you*? If you win, all is well, and you may forget the terror you felt. If you lose . . . well, who cares about losers? I'm not saying competition always has such negative effects, but it's very far from being a universal spur to healthful actions.

For every winner, there must be one or more losers. And before you say losing will spur them to greater efforts next time, think about it. Is that what actually happens? Don't many "losers" resolve never to repeat such humiliation again? Doesn't being branded a loser often cause alienation and wreck people's self-esteem? And doesn't it sometimes drive people to seek to win by any means available, including deceit and even violence?

Of course, competition in sport has another purpose: It's what spectators come to watch. The best game, from the spectators' point of view, is a close-run match where neither player or team seems capable of beating the other. And without spectators and TV audiences, there would be no money. That's why match organizers try so hard to produce games which hang in the balance—even, in the case of some "sports," to the extent of choreographing events and sending players into the game with suitable scripts.

Business isn't—yet—a spectator sport (though Donald Trump and his imitators seem to be trying to make it one), and so rigging the game to win more easily is not much of a problem. If winning is all that counts, as we're often told in the business world, the best game from the player's point of view will always be the one where he or she dominates to such an extent that the opponent never has a chance. Win fast with no effort is the ideal. If you want to be a winner, pick on others who have no chance against you.

That's exactly what happens, only it's usually done by competing against superficially able "opponents" whose ability has been hamstrung in some way—because you're the boss, because you've made it clear you'll destroy their careers if they make you look bad, or because you've rigged the game against them in advance.

Employee competition is rarely "fair" in any objective way. Traditional systems—based as they are on subjective ratings and unstated standards—are heavily rigged in favor of those already in power and their chosen *protégés*. The way to the top depends more on who you know, and how you play the political game, than what you know or how able you are. Businesses are social systems, with all that implies about influence, schmoozing the powerful, and the power of looking good.

Competition for promotion and rewards is often more about how things look than how they are. It's more like a scripted entertainment than a genuine contest. The rules for winning are there, but rarely stated openly, despite all the nonsense about "competencies" and appraisals. Rewards are given out on a largely subjective basis. Those in power make sure the winners are those who they want to win—those who are most useful to them, the ones they like, and probably the ones most like them as well.

Making people compete against one another for rewards, attention, and praise has become traditional, but it's not the only way to set standards or share prizes. There used to be a time when awards were about showing outstanding skill or ability, regardless of other people or winning and losing—when showing your skill and sportsmanship counted for more than coming out on top.

Thanks to the media's obsession with turning everything into a no-holds-barred wrestling match, sport has forgotten sportsmanship, politicians have become die-hard competitors, judges preside over trials that closely resemble gladiatorial contests, and even literary awards are tricked out in the paraphernalia of competition, complete with squabbling judges and post-game slanging matches. And as for the Oscars . . .

It's no surprise that competition has also become the chosen window-dressing of business as well. Let those who don't matter compete as much as possible. They're all "losers" anyway, so who cares who gets hurt? If competition drags out a little extra effort, that's good. If it doesn't, it hardly matters.

The true competition in business has little to do with producing results. It's all about display, playing politics, and destroying those who stand in your way—even if that means hurting the business as well.

In a world of no-holds-barred competition, those who rise to the top are the most ruthless, the most driven, and—all too often—those with the weakest consciences. Who rises to the top? The most able and honorable competitor, or the cheater? Can you tell until it's too late? Does the rash of top executive prosecutions tell you anything about the results of a "winner takes all" outlook?

Competition spurs *some* people to higher effort. It convinces many others it's not worth trying and being humiliated. It causes some to seek to win by honorable means, and others to use every dirty trick they know to cheat their way to the top. When you look at it objectively, competition in business is far from being the best way to encourage individual or team excellence, let alone the only one.

Discussion Questions

1. In what specific ways does competition function in the business world, according to Coyote? Describe specific ways in which you yourself competed or observed someone else compete in a job that you or your acquaintance held.

2. According to Coyote, how do individuals react emotionally to competition? What two rhetorical questions does the author ask about this emotional response? How would you answer each of these questions?

3. What assertions does Coyote make about the value of competition in the business world? Compare his conclusion to the position taken by Pate. Explain your reasons for finding yourself more in agreement with one of these authors than the other.

Assignment #4

"THE IMPORTANCE OF 'SOCIETAL FORGETTING'"

This unit asks you to think about one of the significant aspects of the technological revolution, a relatively recent development in human history that has significantly altered the way we live. The lead essay in the unit is written by Jeffrey Rosen, who asks us to consider the implications for all of us as we inhabit a world where the Internet records and preserves everything that we do online. For Rosen, today's "digital memory bank" dangerously impinges on our fundamental right to privacy and threatens our identity, freedom, growth, and dignity. In order to write a successful essay in response to his argument, you will have to understand what Rosen means by "societal forgetting" and its integral connection to our personal and social growth and health. As you work through this unit, you will have to spend some time thinking about the impact of technology, in all of its forms and in all of the ways that we use it daily—on our fundamental rights to privacy and freedom of speech, which have historically been protected by constitutional amendments. Be sure to consider the arguments put forward in the supporting reading selections at the end of the unit as you develop your own position on the issue. Will you agree with Rosen's argument that privacy is endangered by digital memory, and that it is time to reevaluate and perhaps limit the power unleashed by technology?

Remember to make full use of the stages of the writing process as you work through the authors' ideas and your own. The unit's writing activities will bring you to a new awareness of the importance of the issue that Rosen addresses. After thinking about, writing about, and discussing the activities and reading selections in this unit, you will be prepared to offer an interesting, well-developed, and coherent argument about the importance of "societal forgetting" in the context that Rosen presents. Use the activity pages as guides, and their questions and directions as catalysts for doing a thorough exploration and for developing insightful ideas.

THE IMPORTANCE OF "SOCIETAL FORGETTING"

JEFFREY ROSEN

Jeffrey Rosen is an American academic, writer, and speaker. He earned a BA from Harvard University and a JD degree from Yale. Rosen is a professor in the George Washington University School of Law, and a widely published writer. The following is from an essay he published in 2010.

Four years ago, Stacy Snyder, then a 25-year-old teacher in training at Conestoga Valley High School in Lancaster, Pennsylvania, posted a photo on her MySpace page that showed her at a party wearing a pirate hat and drinking from a plastic cup, with the caption "Drunken Pirate." After discovering the page, her supervisor at the high school told her the photo was "unprofessional," and the dean of Millersville University School of Education, where Snyder was enrolled, said she was promoting drinking in virtual view of her underage students. As a result, days before Snyder's scheduled graduation, the university denied her a teaching degree. Snyder sued, arguing that the university had violated her First Amendment right to free speech by penalizing her for her perfectly legal after-hours behavior. But in 2008, a federal district judge rejected her claim, saying that because Snyder was a public employee whose photo didn't relate to matters of public concern, her "Drunken Pirate" post was not protected speech (Krebs).

When historians of the future look back on the perils of the early digital age, Stacy Snyder may well be an icon. The problem she faced is only one example of a challenge that, in big and small ways, is confronting millions of people around the globe: how best to live our lives in a world where the Internet records everything and forgets nothing—where every online photo, status update, Twitter post, and blog entry by and about us can be stored forever. With websites like *LOL Facebook Moments*, which collects and shares embarrassing personal revelations from Facebook users, ill-advised photos and online chatter are coming back to haunt people months or years after the fact. Examples are proliferating daily: There was the 16-year old British girl who was fired from her office job for complaining on Facebook, "I'm so totally bored" (Levy); there was the 66-year-old Canadian psychotherapist who tried to enter the United States but was turned away at the border—and barred permanently from visiting the country—after a border guard's Internet search found that the therapist had written an article in a philosophy journal describing his experiments 30 years ago with LSD (O'Brien).

According to a recent survey by Microsoft, 75 percent of U.S. recruiters and human-resource professionals report that their companies require them to do online research about candidates, and many use a range of sites when scrutinizing applicants—including search engines, social networking sites, photo- and video-sharing sites, personal websites and blogs, Twitter, and online gaming sites. Seventy percent of U.S. recruiters report that they have rejected candidates because of information found online, like photos and discussion-board conversations and membership in controversial groups.

The fact that the Internet never seems to forget is threatening, at an almost existential level, our ability to control our identities; to preserve the option of reinventing ourselves and starting anew; to overcome our checkered pasts.

In a recent book, *Delete: The Virtue of Forgetting in the Digital Age*, the cyberscholar Viktor Mayer-Schönberger cites Stacy Snyder's case as a reminder of the importance of "societal forgetting." By "erasing external memories," he says in the book, "our society accepts that human beings evolve over time, that we have the capacity to learn from past experiences and adjust our behavior." In traditional societies, where missteps are observed but not necessarily recorded, the limits of human memory ensure that people's sins are eventually forgotten. By contrast, Mayer-Schönberger notes, a society in which everything is recorded "will forever tether us to all our past actions, making it impossible, in practice, to escape them." He concludes that "without some form of forgetting, forgiving becomes a difficult undertaking." It's often said that we live in a permissive era, one with infinite second chances. But the truth is that for a great many people, the permanent memory bank of the Web increasingly means there are no second chances—no opportunities to escape a scarlet letter in your digital past. Now the worst thing you've done is often the first thing everyone knows about you.

It's sobering, now that we live in a world misleadingly called a "global village," to think about privacy in actual villages long ago. In the villages described in the Babylonian Talmud, for example, any kind of gossip or tale-bearing about other people—oral or written, true or false, friendly or mean—was considered a terrible sin because small communities have long memories and every word spoken about other people was thought to ascend to the heavenly cloud. (The digital cloud has made this metaphor literal.) But the Talmudic villages were, in fact, far more humane and forgiving than our brutal global village, where much of the content on the Internet would meet the Talmud's definition of gossip. Although the Talmudic sages believed that God reads our thoughts and records them in the book of life, they also believed that God erases the book for those who atone for their sins by asking forgiveness of those they have wronged. In the Talmud, people have an obligation not to remind others of their past misdeeds, on the assumption they may have atoned and grown spiritually from their mistakes: "If a man was a repentant sinner," the Talmud says, "one must not say to him, 'Remember your former deeds.'"

Works Cited

Krebs, Brian. "Security Fix." *The Washington Post*. 3 Dec. 2008. http://voices.washingtonpost. com/securityfix/2008/12/court_rules_against_teacher_in.html.

Levy, Andrew. "Teenage Office Worker Sacked." *Dailymail.com*. 6 Oct. 2017. http:// www.dailymail.co.uk/news/article-1155971/Teenage-office-worker-sacked-moaning-Facebook-totally-boring-job.html.

Mayer-Schönberger, Viktor. *Delete: The Virtue of Forgetting in the Digital Age*. New Jersey: Princeton University Press, 2009. Print.

O'Brien, Luke. "Canadian Psychologist Who Used LSD Forty Years Ago Permanently Barred From Entering US." *Wired.* 26 Apr. 2007. https://www.wired.com/2007/04/canadian_psycho/.

Essay Topic

According to Rosen, why is "societal forgetting" valuable? What do you think of his views? To develop your own position, be sure to discuss specific examples; those examples can be drawn from anything you've read, as well as from your own observation and experience.

Vocabulary Check

Once again, be sure to use the following activity to ensure that you comprehend the key vocabulary terms in "The Importance of 'Societal Forgetting,'" and the way Rosen uses them. Words can have a variety of meanings, or they can have specialized meanings in certain contexts. Look up the definitions of the following words from the reading. Choose the meaning that you think this author intended when he selected that particular word. Then, explain the way the meaning or concept behind the definition is key to understanding his argument.

1. *violate*

   definition: _____

   _____

   explanation: _____

   _____

   _____

   _____

2. *penalize*

   definition: _____

   _____

   explanation: _____

   _____

   _____

   _____

3. *peril*

   definition: _____

   _____

   explanation: _____

   _____

   _____

   _____

4. *confront*

definition: _____

_____

explanation: _____

_____

_____

_____

5. *ill-advised*

definition: _____

_____

explanation: _____

_____

_____

_____

6. *proliferate*

definition: _____

_____

explanation: _____

_____

_____

_____

7. *bar (v)*

definition: _____

_____

explanation: _____

_____

_____

_____

8. *scrutinize*

definition: _____

_____

explanation: _____

_____

_____

_____

9. *controversial*

definition: _____

_____

explanation: _____

_____

_____

_____

10. *checkered*

definition: _____

_____

explanation: _____

_____

_____

_____

11. *capacity*

definition: _____

_____

explanation: _____

_____

_____

_____

12. *permissive*

definition: _____

_____

explanation: _____

_____

_____

_____

13. *scarlet letter*

definition: _____

_____

explanation: _____

_____

_____

_____

14. *ascend*

definition: _____

_____

explanation: _____

_____

_____

_____

15. *atone*

definition: _____

_____

explanation: _____

_____

_____

_____

16. *obligation*

    definition: _____

_____

    explanation: _____

_____

_____

_____

17. *assumption*

    definition: _____

_____

    explanation: _____

_____

_____

_____

18. *repentant*

    definition: _____

_____

    explanation: _____

_____

_____

_____

Questions to Guide Your Reading

Answer the following questions so you can gain a thorough understanding of "The Importance of 'Societal Forgetting.'"

Paragraph 1

In what ways did posting on social media affect Stacy Snyder's future?

Paragraph 2

Why might future historians, according to Jeffrey Rosen, come to regard Stacy Snyder as an icon?

Paragraph 3

As Rosen points out, what kinds of information attained through online research are of interest to job recruiters and human resource professionals? What do they do with this information?

Paragraph 4

In Rosen's view, what is threatening about the Internet?

Paragraph 5

How does our society differ from traditional societies in terms of second chances? Do we say that we believe in giving people second chances? Do we do what we say?

Paragraph 6

What does Rosen tell us about privacy in small villages of the past? How is this important to his central argument?

Prewriting for a Directed Summary

The first part of the writing topic that follows "The Importance of 'Societal Forgetting'" asks you about a central idea from the essay by Rosen. To answer this part of the writing topic, you will want to write a *directed* summary, meaning one that responds specifically to the writing topic's first question.

first part of the writing topic:

According to Rosen, why is "societal forgetting" valuable?

Hint

Don't forget to look back to Part 1's "A Review of the Guidelines for Writing a Directed Summary."

Focus Questions

1. In "The Importance of 'Societal Forgetting,'" what is the problem that the Internet presents?

2. According to Rosen, how did many small communities in the past handle the misdeeds of their members?

3. At the existential level, what forms does the Internet threat take, according to Rosen? In other words, what deeper effects—effects beyond not getting a job or being criticized for something done many years before— does the Internet's digital memory potentially have on us?

4. In the words of cyberscholar Viktor Mayer-Schönberger, why is erasing the past important to our development as human beings?

Developing an Opinion and Working Thesis Statement

To fully respond to the writing topic that follows "The Importance of 'Societal Forgetting,'" you will have to take a position of your own on the issue Rosen addresses.

writing topic's second part:

What do you think of his views?

Do you agree with Rosen that we must protect ourselves from the Internet's threatening ability to permanently record everything done online? State your position clearly so that it will unify your essay and give it a clear purpose.

It is likely that you aren't yet sure what position you want to take in your essay. If this is the case, you can explore your ideas on a blank page of this book, or go on to the next section and work on developing your ideas through specific evidence drawn from your experience. Then you can come back to this page and work on developing a thesis statement based on the discoveries you made when you explored your ideas more systematically.

1. Use the following thesis frame to identify the basic elements of your working thesis statement:
   a. What is the issue that the writing topic asks you to consider? In other words, what is the main topic the essay is about?

   _____

   b. What is Rosen's opinion about that issue?

   _____

   c. What is your opinion about the issue, and will you agree or disagree with Rosen's opinion?

   _____

   _____

   _____

2. Now use the elements you isolated in the thesis frame to write a thesis statement. You may have to revise it several times until it captures your idea clearly.

   _____

   _____

Prewriting to Find Support for Your Thesis Statement

The last part of the writing topic asks you to support the position you put forward in your thesis statement. Well-developed ideas are crucial when you are making an argument because you will have to be clear, logical, and thorough if you are to be convincing. As you work through the exercises below, you will generate much of the 4Cs material you will need when you draft your essay's body paragraphs.

writing topic's third part:

To develop your own position, be sure to discuss specific examples; those examples can be drawn from anything you've read, as well as from your own observation and experience.

Hint

Complete each section of this prewriting activity; your responses will become the material you will use in the next stage—planning and writing the essay.

1. As you begin to develop some evidence as a basis for the position you decide to take, think about your own connections to the Internet. Use the following to guide your thinking:

   - List all of the ways that you use the Internet in a typical week. Include everything: texting, e-mailing, doing online shopping, doing library research, posting on Facebook, watching YouTube, listening to music, etc.

   - Look over your list and think about the picture of yourself these online activities might give to someone who doesn't know you personally. What impressions might someone draw regarding who you are, what you care about, how strong a job applicant you might make, and so on?

   - Think back to all of the Internet messages, postings, searches, etc. that you have done throughout your life. Consider how you might feel, knowing that almost anyone can access every detail of your online presence—for whatever reason. Does this seem to be a reasonable threat to you? Try to explore your thoughts.

   - How strongly do you feel about protecting your online history? Does it bother you, or do you think that Rosen exaggerates the potential threat of the digital record? Try to give as many reasons as you can for your answers.

- Finally, look over this exercise, and see if you can sum up, in one or two descriptive sentences, the importance of privacy in your life. Do you feel that your privacy, your freedom of speech, or both are threatened by the permanent digital archive? Do some freewriting to explore your thoughts. Spend some focused time, and try to develop your ideas carefully and completely because this step will lead you to not only the position you want to take in your thesis statement but also the evidence you will use to support your position as you outline and draft your essay.

2. Now broaden your focus; consider the people you know well, and consider how each of them might respond to the previous bullet points. Do you know anyone who seems especially vulnerable to potential regrets when it comes to the digital record? Do you know anyone who might operate at the other extreme, i.e., reject some of the convenience of the Internet due to privacy issues? Think about both of these extremes in terms of Rosen's argument about the importance of "societal forgetting." Do Rosen's concerns seem especially relevant to one or more of your family or friends? Jot down any examples that you might use to support the position you take in your essay.

Speculate below on the results of your thinking at this point, and see if you can draw a conclusion based on your findings and insights.

3. If you have read and discussed any of the readings at the end of this unit, list the title of each, and then write just a couple of sentences that capture each reading's perspective on the importance of limiting, or not limiting, the availability of the digital record. Look over your list and determine whether one or more of them will influence your own view and the argument you want to make. Do some freewriting to explore your ideas.

Now you are ready to think about Rosen's argument and to revisit your working thesis statement to see if it still represents your thinking.

Revising Your Thesis Statement

Now that you have spent some time working out your ideas more systematically and developing some supporting evidence for the position you want to take, look again at the working thesis statement you crafted earlier and see if it is still accurate. As your first step, look again at the writing topic, and then write your original working thesis on the lines that follow it.

writing topic:

According to Rosen, why is "societal forgetting" valuable? What do you think of his views? To develop your own position, be sure to discuss specific examples; those examples can be drawn from anything you've read, as well as from your own observation and experience.

working thesis statement:

_____

_____

Remember that your thesis statement must address the second part of the writing topic, but also take into consideration the writing topic as a whole. The first part of the writing topic identifies the issue that is up for debate, and the last part of the topic reminds you that, whatever position you take on the issue, you must be able to support it with specific evidence.

Take some time now to see if you want to revise your thesis statement. Often, after extensive prewriting and focused thought, you will find that the working thesis statement is no longer an accurate reflection of what you plan to say in your essay. Sometimes only a word or phrase must be added or deleted; other times, the thesis statement must be significantly rewritten, as either the subject section or the claim portion or both are inaccurate.

After examining your working thesis statement and completing any necessary revisions, check it one more time by asking yourself the following questions:

a. Does the thesis include an accurate depiction of the position Rosen takes on the importance of "societal forgetting"?

b. Do you make clear your position on the issue?

c. Is your thesis well punctuated, grammatically correct, and precisely worded?

Add any missing elements, correct the grammar errors, and refine the wording. Then, write your polished thesis on the lines below. Try to look at it from your readers' perspective. Is it strong and interesting?

_____

_____

Planning and Drafting Your Essay

Now that you have examined Rosen's argument and thought at length about your own views, draft an essay that responds to all parts of the writing topic. Use the material you developed in this section to compose your draft, and then exchange drafts with a class-mate and use the peer review activity to revise your draft.

Getting started on the draft is often the hardest part of the writing process because this is where you move from exploring and planning to getting your ideas down in a unified, coherent shape. Creating an outline will give you a basic structure for incor-porating all the ideas you have developed in the preceding pages. An outline will also give you a bird's-eye view of your essay and help you spot problems in development or logic. Consult the academic essay diagram in Part 1 of this book, too, to remind yourself of the characteristics of one of the conventional forms of a college essay and its basic parts.

Hint

This outline doesn't have to contain polished writing. You may want to fill in only the basic ideas in phrases or terms.

I. **Introductory Paragraph**

   A. An opening sentence that gives the reading selection's title and author and begins to answer the first part of the writing topic:

      _____

      _____

   B. Main points to include in the directed summary:

     1.

     2.

     3.

     4.

C. Write out your thesis statement. (Look back to "Revising Your Thesis Statement," where you reexamined and refined your working thesis statement.) It should clearly state whether Rosen's claim that, given technology's ability to permanently record everything we do online, we must protect every individual's right to privacy.

_____

_____

II. Body Paragraphs

A. The paragraph's one main point that supports the thesis statement:

_____

1. Controlling idea sentence:

   _____

   _____

2. Corroborating details:

   _____

   _____

   _____

   _____

3. Careful explanation of why the details are relevant:

   _____

   _____

   _____

   _____

   _____

4. Connection to the thesis statement:

   _____

   _____

   _____

B. The paragraph's one main point that supports the thesis statement:

_____

1. Controlling idea sentence:

_____

_____

2. Corroborating details:

_____

_____

_____

_____

3. Careful explanation of why the details are relevant:

_____

_____

_____

_____

4. Connection to the thesis statement:

_____

_____

_____

C. The paragraph's one main point that supports the thesis statement:

_____

1. Controlling idea sentence:

_____

_____

2. Corroborating details:

_____

_____

_____

_____

3. Careful explanation of why the details are relevant:

_____

_____

_____

_____

_____

4. Connection to the thesis statement:

_____

_____

_____

D. The paragraph's one main point that supports the thesis statement:

_____

1. Controlling idea sentence:

_____

_____

2. Corroborating details:

_____

_____

_____

_____

3. Careful explanation of why the details are relevant:

_____

_____

_____

_____

_____

4. Connection to the thesis statement:

_____

_____

_____

Repeat this form for any remaining body paragraphs.

III. Conclusion (For help, see "Conclusions" in Part 1.)

    A. Type of conclusion to be used:

    _____

    B. Key words or phrases to include:

    _____

Getting Feedback on Your Draft

Use the following guidelines to give a classmate feedback on his or her draft. Read the draft through first, and then answer each of the items below as specifically as you can.

Name of draft's author: _____

Name of draft's reader: _____

Discuss the success of the thesis of this draft. Does it provide a clear answer to the writing topic? Is it appropriate? complete? prominently placed?

Discuss the content of this draft. Is each of the supporting ideas relevant and convincing enough to make a credible argument?

Discuss the development of this draft. Is each argument fully defended with the use of concrete examples and further explanations?

Discuss the organization of this draft. Could the paragraphs be ordered in a more reasonable way? Are transitions provided to help the reader move easily from one argument to the next? Does the essay seem to develop in a logical manner?

Discuss the sentence-level fluency of this draft. Are there problems with basic grammar? Do idiom and word choice errors interfere with the reader's comprehension? Does the writer correctly use punctuation marks to identify sentence boundaries?

Final Draft Checklist

Content

_____ My essay has an appropriate title.

_____ I provide an accurate summary of Rosen's position on the issue presented in "The Importance of 'Societal Forgetting.'"

_____ My thesis states a clear position that can be supported by evidence.

_____ I have enough paragraphs and argument points to support my thesis.

_____ Each body paragraph is relevant to my thesis.

_____ Each body paragraph contains the 4Cs.

_____ I use transitions whenever necessary to connect ideas.

_____ The final paragraph of my essay (the conclusion) provides readers with a sense of closure.

Grammar, Punctuation, and Mechanics

_____ I use the present tense to discuss Rosen's argument and examples.

_____ I use verb tenses correctly to show the chronology of events.

_____ I have verb tense consistency throughout my sentences and paragraphs.

_____ I have checked for subject-verb agreement in all of my sentences.

_____ I have revised all fragments and mixed or garbled sentences.

_____ I have repaired all fused (run-on) sentences and comma splices.

_____ I have placed a comma after introductory elements (transitions and phrases) and all dependent clauses that open a sentence.

_____ If I present items in a series (nouns, verbs, prepositional phrases), they are parallel in form.

_____   If I include material spoken or written by someone other than myself, I have correctly punctuated it with quotation marks, using the MLA style guide's rules for citation.

_____   If I include material spoken or written by someone other than myself, I have included a works-cited list that follows the MLA style guide's rules for citation.

Reviewing Your Graded Essay

After your instructor has returned your essay, you may have the opportunity to revise your paper and raise your grade. Many students, especially those whose essays receive nonpassing grades, feel that their instructors should be less "picky" about grammar and should pass the work on content alone. However, most students at this level have not yet acquired the ability to recognize quality writing, and they do not realize that content and writing actually cannot be separated in this way. Experienced instructors know that errors in sentence structure, grammar, punctuation, and word choice either interfere with content or distract readers so much that they lose track of content. In short, good ideas badly presented are no longer good ideas; to pass, an essay must have passable writing. So even if you are not submitting a revised version of this essay to your instructor, it is important that you review your work carefully in order to understand its strengths and weaknesses. This sheet will guide you through the evaluation process.

You will want to continue to use the techniques that worked well for you and to find strategies to overcome the problems that you identify in this sample of your writing. To recognize areas that might have been problematic for you, look back at the scoring rubric in this book. Match the numerical/verbal/letter grade received on your essay to the appropriate category. Study the explanation given on the rubric for your grade.

Write a few sentences below in which you identify your problems in each of the following areas. Then, suggest specific changes you could make that would improve your paper. Don't forget to use your handbook as a resource.

1. Grammar/punctuation/mechanics

    My problem:

    My strategy for change:

2. Thesis/response to assignment

    My problem:

    My strategy for change:

3. Organization
My problem:

My strategy for change:

4. Paragraph development/examples/reasoning
My problem:

My strategy for change:

5. Assessment
In the space below, assign a grade to your paper using the rubric in Part 1 of this book. If your instructor assigned your essay a grade of *High Fail*, you might give it the letter grade you now feel the paper warrants. If your instructor used the traditional letter grade to evaluate the essay, choose a category from the rubric in this book, or any other grading scale that you are familiar with, to show your evaluation of your work. Then, write a short narrative explaining your evaluation of the essay and the reasons it received the grade you gave it.

Grade: _____

Narrative: _____

_____

_____

_____

_____

Extending the Discussion: Considering Other Viewpoints

Reading Selections

"The Digital Person" by Daniel J. Solove
"Failing to Forget" by Viktor Mayer-Schönberger
"Power and Privacy on the Internet" by Ross Douthat
"Is the Fourth Amendment Relevant?" by Christopher Slobogin
"The Future of Identity" by Eric Schmidt and Jared Cohen

THE DIGITAL PERSON

Daniel J. Solove

Daniel J. Solove received his JD from Yale Law School. He is now a law professor at the George Washington University Law School. He is well known for his work in privacy, especially as it intersects with the rise of technology. He has published articles and books, including Nothing to Hide: The False Tradeoff between Privacy and Security *(2011),* The Future of Reputation: Gossip, Rumor, and Privacy on the Internet *(2007), and* The Digital Person: Technology and Privacy in the Information Age *(2004). The following reading selection is an excerpt from that book.*

In earlier times, communities were small and intimate. Personal information was preserved in the memories of friends, family, and neighbors, and it was spread by gossip and storytelling. Today, the predominant mode of spreading information is not through the flutter of gossiping tongues but through the language of electricity, where information pulses between massive record systems and databases. An ever-growing series of records is created about almost every facet of a person's life. As businesses and the government increasingly share personal information, digital dossiers about nearly every individual are being assembled. Yet we know little about how our personal information is being used, and we lack the power to do much about it. Companies use digital dossiers to determine how they do business with us; financial institutions use them to determine whether to give us credit; employers turn to them to examine our backgrounds when hiring; law enforcement officials draw on them to investigate us; and identity thieves tap into them to commit fraud. The information gathered about us has become quite extensive, and it is being used in ways that profoundly affect our lives.

Computers and cyberspace have vastly increased our ability to collect, store, and analyze information. Today, it seems as if everyone is collecting information—the media, employers, businesses, and government. Countless companies maintain computerized records of their customers' preferences, purchases, and activities. There are hundreds of records detailing an individual's consumption. Credit card companies maintain information about one's credit card purchases. Video stores keep records about one's video rentals. Online retailers, such as *Amazon.com*, preserve records of all the books and other items a person buys. And there are hundreds of companies people aren't even aware of that maintain their personal information. For example, Wiland Services maintains a database of about 1,000 different points of information on over 215 million individuals.[1] *Acxiom.com* collects and sells data on consumers to marketers. In its InfoBase, it provides "[o]ver 50 demographic variables . . . including age, income, real property data, children's data, and others." It also contains data on education levels, occupation, height, weight, political affiliation, ethnicity, race, hobbies, and net worth.[2]

A new breed of company is emerging that devotes its primary business to the collection of personal information. Based in Florida, Cataline Marketing Corporation maintains supermarket buying history databases on 30 million households from more than 5,000 stores.[3] These data contain a complete inventory of one's groceries, over-the-counter medications, hygiene supplies, and contraceptive devices, among others. Aristotle, Inc. markets a database of 150 million registered voters. Aristotle's database records voters' names, addresses, phone numbers, party affiliation, and voting frequency. Aristotle combines these data with about 25 other categories of information, such as one's race, income, and employer—even the make and model of one's car. It markets a list of wealthy campaign donors called "Fat Cat." Aristotle boasts: "Hit your opponent in the wallet! Using Fat Cats, you can ferret out your adversary's contributors and slam them with a mail piece explaining why they shouldn't donate money to the other side."[4] Another company manufactures software called GeoVoter, which combines about 5,000 categories of information about a voter to calculate how that individual will vote.[5]

The most powerful database builders construct information empires, sometimes with information on more than half of the American population. For example, Donnelley Marketing Information Services of New Jersey keeps track of 125 million people. Wiland Services has constructed a database containing over 1,000 elements, from demographic information to behavioral data, on over 215 million people. There are around five database compilers that have data on almost all households in the United States.[6]

Beyond marketers, hundreds of companies keep data about us in their record systems. The complete benefits of the Information Age do not simply come to us—we must "plug in" to join in. In other words, we must establish relationships with Internet Service Providers, cable companies, phone companies, insurance companies, and so on. All of these companies maintain records about us. The Medical Information Bureau, a nonprofit institution, maintains a database of medical information on 15 million individuals, which is available to over 700 insurance companies.[7] Credit card companies have also developed extensive personal information databases. Unlike cash, which often does not involve the creation of personally identifiable records, credit cards result in detailed electronic documentation of our purchases.[8]

Increasingly, we rely on various records and documents to assess financial reputation.[9] According to sociologist Steven Nock, this enables reputations to become portable.[10] In earlier times, a person's financial condition was generally known throughout the community. In modern society, however, people are highly mobile, and creditors often lack first-hand experience of the financial condition and trustworthiness of individuals. Therefore, creditors rely upon credit reporting agencies to obtain information about a person's credit history. Credit reports reveal a person's consistency in paying back debts as well as the person's loan defaulting risk. People are assigned a credit score, which impacts whether they will be extended credit, and, if so, what rate of interest will be charged. Credit reports contain a detailed financial history, financial account information, outstanding debts, bankruptcy filings, judgments, liens, and mortgage foreclosures. Today, there are three major credit reporting agencies—Equifax, Experian, and TransUnion. Each agency has compiled extensive dossiers about almost every adult US citizen.[11] Credit reports have become essential to securing a loan, obtaining a job, purchasing a home or a car, applying for a license, or even renting an apartment. Credit reporting agencies also prepare investigative consumer reports, which supplement the credit report with information about an individual's character and lifestyle.[12]

Cyberspace is the new frontier for gathering personal information, and its power has only begun to be exploited. The Internet is rapidly becoming the hub of the personal information market, for it has made the peddling and purchasing of data much easier. Focus USA's website boasts that it has detailed information on 203 million people.[13] Among its over 100 targeted mailing lists are lists of "Affluent Hispanics," "Big-Spending Parents," "First Time Credit Card Holders," "Grown But Still At Home," "Hi-Tech Seniors," "New Homeowners," "Status Spenders," "Big Spending Vitamin Shoppers," and "Waist Watchers."[14] The database contains data about age, gender, income, children, Internet connections, and more.

Targeting is very important for web advertising because a web page is cluttered with information and images all vying for the users' attention. Many websites directly solicit data from their users. Numerous websites require users to register and log in, and registration often involves answering a questionnaire. Online merchants amass data from their business transactions with consumers. For example, I shop on *Amazon.com*, which keeps track of my purchases in books, videos, music, and other items. I can view its records of every item I've ordered, and this goes back well over six years. When I click on this option, I get an alphabetized list of everything I bought and the date I bought it. Amazon uses its extensive records to recommend new books and videos. With a click, I can see dozens of books that Amazon thinks I'll be interested in. It is eerily good, and it can pick out books for me better than my relatives can. It has me pegged.

As we stand at the threshold of an age structured around information, we are only beginning to realize the extent to which our lives can be encompassed within its architecture. "The time will come," predicts one marketer, "when we are well known for our inclinations, our predilections, our proclivities, and our wants. We will be classified, profiled, categorized, and our every click will be watched."[15] Our online personas— captured, for instance, in our web pages and online postings—are swept up as well. We are accustomed to information on the Web quickly flickering in and out of existence, presenting the illusion that it is ephemeral. But little on the Internet disappears or is forgotten, even when we delete or change the information. The amount of personal information archived will only escalate as our lives are increasingly digitized into the electric world of cyberspace. These developments certainly suggest a threat to privacy, but what specifically is the problem? The way this question is answered has profound implications for the way the law will grapple with the problem in the future.

One of the greatest dangers of using information that we generally regard as private is that we often make judgments based on this private information about the person. As legal scholar Kenneth Karst warned in the 1960s, one danger of "a centralized, standardized data processing system" is that the facts stored about an individual "will become the only significant facts about the subject of the inquiry."[16] Legal scholar Jeffrey Rosen aptly observes, "Privacy protects us from being misdefined and judged out of context in a world of short attention spans, a world in which information can easily be confused with knowledge. True knowledge of another person is the culmination of a slow process of mutual revelation."[17]

Increased reliance upon the easily quantifiable and classifiable information available from databases is having profound social effects. The nature and volume of information affects the way people analyze, use, and react to information. Currently, we rely quite heavily on quantifiable data: statistics, polls, numbers, and figures. In the law alone, there is a trend to rank schools; to measure the influence of famous jurists by counting citations to their judicial opinions;[18] to assess the importance of law review articles by tabulating citations to them;[19] to rank law journals with an elaborate system of establishing point values for authors of articles;[20] and to determine the influence of academic movements by checking citations. The goal of this use of empirical data is to eliminate the ambiguity and incommensurability of many aspects of life and try to categorize them into neat, tidy categories. The computer has exacerbated this tendency, for the increase in information and the way computers operate furthers this type of categorization and lack of judgment.[21] Indeed, in legal scholarship, much of this tendency is due to the advent of computer research databases, which can easily check for citations and specific terms.

In our increasingly bureaucratic and impersonal world, we are relying more heavily on records and profiles to assess reputation. As H. Jeff Smith, a professor of management and information technology, contends:

> [D]ecisions that were formerly based on judgment and human factors are instead decided according to prescribed formulas. In today's world, this response is often characterized by reliance on a rigid, unyielding process in which computerized information is given great weight. Facts that actually require substantial evaluation could instead be reduced to discrete entries in preassigned categories.[22]

Certainly, quantifiable information can be accurate and serve as the best way for making particular decisions. Even when quantifiable information is not exact, it is useful for making decisions because of administrative feasibility. Considering all the variables and a multitude of incommensurate factors might simply be impossible or too costly.

Nevertheless, the information in databases often fails to capture the texture of our lives. Rather than provide a nuanced portrait of our personalities, compilations of data capture the brute facts of what we do without the reasons. For example, a record of an arrest without the story or reason is misleading. The arrest could have been for civil disobedience in the 1960s—but it is still recorded as an arrest with some vague label, such as "disorderly conduct." It appears no differently from the arrest of a vandal. In short, we are reconstituted in databases as a digital person composed of data. The privacy problem stems paradoxically from the pervasiveness of these data—the fact that it encompasses much of our lives—as well as from its limitations—how it fails to capture us, how it distorts who we are.

Endnotes

[1] Marcia Stepanek, "How the Data-Miners Want to Influence Your Vote," *Business Week Online*, 26 Oct. 2000, at http://www.businessweek.com/bwdaily/dnflash/oct2000/nf20001026_969.htm.

[2] http://www.acxiom.com.

[3] Robert O'Harrow, Jr., "Behind the Instant Coupons, a Data-Crunching Powerhouse," *Wash. Post*, 31 Dec. 1998, at A20.

[4] Leslie Wayne, "Voter Profiles Selling Briskly as Privacy Issues Are Raised," *N.Y. Times*, 9 Sept. 2000, at A1.

[5] Marcia Stepanek, "How the Data-Miners Want to Influence Your Vote," *Business Week Online*, 26 Oct. 2000, at http://www.businessweek.com/bwdaily/dnflash/oct2000/nf20001026_969.htm.

[6] Hughes, *Database Marketer*, 354.

[7] See, e.g., Garfinkel, *Database Nation*, 137; Givens, *Privacy Rights*, 83.

[8] See Peter P. Swire, "Financial Privacy and the Theory of High-Tech Government Surveillance," 77 *Wash. U.L.Q.* 461, 464–69 (1999).

[9] Smith, *Franklin's Web Site*, 314.

[10] Steven L. Nock, *The Costs of Privacy: Surveillance and Reputation in America* 3 (1993).

[11] For example, Experian has information on 205 million Americans. See http//www.experian.com/corporate/factsheet.html.

[12] See Givens, *Privacy Rights*, 83.

[13] http://www.focus-usa-1.com/lists_az.html.

[14] Id.

[15] Sterne, *People Click*, 255.

[16] Kenneth L. Karst, "'The Files': Legal Controls over the Accuracy and Accessibility of Stored Personal Data," 31 *L & Contemp. Probs.* 342, 361 (1966).

[17] Jeffrey Rosen, *The Unwanted Gaze: The Destruction of Privacy in America* 8 (2000).

[18] See, e.g., Richard A. Posner, *Cardozo: A Study in Reputation* 74–91 (1990) (measuring Benjamin Cardozo's reputation by a Lexis search counting mentions of his name).

[19] See, e.g., Fred R. Shapiro, "The Most-Cited Law Review Articles Revised," 71 Chi-Kent L. Rev. 751, 751 (1996) (listing the "one hundred most-cited legal articles of all time").

[20] See, e.g. Robert M. Jarvis & Phyllis G. Coleman, "Ranking Law Reviews: An Empirical Analysis Based on Author Prominence," 39 *Ariz. L. Rev.* 15 (1997).

[21] See Oscar H. Gandy, Jr., "Exploring Identity and Identification in Cyberspace," 14 *Notre Dame J.L. Ethics & Pub. Pol'y* 1085, 1100 (2000) (arguing that profiles are "inherently conservative" because such profiles "reinforce assessments and decisions made in the past").

[22] H. Jeff Smith, *Managing Privacy: Information Technology and Corporate America* 121 (1994).

Discussion Questions

1. List the various entities Daniel J. Solove mentions in his first paragraph whose collection of our personal information affects our lives. Give an example of a positive way one of them might use the data. Give an example in which the ability to access these data might cause harm.

2. Explain the function of "database builders." What reservations would you personally have about working for or doing business with one of these companies? If you do not see the privacy issue as a problem in the mission of these companies, discuss the value of their services to society.

3. Review one of the "greatest dangers" Solove feels accompanies the use of technological personal information. How do you know that Jeffrey Rosen, whose article about "societal forgetting" is also in this chapter, would likely agree with Solove on this point? Consider the fact that taking words out of context can change their meaning.

4. What do you think Solove means when he says that database information cannot "provide a nuanced portrait of our personalities"? Write two descriptions of yourself or someone you know: construct the first only from database information, and in the second provide important details that capture the "texture" of the person. For someone who had never met the person, which description do you think would better help them know the person? Why?

FAILING TO FORGET

Viktor Mayer-Schönberger

Viktor Mayer-Schönberger is a German-born scholar and writer. He earned two LLM degrees, one from the University of Salzburg and a second from Harvard Law School, and he earned an MA in Economics from the London School of Economics. He was a faculty member for ten years at Harvard Kennedy School and today is Professor of Internet Governance and Regulation at the Oxford Internet Institute at the University of Oxford. He has written and published extensively, including the collaboratively written book Big Data: A Revolution That Will Transform How We Live, Work, and Think *(2009), and* Delete: The Virtue of Forgetting in the Digital Age *(2012), from which the following reading selection has been excerpted.*

For us humans, forgetting has always been the norm and remembering the exception. Because of digital technology and global networks, however, this balance has shifted. Today, with the help of widespread technology, forgetting has become the exception, and remembering the default. On an average day, Facebook receives ten million web requests from users around the world *every second.*[1] As professors John Palfrey and Urs Gasser have eloquently detailed, disclosing one's information—whether these are Facebook entries, personal diaries and commentaries (often in the form of blogs); photos, friendships, and relationships (like "links" or "friends"); content preferences and identification (including online photos or "tags"); one's geographic location (through "geo-tagging" or sites like Dopplr); or just short text updates ("tweets")—has become deeply embedded into youth culture around the world.[2] Should everyone who self-discloses information lose control over that information forever and have no say about whether and when the Internet forgets this information? Do we want a future that is forever unforgiving because it is unforgetting? The demise of forgetting has consequences much wider and more troubling than a frontal onslaught on how humans have constructed and maintained their reputation over time. If all our past activities, transgressions or not, are always present, how can we disentangle ourselves from them in our thinking and decision-making? Might perfect remembering make us as unforgiving to ourselves as to others?

Forgetting plays a central role in human decision-making. It lets us act in time, cognizant of, but not shackled by, past events. Through perfect memory, we may lose a fundamental human capacity—to live and act firmly in the present. Jorge Luis Borges's short story "Funes the Memorious" lays out the argument. Due to a riding accident, a young man, Funes, has lost his ability to forget. Through ferocious reading, he has amassed a huge memory of classic works in literature but fails to see beyond the words. Once we have perfect memory, Borges suggests, we are no longer able to generalize and abstract, and so remain lost in the details of our past.[3]

What Borges only hypothesized, we now know. Researchers have recently published the case of AJ, a 41-year-old woman in California, who does not have the biological gift of forgetting.[4] Since she was 11, she remembers practically every day—not in the sense of a day that passed, but in astonishing, agonizing detail. She remembers what exactly she had for breakfast three decades ago; she recalls who called her and when, and what happened in each episode of the television shows she watched—in the 1980s. She does not have to think hard. Remembering is easy for her—her memory is "uncontrollable, and automatic" like a movie "that never stops."[5] Instead of bestowing AJ with a superb facility, her memory repeatedly restricts her ability to decide and to move on. It seems that those that have the capacity to store and recall unusual amounts of what they experience, feel, and think would like to be able to turn off their capacity to remember—at least temporarily. They feel shackled by their constantly present past, so much so that it constrains their daily lives and limits their decision-making ability as well as their capacity to forge close ties with those who remember less. The effect may be even stronger when caused by more comprehensive and easily accessible external digital memory. Too perfect a recall, even when it is benignly intended to aid our decision-making, may prompt us to become caught up in our memories, unable to leave our past behind, and much like Borges's Funes, incapable of abstract thoughts. It is the surprising curse of remembering.

Forgetting is not just an individual behavior. We also forget as a society. Often, such societal forgetting gives individuals who have failed a second chance. We let people try out new relationships if their previous ones did not make them happy. In business, bankruptcies are forgotten as years pass. In some instances, even criminals have their convictions expunged from their record after sufficient time has passed. Through these and many similar mechanisms of societal forgetting, of erasing external memories, our society accepts that human beings evolve over time, that we have the capacity to learn from past experiences and adjust our behavior.

Despite the central importance of forgetting for humans, the monumental shift we are experiencing in the digital age—from a default of forgetting to one of remembering—this phenomenon has, so far, received limited attention. Back in 1998, J.D. Lasica wrote a remarkable piece in the online magazine *Salon*, titled "The Net Never Forgets," and concluded that "our pasts are becoming etched like a tattoo into our digital skins."[6] More recently, Liam Bannon, as well as Jean-François Blanchette and Deborah Johnson, have begun to uncover the dark side of the demise of forgetting.[7] The shift from forgetting to remembering is monumental, and if left unaddressed, it may cause grave consequences for us individually and for society as a whole. Such a future, however, is not inevitable. It is not technology that forces us to remember. Technology facilitates the demise of forgetting—but only if we humans so want. The truth is, *we* are causing the demise of forgetting, and it is up to *us* to reverse that change.

As humans, we do not travel ignorantly through time. With our capacity to remember, we are able to compare, to learn, and to experience time as change. Equally important is our ability to forget, to unburden ourselves from the shackles of our past, and to live in the present. For millennia, the relationship between remembering and forgetting remained clear. Remembering was hard and costly, and humans had to choose deliberately what to remember. The default was to forget. In the digital age, in what is perhaps the most fundamental change for humans since our humble beginnings, that balance of remembering and forgetting has become inverted. Committing information to digital memory has become the default, and forgetting has become the exception. Digitization has made possible plummeting storage costs, easy information retrieval, and global access to digital memory. For the first time in human history, this has enabled us to make remembering cheaper and easier than forgetting, to reverse the age-old default. It is easy to see why. In the face of our own often failing human memory, wouldn't we all opt for total recall? Wouldn't we all want to preserve our thoughts and impressions for posterity? And so we find ourselves in a "brave new world" of comprehensive digital memory, in which information processors such as Google offer the world access to millions of billions of characters of information, from photos and blog posts to detailed marketing information and high-resolution satellite imagery of ours and our neighbor's backyards. Soon, cases like Stacy Snyder's and Andrew Feldmar's will become common occurrences: lives shattered (or at least dented) by perfect recall of trivial past deeds, individuals exposed to a strangely unforgiving public, not just in North America but around the world.

We must respond to the challenges posed by digital remembering—and I believe we can, by reviving our capacity to forget. I am not advocating an ignorant future, but one that acknowledges that with the passage of time, humans change, our ideas evolve, and our views adjust. I want us to commence a wide-ranging, open, and intense discussion about forgetting, and how we can ensure that we'll remember its importance in our digital future.

Endnotes

[1] Howard, "Analyzing Online Social Networks," 14–16.

[2] Palfrey and Gasser, *Born Digital*.

[3] See Borges, *Collected Fictions*.

[4] See Foer, "Remember This," 32–55; the article is based in part on Parker, Cahill, and McGaugh, "A Case of Unusual Autobiographical Remembering," 35–49.

[5] Parker, Cahill, and McGaugh, 35.

[6] Lasica, "The Net Never Forgets," *Salon*.

[7] See, for example, Blanchette and Johnson, "Data Retention and the Panoptic Society: The Social Benefits of Forgetfulness," 33–45. See also Bannon, "Forgetting As A Feature, Not A Bug: the Duality of Memory and Implications for Ubiquitous Computing," 3–15; Bellia, "The Memory Gap in Surveillance Law," 137.

Discussion Questions

1. Explain the shift in balance between remembering and forgetting. Do you think the shift has had any impact on your ability to memorize not just dates, places, and people from your past, but also data such as phone numbers, mathematical formulas, and vocabulary lists?

2. How can the fact that nothing, not even a single detail, can be forgotten hurt our thinking? Discuss the fictional and actual examples of people with perfect recall related in this article. Which of them did you find more cautionary? convincing? frightening? Why?

3. In what ways, according to Viktor Mayer-Schönberger, has society shown that it gives individuals the option of forgetting their past mistakes? What would be some of the negative consequences of losing this type of "societal forgetting"?

4. Discuss the concepts of time and choice in relation to the Internet and the human psyche. How do you think Jeffrey Rosen could have included the concept of time to support his argument on "societal forgetting"?

POWER AND PRIVACY ON THE INTERNET

Ross Douthat

Ross Douthat is an American writer and journalist, working currently as an op-ed writer for the New York Times. *He earned a BA from Harvard University, and has published three books,* Bad Religion: How We Became a Nation of Heretics *(2012),* Grand New Party *(2008), and* Privilege: Harvard and the Education of the Ruling Class *(2005).*

I'm both disturbed by the expansion of surveillance power in America and pessimistic that the Internet era could really turn out any other way. To explore that pessimism a little more, allow me to pivot off an interesting recent passage from a writer named Jacob Bacharach, who is writing in defense of the Millennial generation's willingness to put it all online:

> . . . we now find not only kids, but adults (especially new adults) getting constantly dinged with the dire warning that Social Media Lasts Forever. I think this is probably patently untrue in a purely physical sense; it strikes me as probable that fifty years from now, the whole electronic record of our era will be largely lost in a sea of forgotten passwords, proprietary systems, faulty hardware, and compatibility issues. But it should also be untrue in, dare I say it, the moral sense. Educators and employers are constantly yelling that you young people have an affirmative responsibility not to post anything where a teacher or principal or, worst of all, boss or potential boss might find it, which gets the ethics of the situation precisely backwards. It isn't your sister's obligation to hide her diary; it's yours not to read it. Your boyfriend shouldn't have to close all his browser windows and hide his cell phone; *you* ought to refrain from checking his history and reading his texts. But, says the Director of Human Resources and the Career Counselor, social media are public; you're *putting it out there*. Yes, well, then I'm sure you won't mind if I join you guys at happy hour with this flip-cam and a stenographer. Privacy isn't the responsibility of individuals to squirrel away secrets; it's the decency of individuals to leave others' lives alone.

> At some point, employers will have to face up to the unavoidability of hiring people whose first Google image is a shirtless selfie. Demographics will demand it. They'll have to get used to it just as surely as they'll have to get used to nose rings and, god help us, neck tattoos. It's a shame, though, that it'll be compulsory and reluctant. We should no more have to censor our

electronic conversations than whisper in a restaurant. I suspect that as my own generation and the one after it finally manage to boot the Boomers from their tenacious hold on the steering wheel of this civilization that they've piloted ineluctably and inexorably toward the shoals, all the while whining about the lazy passengers, we will better understand this, and be better, and more understanding. And I hope that the kids today will refuse to heed the warnings and insist on making a world in which what is actually unacceptable is to "make one's public life little more than a series of polite and carefully maintained lies" (Bacharach 2).

This is an eloquent statement of the way that many people, especially my age and younger, think about their online lives, and how they want others (including institutions as well as individuals) to approach what they share on social media. Certainly the moral case Bacharach makes is a potent one: An employer snooping on employees' Facebook pages, an ex-boyfriend forwarding intimate photos from past relationships to his friends, and yes, a government sifting your social media data are all engaged in something far more indecent than the online behavior they're exploiting. And the society he hopes for is one that *most* of today's young people will probably experience: A world where everyone treats Facebook the way they treat a happy hour with friends is a world where the individual costs of online sharing will be minimized (because everyone is doing it), and where most people's scantily-clad selfies and dumb tweets won't hurt their employment prospects, let alone attract any interest from the government.

But it's still the case that if your boss or your ex-boyfriend or your friendly neighborhood NSA *did* have some reason to exploit your texts and tweets and e-mails and selfies, they would have means and opportunities that no previous era of social interaction has afforded. And that's what's missing from Bacharach's accounting: An acknowledgment that the use of social media is inherently different from offline forms of socializing, not in its content or intent, but in the kind of power it automatically cedes to other people and institutions, to use and exploit as they choose.

You can see this in the analogies he chooses, to restaurant dinners and happy hours. If you go to happy hour with your pals, those pals and maybe a nosy bartender are the only people who can exploit whatever happens there, and if somebody showed up with a flipcam and notebook, you'd notice the weirdness of the situation quickly enough and alter your behavior accordingly. Likewise if you go on a date to a nice restaurant; you'd start censoring yourself pretty quickly if the couple at the next table started writing down everything you said.

If you hold forth with your pals on Gmail or Facebook, though, the flipcam-and-notebook combination is built into the platform you're using, and it belongs to your corporate hosts: You're giving them a semi-permanent record of what you've said and done, and however unethical it might be for them to exploit it, sell it, or allow the government to access it, the power to do so nonetheless exists. Likewise, on a more personal level, what's shared with friends and lovers electronically gives them more power over you than a careless word or even an intimate letter would have done. In both cases, betrayal is possible, but in the online case, it can happen faster and more comprehensively than ever before.

And if there's one thing we know from human history, it's that powers granted rarely go unexploited. You may not be victimized personally; indeed, you probably won't be. But someone will, or many someones, in ways that wouldn't have been possible or even imaginable before the Internet.

This victimization deserves to be condemned rather than just explained: A truly moral person, a truly moral corporation, and a truly moral government would not exploit the kind of information that people now share with one another on the Internet. But it is not sufficient to simply say, with Bacharach and many others who have come of age with the Internet, that privacy is "the decency . . . to leave others' lives alone," and demand that the world and all its powers live up to that ideal. Privacy is also the wisdom to recognize that not all peers and powers are actually decent, and that one's exposure should perhaps be limited accordingly. And it's precisely because the ease and convenience of Internet communication incline us all (myself included) to forget or compromise this wisdom—or else pretend to we're abandoning it out of some higher commitment to honesty and openness that I expect us to make our peace with the surveillance state, now and for many years to come.

Works Cited

Bacharach, Jacob. "Peeping Thomism." https://jacobbacharach.com/2013/05/31/peepig-thomism/

Discussion Questions

1. Paraphrase the first sentence of Ross Douthat's article "Power and Privacy on the Internet." Why does this statement confirm or contradict your own feelings about the Internet?

2. Which of Bacharach's arguments does Douthat find to be "eloquent"? Why does he like to think this point could be valid? Why does he think it isn't? What do you think of his refutation of Bacharach's point? Thinking back to Rosen's idea that we are in an "early digital age" that future historians will study, do you think he might find Bacharach's argument compelling? Explain.

IS THE FOURTH AMENDMENT RELEVANT?

CHRISTOPHER SLOBOGIN

Christopher Slobogin is a law professor at Vanderbilt University Law School. He has written many articles, books, and contributing chapters on criminal law procedure. The following reading selection is an excerpt from one of those chapters. The full article can be found in Constitution 3.0: Freedom and Technological Change *(2011), edited by Jeffrey Rosen and Benjamin Wittes.*

The Fourth Amendment prohibits unreasonable searches of houses, persons, papers, and effects, and further provides that if a warrant is sought authorizing a search, it must be based on probable cause and describe with particularity the place to be searched and the person or thing to be seized. This language is the primary constitutional mechanism for regulating police investigations. The courts have held that when police engage in a search, they must usually have probable cause—about a fifty percent certainty—that the search will produce evidence of crime, and they must usually also have a warrant, issued by an independent magistrate, if there is time to get one. As construed by the US Supreme Court, however, these requirements are irrelevant to many modern practices. The Fourth Amendment's increasing irrelevance stems from the fact that the Supreme Court is mired in precedent decided in another era. Over the past two hundred years, the Fourth Amendment's guarantees have been construed largely in the context of what might be called "physical searches"—entry into a house or car, stopping and frisking a person on the street, or rifling through a person's private papers. But today, with the introduction of devices that can see through walls and clothes, monitor public thoroughfares twenty-four hours a day, and access millions of records in seconds, investigative techniques do not require physical access to premises, people, papers, or effects and can often be carried out covertly from far away. To date, the Supreme Court's interpretation of the Fourth Amendment has failed to anticipate the technological revolution and has continued to ignore it.

Under current law, most virtual searches are not Fourth Amendment searches, or if they are, they can usually be carried out on little or no suspicion if they do not involve interception of communication content. Given the huge amount of information that virtual searches provide about everyone's activities and transactions, traditional physical searches—with their cumbersome warrant and probable cause requirements—are much less necessary than they used to be. American citizens may eventually live, and indeed may already be living, in a world where the Fourth Amendment as currently construed is irrelevant to most investigations. Technological developments have exposed the fact that the courts' view of the Fourth Amendment threatens the entire edifice of search and seizure law.

Some might react to all of this with a shrug of the shoulders. Antipathy toward virtual searches could exist for a number of reasons. First, there is the prototypically

American aversion to overweening government power. As one opponent of the National Security Agency monitoring program inveighs, "Whether the next president is a Republican or a Democrat, there is nothing to prevent him from using this Executive Branch database for his own political purposes. That is a real threat to America. This database needs to be immediately and completely destroyed."[1] From J. Edgar Hoover's misuse of FBI files to Attorney General John Mitchell's illegal authorization of wiretaps on thousands of 1970s dissidents, from recent reports of the FBI's illicit use of National Security Letters to the Bush administration's attempts to access information about anti-war journalists and protesters, history confirms that, as TIA's icon proclaims, knowledge is power.[2] And power can be abused.

The ill effects of virtual searches do not stop with official misuse of information resulting from general searches. Less tangible, but arguably just as important, is the discomfort people feel when they are being watched or monitored even if, or perhaps especially when, they are not sure they are being targeted. In other words, for many individuals, privacy vis-à-vis the government has value in and of itself regardless of whether there is evidence of government abuse, overstepping, or mistake. Thus, when Daniel Solove asked people on his privacy blog how they would respond to someone who claims to be unconcerned about government surveillance because "I've got nothing to hide," he received numerous vigorous retorts: "If you've got nothing to hide, can I see your credit card bills for the last year?" and "If you've got nothing to hide, then you don't have a life."[3]

These sentiments may be associated with real-world impacts even when government makes no use of the surveillance product. Studies of the workplace indicate that panoptic monitoring makes employees, even completely "innocent" ones, more nervous, less productive, and more conformist.[4] And surveillance of public activities—whether via cameras, satellites, or visual means—clearly diminishes the anonymity that people expect not only in the home but as they go about their daily activities in public spaces. As one court—unfortunately, an outlier that is not representative of the typical court on these issues—states in describing the impact of a Q-ball GPS device of the type used in typical cases,

> Disclosed in the data retrieved from the transmitting unit, nearly instantaneously with the press of a button on the highly portable receiving unit, will be trips the indisputably private nature of which takes little imagination to conjure: trips to the psychiatrist, the plastic surgeon, the abortion clinic, the AIDS treatment center, the strip club, the criminal defense attorney, the by-the-hour motel, the union meeting, the mosque, synagogue or church, the gay bar, and on and on. What the technology yields and records with breathtaking quality and quantity, is a highly detailed profile, not simply of where we go, but by easy inference, of our associations—political, religious, amicable, and amorous, to name only a few—and of the pattern of our professional and avocational pursuits.[5]

Most broadly, freedom from random governmental monitoring—of both public spaces and recorded transactions—might be an essential predicate for self-definition and development of the viewpoints that make democracy vibrant.

None of this means that surveillance by the government should be prohibited. But it does suggest that it should be regulated under the Constitution, just as physical searches are. Furthermore, it suggests that backend regulation of virtual searches, through provisions limiting information disclosure and use, will not be sufficient, because it will not prevent the subterranean abuse of information already collected, nor will it eradicate the feeling of being watched and the chilling effects occasioned by surveillance.

Virtual searches are rapidly replacing physical searches of homes, cars, and luggage. Outdoor activities and many indoor ones as well can be caught on camera, monitored using tracking devices, or documented using computers. Yet none of this technological surveillance can be challenged under the Fourth Amendment if its target could conceivably be viewed, with the naked eye or with common technology, by a member of the public, or could be detected using a contraband-specific device, or has been voluntarily surrendered to a human or institutional third party. And even those technological investigations that are considered searches will usually survive Fourth Amendment challenge, if they can be characterized as preventive or intelligence-gathering exercises rather than efforts to solve ordinary crime.

It is time to revert back to first principles. A search involves looking for something. Justification for a search should be proportionate to its intrusiveness except in the rare circumstances when the search is part of a large-scale program authorized by legislation that avoids political process defects or is aimed at preventing specific, imminent, and significant danger. These principles will restore the Fourth Amendment to its place as the primary arbiter of how government investigates its citizens, even when those investigations rely on technology that can be used covertly and from a distance.

Endnotes

[1] Michael Stabeno, letter to the editor, *Portland Oregonian*, May 16, 2006, B09, available at 2006 WLNR (*WestLaw News Resource*) 8457654.

[2] For a description of Hoover's abuses, see Solove, *Digital Person*, 175–87; for Mitchell's, see Frederick S. Lane, *American Privacy* (Boston: Beacon Press, 2009), xvii.

[3] Daniel Solove, "'I've Got Nothing to Hide' and Other Misunderstandings of Privacy," 44 *San Diego Law Review* (2007): 745, 750.

[4] Carl Botan, "Communication Work and Electronic Surveillance: A Model for Predicting Panoptic Effects," 63 *Communications Monographs* (1996): 293–313, 308–309. See Slobogin, *Privacy at Risk*, 257 n129.

[5] *People v. Weaver*, 12 N.Y.3d 433, 882 N.Y.S.2d 357, 909 N.E.2d 1195 (May 12, 2009).

Discussion Questions

1. What protection is guaranteed by the Fourth Amendment? Why do you think our forefathers felt it was important for citizens in a democracy to be shielded in this way? Give a hypothetical example of a situation where someone could be harmed without this right.

2. How has technology made it possible to obstruct the process guaranteed by the Fourth Amendment? Why do you consider this kind of loss more or less concerning than that of the disappearance of "societal forgetting"?

3. What are some of the reasons, according to Christopher Slobogin, that might make people feel "antipathy toward virtual searches"? Explain the negative impact that Slobogin cites to support these reasons. What, in particular, was the court's unusual finding in *People v. Weaver*? Of all the reasons Slobogin offers, which was most effective in convincing you that technological searches pose a problem? If you feel indifferent about the topic, give a reason for your lack of concern.

4. Explain the "first principle" underlying the Fourth Amendment. If that principle were completely restored through application to cyber searches, how would the restoration affect the lack of "societal forgetting" brought about by the Internet that Jeffrey Rosen discusses in "The Importance of 'Societal Forgetting'"? Do you think Rosen would support Slobogin's interpretation of the application of the Fourth Amendment? Why or why not?

THE FUTURE OF IDENTITY

Eric Schmidt and Jared Cohen

Eric Schmidt is an American billionaire businessman, software engineer, and executive chairman of Google. He earned a BS from Princeton University and a PhD from the University of California, Berkeley. He has coauthored two books, including How Google Works *(2014). Jared Cohen is an American writer, the CEO of Jigsaw (formerly Google Ideas), and an Adjunct Senior Fellow at the Council on Foreign Relations. He earned a BA from Stanford University and an MA from Oxford University as a Rhodes Scholar. He has served in various roles in federal politics and has published several books, including* Children of Jihad: A Young American's Travels among the Youth of the Middle East *(2007), and, with Eric Schmidt,* The New Digital Age: Reshaping the Future of People, Nations and Business *(2013). The following reading selection is an excerpt from that book.*

In the next decade, the world's virtual population will outnumber the population of Earth. Practically every person will be represented in multiple ways online, creating vibrant and active communities of interlocking interests that reflect and enrich our world. All of those connections will create massive amounts of data—a data revolution, some call it—and empower citizens in ways never before imagined. Yet despite these advancements, a central and singular caveat exists: The impact of this data revolution will be to strip citizens of much their control over their personal information in virtual space, and that will have significant consequences in the physical world. This may not be true in every instance or for every user, but on a macro level it will deeply affect and shape our world. The challenge we face as individuals is determining what steps we are willing to take to regain control over our privacy and security.

Today, our online identities affect but rarely overshadow our physical selves. What people do and say on their social-networking profiles can draw praise or scrutiny, but for the most part truly sensitive or personal information stays hidden from public view. Smear campaigns and online feuds typically involve public figures, not ordinary citizens. In the future, our identities in everyday life will come to be defined more and more by our virtual activities and associations. Our highly documented pasts will have an impact on our prospects, and our ability to influence and control how we are perceived by others will decrease dramatically. The potential for someone else to access or share or manipulate parts of our online identities will increase, particularly due to our reliance on cloud-based data storage. (In nontechnical language, cloud computing refers to software hosted on the Internet that the user does not need to manage closely. Storing documents or content "in the cloud" means that data are stored on remote servers rather than on local ones or on a person's own computer, and it can be accessed by multiple networks and users. With cloud computing, online activities are faster, quicker to spread, and better equipped to handle traffic loads.) This vulnerability—both perceived and real—will mandate that technology companies work even harder to earn the trust of their users. If they do not exceed expectations in terms of both privacy and security, the result will be either a backlash or abandonment of their product. The technology industry is already hard at work to find creative ways to mitigate risks, such as through two-factor authentication, which requires you to provide two of the following to access your personal data: something you know (e.g., password), have (e.g., mobile device), and are (e.g., thumbprint). We are also encouraged knowing that many of the world's best engineers are hard at work on the next set of solutions. And at a minimum, strong encryption will be nearly universally adopted as a better but not perfect solution. ("Encryption" refers to the scrambling of information so that it can be decoded and used only by someone with the right verification requirements.)

The basics of online identity could also change. Some governments will consider it too risky to have thousands of anonymous, untraceable, and unverified citizens— "hidden people"; they'll want to know who is associated with each online account and will require verification at a state level in order to exert control over the virtual world. Our online identities in the future are unlikely to be represented by simple Facebook pages; instead, our identities will be represented by a constellation of profiles, from every online activity, that will be verified and perhaps even regulated by the government. Imagine all of our accounts—Facebook, Twitter, Skype, Google+, Netflix, *New York Times* subscription—linked to an "official profile." Within search results, information tied to verified online profiles will be ranked higher than content without such verification, which will result in most users naturally clicking on the top (verified) results. The true cost of remaining anonymous, then, might be irrelevance; even the most fascinating content, if tied to an anonymous profile, simply won't be read because of its excessively low ranking.

The shift from having one's identity shaped offline and projected online to an identity that is fashioned online and experienced offline will have implications for citizens, states, and companies as they navigate the new digital world. And how people and institutions handle privacy and security concerns in this formative period will determine the new boundaries for citizens everywhere.

The data revolution will bring untold benefits to the citizens of the future. They will have unprecedented insight into how other people think, behave, and adhere to norms or deviate from them, both at home and in every society in the world. The newfound ability to obtain accurate and verified information online easily, in native languages, and in endless quantity, will usher in an era of critical thinking in societies around the world that before had been culturally isolated. In societies where the physical infrastructure is weak, connectivity will enable people to build businesses, engage in online commerce, and interact with their government at an entirely new level.

The future will usher in an unprecedented era of choices and options. While some citizens will attempt to manage their identity by engaging in the minimum amount of virtual participation, others will find the opportunities to participate worth the risk of the exposure they incur. Citizen participation will reach an all-time high as anyone with a mobile handset and access to the Internet will be able to play a part in promoting accountability and transparency. A shopkeeper in Addis Ababa and a precocious teenager in San Salvador will be able to disseminate information about bribes and corruption, report election irregularities, and generally hold their governments to account. Video cameras installed in police cars will help keep the police honest, if the camera phones carried by citizens don't already. Commerce, education, health care, and the justice system will all become more efficient, transparent, and inclusive as major institutions opt in to the digital age.

People who try to perpetuate myths about religion, culture, ethnicity, or anything else will struggle to keep their narratives afloat amid a sea of newly informed listeners. With more data, everyone gains a better frame of reference. While many worry about the phenomenon of confirmation bias (when consciously or otherwise, people pay attention to sources of information that reinforce their existing worldview) as online sources of information proliferate, a recent Ohio State University study suggests that this effect is weaker than perceived, at least in the American political landscape. In fact, confirmation bias is as much about our responses to information passively received as it is about our tendency to proactively select information sources. So as millions of people come online, we have reason to be optimistic about the social changes ahead.

Identity will be the most valuable commodity for citizens in the future, and it will exist primarily online. Online experience will start with birth, or even earlier. Periods of people's lives will be frozen in time and easily surfaced for all to see. In response, companies will have to create new tools for control of information, such as lists that would enable people to manage who sees their data. The communication technologies we use today are invasive by design, collecting our photos, comments, and friends into giant databases that are searchable and, in the absence of outside regulation, fair game for employers, university admissions personnel, and town gossips. We are what we tweet.

Ideally, all people would have the self-awareness to closely manage their online identities and the virtual lives they lead, monitoring and shaping them from an early age so as not to limit their opportunities in life. Of course, this is impossible. For children and adolescents, the incentives to share will always outweigh the vague, distant risks of self-exposure, even with salient examples of the consequences in public view. By the time a man is in his forties, he will have accumulated and stored a comprehensive online narrative, all facts and fictions, every misstep and every triumph, spanning every phase of his life. Even the rumors will live forever.

In deeply conservative societies where social shame is weighted heavily, we could see a kind of "virtual honor killing"—dedicated efforts to ruin a person's online identity either preemptively (by exposing perceived misdeeds or planting false information) or reactively (by linking his or her online identity to content detailing a crime, real or imagined). Ruined online reputations might not lead to physical violence by the perpetrator, but a young woman facing such accusations could find herself branded with a digital scarlet letter that, thanks to the unfortunate but hard-to-prevent reality of data permanence, she'd never be able to escape. And that public shame could lead one of her family members to kill her.

And what about the role of parents? Being a parent is hard enough, as anyone who has kids knows. While the online world has made it even tougher, it is not a hopeless endeavor. Parents will have the same responsibilities in the future, but they will need to be even more involved if they are going to make sure their children do not make mistakes online that could hurt their physical future. As children live significantly faster lives online than their physical maturity allows, most parents will realize that the most valuable way to help their child is to have the privacy-and-security talk even before the sex talk. The old-fashioned tactic of parents talking to their children will retain enormous value.

Certainly some parents will try to game the system as well with more algorithmic solutions that may or may not have an effect. The process of naming a child offers one such example. As the functional value of online identity increases, parental supervision will play a critical role in the early stages of life, beginning with a child's name. Steven D. Levitt and Stephen J. Dubner, the authors of the popular economics book *Freakonomics*, famously dissected how ethnically popular names (specifically, names common in African-American communities) can be an indicator of children's chances for success in life.[1] Looking ahead, parents will also consider how online search rankings will affect their child's future. The truly strategic will go beyond reserving social-networking profiles and buying domain names (e.g., *www.JohnDavidSmith.com*), and instead select names that affect how easy or hard it will be to find their children online. Some parents will deliberately choose unique names or unusually spelled traditional names so that their children have an edge in search results, making them easy to locate and promotable online without much direct competition. Others will go the opposite route, choosing basic and popular names that allow their children to live in an online world with some degree of shelter from Internet indexes—just one more "Jane Jones" among thousands of similar entries.

We'll also see a proliferation of businesses that cater to privacy and reputation concerns. This industry exists already, with companies like *Reputation.com* using a range of proactive and reactive tactics to remove or dilute unwanted content from the Internet. During the 2008 economic crash, it was reported that several Wall Street bankers hired online reputation companies to minimize their appearance online, paying up to $10,000 per month for the service. In the future, this industry will diversify as the demand explodes, with identity managers becoming as common as stockbrokers and financial planners. Active management of one's online presence—say, by receiving quarterly reports from one's identity manager tracking the changing shape of one's online identity—will become the new normal for the prominent and those who aspire to be prominent.

A new realm of insurance will emerge, too. Companies will offer to insure our online identity against theft and hacking, fraudulent accusations, misuse, or appropriation. For example, parents may take out an insurance policy against reputational damage caused by what their children do online. Perhaps a teacher will take out an insurance policy that covers her against a student hacking into her Facebook account and changing details of her online profile to embarrass or defame her. We have identity-theft protection companies today; in the future, insurance companies will offer customers protection against very specific misuses. Any number of people could be attracted to such an insurance policy, from the genuinely in need to the generally paranoid.

Online identity will become such a powerful currency that we will even see the rise of a new black market where people can buy real or invented identities. Citizens and criminals alike will be attracted to such a network, since the false identity that could provide cover for a known drug smuggler could also shelter a political dissident. The identity will be manufactured or stolen, and it will come complete with backdated entries and IP (Internet protocol) activity logs, false friends and sales purchases, and other means of making it appear convincing. If a Mexican whistle-blower's family needs to flee the violence of Ciudad Juárez and fears cartel retribution, a set of fake online identities will certainly help cover their tracks and provide them with a clean slate.

Some people will cheer for the end of control that connectivity and data-rich environments engender.[2] They are the people who believe that information wants to be free, and that greater transparency in all things will bring about a more just, safe, and free world. For a time, WikiLeaks' cofounder Julian Assange was the world's most visible ambassador for this cause, but supporters of WikiLeaks and the values it champions come in all stripes, including right-wing libertarians, far-left liberals, and apolitical technology enthusiasts. While they don't always agree on tactics, to them, data permanence is a failsafe for society. Despite some of the known negative consequences of this movement (threats to individual security, ruined reputations, and diplomatic chaos), some free-information activists believe the absence of a delete button ultimately strengthens humanity's progress toward greater equality, productivity, and self-determination. We believe, however, that this is a dangerous model, especially given that there is always going to be someone with bad judgment who releases information that will get people killed. This is why governments have systems and valuable regulations in place that, while imperfect, should continue to govern who gets to make the decision about what is classified and what is not.

Security and privacy are a shared responsibility between companies, users, and the institutions around us. Companies like Google, Apple, Amazon, and Facebook are expected to safeguard data, prevent their systems from being hacked into, and provide the most effective tools for users to maximize control of their privacy and security. But it is up to us users to leverage these tools. Each day we choose not to utilize them, we will experience some loss of privacy and security as the data keep piling up. And we cannot assume there is a simple delete button. The option to "delete" data is largely an illusion—lost files, deleted e-mails, and erased text messages can be recovered with minimal effort. Data are rarely erased on computers; operating systems tend to remove only a file's listing from the internal directory, keeping the file's contents in place until the space is needed for other things. (And even after a file has been overwritten, it's still occasionally possible to recover parts of the original content due to the magnetic properties of disc storage. This problem is known as "data remanence" by computer experts.) Cloud computing only reinforces the permanence of information, adding another layer of remote protection for users and their information.

Such mechanisms of retention were designed to save us from our own carelessness when operating computers. In the future, people will increasingly trust cloud storage—like ATMs in bands—over physical machinery, placing their faith in companies to store some of their most sensitive information, avoiding risks of hard-drive crashes, computer theft, or document loss. This multilayer backup system will make online interactions more efficient and productive, not to mention less emotionally fraught.

Near-permanent data storage will have a big impact on how citizens operate in virtual space. There will be a record of all activity and associations online, and everything added to the Internet will become part of a repository of permanent information. The possibility that one's personal content will be published and become known one day—either by mistake or through criminal interference—will always exist. People will be held responsible for their virtual associations, past and present, a responsibility that raises the risk for nearly everyone since people's online networks tend to be larger and more diffuse than their physical ones. The good and bad behavior of those they know will affect them positively or negatively. (And, no—stricter privacy settings on social-networking sites will not suffice.)

Since information wants to be free, don't write anything down you don't want read back to you in court or printed on the front page of a newspaper, as the saying goes. In the future, this adage will broaden to include not just what you say and write, but the websites you visit, whom you include in your online network, what you "like," and what others who are connected to you do, say, and share.

People will become obsessively concerned about where personal information is stored. A wave of businesses and start-ups will emerge, promising to offer solutions, from present-day applications such as *Snapchat*, which automatically deletes a photo or message after ten seconds, to more creative solutions that also add a layer of encryption and a shorter countdown. At best, such solutions will only mitigate the risk of private information being released more broadly. Part of this is due to counter-innovations such as apps that will automatically take a screenshot of every message and photo sent faster than your brain can instruct your fingers to command your device. More scientifically, attempts to keep personal information private are always going to be defeated by attacking the analog hole, which stipulates that information must eventually be seen if it is to be consumed. As long as this holds true, there will always be the risk of someone taking a screenshot or proliferating the content.

If we are on the Web, we are publishing, and we run the risk of becoming public figures—it's only a question of how many people are paying attention, and why. Individuals will still have some discretion over what they share from their devices, but it will be impossible to control what others capture and share.

Endnotes

[1] Steven D. Levitt and Stephen J. Dubner. *Freakonomics.* New York: William Morrow Publishing, 2006.

[2] This dictum is commonly attributed to Stewart Brand, the founder and editor of the *Whole Earth Catalog*, recorded at the first Hackers' Conference, in 1984.

Discussion Questions

1. When and why will the world's virtual population outnumber the actual population of the earth? What will be the impact of this population difference? How do you personally plan to respond to the challenge that Eric Schmidt and Jared Cohen claim this situation will pose?

2. Imagine a possible scenario in which an individual's (yours or a hypothetical person's) online identity was manipulated. How would his or her personal and professional life be affected? What recourse would he or she have?

3. List and discuss the benefits of the data revolution identified by Schmidt and Cohen. Which of them are we already experiencing? Which do you think will have the biggest global impact? Which do you think will bring about the biggest change in your life? Which of these benefits do you think Rosen or any other authors in this unit would not think was necessarily a positive result of the data revolution?

4. What will be some of the reactions and results when online identity becomes a commodity?

5. Discuss the concept that "information wants to be free" as it relates to the argument in this article and at least one other article in this unit in which it is discussed.

Assignment #5

"COLLEGE IN AMERICA"

This assignment requires you to write a response to the central argument in Caroline Bird's reading selection "College in America." Be sure to read the essay carefully and think about its ideas as you complete the supporting activities. Also, carefully read the background readings in the "Extending the Discussion" section to see what others have to say about college in America. After you have read critically and done the prewriting activities in this section, you will be ready to develop your own essay in response to the writing topic that follows Bird's reading selection.

COLLEGE IN AMERICA

CAROLINE BIRD

Caroline Bird (1915–2011) earned a BA in American history from the University of Toledo in 1938 and an MA in comparative literature from the University of Wisconsin in 1939. Bird's controversial 1975 book The Case Against College *is still an influential work that generates discussion and debate. She is also known for her feminism and writings on women's issues; her book* Born Female: The High Cost of Keeping Women Down *broke new ground in 1968, and she later wrote books and articles about issues concerning women and aging. The following is taken from a* Psychology Today *essay that Bird wrote in 1975.*

The premise that college is the best place for all high school graduates grew out of a noble American ideal. Just as the United States was the first nation to aspire to teach every small child to read and write, so during the 1950s we became the first and only great nation to aspire to higher education for all. During the 1960s, we damned the expense and built great state university systems as fast as we could. And adults—parents, employers, high-school counselors—began to push, shove, and cajole youngsters to "get an education."

We have come to expect that we can bring about social equality by putting all young people through four years of academic rigor. However, at best, this use of college is a roundabout and expensive way to narrow the gap between the highest and lowest in our society. At worst, equalizing opportunity through universal higher education pressures the whole population to do a type of intellectual work natural only to a few. Moreover, it violates the fundamental principle of respect for the differences between people because it leads to the assumption that academic work in college is the only way to establish one's identity in society.

Of course, most parents aren't thinking of the "higher" good at all. They send their children to college because they are convinced young people benefit financially from those four years of higher education. But if money is the only goal, college is the dumbest investment one can make. If a 1972 Princeton-bound high-school graduate had put the $34,181 that his four years of college would have cost him into a savings bank at 7.5% interest compounded daily, he would have had at age sixty-four a total of $1,129,200, or $528,200 more than the earnings of a male college graduate, and more than five times as much as the $199,000 extra the more educated man could expect to earn between twenty-two and sixty-four.

Of course, some people would argue that college is the doorway to the elite professions, especially medicine and law. But only a minority of college graduates can enter law or medical school, and many experts have begun to wonder whether society will support so many lawyers and doctors once they graduate. The American Enterprise Institute estimated in 1971 that there would be more than the target ratio of one hundred doctors

From *Psychology Today,* May 1975 by Caroline Bird.

for every hundred thousand people in the population by 1980. And the odds are little better for would-be lawyers. Law schools are already graduating twice as many new lawyers every year as the Department of Labor thinks will be needed, and the oversupply is growing every year.

It could be argued that many Americans today are looking less to high status and high pay than to finding a job that is "interesting," that permits them "to make a contribution, express themselves" and "use their special abilities." They think college will help them find it. But colleges fail to warn students that jobs of these kinds are hard to come by, even for qualified applicants, and they rarely accept the responsibility of helping students choose a career that will lead to a job. When a young person says he is interested in helping people, his counselor tells him to become a psychologist. But jobs in psychology are scarce. The Department of Labor, for instance, estimated there would be 4,300 new jobs for psychologists in 1975, while colleges were expected to turn out 58,430 BAs in psychology that year.

And it's not at all apparent that what is actually learned in the process of majoring in a field like engineering is necessary for success. Successful engineers and others I talked to said they find that on the job they rarely use what they learned in school. In order to see how well college prepared engineers and scientists for actual paid work in their fields, the Carnegie Commission queried all the employees with degrees in these fields in two large firms. Only one in five said the work they were doing bore a "very close relationship" to their college studies, while almost a third saw "very little relation at all." An overwhelming majority could think of many people who were doing their same work, but had majored in different fields.

Majors in nontechnical fields report even less relationship between their studies and their jobs. Charles Lawrence, a communications major in college and now the producer of *Kennedy & Co.*, the Chicago morning television show, says, "You have to learn all that stuff and you never use it again. I learned my job doing it." Others employed as architects, nurses, teachers, and other members of the so-called learned professions report the same thing.

If college is so expensive and contributes so little to what happens after graduation, how can society justify spending so much money on it? More importantly, how can we defend the immense social pressures—pressures generated by that investment—that manipulate many young people's priorities so that they go to college against their better judgment? We ought to find alternative ways for young people to grow into adulthood, and we ought to give them more realistic preparation for the years ahead.

Writing Topic

Why does Bird think that a college education may not be the best choice for all high school graduates? Does her argument, written in 1975, apply to high school graduates in the twenty-first century? Be sure to support your position with specific examples drawn from your observations, experiences, and readings.

Vocabulary Check

In order for you to understand a reading selection, it is important to think about its key vocabulary terms and the way they are used by the writer. Words can have a variety of meanings, or they can have specialized meanings in certain contexts. Look up the definitions of the following words or phrases from the reading. Choose the meaning that you think Bird intended when she selected that particular word or phrase. Then explain the way the meaning or concept behind the definition is key to understanding her argument.

1. *premise*

   definition: _____

   _____

   explanation: _____

   _____

   _____

   _____

2. *aspire*

   definition: _____

   _____

   explanation: _____

   _____

   _____

   _____

3. *cajole*

   definition: _____

   _____

   explanation: _____

   _____

   _____

4. *elite*

   definition: _____

   _____

   explanation: _____

   _____

   _____

   _____

5. *apparent*

   definition: _____

   _____

   explanation: _____

   _____

   _____

   _____

6. *manipulate*

   definition: _____

   _____

   explanation: _____

   _____

   _____

   _____

Questions to Guide Your Reading

Answer the following questions so you can gain a thorough understanding of "College in America."

Paragraphs 1–2

Explain the reason that Americans believe every high school graduate should attend college. Trace the educational history that resulted in this egalitarian ideal.

Paragraph 2

In what way does Bird think that sending all young people to college fails to respect difference? Consider some of the ways this argument could be used to help or hurt some of the youth.

Paragraph 3

Why, according to the author, do most parents want their children to go to college? If your parents have encouraged you to continue your education at a four-year college, what were their reasons? Do their reasons support Bird's assertion?

Paragraph 4

According to the author, why might an education preparing for the legal and medical professions be a poor investment? How would you respond to her contention?

Paragraph 5

What other kinds of jobs do Americans believe going to college will help them find? Why does the author think this belief is a false one?

Paragraphs 6–7

Why does the author find a college education to be useless in preparing people for careers in engineering, science, and nontechnical fields? How well do you feel she supports her assertion about the relationship between college and these jobs?

Paragraph 8

In her conclusion, what change does the author want us to make?

Prewriting for a Directed Summary

The first part of the writing topic that follows "College in America" asks you about a central idea from Bird's essay. To answer this part of the writing topic, you will want to write a *directed* summary, meaning one that responds specifically to the writing topic's first question.

first question in the writing topic:

Why does Bird think that a college education may not be the best choice for all high school graduates?

Focus Questions

1. What does Bird find inherently disrespectful about the ideal that prompts Americans to believe that all students should go to college after high school?

2. What do most people say is the major benefit of a college education, and why does Bird find that idea unsound?

3. Why are some of the other reasons for attending college equally false, according to Bird?

Developing an Opinion and Working Thesis Statement

The second question in the writing topic for "College in America" asks you to take a position of your own. Your response to this part of the writing topic will become the thesis statement of your essay, so it is important to spend some time ensuring that it reflects the position you want to take on the importance of a college education in today's world.

The framework below will help you develop your working thesis. But keep an open mind as you complete the prewriting pages that follow this one and read the positions other writers take in the essays in the "Extending the Discussion" section of this chapter. You may find that, after giving more thought to the issue, you want to modify your position.

writing topic's second question:

Does her argument, written in 1975, apply to high school graduates in the twenty-first century?

Do you agree with Bird that going on to four years of college may not be the best choice for all high school graduates and that we should encourage some to find alternative ways to prepare for adulthood? As you think about the position you want to take in your working thesis statement, keep in mind Bird's ideas, the ideas of some of the writers in the "Extending the Discussion" section of this unit, and your own experiences.

1. Use the following thesis frame to identify the basic elements of your working thesis statement:
    a. What is the issue of "College in America" that the writing topic's first question asks you to consider?

    _____

    b. What is Bird's position on that issue?

    _____

    c. Will your position be that Bird's claim about high school graduates going to college applies, or doesn't apply, to high school graduates today? _____

    _____

    _____

2. Now use the elements you isolated in 1a, b, and c to write a thesis statement. You may have to revise it several times until it captures your idea clearly.

    _____

    _____

Prewriting to Find Support for Your Thesis Statement

The last part of the writing topic asks you to support the position you put forward in your thesis statement. Well-developed ideas are crucial when you are making an argument because you will have to be clear, logical, and thorough if you are to be convincing. As you work through the exercises below, you will generate much of the 4Cs material you will need when you draft your essay's body paragraphs.

writing topic's last question:

> *Be sure to support your position with specific examples drawn from your observations, experiences, and readings.*

Complete each section of this prewriting activity; your responses will become the material you will use in the next stage—planning and writing the essay.

1. As you begin to develop your own examples, think about how going to college connects to your own life and the lives of those you know. In the space below, make a list of personal experiences you or others have had with making choices after high school. How significant are Bird's observations when it comes to your life and in the lives of those you know? What strategies have you or others used to make choices about your futures? Any experience you have had that says something about this central idea can provide you with an example to support your thesis. List as many ideas as you can, and freewrite about the significance of each.

   Once you've written your ideas, look them over carefully. Try to group your ideas into categories. Then, give each category a label. In other words, cluster ideas that seem to have something in common and, for each cluster, identify that shared quality by giving it a title.

2. Now make another list, but this time focus on examples from your studies, the media, your reading (especially the supplemental readings in this section), and your knowledge of contemporary society. Do any of these examples affirm Bird's ideas? Do any of the examples challenge her views? As you think about society as a whole, consider the many ways people make a living, and the skills they need to do a good job. Think, too, about how you might rank some of those jobs in terms of their importance to society. Do you think a college degree is essential to high achievement in most or all of those jobs you consider to be important? Be sure to note your ideas as fully as possible.

What views do the supplemental essays in this section take? Review their arguments and supporting evidence, and compare them to Bird's. Are any of them especially convincing for you? If so, list them here. (If you refer to any of their ideas in your essay, be sure to cite them.) List and/or freewrite about all the relevant ideas you can think of, even those about which you are hesitant.

Once you've written down your ideas, look them over carefully. Try to group your ideas into categories. Then, give each category a label. In other words, cluster ideas that seem to have something in common and, for each cluster, identify that shared quality by giving the group of ideas a title.

3. Now that you've developed categories, look through them and select two or three to develop in your essay. Make sure they are relevant to your thesis and are important enough to persuade your readers. Then, in the space below, briefly summarize each item in your categories and explain how it supports your thesis statement.

   The information and ideas you develop in this exercise will become useful when you turn to planning and drafting your essay.

Revising Your Thesis Statement

Now that you have spent some time working out your ideas more systematically and developing some supporting evidence for the position you want to take, look again at the working thesis statement you crafted earlier to see if it is still accurate. As your first step, look again at the writing topic, and then write your original working thesis on the lines that follow it.

writing topic:

Why does Bird think that a college education may not be the best choice for all high school graduates? Does her argument, written in 1975, apply to high school graduates in the twenty-first century? Be sure to support your position with specific examples drawn from your observations, experiences, and readings.

working thesis statement:

_____

_____

Remember that your thesis statement must answer the second question in the writing topic, but take into consideration the writing topic as a whole. The first question in the topic identifies the issue that is up for debate, and the last question reminds you that, whatever position you take on the issue, you must be able to support it with specific examples.

Take some time now to revise your thesis statement. Consider whether you should change it significantly because it no longer represents your position, or whether only a word or phrase should be added or deleted to make it clearer.

Now, check it one more time by asking yourself the following questions:

a. Does the thesis statement directly identify Bird's argument?

b. Does your thesis state your position on the issue?

c. Is your thesis well punctuated, grammatically correct, and precisely worded?

Add any missing elements, correct the grammar errors, and refine the wording. Then write your polished thesis on the lines below. Try to look at it from your readers' perspective. Is it strong and interesting?

_____

_____

Planning and Drafting Your Essay

You may not be in the habit of outlining or planning your essay before you begin drafting it, and some of you may avoid outlining altogether. If you haven't been using an outline as you move through the writing process, try using it this time. Creating an outline will give you a clear and coherent structure for incorporating all of the ideas you have developed in the preceding pages. It will also show you where you may have gone off track, left logical holes in your reasoning, or failed to develop one or more of your paragraphs.

Your outline doesn't have to use Roman numerals or be highly detailed. Just use an outline form that suits your style and shows you a bird's-eye view of your argument. Below is a form that we think you will find useful. Consult the academic essay diagram in Part 1 of this book, too, to remind yourself of the conventional form of a college essay and its basic parts.

Creating an Outline for Your Draft

I. Introductory Paragraph

A. An opening sentence that gives the reading selection's title and author and begins to answer the first part of the writing topic:

_____

B. Main points to include in the directed summary:

1.

2.

3.

4.

C. Write out your thesis statement. (Look back to "Revising Your Thesis Statement," where you reexamined and refined your working thesis statement.) It should clearly whether Bird's claim about high school graduates going to college applies, or doesn't apply, to high school graduates today.

_____

II. Body Paragraphs

A. The paragraph's one main point that supports the thesis statement:

_____

1. Controlling idea sentence:

_____

_____

2. Corroborating details:

_____

_____

_____

_____

3. Careful explanation of why the details are significant:

_____

_____

_____

_____

4. Connection to the thesis statement:

_____

_____

_____

_____

B. The paragraph's one main point that supports the thesis statement:

_____

1. Controlling idea sentence:

_____

_____

2. Corroborating details:

_____

_____

_____

_____

3. Careful explanation of why the details are significant:

_____

_____

_____

_____

4. Connection to the thesis statement:

_____

_____

_____

_____

C. The paragraph's one main point that supports the thesis statement:

_____

1. Controlling idea sentence:

_____

_____

2. Corroborating details:

_____

_____

_____

_____

3. Careful explanation of why the details are significant:

_____

_____

_____

_____

4. Connection to the thesis statement:

_____

_____

_____

_____

D. The paragraph's one main point that supports the thesis statement:

_____

1. Controlling idea sentence:

_____

_____

2. Corroborating details:

_____

_____

_____

_____

3. Careful explanation of why the details are significant:

_____

_____

_____

_____

4. Connection to the thesis statement:

_____

_____

_____

_____

Repeat this form for any remaining body paragraphs.

III. Conclusion

A. Type of conclusion to be used:

_____

B. Key words or phrases to include:

_____

Use the following guidelines to give a classmate feedback on his or her draft. Read the draft through first, and then answer each of the items below as specifically as you can.

Name of draft's author: _____

Name of draft's reader: _____

The Introduction

1. Within the opening sentences:
   a. Bird's first and last name are given.   yes   no
   b. Bird's title is given and placed within quotation marks.   yes   no
2. The opening contains a summary that:
   a. explains Bird's position on going to college.   yes   no
   b. explains why Bird takes this position.   yes   no
3. The opening provides a thesis that makes clear the writer's
   opinion regarding Bird's argument.   yes   no

If the answer to #3 above is yes, state the thesis below as it is written. If the answer is no, explain to the writer what information is needed to make the thesis complete.

_____

_____

_____

The Body

1. How many paragraphs are in the body of this essay? _____
2. To support the thesis, this number is   sufficient   not enough
3. Do paragraphs contain the 4Cs?

Paragraph 1	Controlling idea sentence	yes	no
	Corroborating details	yes	no
	Careful explanation of why the details are significant	yes	no
	Connection to the thesis statement	yes	no
Paragraph 2	Controlling idea sentence	yes	no
	Corroborating details	yes	no
	Careful explanation of why the details are significant	yes	no
	Connection to the thesis statement	yes	no

Paragraph 3	Controlling idea sentence	yes	no
	Corroborating details	yes	no
	Careful explanation of why the details are significant	yes	no
	Connection to the thesis statement	yes	no
Paragraph 4	Controlling idea sentence	yes	no
	Corroborating details	yes	no
	Careful explanation of why the details are significant	yes	no
	Connection to the thesis statement	yes	no
Paragraph 5	Controlling idea sentence	yes	no
	Corroborating details	yes	no
	Careful explanation of why the details are significant	yes	no
	Connection to the thesis statement	yes	no

(Continue as needed.)

4. Identify any of the above paragraphs that are underdeveloped (too short). _____

5. Identify any of the above paragraphs that fail to support the thesis. _____

6. Identify any of the above paragraphs that are redundant or repetitive. _____

7. Suggest any ideas for additional paragraphs that might improve this essay.

_____

_____

_____

The Conclusion

1. Does the final paragraph avoid introducing new ideas
   and examples that really belong in the body of the essay?   yes   no
2. Does the conclusion provide closure (let readers know
   that the end of the essay has been reached)?   yes   no
3. Does the conclusion leave readers with an understanding
   of the significance of the argument?   yes   no

4. State in your own words what the draft writer considers to be important about his
   or her argument.

_____

_____

5. Identify the type of conclusion used (see the guidelines for conclusions in Part 1).

Editing

1. During the editing process, the writer should pay attention to the following problems in sentence structure, punctuation, and mechanics:

    fragments
    misplaced and dangling modifiers
    fused (run-on) sentences
    comma splices
    misplaced, missing, and unnecessary commas
    misplaced, missing, and unnecessary apostrophes
    incorrect quotation mark use
    capitalization errors
    spelling errors

2. While editing, the writer should pay attention to the following areas of grammar:

    verb tense
    subject-verb agreement
    irregular verbs
    pronoun type
    pronoun reference
    pronoun agreement
    noun plurals
    prepositions

Final Draft Checklist

Content

_____ My essay has an appropriate title.

_____ I provide an accurate summary of Bird's position on the issue presented in "College in America."

_____ My thesis states a clear position that can be supported by evidence.

_____ I have enough paragraphs and argument points to support my thesis.

_____ Each body paragraph is relevant to my thesis.

_____ Each body paragraph contains the 4Cs.

_____ I use transitions whenever necessary to connect ideas.

_____ The final paragraph of my essay (the conclusion) provides readers with a sense of closure.

Grammar, Punctuation, and Mechanics

_____ I use the present tense to discuss Bird's argument and examples.

_____ I use verb tenses correctly to show the chronology of events.

_____ I have verb tense consistency throughout my sentences.

_____ I have checked for subject-verb agreement in all of my sentences.

_____ I have revised all fragments and mixed or garbled sentences.

_____ I have repaired all fused (run-on) sentences and comma splices.

_____ I have placed a comma after introductory elements (transitions and phrases) and all dependent clauses that open a sentence.

_____ If I present items in a series (nouns, verbs, prepositional phrases), they are parallel in form.

_____ If I include material spoken or written by someone other than myself, I have correctly punctuated it with quotation marks, using the MLA style guide's rules for citation.

Reviewing Your Graded Essay

After your instructor has returned your essay, you may have the opportunity to revise your paper and raise your grade. Many students, especially those whose essays receive nonpassing grades, feel that their instructors should be less "picky" about grammar and should pass the work on content alone. However, most students at this level have not yet acquired the ability to recognize quality writing, and they do not realize that content and writing actually cannot be separated in this way. Experienced instructors know that errors in sentence structure, grammar, punctuation, and word choice either interfere with content or distract readers so much that they lose track of content. In short, good ideas badly presented are no longer good ideas; to pass, an essay must have passable writing. So even if you are not submitting a revised version of this essay to your instructor, it is important that you review your work carefully in order to understand its strengths and weaknesses. This sheet will guide you through the evaluation process.

You will want to continue to use the techniques that worked well for you and to find strategies to overcome the problems that you identify in this sample of your writing. To recognize areas that might have been problematic for you, look back at the scoring rubric in this book. Match the numerical/verbal/letter grade received on your essay to the appropriate category. Study the explanation given on the rubric for your grade.

Write a few sentences below in which you identify your problems in each of the following areas. Then, suggest specific changes you could make that would improve your paper. Don't forget to use your handbook as a resource.

1. Grammar/punctuation/mechanics
   My problem:

   My strategy for change:

2. Thesis/response to assignment
   My problem:

   My strategy for change:

3. Organization
   My problem:

   My strategy for change:

4. Paragraph development/examples/reasoning
   My problem:

   My strategy for change:

5. Assessment

In the space below, assign a grade to your paper using a rubric other than the one used by your instructor. In other words, if your instructor assigned your essay a grade of *High Fail*, you might give it the letter grade you now feel the paper warrants. If your instructor used the traditional letter grade to evaluate the essay, choose a category from the rubric in this book, or any other grading scale that you are familiar with, to show your evaluation of your work. Then, write a short narrative explaining your evaluation of the essay and the reasons it received the grade you gave it.

Grade: _____

Narrative: _____

_____

_____

_____

_____

*Extending the Discussion:
Considering Other Viewpoints*

Reading Selections

"See Workers as Workers, Not As a College Credential" by NY Times Editorial
Board
"My College Students Are Not OK" by Jonathan Malesic
"The American Scholar" by Ralph Waldo Emerson
"White-Collar Blues" by Benedict Jones
"America's Anxious Class" by Robert Reich
"Marketing Techniques Go to College" by Penny Singer
Berkeley College Ad
St. Joseph's College Ad
Virginia Intermont College Ad
Hofstra University Ad
Columbia University Ad

SEE WORKERS AS WORKERS, NOT AS A COLLEGE CREDENTIAL

The New York Times Editorial Board

The New York Times editorial board is composed of a group of politically-driven liberal journalists who share values and a commitment to write in support of those values as they impact important issues such as civil rights, honest governance, and defense of society's marginalized populations. The opinions of the editorial board do not represent The NY Times *as a whole in their free exchange of viewpoints and information. The board was founded in 1896 and continues today. The board members authored the following article, which appeared in* The Times *in January of 2023.*

In one of the richest nations on earth, the path to prosperity has narrowed significantly in recent decades—especially for those without a college education. More than 62 percent of Americans ages 25 and up do not hold bachelor's degrees, and the earnings gap between those with a college education and those without one has never been wider. In 2021, the difference between the median earnings of younger workers with bachelor's degrees and workers of the same age with high-school diplomas only was $22,000 —the largest since the Federal Reserve Bank of New York began tracking earnings in 1990. That's happening even as the cost of college spirals upward, putting it out of reach for many. This has fueled anxiety, bitterness, and a sense of alienation among the millions who see themselves as shut out of an economy that does not value them.

Making college more affordable is important, but there are other keys to the doors of opportunity as well. With an executive order issued on January 18, his first full day as governor, Josh Shapiro of Pennsylvania used one of them: He eliminated the requirement of a four-year college degree for the vast majority of jobs in the state government, a change similar to one that Maryland and Utah made last year (1). This demonstrates both good policy and good leadership, representing a concrete change in hiring philosophy that stops reducing people to a credential and conveys that everyone—college-educated or not—has experience and worth that employers should consider. It is a step—and a mindset—that other leaders should consider as well.

The decision was driven in part by the realities of a tight labor market. Unemployment in Pennsylvania is 3.9 percent—close to the national average of 3.5 percent—and lower than it was before the pandemic. Public and private employers have been struggling to find qualified applicants, prompting a reevaluation of hiring criteria. As Mr. Shapiro's order notes, "In the modern labor market, applicants gain knowledge, skills, and abilities through a variety of means, including apprenticeships, on-the-job training, military training, and trade schools" (2).

His move opens up 92 percent of state government jobs—approximately 65,000 positions—to anyone with "the relevant work experience and skills-based training, regardless of their educational attainment." Job postings will emphasize experience over education. The nonprofit organization Opportunity@Work has been promoting the idea of skills- and experience-based hiring since 2015. It estimates that 50 percent of the American work force comprises workers who have gained their skills through alternative routes such as apprenticeships, military service, trade schools, certificate programs, and on-the-job training rather than acquiring bachelor's degrees—a deep pool of underutilized and undercompensated talent. If employers don't have a strategy for engaging this pool, said Byron Auguste, the group's chief executive and cofounder, "they don't have a talent strategy—they only have half a talent strategy."

If the United States can't find ways to tap into all of this talent, we will not be able to solve our most urgent problems, like climate change and pandemic preparedness, or build a stronger and fairer country. Too many Americans see our society and economy as profoundly unfair, set up to serve the needs of well-connected elites and providing more benefits to people who went to college or know how to work the system. And too many feel that political leaders don't care about them and that government and institutions don't work for them. Opening up jobs may seem small-bore, but it shows that government is listening and helps build trust among those who may feel unseen or looked down upon by parts of the labor market.

The private sector has been moving gradually in this direction already. Major players to embrace skill-based hiring include General Motors, Bank of America, Google, Apple, and Accenture. IBM is recognized as a particular leader; about half of its U.S. job openings no longer require a four-year degree (3). This trend has been concentrated among what is termed "middle-skill jobs," which call for some education or training beyond high school, according to a 2022 report by researchers from Harvard Business School and Emsi Burning Glass, a labor market data firm. These middle-skill jobs, the report notes, "have long served as an important stepping stone to the middle class" (4.)

During the Great Recession, many of those steppingstones were removed. Unemployment was high, and many employers responded with "degree inflation"—larding college education requirements onto jobs that previously had not called for them—even though the work involved remained the same. As a result, the report notes, "key avenues for upward mobility were closed to roughly 80 million prime working age Americans at a time when income inequality was already widening." Over the last few years, this degree inflation has begun to recede. If this "degree reset" continues, many more jobs may be opened to workers without college degrees over the next five years.

This could also help make the American work force more diverse and inclusive in several ways. Black and Hispanic job-seekers are less likely to have bachelor's degrees than non-Hispanic whites and Asian Americans (5). Rural Americans would also benefit; only 25 percent of them hold a bachelor's degree or higher. "No part of the country is more disadvantaged by degree screening than rural America," Mr. Auguste said (6). The public sector should join this reset more aggressively. In June 2020, President Donald Trump issued an executive order to make skills more important than degrees in federal hiring (7). The Biden administration has also taken a couple of steps in that direction (8).

Getting more states on board could provide a valuable boost; state governments are among the largest employers in many states, so their hiring criteria play a special role in validating workers without college degrees. Last March, Larry Hogan of Maryland became the first governor to announce that his state was doing away with college degree requirements for many jobs. In December, his fellow Republican, Spencer Cox of Utah, followed suit. "Degrees have become a blanketed barrier to entry in too many jobs," Mr. Cox said. "Instead of focusing on demonstrated competence, the focus too often has been on a piece of paper" (9).

With Mr. Shapiro, a Democrat, weighing in for Pennsylvania, the nation's fifth most populous state, the movement's bipartisan credentials have been burnished. It is a move that Americans in every state should actively encourage. Expanding the terms for who can get hired is a change that would reverberate far beyond individual jobs and job seekers. It would bring a greater degree of openness and fairness into the labor market and send a message about government's ability to adapt and respond to the concerns of its citizens. In a country where a majority of people do not have bachelor's degrees, policies that automatically close off jobs to so many people contribute to the perception that the system is rigged against them.

A healthy democracy recognizes and promotes opportunity for everyone. Americans need to hear that message.

Works Cited

1. https://www.post-gazette.com/news/politics-state/2023/01/18/josh-shapiro-college-degree-requirement-jobs-workforce/stories/202301180096
2. https://www.governor.pa.gov/wp-content/uploads/2023/01/20230117_EO%20 2023-03_Final_EXECUTED.pdf
3. https://www.gallup.com/workplace/344621/why-ibm-chooses-skills-degrees.aspx
4. https://www.hbs.edu/managing-the-future-of-work/Documents/research/emerging_degree_reset_020922.pdf
5. https://www.census.gov/newsroom/press-releases/2022/educational-attainment.html
6. https://nces.ed.gov/programs/coe/indicator/lbc/educational-attainment-rural?tid=1000
7. https://www.federalregister.gov/documents/2020/07/01/2020-14337/modernizing-and-reforming-the-assessment-and-hiring-of-federal-job-candidates
8. https://www.axios.com/2022/05/19/white-house-prods-agencies-to-focus-on-skills-in-hiring
9. https://www.abc4.com/news/local-news/gov-spencer-cox-removes-bachelors-degree-requirement-for-state-government-jobs/

Discussion Questions

1. What is the difference in median earnings between workers with a college degree and those without one? How do the members of *The New York Times* Editorial Board believe this discrepancy makes the less educated feel? Do you see this situation as a societal problem? Explain.

2. What moves have some state governments, as well some companies in the private sector, made to address this problem? What effect do you think these changes will have on the number of students who enroll in college? If these changes were already in place, would you have made a different decision about pursuing a degree in higher education? Explain your answer.

3. What alternatives are being considered as possible replacements for a college degree? Evaluate each of these alternatives in terms of the preparation needed to perform your desired future job.

4. Discuss and compare Peter Kirsanow's and Jonathan Klemens's understanding of the American work ethic. How does each writer's ideas support, or challenge, the revision of job requirements discussed by the Times editorial board in the above article?

MY COLLEGE STUDENTS ARE NOT OKAY

JONATHAN MALESIC

Jonathan Malesic earned a PhD in religious studies from the University of Virginia, and he is currently a teacher of writing and religion at the college level. He is also an essayist and journalist, and his articles have appeared in places such as The New York Times, The Chronicle of Higher Education, *and* The Washington Post. *He won a book of the Year Award for his book* Secret Faith in the Public Square *(2009). He is the author of the book* The End of Burnout: Why Work Drains Us and How to Build Better Lives *(2022). The following article appeared in* The New York Times *in 2022.*

In my classes last fall, a third of the students were missing nearly every time, and usually not the same third. Students buried their faces in their laptop screens and let my questions hang in the air unanswered. My classes were small, with nowhere to hide, yet some students openly slept through them.

I was teaching writing at two very different universities: one private and wealthy, its lush lawns surrounded by towering fraternity and sorority houses; the other public, with a diverse array of strivers milling about its largely brutalist campus. The problems in my classrooms, though, were the same. Students just weren't doing what it takes to learn.

By several measures—attendance, late assignments, quality of in-class discussion—they performed worse than any students I had encountered in two decades of teaching. They didn't even seem to be trying. At the private school, I required individual meetings to discuss their research paper drafts; only six of fourteen showed up. Usually, they all do.

I wondered if it was me, if I was washed up. But when I posted about this on Facebook, more than a dozen friends teaching at institutions across the country gave similar reports. Last month, *The Chronicle of Higher Education* received comments from more than 100 college instructors about their classes. They, too, reported poor attendance, little discussion, missing homework, and failed exams.

The pandemic certainly made college more challenging for students, and over the past two years, compassionate faculty members have loosened course structures in response: They have introduced recorded lectures, flexible attendance and deadline policies, and lenient grading. In light of the widely reported mental health crisis on campuses, some students and faculty members are calling for those looser standards and remote options to persist indefinitely, even as vaccines and COVID-19 therapies have made it relatively safe to return to prepandemic norms.

I also feel compassion for my students, but the learning breakdown has convinced me that continuing to relax standards would be a mistake. Looser standards are contributing to the problem, because they make it too easy for students to disengage from classes.

Student disengagement is a problem for everyone, because everyone depends on well-educated people. College prepares students for socially essential careers—including as engineers and nurses—and to be citizens who bring high-level intellectual habits to bear on big societal problems, from climate change to the next political crisis. On a more fundamental level, it also prepares many students to be responsible adults: to set goals and figure out what help they need to attain them.

Higher education is now at a turning point. The accommodations for the pandemic can either end or be made permanent. The task won't be easy, but universities need to help students rebuild their ability to learn. And to do that, everyone involved—students, faculties, administrators and the public at large—must insist on in-person classes and high expectations for fall 2022 and beyond.

In March 2020, essentially all of U.S. higher education went remote overnight. Faculties, course designers, and educational technology staffs scrambled to move classes online, developing new techniques on the fly. The changes often entailed a loosening of requirements. A study by Canadian researchers found that nearly half of U.S. faculty members reduced their expectations for the quantity of work in their classes in spring 2020, and nearly a third lowered quality expectations. That made sense in those emergency conditions; it seemed to me that students and faculties just needed to make it through.

That fall, most students were learning at least partly online. Simultaneously, colleges gave undergraduate students more autonomy and flexibility over how they learned, with options to go remote or asynchronous.

Faculty members and students across the Dallas-Fort Worth area, where I live, described a widespread breakdown in learning that year. Matthew Fujita, a biology professor at the University of Texas at Arlington, said the results of the first exam in his fall 2020 genetics class, a large lecture course, reflected "the worst performance I'd ever seen on a test."

Amy Austin, who teaches Spanish at U.T.A., began calling her students her "divine little silent circles"—a reference to Dante Alighieri's *Divine Comedy*—because she would typically see only their initials in a circle on her computer screen, none of them speaking.

Students' self-reports track with these observations. A June 2021 survey by *Inside Higher Ed* found that more than half of students said they learned less that academic year than they did before the pandemic.

There is much evidence that students learn less online than they do in person, in part because online courses demand considerable self-discipline and motivation. And some lessons just don't translate to a remote format. "You can't learn how to use a microscope online," said Melissa Walsh, who teaches biology and environmental science at U.T.A. "You just can't."

It's no surprise, then, that in one of the first studies to examine broad-scale learning outcomes during the pandemic, researchers found that the switch to online learning resulted in more course failures and withdrawals in the Virginia community-college system, even despite more lenient grading. Students nationwide reported a greater willingness to cheat, too.

It's bad enough that so many students had to take classes through a medium where they don't do their best. More disconcerting is that when classes returned to mainly in-person in fall 2021, student performance did not bounce back. The problem isn't only that students learn poorly online. It's also that when they go through a year or more of remote classes, they develop habits that harm their ability to learn offline, too.

Dr. Austin said the quality of her students' work had not recovered after the return to campus. On grammar tests, students continued to score lower than they did before the pandemic. Now, she told me, the students in her classroom often met her questions with blank stares. "This is like being online!" she said. That was my experience, too. In my classes, it often seemed as if my students thought they were still on Zoom with their cameras off, as if they had muted themselves.

Many students got out of the habit of coming to class at all. Dr. Walsh estimated that in her biology course for non-majors this spring, just 30 percent to 40 percent of students attended class, and only a handful watched her recorded lectures. The students who don't attend class are missing out on the best of Dr. Walsh, who recently won a campuswide teaching award.

"What makes me an effective instructor," she said, "has a lot to do with my personality, how I engage in the classroom, using humor. I'm very animated. I like to walk around the classroom and talk with students." Doing so is a way not just to get them engaged but also to test their learning and adjust her teaching on the fly. "I'm not able to do that with students who don't come to the classroom," she said.

Dr. Walsh added that if students aren't in the classroom, she can't recruit them to collaborate with her on research, an invaluable learning experience. She also has little to go on when writing recommendations for medical school.

The problem is bigger than any one professor's class. It's hard to insist on in-person attendance when colleagues are demanding flexibility or, as Dr. Walsh noted, when non-tenure-track faculty members like her are evaluated for contract renewal and promotion based on student evaluations. If students expect recorded lectures—even ones they won't watch—then instructors will feel pressure to provide them.

It's true that some students thrive with the flexibility and freedom afforded by COVID-era policies. Jeffrey Vancil, a sophomore at the University of Texas at Dallas (where my wife teaches and where I taught last year), said that in his first year, he could study more efficiently by watching lecture recordings on his own schedule and at faster speeds. He didn't have to waste time moving from building to building. And with the extra time, he could work for political groups and as a volunteer firefighter.

After his classes went mostly in-person, he said, he had to pull back on his extracurriculars, and his grades suffered. The best approach, in his view, would be to "let people choose" how to take their classes, "because we now have the infrastructure in place that we can record lectures and have in-person ones for people who learn best each way."

Remote and recorded classes can also enable students who work or care for children to fit school into their schedules. Ahlam Atallah, a senior at U.T.A., said that online courses allowed her to take classes while her two children were at home. She also didn't have to commute to or find parking on the vast suburban campus.

But she found that taking classes at home divided her attention. "You can't talk about this novel you're reading when you have a two-year-old running around, asking, 'Mom, Mom, can I have a snack?'" Ms. Atallah said. This past academic year, with both children at school in person, she went to nearly all her in-person classes, even those with recorded lectures. In the classroom, she said, "I can give my full attention to the class, to my professor and my fellow students."

For most students, including those with children, being in person helps them focus and excel. Mr. Vancil told me he had already developed good learning habits by the time he got to college. In my experience, most students haven't. And so it's worrying to hear students call for more remote classes and more flexibility. They are asking for conditions in which they are, on average, more likely to fail.

Some instructors are taking on extra work to offer students chances to close the learning gap. Dr. Walsh described her workload as "astronomical, exhausting." Dr. Austin allowed students to rewrite papers in the past, but she extended the policy to exams. She found that many more students needed to rewrite their assignments. She estimated that grading the rewrites "doubled" her workload. But, she added, "If I didn't do the rewrites, I'd have more people failing my classes."

Because it is students whose educations are at stake, they bear much of the responsibility for remaking their ability to learn. But faculty members and administrators need to give students an environment that encourages intellectual habits like curiosity, honesty, and participation in a community of inquiry. These habits aren't only the means to a good education; to a large extent, they are the education.

To build a culture that will foster such habits, colleges might draw lessons from what may seem an unusual source: the University of Dallas, a small Catholic university with a great-books curriculum and a reputation for conservatism. Several of its faculty members told me the nationwide learning breakdown simply wasn't happening there.

As everywhere else, University of Dallas classes went remote in March 2020. But most were in person again that fall. Returning so quickly was an unconventional move, though one that people at the university said was consistent with the institutional culture. In September 2020, a student wrote in an op-ed in the campus newspaper, "The anticipation of returning to campus this August made me wonder, 'Is this how Odysseus felt as he returned home after ten years?'"

Anthony Nussmeier, who teaches Italian at the university, praised its response to the pandemic as exhibiting a holistic understanding of care for students, balancing "the immediate health imperative with other imperatives that are no less important: the importance of mental health, the importance of friendship, the importance of physical proximity to other human beings for most of us."

As a result of the school's decision, its students didn't have as much time to develop the habits of disengagement that their peers in Zoom U. did.

Gabriella Capizzi, a junior at the University of Dallas, said the accountability of attending classes in person pushed her to work harder and learn more. In person, Ms. Capizzi said, a positive sense of anxiety motivates her to prepare for class discussion, because some professors cold-call students. "You go in with yourself, and you have a notebook, but you either know it or you don't," she said. "There's a rush of adrenaline when you get something right. You're actually moving forward and learning."

Last month at the school, I visited Scott Crider's Literary Traditions II, a required first-year English course that reads Dante, Milton, and Shakespeare. The sixteen students—two were absent—sat in a rough circle, their wheeled desks backed up to the walls. No laptops or phones were visible. (Dr. Crider said he prohibits both—a common custom at the university.) Students intently marked up their spiral-bound notebooks and copies of sonnets.

Two students debated the syllabic rhythm in the last two lines of *Paradise Lost*. Others craned their necks to watch their classmates work at the whiteboard. Parsing out poetic meter is not everyone's idea of a good time, but the students looked anything but bored. They laughed at Dr. Crider's humor. Just about everyone spoke up, sharing observations, questions and even a complaint about a William Carlos Williams poem. I didn't want class to end.

To the people I spoke with at the University of Dallas, the personal, relational character of education is inseparable from high intellectual standards. Ms. Capizzi recalled a literature course she took with a professor who was known as a hard grader. She visited his office at least once a week to talk about the material, and even more often when there was a paper due. "Him having a high standard for each of us was good, but then we have the standard for ourselves," she said. "It's difficult, but you want it to be difficult, and you want to be a part of it because it's difficult."

Ms. Capizzi's comments echo those of the sociologists Daniel F. Chambliss and Christopher G. Takacs, who in their 2014 book *How College Works* found that students learn when they're motivated and that "the strongest motivation to work on basic skills comes from an emotionally based face-to-face relationship with specific other people—for instance, the one-on-one writing tutorial with a respected professor who cares about this student's work."

Those relationships are much harder to forge remotely, and students who don't discover early on that they learn through relationships will never know to seek them out. Even Mr. Vancil, who wishes he could take all his classes remotely, said he learns a great deal from his frequent visits to his professors' office hours.

Professors must recognize that caring for students means wanting to see them thrive. That entails high expectations and a willingness to help students exceed them. Administrators will need to enact policies that put relationships at the center. That will mean resisting the temptation to expand remote learning, even if students demand it, and ensuring that faculty workloads leave time for individual attention to students.

"Young people are the hope of the world," Dr. Crider told me. Current students, he added, "are capable of rising to the same standards as before, and we do them a disservice when we presume they're too mentally ill or too traumatized to function."

A mantra of teaching, at any level, is "Meet the students where they are." But if education is built on relationships, then colleges must equally insist students meet their teachers where they are. The classroom, the lab, and the office are where we instructors do our best and where a vast majority of students can do their best, too. Our goal is to take students somewhere far beyond where they meet us.

Discussion Questions

1. In Jonathan Malesic's classes, in what ways have students changed since the return to campus after the pandemic lockdown? Do you think the behaviors he has observed are now common on your own campus? How has your behavior altered in response to having experienced the lockdown?

2. How have many compassionate instructors changed their courses for their post pandemic students? What is Malesic's response to their adaptations? Do you think that Malesic cares more or less about students than the "compassionate" teachers?

3. What does the evidence suggest about student learning online versus in-person? Compare your own in-person and online learning experiences. Which did you prefer? Why?

4. What disadvantages, other than just coverage of course material, are pointed out by Dr. Walsh and Ms. Atallah? Do you believe these disadvantages outweigh the flexibility of online classes? Explain your answer.

THE AMERICAN SCHOLAR

Ralph Waldo Emerson

Ralph Waldo Emerson (1803-1882) was an influential American man of letters and an indispensable figure in the Transcendentalist movement. His essay "Self-Reliance" is widely considered a classic. The excerpt below is from another essay, originally a speech given to Harvard's Phi Beta Kappa Society and titled "An Oration Delivered before the Phi Beta Kappa Society, at Cambridge, [Massachusetts,] August 31, 1837." He published the speech under its original title as a pamphlet but later changed the title to "The American Scholar" to broaden its appeal.

Mr. President and Gentlemen,

I greet you on the re-commencement of our literary year. Our anniversary is one of hope, and, perhaps, not enough of labor. We do not meet for games of strength or skill, for the recitation of histories, tragedies, and odes, like the ancient Greeks; for parliaments of love and poesy, like the Troubadours; nor for the advancement of science, like our contemporaries in the British and European capitals. Thus far, our holiday has been simply a friendly sign of the survival of the love of letters amongst a people too busy to give to letters any more. As such, it is precious as the sign of an indestructible instinct. Perhaps the time is already come, when it ought to be, and will be, something else; when the sluggard intellect of this continent will look from under its iron lids, and fill the postponed expectation of the world with something better than the exertions of mechanical skill. Our day of dependence, our long apprenticeship to the learning of other lands, draws to a close.

The millions, that around us are rushing into life, cannot always be fed on the sere remains of foreign harvests. Events, actions arise, that must be sung, that will sing themselves. Who can doubt, that poetry will revive and lead in a new age, as the star in the constellation Harp, which now flames in our zenith, astronomers announce, shall one day be the pole-star for a thousand years?

In this hope, I accept the topic which not only usage, but the nature of our association, seem to prescribe to this day, —the AMERICAN SCHOLAR. Year by year, we come up hither to read one more chapter of his biography. Let us inquire what light new days and events have thrown on his character, and his hopes.

It is one of those fables, which, out of an unknown antiquity, convey an unlooked-for wisdom, that the gods, in the beginning, divided Man into men, that he might be more helpful to himself; just as the hand was divided into fingers, the better to answer its end.

The old fable covers a doctrine ever new and sublime; that there is One Man, — present to all particular men only partially, or through one faculty; and that you must take the whole society to find the whole man. Man is not a farmer, or a professor, or an engineer, but he is all. Man is priest, and scholar, and statesman, and producer, and soldier. In the *divided* or social state, these functions are parceled out to individuals, each of whom aims to do his stint of the joint work, whilst each other performs his. The fable implies, that the individual, to possess himself, must sometimes return from his own labor to embrace all the other laborers. But unfortunately, this original unit, this fountain of power, has been so distributed to multitudes, has been so minutely subdivided and peddled out, that it is spilled into drops, and cannot be gathered. The state of society is one in which the members have suffered amputation from the trunk, and strut about so many walking monsters, —a good finger, a neck, a stomach, an elbow, but never a man.

Man is thus metamorphosed into a thing, into many things. The planter, who is Man sent out into the field to gather food, is seldom cheered by any idea of the true dignity of his ministry. He sees his bushel and his cart, and nothing beyond, and sinks into the farmer, instead of Man on the farm. The tradesman scarcely ever gives an ideal worth to his work, but is ridden by the routine of his craft, and the soul is subject to dollars. The priest becomes a form; the attorney, a statute-book; the mechanic, a machine; the sailor, a rope of a ship.

In this distribution of functions, the scholar is the delegated intellect. In the right state, he is, *Man Thinking*. In the degenerate state, when the victim of society, he tends to become a mere thinker, or, still worse, the parrot of other men's thinking.

In this view of him, as Man Thinking, the theory of his office is contained. Him nature solicits with all her placid, all her monitory pictures; him the past instructs; him the future invites.

Is not, indeed, every man a student, and do not all things exist for the student's behoof? And, finally, is not the true scholar the only true master? But the old oracle said, "All things have two handles: beware of the wrong one." In life, too often, the scholar errs with mankind and forfeits his privilege. Let us see him in his school, and consider him in reference to the main influences he receives.

I. The first in time and the first in importance of the influences upon the mind is that of nature. Every day, the sun; and, after sunset, night and her stars. Ever the winds blow; ever the grass grows. Every day, men and women, conversing, beholding and beholden. The scholar is he of all men whom this spectacle most engages. He must settle its value in his mind. What is nature to him? There is never a beginning, there is never an end, to the inexplicable continuity of this web of God, but always circular power returning into itself. Therein it resembles his own spirit, whose beginning, whose ending, he never can find, —so entire, so boundless. Far, too, as her splendors shine, system on system shooting like rays, upward, downward, without center, without circumference, —in the mass and in the particle, nature hastens to render account of herself to the mind. Classification begins. To the young mind, everything is individual, stands by itself. By and by, it finds how to join two things, and see in them one nature; then three, then three thousand; and so, tyrannized over by its own unifying instinct, it goes on tying things together, diminishing anomalies, discovering roots running under ground, whereby contrary and remote things cohere, and flower out from one stem. It presently learns, that, since the dawn of history, there has been a constant accumulation and classifying of facts. But what is classification but the perceiving that these objects are not chaotic, and are not foreign, but have a law which is also a law of the human mind?

The astronomer discovers that geometry, a pure abstraction of the human mind, is the measure of planetary motion. The chemist finds proportions and intelligible method throughout matter; and science is nothing but the finding of analogy, identity, in the most remote parts. The ambitious soul sits down before each refractory fact; one after another, reduces all strange constitutions, all new powers, to their class and their law, and goes on for ever to animate the last fiber of organization, the outskirts of nature, by insight.

Thus to him, to this school-boy under the bending dome of day, is suggested, that he and it proceed from one root; one is leaf and one is flower; relation, sympathy, stirring in every vein. And what is that Root? Is not that the soul of his soul? —A thought too bold, —a dream too wild. Yet when this spiritual light shall have revealed the law of more earthly natures, —when he has learned to worship the soul, and to see that the natural philosophy that now is, is only the first gropings of its gigantic hand, he shall look forward to an ever expanding knowledge as to a becoming creator. He shall see, that nature is the opposite of the soul, answering to it part for part. One is seal, and one is print. Its beauty is the beauty of his own mind. Its laws are the laws of his own mind. Nature then becomes to him the measure of his attainments. So much of nature as he is ignorant of, so much of his own mind does he not yet possess. And, in fine, the ancient precept, "Know thyself," and the modern precept, "Study nature," become at last one maxim.

II. The next great influence into the spirit of the scholar, is, the mind of the Past, —in whatever form, whether of literature, of art, of institutions, that mind is inscribed. Books are the best type of the influence of the past, and perhaps we shall get at the truth, —learn the amount of this influence more conveniently, —by considering their value alone.

The theory of books is noble. The scholar of the first age received into him the world around; brooded thereon; gave it the new arrangement of his own mind, and uttered it again. It came into him, life; it went out from him, truth. It came to him, short-lived actions; it went out from him, immortal thoughts. It came to him, business; it went from him, poetry. It was dead fact; now, it is quick thought. It can stand, and it can go. It now endures, it now flies, it now inspires. Precisely in proportion to the depth of mind from which it issued, so high does it soar, so long does it sing.

Or, I might say, it depends on how far the process had gone, of transmuting life into truth. In proportion to the completeness of the distillation, so will the purity and imperishableness of the product be. But none is quite perfect. As no air-pump can by any means make a perfect vacuum, so neither can any artist entirely exclude the conventional, the local, the perishable from his book, or write a book of pure thought, that shall be as efficient, in all respects, to a remote posterity, as to contemporaries, or rather to the second age. Each age, it is found, must write its own books; or rather, each generation for the next succeeding. The books of an older period will not fit this.

Yet hence arises a grave mischief. The sacredness which attaches to the act of creation, —the act of thought, —is transferred to the record. The poet chanting, was felt to be a divine man: henceforth the chant is divine also. The writer was a just and wise spirit: henceforward it is settled, the book is perfect; as love of the hero corrupts into worship of his statue. Instantly, the book becomes noxious: the guide is a tyrant. The sluggish and perverted mind of the multitude, slow to open to the incursions of Reason, having once so opened, having once received this book, stands upon it, and makes an outcry, if it is disparaged. Colleges are built on it. Books are written on it by thinkers, not by Man Thinking; by men of talent, that is, who start wrong, who set out from accepted dogmas, not from their own sight of principles. Meek young men grow up in libraries, believing it their duty to accept the views, which Cicero, which Locke, which Bacon, have given, forgetful that Cicero, Locke, and Bacon were only young men in libraries, when they wrote these books.

Hence, instead of Man Thinking, we have the bookworm. Hence, the book-learned class, who value books, as such; not as related to nature and the human constitution, but as making a sort of Third Estate with the world and the soul. Hence, the restorers of readings, the emendators, the bibliomaniacs of all degrees.

Books are the best of things, well used; abused, among the worst. What is the right use? What is the one end, which all means go to effect? They are for nothing but to inspire. I had better never see a book, than to be warped by its attraction clean out of my own orbit, and made a satellite instead of a system. The one thing in the world, of value, is the active soul. This every man is entitled to; this every man contains within him, although, in almost all men, obstructed, and as yet unborn. The soul active sees absolute truth; and utters truth, or creates. In this action, it is genius; not the privilege of here and there a favorite, but the sound estate of every man. In its essence, it is progressive. The book, the college, the school of art, the institution of any kind, stop with some past utterance of genius. This is good, say they, —let us hold by this. They pin me down. They look backward and not forward. But genius always looks forward. The eyes of man are set in his forehead, not in his hindhead. Man hopes. Genius creates. To create, —to create, —is the proof of a divine presence. Whatever talents may be, if the man create not, the pure efflux of the Deity is not his; —cinders and smoke there may be, but not yet flame. There are creative manners, there are creative actions, and creative words; manners, actions, words, that is, indicative of no custom or authority, but springing spontaneous from the mind's own sense of good and fair.

On the other part, instead of being its own seer, let it receive from another mind its truth, though it were in torrents of light, without periods of solitude, inquest, and self-recovery, and a fatal disservice is done. Genius is always sufficiently the enemy of genius by over influence. The literature of every nation bear me witness. The English dramatic poets have Shakespearized now for two hundred years.

Undoubtedly there is a right way of reading, so it be sternly subordinated. Man Thinking must not be subdued by his instruments. Books are for the scholar's idle times. When he can read God directly, the hour is too precious to be wasted in other men's transcripts of their readings. But when the intervals of darkness come, as come they must, —when the sun is hid, and the stars withdraw their shining, —we repair to the lamps which were kindled by their ray, to guide our steps to the East again, where the dawn is. We hear, that we may speak. The Arabian proverb says, "A fig tree, looking on a fig tree, becometh fruitful."

It is remarkable, the character of the pleasure we derive from the best books. They impress us with the conviction, that one nature wrote and the same reads. We read the verses of one of the great English poets, of Chaucer, of Marvell, of Dryden, with the most modern joy, —with a pleasure, I mean, which is in great part caused by the abstraction of all *time* from their verses. There is some awe mixed with the joy of our surprise, when this poet, who lived in some past world, two or three hundred years ago, says that which lies close to my own soul, that which I also had wellnigh thought and said. But for the evidence thence afforded to the philosophical doctrine of the identity of all minds, we should suppose some preestablished harmony, some foresight of souls that were to be, and some preparation of stores for their future wants, like the fact observed in insects, who lay up food before death for the young grub they shall never see.

I would not be hurried by any love of system, by any exaggeration of instincts, to underrate the Book. We all know, that, as the human body can be nourished on any food, though it were boiled grass and the broth of shoes, so the human mind can be fed by any knowledge. And great and heroic men have existed, who had almost no other information than by the printed page. I only would say, that it needs a strong head to bear that diet. One must be an inventor to read well. As the proverb says, "He that would bring home the wealth of the Indies, must carry out the wealth of the Indies." There is then creative reading as well as creative writing. When the mind is braced by labor and invention, the page of whatever book we read becomes luminous with manifold allusion. Every sentence is doubly significant, and the sense of our author is as broad as the world. We then see, what is always true, that, as the seer's hour of vision is short and rare among heavy days and months, so is its record, perchance, the least part of his volume. The discerning will read, in his Plato or Shakespeare, only that least part, —only the authentic utterances of the oracle; —all the rest he rejects, were it never so many times Plato's and Shakespeare's.

Of course, there is a portion of reading quite indispensable to a wise man. History and exact science he must learn by laborious reading. Colleges, in like manner, have their indispensable office, —to teach elements. But they can only highly serve us, when they aim not to drill, but to create; when they gather from far every ray of various genius to their hospitable halls, and, by the concentrated fires, set the hearts of their youth on flame. Thought and knowledge are natures in which apparatus and pretension avail nothing. Gowns, and pecuniary foundations, though of towns of gold, can never countervail the least sentence or syllable of wit. Forget this, and our American colleges will recede in their public importance, whilst they grow richer every year.

III. There goes in the world a notion, that the scholar should be a recluse, a valetudinarian, —as unfit for any handiwork or public labor, as a penknife for an axe. The so-called "practical men" sneer at speculative men, as if, because they speculate or *see*, they could do nothing. I have heard it said that the clergy, —who are always, more universally than any other class, the scholars of their day, —are addressed as women; that the rough, spontaneous conversation of men they do not hear, but only a mincing and diluted speech. They are often virtually disfranchised; and, indeed, there are advocates for their celibacy. As far as this is true of the studious classes, it is not just and wise. Action is with the scholar subordinate, but it is essential. Without it, he is not yet man. Without it, thought can never ripen into truth. Whilst the world hangs before the eye as a cloud of beauty, we cannot even see its beauty. Inaction is cowardice, but there can be no scholar without the heroic mind. The preamble of thought, the transition through which it passes from the unconscious to the conscious, is action. Only so much do I know, as I have lived. Instantly we know whose words are loaded with life, and whose not.

The world, —this shadow of the soul, or *other me*, lies wide around. Its attractions are the keys which unlock my thoughts and make me acquainted with myself. I run eagerly into this resounding tumult. I grasp the hands of those next me, and take my place in the ring to suffer and to work, taught by an instinct, that so shall the dumb abyss be vocal with speech. I pierce its order; I dissipate its fear; I dispose of it within the circuit of my expanding life. So much only of life as I know by experience, so much of the wilderness have I vanquished and planted, or so far have I extended my being, my dominion. I do not see how any man can afford, for the sake of his nerves and his nap, to spare any action in which he can partake. It is pearls and rubies to his discourse. Drudgery, calamity, exasperation, want, are instructors in eloquence and wisdom. The true scholar grudges every opportunity of action past by, as a loss of power.

It is the raw material out of which the intellect molds her splendid products. A strange process too, this, by which experience is converted into thought, as a mulberry leaf is converted into satin. The manufacture goes forward at all hours.

The actions and events of our childhood and youth, are now matters of calmest observation. They lie like fair pictures in the air. Not so with our recent actions, —with the business which we now have in hand. On this we are quite unable to speculate. Our affections as yet circulate through it. We no more feel or know it, than we feel the feet, or the hand, or the brain of our body. The new deed is yet a part of life, —remains for a time immersed in our unconscious life. In some contemplative hour, it detaches itself from the life like a ripe fruit, to become a thought of the mind. Instantly, it is raised, transfigured; the corruptible has put on incorruption. Henceforth it is an object of beauty, however base its origin and neighborhood. Observe, too, the impossibility of antedating this act. In its grub state, it cannot fly, it cannot shine, it is a dull grub. But suddenly, without observation, the selfsame thing unfurls beautiful wings, and is an angel of wisdom.

So is there no fact, no event, in our private history, which shall not, sooner or later, lose its adhesive, inert form, and astonish us by soaring from our body into the empyrean. Cradle and infancy, school and playground, the fear of boys, and dogs, and ferules, the love of little maids and berries, and many another fact that once filled the whole sky, are gone already; friend and relative profession and party, town and country, nation and world, must also soar and sing.

Of course, he who has put forth his total strength in fit actions, has the richest return of wisdom. I will not shut myself out of this globe of action, and transplant an oak into a flowerpot, there to hunger and pine; nor trust the revenue of some single faculty, and exhaust one vein of thought, much like those Savoyards, who, getting their livelihood by carving shepherds, shepherdesses, and smoking Dutchmen, for all Europe, went out one day to the mountain to find stock, and discovered that they had whittled up the last of their pine-trees. Authors we have, in numbers, who have written out their vein, and who, moved by a commendable prudence, sail for Greece or Palestine, follow the trapper into the prairie, or ramble round Algiers, to replenish their merchantable stock. If it were only for a vocabulary, the scholar would be covetous of action. Life is our dictionary. Years are well spent in country labors; in town, —in the insight into trades and manufactures; in frank intercourse with many men and women; in science; in art; to the one end of mastering in all their facts a language by which to illustrate and embody our perceptions. I learn immediately from any speaker how much he has already lived, through the poverty or the splendor of his speech. Life lies behind us as the quarry from whence we get tiles and copestones for the masonry of to-day. This is the way to learn grammar. Colleges and books only copy the language which the field and the work-yard made.

But the final value of action, like that of books, and better than books, is, that it is a resource. That great principle of Undulation in nature, that shows itself in the inspiring and expiring of the breath; in desire and satiety; in the ebb and flow of the sea; in day and night; in heat and cold; and as yet more deeply ingrained in every atom and every fluid, is known to us under the name of Polarity, —these "fits of easy transmission and reflection," as Newton called them, are the law of nature because they are the law of spirit.

The mind now thinks; now acts; and each fit reproduces the other. When the artist has exhausted his materials, when the fancy no longer paints, when thoughts are no longer apprehended, and books are a weariness, —he has always the resource to *live*. Character is higher than intellect. Thinking is the function. Living is the functionary. The stream retreats to its source. A great soul will be strong to live, as well as strong to think. Does he lack organ or medium to impart his truths? He can still fall back on this elemental force of living them. This is a total act. Thinking is a partial act. Let the grandeur of justice shine in his affairs. Let the beauty of affection cheer his lowly roof. Those "far from fame," who dwell and act with him, will feel the force of his constitution in the doings and passages of the day better than it can be measured by any public and designed display. Time shall teach him, that the scholar loses no hour which the man lives. Herein he unfolds the sacred germ of his instinct, screened from influence. What is lost in seemliness is gained in strength. Not out of those, on whom systems of education have exhausted their culture, comes the helpful giant to destroy the old or to build the new, but out of unhandselled savage nature, out of terrible Druids and Berserkirs, come at last Alfred and Shakespeare.

I hear therefore with joy whatever is beginning to be said of the dignity and necessity of labor to every citizen. There is virtue yet in the hoe and the spade, for learned as well as for unlearned hands. And labor is everywhere welcome; always we are invited to work; only be this limitation observed, that a man shall not for the sake of wider activity sacrifice any opinion to the popular judgments and modes of action.

I have now spoken of the education of the scholar by nature, by books, and by action. It remains to say somewhat of his duties. They are such as become Man Thinking. They may all be comprised in self-trust. The office of the scholar is to cheer, to raise, and to guide men by showing them facts amidst appearances. He plies the slow, unhonored, and unpaid task of observation. Flamsteed and Herschel, in their glazed observatories, may catalogue the stars with the praise of all men, and, the results being splendid and useful, honor is sure. But he, in his private observatory, cataloguing obscure and nebulous stars of the human mind, which as yet no man has thought of as such, —watching days and months, sometimes, for a few facts; correcting still his old records; —must relinquish display and immediate fame. In the long period of his preparation, he must betray often an ignorance and shiftlessness in popular arts, incurring the disdain of the able who shoulder him aside. Long he must stammer in his speech; often forego the living for the dead. Worse yet, he must accept,—how often! poverty and solitude. For the ease and pleasure of treading the old road, accepting the fashions, the education, the religion of society, he takes the cross of making his own, and, of course, the self-accusation, the faint heart, the frequent uncertainty and loss of time, which are the nettles and tangling vines in the way of the self-relying and self-directed; and the state of virtual hostility in which he seems to stand to society, and especially to educated society. For all this loss and scorn, what offset? He is to find consolation in exercising the highest functions of human nature. He is one, who raises himself from private considerations, and breathes and lives on public and illustrious thoughts. He is the world's eye.

He is the world's heart. He is to resist the vulgar prosperity that retrogrades ever to barbarism, by preserving and communicating heroic sentiments, noble biographies, melodious verse, and the conclusions of history. Whatsoever oracles the human heart, in all emergencies, in all solemn hours, has uttered as its commentary on the world of actions, —these he shall receive and impart. And whatsoever new verdict Reason from her inviolable seat pronounces on the passing men and events of to-day, —this he shall hear and promulgate.

These being his functions, it becomes him to feel all confidence in himself, and to defer never to the popular cry. He and he only knows the world. The world of any moment is the merest appearance. Some great decorum, some fetish of a government, some ephemeral trade, or war, or man, is cried up by half mankind and cried down by the other half, as if all depended on this particular up or down. The odds are that the whole question is not worth the poorest thought which the scholar has lost in listening to the controversy. Let him not quit his belief that a popgun is a popgun, though the ancient and honorable of the earth affirm it to be the crack of doom. In silence, in steadiness, in severe abstraction, let him hold by himself; add observation to observation, patient of neglect, patient of reproach; and bide his own time, —happy enough, if he can satisfy himself alone, that this day he has seen something truly. Success treads on every right step. For the instinct is sure, that prompts him to tell his brother what he thinks. He then learns, that in going down into the secrets of his own mind, he has descended into the secrets of all minds. He learns that he who has mastered any law in his private thoughts, is master to that extent of all men whose language he speaks, and of all into whose language his own can be translated. The poet, in utter solitude remembering his spontaneous thoughts and recording them, is found to have recorded that, which men in crowded cities find true for them also. The orator distrusts at first the fitness of his frank confessions, —his want of knowledge of the persons he addresses, —until he finds that he is the complement of his hearers; —that they drink his words because he fulfills for them their own nature; the deeper he dives into his privatest, secretest presentiment, to his wonder he finds, this is the most acceptable, most public, and universally true. The people delight in it; the better part of every man feels, This is my music; this is myself.

In self-trust, all the virtues are comprehended. Free should the scholar be, —free and brave. Free even to the definition of freedom, "without any hindrance that does not arise out of his own constitution." Brave; for fear is a thing, which a scholar by his very function puts behind him. Fear always springs from ignorance. It is a shame to him if his tranquility, amid dangerous times, arise from the presumption, that, like children and women, his is a protected class; or if he seek a temporary peace by the diversion of his thoughts from politics or vexed questions, hiding his head like an ostrich in the flowering bushes, peeping into microscopes, and turning rhymes, as a boy whistles to keep his courage up. So is the danger a danger still; so is the fear worse. Manlike let him turn and face it. Let him look into its eye and search its nature, inspect its origin, —see the whelping of this lion, —which lies no great way back; he will then find in himself a perfect comprehension of its nature and extent; he will have made his hands meet on the other side, and can henceforth defy it, and pass on superior. The world is his, who can see through its pretension. What deafness, what stone-blind custom, what overgrown error you behold, is there only by sufferance, —by your sufferance. See it to be a lie, and you have already dealt it its mortal blow.

Discussion Questions

1. What, according to Emerson, is the difference between "*Man Thinking*" and "a mere thinker"? Which kind of scholar has your college prepared you to be? How has it taught you to be one or the other?

2. Why does Emerson think that in spite of the many books already in existence, it is essential that each generation write books? Do you think new books need to continually be written? Explain your answer.

3. How does Emerson explain his assertion that books are among both the best and worst of things? What reasons would you offer to explain the value of books in our society?

4. What does Emerson see as the true mission of colleges? How does he think they should accomplish their mission? What should be the goal of a college education? Explain ways your college is succeeding or failing in meeting this goal.

5. In section II, how does Emerson differentiate between talent and genius?

6. Near the end of this section, what does he say is the role of colleges with regard to genius? Do you agree? Explain your answer.

7. What does Emerson feel is the relationship between "nature, books, and action"?

WHITE-COLLAR BLUES

BENEDICT JONES

Benedict Jones received a bachelor's degree with a double major from the University of California, San Diego, and earned an English MA at the University of California, Riverside, where he is now a lecturer in the University Writing Program. His scholarly work focuses on Victorian-era prehistoric fiction and evolutionary theories, but he has written articles, reviews, and conference papers on a variety of topics.

A very smart engineer friend of mine (I'll call him Bob) is fond of saying, "College has ruined many a good truck driver." He doesn't mean that truck drivers shouldn't go to college or that a college-educated truck driver is useless. He means that some people who are cut out to be happy, skilled, and productive blue-collar workers aspire to careers that don't suit their talents, all because American society has filled our heads with all sorts of pro-college, anti-blue-collar snobbery.

Some people disagree with Bob. When he makes his pronouncement in public, I hear shocked responses. One person might offer no constructive criticism or argument and just gasp, "You're so elitist! How can you say that?" Someone else will opine that we *all* need equal access to higher education and to highly valued white-collar, service-sector, and professional jobs. Under the misapprehension that college is for everyone, another person might trot out a perennial motto from the United States Army and argue that every one of our esteemed citizens should have the chance to "be all that they can be." College, they think, will do that for everyone, with few exceptions.

I respect their right to their opinion. But I submit that somewhere along the line, this country ran astray. We've demonized blue-collar jobs and democratized higher education to such an extent that many people see physical work as demeaning and view college—particularly four-year colleges and universities—as the only route to success, respectability, and happiness.

You do remember happiness? That elusive quality that we all pursue, especially if we are fans of the Declaration of Independence? I think that happiness is misunderstood in this country. Things have gotten so bad that instead of looking inside ourselves for fulfillment, we look to the latest deodorant or detergent or designer jeans. We follow the latest gossip on our favorite (or least favorite) celebrities. We invest ourselves in a particular football team. We spend thousands of dollars on cosmetics and gym equipment and even plastic surgery—not so much because we want to see a prettier reflection but so that others will see it.

It doesn't work, of course. Buying the latest version of Sure may stave off sweat for a few hours, but it does not improve us as humans. We get caught up in the lives of public figures and think of them as allies when they don't even know us or care about us. We are elated when "our" team wins the championship or our screen idol wins the Oscar, but we're deflated when "our" side loses. We may eliminate the gray in our hair, but we cannot erase the gray disquiet in our souls.

To achieve true happiness, we have to find our place in life. Most of us want romantic relationships. Family is often a factor. Ethics, religion, or spirituality is usually key. Community can be important. And there's always something to be said for having our basic needs met, not to mention a few little luxuries here and there.

So most of us have to work. But I don't see how anyone can be happy in life who is unhappy in work, and so many Americans today are unsatisfied with their jobs. Too many people try to cram themselves into careers for which they are ill-suited—jobs that will not bring happiness or fulfillment. Some people who would make excellent plumbers, electricians, or technicians are doggedly determined to earn a four-year degree so that they can land a mind-numbing and stultifying desk job that doesn't even begin to capitalize on their real gifts and talents.

I haven't even mentioned the huge number of eighteen-year-old pre-med and pre-law hopefuls whose dearest wish (or their families' dearest wish?) is to earn a professional degree that will grant them money and status. In addition to the enormous expense of graduate and professional schools and the unlikelihood that a reputable program will be thrilled with a 2.7 undergraduate GPA, I suspect that many of these young people have no realistic idea what doctors or lawyers actually do all day. For example, I am consistently amazed by the number of students who dislike reading and have poor writing skills but think they want to be lawyers. In addition, a veterinarian I know recently confided in me that veterinary school had not prepared him for the comparatively little time he would spend with animals, doing actual veterinary work—half of his job entails dealing with people and not their pets. I have no doubt that he enjoys his job, but I am pretty sure that the lower-paid animal health technicians spend more time working with the animals than he does and have less stress and less debt to boot. I wonder whether the veterinary school hopefuls in my own classes know this.

Many blue-collar workers are highly skilled and make very respectable incomes. One big problem, in many people's eyes, is that such workers are not "professionals." They work with their hands. They wear work clothes, maybe a uniform. They often get dirty. But think about it: If you're not interested in book learning and are miserable taking two years of general education courses, why not find a hands-on career that will make use of your unbookish talents and truly make you happy? Would you rather be a barely adequate and unfulfilled desk jockey (probably with a huge college loan to pay off), or a skilled, appreciated, and contented electrician, inventory specialist, or welder?

More to the point, for students who aren't academically inclined, would you rather turn your nose up at a practical, hands-on education; rack up tens of thousands in debt because of societal expectations; and only then start investigating other options after you discover that your professional career path really doesn't suit your needs? Or perhaps feel stuck in an unfulfilling career forever? Or would you prefer to keep an open mind and an honest heart, and explore the possibilities before you are disillusioned and heavily in debt?

I realize that the situation is not quite that simple for everyone. I seem to be setting up a false dilemma for some individuals. But I don't mean to imply that all young people must choose between a college education and a job that involves working with their hands. There's no reason artisans, craftsmen, and technicians shouldn't acquire a little more book-learning (or a lot) if the spirit moves them. Education can be valuable for anyone. But it is counterproductive to expect all people to aspire to the same college dream when human beings have such widely varying strengths, abilities, and interests. The college-fits-all approach is especially injurious in the United States, where we claim to celebrate diversity. If we revel in America's sexual, ethnic, racial, and religious differences, we should support occupational variety as well. And that means embracing more occupations that do not require a university degree and take place at a desk.

I'm not singing the praises of unskilled labor or assembly-line jobs requiring limited skills. Nor am I trying to keep people down who are trying to get ahead. I'm talking about people who, in a snobbery-free America, would much prefer jobs requiring hands-on skills and talents—and often creativity. I mean jobs that might require an apprenticeship, on-the-job training, or a degree or credential from a trade school, technical college, or community college. I was once startled to hear that one of my university students wanted to be a chef—an occupation requiring true passion, years of dedication, and specialized training. But he was enrolled in a four-year university with no courses to aid him in his ambition. Further discussion revealed that his parents, expecting him to pursue a more prestigious career, had pushed him into the university and refused to help fund him through culinary school. I have since lost track of this young man, so I don't know how it all worked out. But I often wonder about him.

I have also encountered similar stories from young people who wanted to become artists, musicians, computer technicians, dental assistants, electricians, automobile mechanics, and so on. And these are just the students who haven't quite swallowed the college dream and repressed their true longings. After years of hearing "My parents want me to be a doctor/lawyer/other professional" and seeing the anxiety and discontent of students who no longer know their real gifts and passions, I despair that they will ever be happy.

Bob, too, sees the snobbery at his job every day. In a recent e-mail, he writes that his employer exhibits "a blatant and overt dismissal of 'infrastructure' and 'support' roles . . . as neither important nor career paths." He concludes, "It's a disastrous situation with no remedy in sight, but inculcated at the very highest level." This disaster might be avoided if his employer could resist the seductive concept of universal college education and thus offer respect for expert support personnel. Such workers do know what they are doing, but for the boss, college always trumps knowledge.

Lest anyone think that I, a college instructor with an advanced degree, am romanticizing hands-on workers, I should point out that I was a blue-collar employee for fifteen years and worked for eight years as a skilled printer for an international company. I got up early (or stayed up late, when I worked second shift); wore steel-toed shoes; worked with machinery, ink, and tools; and got dirty every day. I went into printing because I was interested in it. I did always expect to finish college, so I never planned to make a career of printing, but I wound up spending twelve years with the same company, and I retained a sense of pride for the product that I delivered day after day. If this had been my true calling, I would have willingly spent twenty or thirty years at the same job. Although I have traded the physically demanding job for one that is more mentally exhausting, I am proud of my years of craftsmanship, even when other people seemed embarrassed by my work. "You're not planning to do this for the rest of your life, are you?" asked a college student who once temped for us. I hastened to assure her that I was not, but a little voice inside said, "I am good at what I do, even if I don't plan to do it forever. Why be ashamed?" What's important is that the individual be satisfied with what he or she does, regardless of what others might think.

Artisans, craftsmen, support personnel, and technicians have something to offer the world. They have real skills and talents, and we need their services. I am deeply grateful to the plumber who repairs a leak that I haven't the skill to fix. I love the CalTrans workers who improve our freeways at night, when fewer drivers are inconvenienced. I treasure the mechanics who keep my car in top form; like most Southern Californians, I would find it difficult to get around efficiently without my horseless carriage. And who can forget our 9/11 adulation of firefighters, police officers, and EMTs? They're not precisely blue-collar employees, but most of them do not have four-year degrees. Lest you forget, these folks are still going strong, serving America, and saving lives.

It's wrong of us to look down on these workers just because we've all bought into the whole college dream. For many young people, four years of college is a nightmare—one whose poisonous effects can derail them for years (or even for their entire lives) and dissuade them from pursuing fulfilling careers. Those who say otherwise have simply succumbed to the snobbery.

So I'm with Bob. College has ruined many a good mechanic, plumber, contractor, facilities manager, IT technician, chef.

Oh, and don't forget the truck drivers.

Discussion Questions

1. Define the attitude toward certain kinds of occupations that Benedict Jones recognizes in the comment of his friend. To what degree do you feel this attitude is responsible for your choice of going to college and your future career goals?

2. What, according to the author, are the essential elements of happiness? What would you like to add or eliminate from this list? Make a prioritized list of the things that you feel are important for your own happiness.

3. Why does the author claim that education snobbery is detrimental to our society as a whole? Imagine a country where everyone had a college education and a professional career, and then describe some specific problems that would result in everyday life.

4. Study and discuss the following quotations, the first from "White-Collar Blues" and the second from "College in America." Then, see if you can find points of agreement between the two writers. Read each passage closely and consider all the nuances of the word choices and expressions, as well as the ideas themselves. Look for common ground, and for possible points of difference. Then discuss your conclusions.

Jones:
"There's no reason artisans, craftsmen, and technicians shouldn't acquire a little more book-learning (or a lot) if the spirit moves them. Education can be valuable for anyone. But it is counterproductive to expect all people to aspire to the same college dream when human beings have such widely varying strengths, abilities, and interests."

Bird:
"It could be argued that many Americans today are looking less to high status and high pay than to finding a job that is 'interesting,' that permits them 'to make a contribution, express themselves' and 'use their special abilities.' They think college will help them find it. But colleges fail to warn students that jobs of these kinds are hard to come by, even for qualified applicants, and they rarely accept the responsibility of helping students choose a career that will lead to a job."

AMERICA'S ANXIOUS CLASS

ROBERT REICH

Robert Reich earned a bachelor's degree from Dartmouth and a JD from Yale; he also studied at Oxford on a Rhodes Scholarship. He has held professorships at Harvard University and Brandeis University, and he currently teaches at UC Berkeley at the prestigious Goldman School of Public Policy. In addition to serving under Presidents Ford and Carter, he was Secretary of Labor during the first Clinton administration. He is an influential lecturer and writer with over a dozen books, several of them bestsellers on politics and the economy.

The American middle class is disintegrating and turning into three new groups: an underclass largely trapped in central cities and isolated from the growing economy; an overclass profitably positioned to ride the waves of change; and an anxious class, most of whom hold jobs but are justifiably uneasy about their own standing and fearful for their children's future.

What divides the over, the under, and the anxious classes is both the quality of their formal educations and their capacity and opportunity to learn throughout their working lives. Skills have always been relevant to earnings, of course. But they have never been as important as they are today. Only fifteen years ago, a male college graduate earned 49% more than a man with only a high school degree. That's a sizable difference, but it's a divide small enough for both men to occupy terrain each would call middle class. In 1992, a male college graduate outearned his high school graduate counterpart by 83%—a difference so great that they no longer inhabit common territory or share common perspectives. Women are divided along similar, though slightly less stark, lines.

Traditionally, membership in the American middle class included not only a job with a steadily increasing income, but a bundle of benefits that came with employment. But a gap has grown here as well. Employer-sponsored health coverage for workers with college degrees has declined only slightly, from 79% in 1979 to 76% in 1993. But for high school graduates, rates have fallen further: 68% to 60% over the same period. And rates for high school dropouts have plunged—from an already low 52% in 1979 to only 36% last year. . . .

But earnings and benefits don't tell the complete story. Merely getting a job and holding onto it depend ever more on strong skills. In the 1970s, the average unemployment rate for people who had not completed high school was 7%; by 1993 it had passed 12%. Job loss for high school graduates has followed a comparable trajectory. By contrast, the unemployment rate for workers with at least a college education has remained around 3%. . . .

As they take hold in the neighborhoods and workplaces of America, these forces are ominous. Consider the physical separation they have already helped forge. The overclass has moved to elite suburbs—occasionally into their own gated communities or residential compounds policed by their own security forces. The underclass finds itself quarantined in surroundings that are unspeakably bleak and often violent. And the anxious class is trapped, too—not only by houses and apartments often too small for growing families, but also by the frenzy of effort it takes to preserve their standing, with many families needing two or three paychecks to deliver the living standard one job used to supply. In other words, even as America's economic tide continues to rise, it no longer lifts all the boats. Only a small portion of the American population benefited from the economic growth of the 1980s. The restructurings and capital investments launched during the 1980s and continuing through the 1990s have improved the productivity and competitiveness of American industry, but not the prospects of most Americans. And the people left behind have unleashed a wave of resentment and distrust—a wave buffeting government, business, and other institutions that the anxious class believes has betrayed them.

This creates fertile soil for the demagogues and conspiracy theorists who often emerge during anxious times. People in distress, people who fear for their future, naturally cling to what they have and often resist anything that threatens it. People who feel abandoned—by a government that has let them slide or a company that has laid them off—respond to opportunists peddling simplistic explanations and sinister solutions. Why are you having trouble making ends meet? We're letting in too many immigrants. Why are you struggling to pay your bills? Affirmative action tilts things in favor of African Americans and Hispanics. Why is your job at risk? Our trade policies have not been sufficiently protectionist.

As a solution, we can't turn back the clock and return to the safe old world of routine mass production that dominated postwar America. Efforts to do so—say, by keeping foreign investment and goods outside of our borders or by stifling technological advancements—would not resurrect the old middle class. They would only inhibit the ability of every American to prosper and change. The real solution is to give all Americans a stake in economic growth, to ensure that everyone benefits from our newfound competitiveness. This economy will not be at full capacity until we tap the potential of all our citizens to be more productive.

Individuals and families shoulder much of the responsibility here, of course. Ultimately, they must face the realities of the new economy and ensure that they and their children have the basic intellectual tools to prosper in it. Government has a role, too. It can clear away some of the obstacles—improving the quality of public education, setting skills standards, and smoothing the transition from school to work and from job to job. But individuals, however resourceful, and governments, however reinvented, can't build a new middle class on their own. Business has an indispensable role to play. Unless business joins in a compact to rebuild America's middle class—training and empowering ordinary workers to be productive and innovative—this task cannot succeed.

Discussion Questions

1. What three classes does Reich say compose American society? Describe the living conditions and the resulting attitudes from these conditions generally experienced by each class. How does Reich's classification compare with your own experiences of American society?

2. According to Reich, what benefits is a middle-class college-educated worker more likely to receive than a middle-class high-school graduate? Consider his statistics in relation to Bird's, and discuss their similarities and differences. How do you account for any discrepancies you might notice?

3. What does Reich predict from America's rising economic tide? What evidence from your own experience confirms or contradicts his prediction? What role do you think education should play in our country's economic future?

4. What do the ideas of Reich and Bird have in common? Do you think they would generally agree if they met and discussed America's youth and the future prospects of America? Do you see any potential areas of disagreement between them? Explain.

MARKETING TECHNIQUES GO TO COLLEGE

PENNY SINGER

Penny Singer was a journalist who wrote for the New York Times. *This article was published in the* New York Times *in 1987.*

Can colleges be sold like cars? At one time, academics shuddered at the idea, but times have changed. Faced with shrinking pools of students and rising operating costs, educators are finding that advertising their wares is not only respectable but essential.

Colleges and universities from coast to coast are retaining advertising agencies, and are using some of the most sophisticated marketing techniques available, to help them sell in a buyer's market. For instance, what was formerly known as the Admissions Office is now the Office of Enrollment Management at the College of New Rochelle. "Enrollment management involves not only recruiting students but retaining them as well," says Nancy Haiduck, director of college recruitment. "We have adapted marketing principles and practices to our own needs to attract students."

To attract the undergraduate student most likely to spend four years at the College of New Rochelle, Dr. Joan Baily, Assistant Vice President of Academic Affairs and in charge of enrollment management, says the college has combined traditional methods of recruiting—such as maintaining alumni contacts and sending admissions counselors to college fairs and high schools—with untraditional sophisticated advertising and marketing campaigns. "In our marketing campaigns, we use a lot of direct mail," Dr. Baily says. "By taking a rifle approach, we make mailings only to a predefined target audience. We buy our list from the College Board in Princeton, New Jersey, which charges us about fifteen cents for a name. The success of the direct-mail program depends on the quality and quantity of the mailing list. Returns from direct mail are put in with other inquiries to generate our list." The College Board, which prepares the Scholastic Aptitude Test, is one of the largest suppliers of lists to colleges. It has the names of more than a million high school juniors and seniors who have agreed to have their names placed on a computer roster. About nine hundred colleges nationwide buy the names of high school students from the Student Search Service, a lucrative arm of the College Board.

The College of New Rochelle's direct-mail series includes several brochures with information on and pictures of the college, plus direct-mail letters—including one from the college president, one from the director of financial aid, and a personal letter from the chairmen of various departments. The cost of the recruiting effort, according to Dr. Baily's estimate, is about $1,100 per entering freshman. "That places us in the middle range; the average cost of recruiting a student is $1,300 at most private colleges, even higher for the Ivies," she says, citing statistics from the National Association of Colleges.

However, the recruitment effort pays off in more than one way. "It helps us hold our own with admissions in a declining market," Dr. Baily says, "and, most important, our retention rate is very high. Most of our entering freshmen graduate four years later."

Print advertising plays only a small role in the recruitment efforts of the School of Arts and Science and the School of Nursing, the two undergraduate schools that enroll the eighteen- to twenty-two-year-old students on the New Rochelle campus. "We do use some institutional ads for that market," Dr. Baily says, "but most of our advertising is aimed at adult students for our School of New Resources, which is one of the first in the country designed exclusively for adults, and the graduate school."

A number of factors—such as job opportunities in a time of high employment, and a lack of financial aid—have caused enrollments of adult students to decline, Dr. Baily says, and have prompted the recent advertising campaigns by the College of New Rochelle and others. "We're running ads in tune with the times, with emphasis on promoting course offerings aimed at the out-of-work executive that will lead to a second career and teaching degrees, for those looking for career changes. Teachers are in short supply right now. We do use an advertising agency—Ruder Finn & Rotman in Manhattan. We also do some radio advertising for the School of New Resources."

The communications-information office at Pace University's Pleasantville campus can compare with a small outside advertising agency, billing about $5 million a year. Headed by Frances A. Keegan, the vice president for university communications, the department, with forty full-time employees, works with a budget of $3.5 million a year for publications and marketing of the three Pace undergraduate schools and its six graduate schools. Ms. Keegan, who is aided by Herbert Falk, director of information, represents a new breed of university vice president: the marketing professional. Formerly vice president in charge of advertising for the Book of the Month Club, Ms. Keegan, a direct-mail marketing specialist, worked for one of the leading advertising agencies in the field, Wunderman, Ricotta & Kline, for a number of years before she was recruited by the Book-of-the-Month Club. "I came to Pace eight years ago" she says, "originally as a trustee who was asked to help reorganize the university's marketing effort. Then I stayed on as a full-time employee."

According to Ms. Keegan, the competition for students is keen among colleges in the area. "Our chief rivals are Fordham, Iona, St. John's, and the State University of New York at Purchase," she says, "and according to a recent newsletter, the years 1989 and 1990 will be extremely difficult for recruiting; the supply of potential students will hit rock bottom owing to the low birth rate of eighteen years before."

The Pace Communications Office is busy year-round. The first in a series of five mailings to high school students for the freshman class of 1988 was made on November 18, Ms. Keegan says. The College Board is the major supplier of names of high school students to Pace, she says. "We also make mailings for our graduate schools; some 50,000 pieces go to 9,500 adults every year," she says. "We consult with advisers, professors, and deans in each of the graduate schools to get us 'psychographic' profiles of the type of student most likely to be recruited. Then we buy the specially targeted names from a list broker we have under contract. For instance, for the law school we get the names of prelaw students from 2,000 colleges."

The psychographic profile is a refinement of the demographic profile, Ms. Keegan explains, and is especially valuable for use in retaining students. "The more you know about a prospective student, the more successful the retention effort." In addition, Mr. Falk says, "It's one thing to get incoming freshmen, another thing to have outgoing seniors." Achieving that result "is what is meant by enrollment management."

Applications for 1988 at the Pace campuses are up, Ms. Keegan says. "Direct-mail efforts have paid off, judging from the number of inquiries we're getting. Nevertheless, it's hard to estimate how many applications will result in matriculating students. But if we can gauge by demand for dormitory space, which is running surprisingly strong, we should more than hold our own next year in the undergraduate college." With the exception of the Pace Law School in White Plains, which Ms. Keegan says is still getting ample numbers of applications, the numbers of adults returning to school has dropped steadily since 1982, a peak year. "We've earmarked a budget of over a million dollars for advertising to the adult market primarily," she says. "AC&R, a division of Saatchi and Saatchi, handles our newspaper and radio advertising campaign. Adults make the decision to enroll in a particular school fairly quickly. They respond to good advertising."

Discussion Questions

1. What is the answer Penny Singer expects to the rhetorical question she uses to open her essay? How useful, effective, or attention-grabbing do you find her analogy to be?

2. Rampell and Bird mention similar connections; Construct a comparison chart using Reeves, Rampell, and Bird and discuss your findings.

3. As a prospective student, choose from the following advertisements the ones that would have appealed to you the most and the least. Explain the reasons for your selections.

4. In what way does Singer's argument support Bird's? How might Bird respond to college ads such as the ones below?

College Advertisements

Below are some college ads. Examine them carefully and see what messages—directly and indirectly—are contained in their images and text. How are they attempting to "sell" a college degree to prospective students and their parents and families?

Virginia Intermont College

Assignment #6
___

"THE PROTESTANT WORK ETHIC: JUST ANOTHER 'URBAN LEGEND'?"

This assignment focuses on the subject of work and its place in our lives. As you explore the reading selections in this unit, note the definitions of work each one presents, and the importance each places on work. Think about the work you do in your life, perhaps in a paid job, in your dedication to your studies, at home, or in playing a sport or a musical instrument. You will have to decide how you will define work and how you will evaluate it in your life.

Begin by carefully reading the lead reading selection, "The Protestant Work Ethic: Just Another 'Urban Legend'?"—we recommend that you read it more than once—and pay attention to Klemens's definition of work and the position he takes on it. Also note the kinds of evidence he uses to support his position, and decide just how compelling you find his argument overall. Then, look carefully at the writing topic that follows it, and spend some time thinking about how you might respond. If you don't yet know what position you want to take, your ideas will develop as you move through the writing process using the activities pages that follow Klemens's essay. The group of reading selections that you will find at the end of the unit will be helpful, too, as you work out your own views and try to formulate a thesis statement and supporting evidence for your position.

THE PROTESTANT WORK ETHIC: JUST ANOTHER "URBAN LEGEND"?

JONATHAN KLEMENS

Jonathan Klemens is a practicing pharmacist currently serving as clinical pharmacist at CVS/Caremark. In the past, he has been a pharmacy instructor and a director of pharmacy. Also a writer, he has published many essays, articles, and works of fiction. The essay below was first published on eZine *in 2008.*

"Hi Ho! Hi Ho! It's off to work we go!" Like the words in the Disney cartoon melody, every day some people merrily trek to a job they apparently enjoy. Are these people misguided social dwarfs out of synch with the rest of the workforce? Even though we often give lip service to the work ethic, it really does exist, and it is stronger than one might expect. Frank Lloyd Wright, the famous twentieth-century architect, stated, "I know the price of success: dedication, hard work, and an unremitting devotion to the things you want to see happen."[1]

The work ethic is personified by those who have found work that provides both a service to society and personal satisfaction. It is their passion—their life calling. Our calling can follow any career path—writer, accountant, missionary, teacher, auto mechanic, carpenter, cook, social worker, attorney, or brain surgeon. It takes commitment and hard work, but we enjoy it and it feels like the right fit. We may actually become so intensively involved and committed that our calling becomes one with the company or organization's mission. Encompassing centuries, this commitment and dedication to hard work has been exemplified in such societies as the Amish, Mennonites, Hutterites, and Shakers. The Shaker phrase attributed to Mother Ann Lee, the founder of the Shaker sect—"Put your hands to work, and your hearts to God"—encourages a simple life of hard work and spirituality. We might also identify with Ben Franklin, who espoused his philosophy of avarice and a strong work ethic.

How could this concept of a work ethic develop and endure in a society where the concept of entitlement now seems to be so prevalent? The roots begin with Max Weber, one of the leading founders of modern sociology, and his renowned work on modern social science, *The Protestant Ethic and the Spirit of Capitalism.* In the 1930s, after the book was translated into English, the US workforce began its ongoing love affair with the work ethic—a social trait that would become the backbone of American enterprise and world leadership. The arduous work of capitalism, according to Weber, is closely associated with intrinsic Protestant religious beliefs and behavior. He states, "However, all the peculiarities of Western capitalism have derived their significance in the last analysis only from their association with the capitalistic organization of labor."[2] Only in the West has rationalization in science, law, and culture developed to the extent where political, technical, and economic conditions depend on highly trained government officials.

Historically, certain Protestant denominations had a strong influence on the members' development of business acumen and the ethic of hard work. These Protestants developed a sense of economic rationalism that emphasized diligent and dedicated work. Each and every Sunday, Methodist and Presbyterian ministers extolled the virtues of the work ethic to their congregations through lengthy and tedious sermons. According to Weber, the following traits characterize a strong work ethic:

- Focus on Work
  We know how precious our time is and that it is limited. We must have a passion and must strive for excellence in our work. Work time should be used efficiently and wisely with a desire to make money as a fruit of our labor and not spend it irresponsibly.

- Unpretentious and Modest Comportment
  We should act and dress appropriately—dress should not be flashy to attract attention or cause distraction to others.

- Honesty and Ethics
  One should possess and exhibit strong ethical beliefs and a moral code of behavior, i.e., the Ten Commandments. We must do the "right thing" when no one is watching.[3]

The power of a free labor force has made capitalism a very powerful force in our society. Riding high on the wave of post-WWII patriotism and intense business competition, we became rightfully proud of our fast-growing economy and the image of hardworking Americans. We take pride in who we were and what we produce as a nation, the greatest and most successful nation on earth. Although the original religious aspects eventually faded, the work ethic is firmly entrenched as a powerful and valued American social trait.

Unquestionably, we do not desire a workforce dominated by mindless "robots" even with a good work ethic. We need innovative thinkers and committed leaders that can guide us through the twenty-first-century and beyond. It is essential that we continue to build a strong labor force committed to an indomitable work ethic—workers that are honest, ethical, and rational. We also need leaders that will not be afraid to work and who will take the responsibility to guide new projects and develop employee potential to exceed projected goals. We need people passionate about a mission. A good work ethic is essential to a strong economy and a strong vibrant society.

Notes:

[1]ThinkExist.com Quotations Online 1 Jan. 2011. 2 Feb. 2011 http://thinkexist.com/quotes/frank_lloyd_wright/

[2]Weber, Max. *The Protestant Ethic and the Spirit of Capitalism.* BN Publishing, 2008, p. 22.

[3]Weber 35.

Writing Topic

Explain Klemens's definition of the American work ethic. Do you agree with his claim that this work ethic is "firmly entrenched as a powerful and valued American social trait"? Be sure to support your position with specific details taken from your own experiences, the media, your observations of others, and your reading, including the reading selections from this course.

Vocabulary Check

Good writers choose their words carefully so that their ideas will be clear. In order for you to understand Klemens's ideas, it is important to think about the key vocabulary terms and the way he uses them to communicate his argument. Words can have a variety of meanings, or they can have specialized meanings in certain contexts. Look up the definitions of the following words or phrases from "The Protestant Work Ethic: Just Another 'Urban Legend'?" Choose the meaning that you think Klemens intended when he selected that particular word or phrase for use in this reading selection. Then, explain the way the meaning or concept behind the definition is key to understanding Klemens's argument.

1. *unremitting*

   definition: _____

   _____

   explanation: _____

   _____

   _____

   _____

2. *personify*

   definition: _____

   _____

   explanation: _____

   _____

   _____

   _____

3. *espouse*

   definition: _____

   _____

   explanation: _____

   _____

   _____

   _____

4. *prevalent*

definition: _____

_____

explanation: _____

_____

_____

_____

5. *arduous*

definition: _____

_____

explanation: _____

_____

_____

_____

6. *intrinsic*

definition: _____

_____

explanation: _____

_____

_____

_____

7. *derive*

definition: _____

_____

explanation: _____

_____

_____

_____

8. *acumen*

   definition: _____

   _____

   explanation: _____

   _____

   _____

   _____

9. *extoll*

   definition: _____

   _____

   explanation: _____

   _____

   _____

   _____

10. *entrench*

    definition: _____

    _____

    explanation: _____

    _____

    _____

    _____

11. *indomitable*

    definition: _____

    _____

    explanation: _____

    _____

    _____

    _____

Questions to Guide Your Reading

Answer the following questions to gain a thorough understanding of "The Protestant Work Ethic: Just Another 'Urban Legend'?"

Paragraph 1

How do the lyrics from a song from Disney's *Snow White and the Seven Dwarfs* relate to Klemens's view of work?

Paragraph 2

According to Klemens, what qualities are shared by groups and individuals who exhibit a strong work ethic? What do they give to their work, and what does their work give back to them?

Paragraph 3

What are the historical roots of the work ethic, as Klemens presents them? Explain the place the work ethic has in the American economic system.

Paragraph 4

Based on Klemens's essay, identify and explain Max Weber's understanding of what constitutes a strong work ethic.

Paragraph 5

According to Klemens, what kind of a workforce is important both to society and its economy?

Prewriting for a Directed Summary

Now that you have used the questions above to understand "The Protestant Work Ethic: Just Another 'Urban Legend'?" as a whole, use the following questions as a guide to focus your attention on a particular perspective in the essay. This perspective will be important when you are working on your own essay in response to the writing topic for this assignment. Be sure to use the answers you give below when it is time to write a clear and coherent directed summary in response to the writing topic's first question:

> first part of the writing topic:
>
> *Explain Klemens's definition of the American work ethic.*

This first part asks you to explain Klemens's explanation of a particular concept. It doesn't ask you to summarize his entire essay. Be sure to keep two aspects in mind as you construct your answer: you will have to *explain*, not just identify, the meaning of the American work ethic *as Klemens defines it.*

Don't forget to look back to Part 1's "A Review of the Guidelines for Writing a Directed Summary."

Focus Questions

1. What particular behaviors and beliefs developed into the work ethic, according to Klemens?

2. What characteristics does Klemens associate with a strong work ethic?

3. In Klemens's view, how do these traits produce a strong economy and society?

Developing an Opinion and Working Thesis Statement

The second question in the writing topic for "The Protestant Work Ethic: Just Another 'Urban Legend'?" asks you to take a position of your own. Your response will form the thesis statement of your essay, so it is important to spend some time ensuring that what you write is an accurate reflection of the position you want to take on the place of work in people's lives. Use the framework below to develop your working thesis, but keep an open mind as you complete the prewriting pages that follow this one and read the positions other writers take in the essays in the "Extending the Discussion" section of this unit. You may find that, after giving more thought to the idea of work, you want to modify your position.

second part of the writing topic:

> *Do you agree with his claim that this work ethic is "firmly entrenched as a powerful and valued American social trait"?*

Do you agree with Klemens that the work ethic is a pervasive value in the lives of most Americans? As you think about the position you want to take in your working thesis statement, keep in mind that the topic asks you to take a position on whether Klemens's idea of a work ethic is still a dominant American trait. In other words, do Americans *today*—not historically or in the recent past—demonstrate that the work ethic is still valued and continues to shape the way they live? Do notice the writing topic's use of the terms "firmly entrenched," "powerful," and "valued" as you develop your thoughts and decide on the position you will take in your essay.

1. Use the following thesis frame to identify the basic elements of your working thesis statement:
   a. What is the issue of "The Protestant Work Ethic: Just Another 'Urban Legend'?" that the writing topic question asks you to consider?

   _____

   b. What is Klemens's opinion about that issue?

   _____

   c. What is your position on the issue, and will you agree or disagree with Klemens's opinion?

   _____

   _____

   _____

2. Now use the elements you isolated in 1a, b, and c to write a thesis statement. You may have to revise it several times until it captures your idea clearly.

   _____

   _____

Prewriting to Find Support for Your Thesis Statement

The last part of the writing topic asks you to support the position you put forward in your thesis statement. Well-developed ideas are crucial when you are making an argument because you will have to be clear, logical, and thorough if you are to be convincing. As you work through the exercises below, you will generate much of the 4Cs material you will need when you draft your essay's body paragraphs.

You might want to take some time now to go back to Part 1 and review the 4Cs.

last part of the writing topic:

Be sure to support your position with specific details taken from your own experiences, the media, your observations of others, and your reading, including the reading selections from this course.

Complete each section of this prewriting activity; your responses will become the material you will use in the next stage—planning and writing the essay.

1. As you begin to develop your own examples, consider, first, your own work ethic.

    •   How much value do you place on work, and what kinds of work do you think are important? Note that the concept of work doesn't just refer to a particular job. It can also refer to anything that requires a commitment of your time and energy in the completion of a task.

    •   Where and how did you learn the values you have about work? Do you find a value in the many kinds of work you have done?

    •   Do you believe that you already work hard enough, or are you always trying to push yourself to do more? How much of your day, on average, is spent working? Write out your thoughts.

    •   How do you make decisions about scheduling relaxation or fun time into your week? Do you think you have enough relaxation time? Does it intrude on your ability to get your work done? How do you feel about this? Write out your thoughts and try to get a sense of your own commitment to a work ethic.

    •   List or freewrite about personal experiences that involved your friends and your family in regard to work. Can you recall ways that you think demonstrate how strongly they have internalized a work ethic?

Once you've written your ideas, look them over carefully. Try to group your ideas into categories. Then, give each category a label. In other words, cluster ideas that seem to have something in common and, for each cluster, identify that shared quality by giving it a title.

2. The writing topic asks you to consider how influential the work ethic is in American society as a whole, so you will want to broaden your focus to extend beyond you and your family and friends. Individuals in your life may be exceptions to a rule that is more pervasive. List or freewrite about examples from your studies, your readings, and your knowledge of current events.

- Do you see a value placed on work in the training of the young people around you? What observations can you make about that training? Try to include specific examples that demonstrate your ideas.
- Have you observed any people new to this country? How do you think they respond to the culture of work in America? Note one or two specific examples you can use to support your conclusions.
- What message about hard work do we get when we watch or read the news? What do we learn to be especially proud of as Americans? How do young people come to understand what makes a good, successful life? How is that reflected in the media?
- Think about TV shows, movies, ads, music, and books you are familiar with. Do any of them suggest, directly or indirectly, that hard work has value? Spend some time analyzing one or two examples that you think are especially relevant. What messages about work do these examples give us?

Now think about examples of a work ethic in a larger context. What different perceptions of work do you see in others? How does a person's work ethic appear to influence his or her life? Do you think the people you know and observe work hard simply for the benefits of hard work, or do they work hard only because they need money? What specific observations have led you to your impressions? Is the difference in motivation significant? Why? Based on your observations, try to come to a conclusion about how pervasive the work ethic is in the people around you.

Once you've written your ideas, look them over carefully. Try to group your ideas into categories. Then, give each category a label. In other words, cluster ideas that seem to have something in common and, for each cluster, identify that shared quality by giving it a title.

3. Now that you've created topics by clustering your ideas into categories, go through them and pick two or three specific ones to develop in your essay. Make sure that they are relevant to your thesis and that they have enough substance to be compelling to your reader. Then, in the space below, briefly summarize each item.

Hint

Once you've decided which categories and items you will use in your essay, take some time to explain below how each category and its items connect to your thesis statement. You will use these details for the next stage.

Revising Your Thesis Statement

Now that you have spent some time working out your ideas more systematically and developing some supporting evidence for the position you want to take, look again at the working thesis statement you crafted earlier to see if it is still accurate. As your first step, look again at the writing topic and then write your original working thesis on the lines that follow it:

writing topic:

Explain Klemens's definition of the American work ethic. Do you agree with his claim that this work ethic is "firmly entrenched as a powerful and valued American social trait"? Be sure to support your position with specific details taken from your own experiences, the media, your observations of others, and your reading, including the reading selections from this course.

working thesis statement:

_____

_____

Remember that your thesis statement must answer the second question in the writing topic while taking into consideration the writing topic as a whole. The first question in the topic identifies the issue that is up for debate, and the last question reminds you that, whatever position you take on the issue, you must be able to support it with specific examples.

Now that you've completed the prewriting exercises and given the writing topic some extensive and focused thought, you might find that the working thesis statement is no longer an accurate reflection of your ideas and of the position you want to take in your essay. You might need to change only a few words or phrases to correct the problem, but it's possible that the thesis statement must be significantly rewritten. Don't try to force your thoughts to fit a working thesis statement that no longer reflects your beliefs; instead, take some time and make your thesis the best representation of your thoughts. The subject or the claim portion may be unclear, vague, or even inaccurate. Look at your working thesis statement through the eyes of your readers and see if it actually says what you want it to say.

After examining it and completing any necessary revisions, check it one more time by asking yourself the following questions:

a. Does the thesis directly identify Klemens's argument?

b. Do you make clear your opinion about the issue?

c. Is your thesis well punctuated, grammatically correct, and precisely worded?

Write your polished thesis on the lines below and look at it again. Is it strong and interesting?

_____

_____

Planning and Drafting Your Essay

The rough draft of an essay is often the most difficult part of the writing process because this is where you move from exploring and planning to getting your ideas down in a unified, coherent shape. Be sure to begin with an outline because it will give you a basic structure to follow as you try to incorporate all the ideas you have developed in the preceding pages. An outline will also give you a bird's-eye view of your essay and help you spot problems in development or logic.

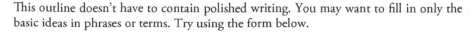

This outline doesn't have to contain polished writing. You may want to fill in only the basic ideas in phrases or terms. Try using the form below.

Creating an Outline for Your Draft

I. **Introductory Paragraph:**

    A. An opening sentence that gives the reading selection's title and author and begins to answer the writing topic question:

    _____

    B. Main points to include in the directed summary:

       1.

       2.

       3.

       4.

       (Continue as necessary.)

    C. Write out your thesis statement. (Look back to "Revising Your Thesis Statement," where you reexamined and refined your working thesis statement.) It should clearly agree or disagree with "The Protestant Work Ethic: Just Another 'Urban Legend'?" and state a clear position using your own words.

II. **Body Paragraphs**

    A. The paragraph's one main point that supports the thesis statement:

    _____

1. Controlling idea sentence:

   _____

   _____

2. Corroborating details:

   _____

   _____

   _____

   _____

3. Careful explanation of why the details are significant:

   _____

   _____

   _____

   _____

4. Connection to the thesis statement:

   _____

   _____

   _____

   _____

B. The paragraph's one main point that supports the thesis statement:

   _____

1. Controlling idea sentence:

   _____

   _____

2. Corroborating details:

   _____

   _____

   _____

   _____

3. Careful explanation of why the details are significant:

_____

_____

_____

_____

4. Connection to the thesis statement:

_____

_____

_____

_____

C. The paragraph's one main point that supports the thesis statement:

_____

1. Controlling idea sentence:

_____

_____

2. Corroborating details:

_____

_____

_____

_____

3. Careful explanation of why the details are significant:

_____

_____

_____

_____

4. Connection to the thesis statement:

_____

_____

_____

_____

D. The paragraph's one main point that supports the thesis statement:

_____

1. Controlling idea sentence:

_____

_____

2. Corroborating details:

_____

_____

_____

_____

3. Careful explanation of why the details are significant:

_____

_____

_____

_____

4. Connection to the thesis statement:

_____

_____

_____

_____

Repeat this form for any remaining body paragraphs.

III. Conclusion

A. Type of conclusion to be used:

_____

B. Key words or phrases to include:

_____

Use the following guidelines to give a classmate feedback on his or her draft. Read the draft through first, and then answer each of the items below as specifically as you can.

Name of draft's author: _____

Name of draft's reader: _____

The Introduction

1. Within the opening sentences,
   a. Klemens is correctly identified by first and last name.   yes   no
   b. the writing selection's title is included and placed within
      quotation marks.   yes   no
2. The opening contains a summary that
   a. explains Klemens's definition of a "work ethic"   yes   no
   b. explains the importance Klemens places on this ethic   yes   no
3. The opening provides a thesis that
   a. offers a concise summary of Klemens's thesis.   yes   no
   b. gives the draft writer's position on the issue.   yes   no

If the answers to #3 above are yes, state the thesis below as it is written. If the answer to one or both of these questions is no, explain to the draft writer what information is needed to make the thesis complete.

_____

_____

_____

The Body

1. How many paragraphs are in the body of this essay? _____
2. To support the thesis, this number is   sufficient   not enough
3. Do paragraphs contain the 4Cs?

Paragraph 1	Controlling idea sentence	yes	no
	Corroborating details	yes	no
	Careful description of why the details are significant	yes	no
	Connection to the thesis statement	yes	no

Paragraph 2	Controlling idea sentence	yes	no
	Corroborating details	yes	no
	Careful description of why the details are significant	yes	no
	Connection to the thesis statement	yes	no
Paragraph 3	Controlling idea sentence	yes	no
	Corroborating details	yes	no
	Careful description of why the details are significant	yes	no
	Connection to the thesis statement	yes	no
Paragraph 4	Controlling idea sentence	yes	no
	Corroborating details	yes	no
	Careful description of why the details are significant	yes	no
	Connection to the thesis statement	yes	no
Paragraph 5	Controlling idea sentence	yes	no
	Corroborating details	yes	no
	Careful description of why the details are significant	yes	no
	Connection to the thesis statement	yes	no

(Continue as needed.)

4. Identify any of the above paragraphs that are underdeveloped (too short). _____

5. Identify any of the above paragraphs that fail to support the thesis. _____

6. Identify any of the above paragraphs that are redundant or repetitive. _____

7. Suggest any ideas for additional paragraphs that might improve this essay.

_____

_____

_____

The Conclusion

1. Does the final paragraph avoid introducing new ideas and examples that really belong in the body of the essay?	yes	no
2. Does the conclusion provide closure (let readers know that the end of the essay has been reached)?	yes	no
3. Does the conclusion leave readers with an understanding of the significance of the argument?	yes	no

4. State in your own words what the draft writer considers to be important about his or her argument.

_____

_____

_____

5. Identify the type of conclusion used (see the guidelines for conclusions in Part 1).

_____

Editing

1. During the editing process, the writer should pay attention to the following problems in sentence structure, punctuation, and mechanics:
   fragments
   misplaced and dangling modifiers
   fused (run-on) sentences
   comma splices
   misplaced, missing, and unnecessary commas
   misplaced, missing, and unnecessary apostrophes
   incorrect quotation mark use
   capitalization errors
   spelling errors

2. While editing, the writer should pay attention to the following areas of grammar:
   verb tense
   subject-verb agreement
   irregular verbs
   pronoun type
   pronoun reference
   pronoun agreement
   noun plurals
   prepositions

Final Draft Checklist

Content

_____ My essay has an appropriate title.

_____ I provide an accurate summary of Klemens's position on the topic presented in "The Protestant Work Ethic: Just Another 'Urban Legend'?"

_____ My thesis states a clear position that can be supported by evidence.

_____ I have enough paragraphs and concrete examples to support my thesis.

_____ Each body paragraph is relevant to my thesis.

_____ Each body paragraph contains the 4Cs.

_____ I use transitions whenever necessary to connect ideas to each other.

_____ The final paragraph of my essay (the conclusion) provides readers with a sense of closure.

Grammar, Punctuation, and Mechanics

_____ I use the present tense to discuss Klemens's argument and examples.

_____ I use verb tenses correctly to show the chronology of events.

_____ I have verb tense consistency throughout my sentences.

_____ I have checked for subject-verb agreement in all of my sentences.

_____ I have revised all fragments and mixed or garbled sentences.

_____ I have repaired all fused (run-on) sentences and comma splices.

_____ I have placed a comma after introductory elements (transitions and phrases) and all dependent clauses that open a sentence.

_____ If I present items in a series (nouns, verbs, prepositional phrases), they are parallel in form.

_____ If I include material spoken or written by someone other than myself, I have correctly punctuated it with quotation marks, using the MLA style guide's rules for citation.

Reviewing Your Graded Essay

After your instructor has returned your essay, you may have the opportunity to revise your paper and raise your grade. Many students, especially those whose essays receive nonpassing grades, feel that their instructors should be less "picky" about grammar and should pass the work on content alone. However, most students at this level have not yet acquired the ability to recognize quality writing, and they do not realize that content and writing actually cannot be separated in this way. Experienced instructors know that errors in sentence structure, grammar, punctuation, and word choice either interfere with content or distract readers so much that they lose track of content. In short, good ideas badly presented are no longer good ideas; to pass, an essay must have passable writing. So, even if you are not submitting a revised version of this essay to your instructor, it is important that you review your work carefully in order to understand its strengths and weaknesses. This sheet will guide you through the evaluation process.

You will want to continue to use the techniques that worked well for you and to find strategies to overcome the problems that you identify in this sample of your writing. In order to help yourself recognize areas that might have been problematic for you, look back at the scoring rubric in this book. Match the numerical/verbal/letter grade received on your essay to the appropriate category. Study the explanation given on the rubric for your grade.

Write a few sentences below in which you identify your problems in each of the following areas. Then, suggest specific changes you could make that would improve your paper. Don't forget to use your handbook as a resource.

1. **Grammar/punctuation/mechanics**
   My problem:

   My strategy for change:

2. **Thesis/response to assignment**
   My problem:

   My strategy for change:

3. Organization
My problem:

My strategy for change:

4. Paragraph development/examples/reasoning
My problem:

My strategy for change:

5. Assessment
In the space below, assign a grade to your paper using a rubric other than the one used by your instructor. In other words, if your instructor assigned your essay a grade of *High Fail*, you might give it the letter grade you now feel the paper warrants. If your instructor used the traditional letter grade to evaluate the essay, choose a category from the rubric in this book, or any other grading scale that you are familiar with, to show your evaluation of your work. Then, write a short narrative explaining your evaluation of the essay and the reasons it received the grade you gave it.

Grade: _____

Narrative: _____

_____

_____

_____

_____

Extending the Discussion:
Considering Other Viewpoints

Readings

"The Magic Number: 32 Hours a Week" by Binyamin Appelbaum
"Vagabonding" by Rolf Potts
"The American Work Ethic" by Peter Kirsanow
"Work in an Industrial Society" by Eric Fromm
"The Ethics of Work-Life Balance" by Bruce Weinstein
"Time Off for the Overworked American" by Courtney E. Martin
"The Importance of Work" by Betty Friedan
"Men at Work" by Anna Quindlen

THE MAGIC NUMBER: 32 HOURS A WEEK

BINYAMIN APPELBAUM

Binyamin Appelbaum is an author and journalist with a focus on business and economics. He earned a BA in history from the University of Pennsylvania. He writes for The New York Times, *having started as a Washington correspondent, and then becoming a member of the editorial board in 2019. His exposés have drawn attention to issues such as housing foreclosures, the subprime mortgage crisis, and the Federal Reserve. His reporting on subprime lending earned him a finalist position for the 2008 Pulitzer Prize in public service. His book* The Economists' Hour *(2019) is a history of the global rise of the economists and the role of their ideas in shaping the modern world's governments and corporations.*

The autoworkers picketing factories across America aren't just seeking higher pay. They are also, audaciously, demanding the end of the standard 40-hour workweek. They want a full week's pay for working 32 hours across four days. And we'll all benefit if they succeed.

Americans spend too much time on the job. A shorter workweek would be better for our health, better for our families, and better for our employers, who would reap the benefits of a more motivated and better-rested work force. Other countries may seek an advantage in the global marketplace by wringing every drop of labor from their workers; American companies have to be more productive, and that means taking better care of their workers.

In 2015, the city of Gothenburg, Sweden, decided to reduce the workweek for 68 nurses at a city-owned elder-care facility. Instead of eight-hour days, the nurses worked for six hours, and the city hired 15 additional nurses to maintain the same level of staffing. As one might expect, the nurses were happier and healthier. The patients were happier and healthier, too.

A growing number of similar experiments by companies in other developed countries have yielded similar results. Working less improves the lives of workers—and it also benefits employers. Of the 61 British firms that participated in a six-month experiment with shorter workweeks last year, 56 decided to let employees continue to work less (1).

While unions have lost much of their power to set standards in the workplace, they can still play a useful role in pioneering changes. The United Auto Workers can establish an example for policymakers to extend to other, nonunion workers through legislation.

Politicians are a cautious bunch when it comes to labor disputes, but President Biden hasn't hesitated to pick a side in the fight between the United Auto Workers and the "Big Three" automakers. On Tuesday, after joining General Motors workers on the picket line in Belleville, Mich., he was asked whether they deserved a 40 percent raise. He said yes (2).

Mr. Biden ought to be equally vocal in supporting the shift to a 32-hour work-week—and not just for those in the auto industry. He ought to back federal legislation redefining the standard week for all hourly workers. Representative Mark Takano, Democrat of California, introduced a 32-hour bill earlier this year. As Mr. Takano has noted, changing the law is particularly important to help blue-collar workers, generally subject to more rigid workplace rules (3).

Though the 40-hour week may feel like an immutable law of nature, it's barely a century old.

American workers fought to establish the eight-hour workday around the turn of the last century, campaigning on the catchy slogan "Eight hours for work, eight hours for rest, eight hours for what you will." But the workweek then was six days long for almost everyone.

In 1922, when Ford became one of the first major employers to commit to a five-day workweek, the announcement made the front page of this newspaper. "'Every man needs more than one day a week for rest and recreation,' said Edsel Ford, the company's president at the time. 'The Ford Company has always sought to promote more time to spend with his family'"(4). It took until 1940 for Congress to legislate a 40-hour week. The law said that hourly employees who worked longer got overtime pay.

The union movement back then had an even shorter week high on its list of priorities. In 1933, the Senate passed a bill establishing a 30-hour standard as part of the great rush of legislation at the beginning of President Franklin Roosevelt's first term. But it went no further, and the 40-hour week soon became conventional.

The revival of the idea partly reflects a shift in societal priorities. Americans have become more protective of their health, more inclined to define themselves in terms of their lives outside work—and perhaps more willing to accept leisure as a substitute for higher pay.

Also, there is less work to go around. In a famous 1930 essay, the British economist John Maynard Keynes predicted that by 2030, people would work only 15 hours a week because technological progress would reduce the amount of labor required to meet people's wants and needs (5). Keynes greatly underestimated both the will to work and the human capacity to want more stuff. But he wasn't entirely wrong. The share of Americans who work has been in decline for decades, and while workers still log long hours, the reality of many jobs is better captured by *The Office* than, say, *The Jungle*.

People need time for rest and "what you will," but they still need jobs, too. Work is not just a source of income; it is an essential part of what it means to be human. A shorter workweek would distribute the available opportunities among more people. At the moment, with unemployment low and many employers struggling to find enough workers, that may not seem like an advantage. But as technological progress continues to reduce or eliminate some kinds of work, it makes sense to share what is left.

It would be fitting for Ford and its workers to once again take the first step into the future.

Works Cited

1. https://static1.squarespace.com/static/60b956cbe7bf6f2efd86b04e/t/63f3df5627
6b3e6d7870207e/1676926845047/UK-4-Day-Week-Pilot-Results-Report-2023.
pdf
2. https://www.nytimes.com/2023/09/26/us/politics/biden-uaw-strike-picket-michi-
gan.html
3. https://takano.house.gov/newsroom/press-releases/
congressman-takano-reintroduces-32-hour-workweek-act
4. https://www.nytimes.com/1922/03/25/archives/5day-40hour-week-for-ford-
employes-new-permanent-working-policy.html
5. https://www.aspeninstitute.org/wp-content/uploads/files/content/upload/Intro_
and_Section_I.pdf

Discussion Questions

1. According to Binyamin Appelbaum, in what ways do workers benefit from a 32-hour work week? Explain his claim that a shorter work week benefits the employers as well.

2. Trace the history of the 40-hour workweek in this country. Identify a country that you are acquainted with or have heard about where the workers usually spend more days and/or longer hours at their job. Tell why you believe that these workers are less, equally, or more productive than American workers.

3. Discuss Appelbaum's example of the Swedish nurses. To what degree did his example help convince you of the validity of his thesis? Do you think their work schedule should be implemented in all American hospitals? Why?

4. Review the other readings in this unit. Choose two of them to discuss in terms of their support or contradiction of Appelbaum's argument.

VAGABONDING

Rolf Potts

Rolf Potts is an American author and travel writer. He earned a degree in writing and literature from George Fox University, and he has published two books, Vagabonding: An Uncommon Guide to the Art of Long-Term World Travel *(2003) and* Marco Polo Didn't Go There *(2008). His numerous articles have appeared in a variety of prestigious publications, including* The New Yorker, National Geographic, *the* New York Times Magazine, The Nation, *and* The Atlantic. *The following reading selection is from his book* Vagabonding.

Ironically, the best litmus test for measuring your vagabonding gumption is found not in travel but in the process of earning your freedom to travel. Earning your freedom, of course, involves work—and work is intrinsic to vagabonding for psychic reasons as much as financial ones.

To see the psychic importance of work, one need look no further than people who travel the world on family money. Sometimes referred to as "trustafarians," these folks are among the most visible and least happy wanderers in the travel milieu. Draping themselves in local fashions, they flit from one exotic travel scene to another, compulsively volunteering in local political causes, experimenting with exotic intoxicants, and dabbling in every non-Western religion imaginable. Talk to them, and they'll tell you they're searching for something "meaningful."

What they're really looking for, however, is the reason why they started traveling in the first place. Because they never worked for their freedom, their travel experiences have no personal reference—no connection to the rest of their lives. They are spending plenty of time and money on the road, but they never spent enough of themselves to begin with. Thus, their experience of travel has a diminished sense of value.

Thoreau touches on this same notion in *Walden*. "Which would have advanced the most at the end of a month," he posits, "the boy who had made his own jackknife from the ore which he had dug and smelted, reading as much as would be necessary for this—or the boy who had . . . received a Rodgers' penknife from his father? Which would be most likely to cut his fingers?"

At a certain level, the idea that freedom is tied to labor might seem a bit depressing. It shouldn't be. For all the amazing experiences that await you in distant lands, the "meaningful" part of travel always starts at home, with a personal investment in the wonders to come.

"I don't like work," says Marlow in Joseph Conrad's *Heart of Darkness*, "but I like what is in the work—the chance to find yourself." Marlow isn't referring to vagabonding, but the notion still applies. Work is not just an activity that generates funds and creates desire; it's the vagabonding gestation period, wherein you earn your integrity, start making plans, and get your proverbial act together. Work is a time to dream about travel and write notes to yourself, but it's also the time to tie up your loose ends. Work is when you confront the problems you might otherwise be tempted to run away from. Work is how you settle your financial *and* emotional debts—so that your travels are not an escape from your real life but a *discovery* of your real life.

On a practical level, there are countless ways to earn your travels. On the road, I have met vagabonders of all ages, from all backgrounds and walks of life. I've met secretaries, bankers, and policemen who've quit their jobs and are taking a peripatetic pause before starting something new. I've met lawyers, stockbrokers, and social workers who have negotiated months off as they take their careers to new locations. I've met talented specialists—waiters, Web designers, strippers—who find they can fund months of travel on a few weeks of work. I've met musicians, truck drivers, and employment counselors who are taking extended time off between gigs. I've met semiretired soldiers and engineers and businessmen who've reserved a year or two for travel before dabbling in something else. Some of the most prolific vagabonders I've met are seasonal workers—carpenters, park service workers, commercial fishermen—who winter every year in warm and exotic parts of the world. Other folks—teachers, doctors, bartenders, journalists—have opted to take their very careers on the road, alternating work and travel as they see fit.

Of all the antisabbaticals that funded my travels, however, no experience was quite as vivid as the two years I spent teaching English in Pusan, South Korea. In addition to learning tons about Asian social customs through my work, I discovered that the simple act of *walking to work* was itself an exercise in possibility. On a given day in Korea, I was equally likely to be greeted by a Buddhist monk wearing Air Jordans as I was by a woman in a stewardess uniform handing out promotional toilet tissue. I eventually stopped noticing such details as children screaming "hello," old men urinating in public, and vegetable-truck loud-speakers blasting "Edelweiss." After two years on the job, I actually found myself fighting boredom as I crooned "California Dreaming" with my salaryman tutees and a roomful of miniskirted seventeen-year-old karaoke "hostesses." And on top of all this, the pay was pretty good.

However you choose to fund your travel freedom, keep in mind that your work is an active part of your travel attitude. Even if your antisabbatical job isn't your life's calling, approach your work with a spirit of faith, mindfulness, and thrift. In such a manner, Thoreau was able to meet all his living expenses at Walden Pond by working just six weeks a year. Since vagabonding is more involved than freelance philosophizing, however, you might have to invest a bit more time in scraping together your travel funds.

Regardless of how long it takes to earn your freedom, remember that you are laboring for more than just a vacation.

A vacation, after all, merely rewards work. Vagabonding justifies it.

Ultimately, then, the first step of vagabonding is simply a matter of making work serve your interests, instead of the other way around. Believe it or not, this is a radical departure from how most people view work and leisure.

Discussion Questions

1. Discuss the relationship Rolf Potts identifies between work and travel. How are they connected? Why does he believe those with family money miss out on this connection? Do you think it is possible to be independently wealthy and still be a vagabond? Why?

2. How specifically does Potts explain the tie between freedom and labor? What are some of the examples he gives of ways people earned the chance to become a vagabond? Why does the idea of leaving your future chosen profession for a lengthy amount of time to wander appeal or not appeal to you?

3. Why do you the the time Potts spent in Korea on what he calls an "antisabbatical" was more like labor or vagabonding?

4. In what ways does Potts's attitude run counter to the Protestant work ethic? In what ways do you think his actions support it?

5. Discuss Potts's decision not to include a list of his outside references. Why do you think he made this decision, and do you agree with it? Explain.

THE AMERICAN WORK ETHIC

Peter Kirsanow

Peter N. Kirsanow received his BA from Cornell University and his JD from Cleveland State University's Cleveland-Marshall College of Law, where he also acted as articles editor of the Cleveland State Law Review, *a scholarly journal focusing on legal scholarship and research. He is a practicing attorney, a partner in a law firm, and a member of the US Commission on Civil Rights. In addition, he served on the National Labor Relations Board from 2006 to 2008. This 2013 article was published in the* National Review Online *in the magazine's blog, called* The Corner.

For more than a century, much of the world has marveled at the American work ethic and American productivity. How long will that continue?

Probably like most *Corner* readers, as a kid, when I wasn't in school, I worked. Starting at age five, I began doing yard work and odd jobs for neighbors and local businesses. When I got a bit older, I got summer and after-school jobs (the latter when not involved in sports). Obviously, I had no skills, so most of the jobs involved manual labor, much of it fairly arduous.

On the occasions when I couldn't find a job, I became self-employed—painting houses, digging trenches, mowing lawns, putting up fences. Almost all of my friends had jobs or were self-employed also. Not working was a source of deep embarrassment. Once, the summer after eighth grade, I had no work for maybe one to two weeks, and not for lack of effort (we typically began lining up summer jobs the preceding October and November). One of my best friends chided me for "being on welfare." The statement stung so much—so profound was the stigma of not working—that we almost came to blows.

Is that changing? An observation: When I bought my house years back, two neighborhood boys appeared almost instantly to rake leaves, cut grass, paint the tool shed, and so on. They worked hard and well—both after school and during breaks. When they moved away, another boy performed some of the same work for about a year.

For the last twenty years, however, no one's asked to do any work, even though it's clear to anyone in the neighborhood there's work to be had. I've sought kids out who, it's plain to see, have no jobs, but I have been largely unsuccessful. For example, I recently asked two teenage boys who'd spent most of the summer playing basketball at a nearby playground if they wanted to earn some cash doing some yard work. They promised to come over on the following Saturday morning, but when Saturday arrived, they didn't arrive or call. I tried again the next week, received more promises, but again, no call, no show.

I've heard similar stories in recent years from lots of friends and employers. Yes, several anecdotes don't amount to statistical evidence, and I encounter hardworking kids all the time. But the *expectation*, the *presumption* of hard work doesn't appear to be anywhere near as pervasive as in the past.

Is it more likely or less likely that this phenomenon will persist (or perhaps get worse) when much of the major media and an entire political party drive a narrative that productive Americans aren't "paying their fair share"; when a president lauds a twenty-six-year-old's ability to stay on his parents' insurance plan; when nearly fifty million Americans access food stamps benefits with a slick-looking card; when unemployment benefits continue interminably; when government encourages citizens to access "free" benefits; when stigma or shame attaches almost as readily to the productive as the nonproductive?

Discussion Questions

1. According to Peter Kirsanow, how does the rest of the world view America in terms of work habits and the results they produce? Discuss the work ethic in the community where you grew up, whether here in the United States or elsewhere.

2. From his experiences and those of his friends, how does he think American children have changed in their attitude towards work? What specific personal examples have led him to his conclusion? Explain why you think that the anecdotes on which he bases his conclusion are sufficient or insufficient to warrant such a conclusion. Relate an anecdote of your own that supports or contradicts his conclusion.

3. Who does the author feel is at least partially responsible for the changing attitude toward work? What specifics does he point out as evidence? What concerns do you think Klemens would have about the effect of these things on America's future?

WORK IN AN INDUSTRIAL SOCIETY

ERICH FROMM

Erich Fromm was born in Germany and trained as a psychoanalyst in Berlin. He taught at Yale and Columbia and became a well-known psychoanalyst and writer. The following essay is adapted from his book The Sane Society *(1955).*

Craftsmanship, especially as it developed in the thirteenth and fourteenth centuries, constitutes one of the peaks in the evolution of creative work in Western history. During the Middle Ages, the Renaissance, and the eighteenth century, work was not only a useful activity, but one which carried with it a profound satisfaction. The main features of craftsmanship as it existed before the Industrial Revolution have been very lucidly expressed by C. W. Mills:

> There is no ulterior motive in work other than the product being made and the processes of its creation. The details of daily work are meaningful because they are not detached in the worker's mind from the product of the work. The worker is free to control his own working action. The craftsman is thus able to learn from his work; and to use and develop his capacities and skills in its prosecution. There is no split of work and play, or work and culture. The craftsman's way of livelihood determines and infuses his entire mode of living. (220)

By contrast, what happens to the industrial worker today, in 1955? He spends his best energy for seven or eight hours a day in producing "something." He needs his work in order to make a living, but his role is essentially a passive one. He fulfills a small, isolated function in a complicated and highly organized process of production, and is never confronted with "his" product as a whole—at least not as a producer, but only as a consumer, provided he has the money to buy "his" product in a store. He is concerned neither with the whole product in its physical aspects nor with its wider economic and social aspects. He is put in a certain place, has to carry out a certain task, but does not participate in the organization or management of the work. He is not interested in, nor does he know, why he produces this commodity instead of another one—what relation it has to the needs of society as a whole. The shoes, the cars, the electric bulbs, are produced by "the enterprise," using the machines. He is part of the machine, rather than its master as an active agent.

For today's industrial worker, work is a means of getting money, not in itself a meaningful human activity. P. Drucker, observing workers in the automobile industry, expresses this idea very succinctly:

> For the great majority of automobile workers, the only meaning of the job is in the pay check, not in anything connected with the work or the product. Work appears as something unnatural, a disagreeable, meaningless, and stultifying condition of getting the pay check, devoid of dignity as well as of importance.

No wonder that this puts a premium on slovenly work, on slowdowns, and on other tricks to get the same pay check with less work. No wonder that this results in an unhappy and discontented worker—because a pay check is not enough to base one's self-respect on. (179)

The alienated and profoundly unsatisfactory character of modern industrial work results in two reactions: one, the ideal of complete laziness; the other, a deep-seated, though often unconscious, hostility toward work and everything and everybody connected with it.

It is not difficult to recognize the widespread longing for the state of complete laziness and passivity. Our advertising appeals to it even more than to sex. There are, of course, many useful and labor-saving gadgets. But this usefulness often serves only as a rationalization for their appeal to complete passivity and receptivity. A package of breakfast cereal is advertised as "new—easier to eat." An electronic toaster is advertised with these words: "the most distinctly different toaster in the world! Everything is done for you with this new toaster. You need not even bother to lower the bread. Power-action, through a unique electric motor, gently takes the bread right out of your fingers!" Everybody knows the picture of the elderly couple in an advertisement of a life-insurance company, who have retired at the age of sixty, and spend their life in the complete bliss of having nothing to do except just travel.

But there is a far more serious and deep-seated reaction to the meaninglessness and boredom of work. It is hostility toward work that is much less conscious than our craving for laziness and inactivity. Many a businessman feels himself the prisoner of his business and the commodities he sells; he has a feeling of fraudulence about his product and a secret contempt for it. He hates his customers, who force him to put up a show in order to sell. He hates his competitors because they are a threat; he hates his employees as well as his superiors because he is in a constant competitive fight with them. Most important of all, he hates himself because he sees his life passing by without making any sense beyond the momentary intoxication of success. Of course, this hate and this contempt—for others and for oneself, and for the very things one produces—are mainly unconscious. Only occasionally do these feelings come up to awareness in a fleeting thought that is sufficiently disturbing to be set aside as quickly as possible.

Works Cited

Drucker, Peter. *Concept of the Corporation*. New York: The John Day Company, 1946. Print.

Mills, C. Wright. *White Collar: The American Middle Classes*. 1951. New York: Oxford UP, 2002.

Discussion Questions

1. According to Fromm, in what ways did the relationship between worker, work, and product differ during preindustrial times from what it was in Fromm's day (1955)? Do you think he may be idealizing the past? Explain your answer. Give your assessment of the relationship that exists today between worker and work.

2. What two reactions does Fromm suggest are the result of performing work in an industrialized society? Relate examples in which you demonstrated one of these reactions yourself or were the recipient of behavior resulting from one of these reactions.

3. Explain the differences in the relationships between workers and work in the discussions of Fromm and Klemens. How would what Klemens calls a "strong work ethic" alter the way the automobile factory workers, observed by Drucker, see themselves and their work?

THE ETHICS OF WORK-LIFE BALANCE

BRUCE WEINSTEIN

Bruce Weinstein received a BA from Swarthmore College and a PhD from Georgetown University. From 2006 to 2012, he contributed to Bloomberg Businessweek's *online edition, which also posted his twelve-episode series* Ask the Ethics Guy. *He is now a blogger at the* Huffington Post *and is a professional public speaker, lecturing on ethics and leadership. His latest book,* Ethical Intelligence, *was published in 2011. The essay below appeared on* Bloomberg Businessweek *in 2009.*

We are a nation in pain. According to a March 12 Gallup poll, the number of people in this country classified as "suffering" has increased by three million over the past year. Managers and business owners experienced the greatest loss of well-being; 60.8% of businesses were thriving in the first quarter of 2008, but this number decreased by almost 14% by the fourth quarter. Given the difficult economic climate and the number of jobs being lost daily, most of us are feeling the pressure to work harder than ever. But in spite of the increasing intensity of our economic crisis, it is not only unfortunate to give in to such pressure. It's unethical.

It's not too late to make a change for the better, though.

It may seem misplaced to discuss work-life balance in a column about ethics. But recall that one of five fundamental ethical principles is fairness, and that we demonstrate fairness in everyday life by how we allocate scarce resources. The most precious commodity you have is time, both in your professional and your personal life. It's also your most critical nonrenewable resource. As a manager, you must constantly ask yourself how you should allocate your time. You know it's wrong to spend so much time on one project at the expense of equally critical ones, or to spend so much time managing one employee that you're unable to manage others.

But a good manager should be, first and foremost, a good human being. Just as managing your career well means allocating your time wisely among the different projects and people you oversee, managing your life wisely means giving due time not just to work but to family, friends, community, self, and spirit. You wouldn't think of spending most of your work day talking with one client on the phone. Why, then, is it okay to devote so much time to your job when you don't give non-work-related things the attention they deserve?

Ethics isn't just about how you treat others. It's also about how you treat yourself—at work and beyond. You're not being fair to others and yourself if you haven't had a vacation in a long time, or if you force yourself to work when you've got the flu. You're also not being fair to others and yourself if you spend so much time being a good manager that you're not able to be a good parent, spouse, or friend. And let's face it: You can't do your job to the best of your ability if you're thoroughly exhausted, and that's not fair to your coworkers or your employer. But working to the exclusion of all else isn't just unfair (and thus unethical). It's also tragic, because the time you spend away from the other meaningful relationships in your life is time you can never get back.

Let's now look at some of the common excuses people give for working so much and how to get beyond them.

"I want to make sure I keep my job."

More than 2.5 million jobs were lost in 2008, and the losses continue to mount. What could be wrong with working all the time in such a climate if it will mean hanging onto your job? Speaking of ethics, isn't there an ethical obligation to keep your job? After all, what would be ethical about not paying bills, or your mortgage, or not being able to take care of your family?

Of course it's important to remain an employee in good standing. But you shouldn't assume that there is a direct correlation with the number of hours you work and the likelihood that you'll hold onto your job. Downsizing is largely a function of economics rather than of job performance; companies are letting people go to cut their losses and hit budget targets. (And yes, letting go of good employees raises other ethical issues, but that deserves its own column.) Working twelve-hour days six or seven days a week isn't going to guard against getting downsized.

In fact, it could even backfire. You might look like someone who can't manage his or her time or isn't up to the responsibilities of the job. And if you work without any letup, you will reach the point of diminishing returns. This isn't a time to be less than a stellar employee, but working overtime won't get you there.

"I need to work more to make what I did last year."

Many of the recently downsized are taking lower-paying jobs because that's all that is available. Some are even taking second jobs and still not making what they did a year ago. But how important is it now to live in the manner to which you have become accustomed? It's one thing to have to work seventy hours a week just to put food on the table and pay the rent or mortgage. It's another to work so much to be able to afford lavish trips, expensive clothes, or a certain lifestyle. Instead of working longer, couldn't you shift your priorities so that you're able to spend more time with family and friends, exercise more often, or even just read some of those books you've been thinking about?

"I have a demanding job."

Gone are the days when leaving your office meant leaving work behind. Many of us choose to use our BlackBerrys, iPhones, laptops, and social networking sites to remain constantly available to our bosses, clients, and colleagues, but this can get out of control. It's flattering to believe that you're indispensable to your company, and that only you can do the work you spend so much time doing. This is rarely true, however painful that may be to accept. Be honest with yourself: Are you spending so much time on the job because you must, or because of habit, ego, or some other reason? We owe it to ourselves and the people we care about (and who care about us) to work smarter, not harder.

"I just love to work."

It's a blessing to be able to say this, but all passions should have limits. A fully human life is a life in balance, and that means giving due time to all of the things that enrich us, fulfill us, and make our lives worth living. When Freud said that work and love were essential components of a happy life, he didn't mean that these were one and the same thing.

There is a time to work and a time to leave work behind. The good manager leaves time to do both.

Works Cited

Adkins, Amy. "U.S. Employee Engagement Dips in March." *Gallup*. April 9, 2015. http://news.gallup.com/poll/182357/employee-engagement-dips-march.aspx

Discussion Questions

1. On what basis does Bruce Weinstein claim that we are "a nation in pain"? From what he and other authors you have read in this unit have to say, offer what evidence you can find to support his statement.

2. From your own experiences and observations, in real life and the media, provide a detailed example of one individual's overcommitment to work and the effects on the people around him or her.

3. What principle of ethics does Weinstein apply to overwork? How does he believe Americans are being unethical in this regard? Discuss his assessment of the excuses and their validity that people give for violating this principle. Explain how one or more of the characteristics of a strong work ethic, which are detailed in Klemens's essay, are being violated by the unethical work behavior that concerns Weinstein.

4. How might Klemens respond to Weinstein?

TIME OFF FOR THE OVERWORKED AMERICAN

COURTNEY E. MARTIN

Courtney E. Martin received a BA in political science and sociology from Barnard College and earned an MA in writing and social change from New York University's Gallatin School of Individualized Study. Her latest book, Do It Anyway: The New Generation of Activists *(2010), focuses on Martin's main passion, social change. She has written many articles for various publications, including the* New York Times, *the* Washington Post, *and the* American Prospect, *whose online division published the article below in 2007. In addition, she is an accomplished public speaker who often addresses issues of body image and youth, also the focus of her first book.*

Remember riding hip to hip with your brothers and sisters in the back of the family van, eating the snacks too soon, fighting over the music selection, losing tiny, indispensable pieces of travel games? Or maybe your family was not of the road trip ilk. Perhaps you remember exciting trips on airplanes, a special pin from the stewardess, watching the clouds take shape out of your own oval window, your grandparents waiting feverishly for your arrival in the sprawling Portland or Poughkeepsie or even Paris airport. As much as you may have resented it then, the family vacation is as quintessentially American as homemade apple pie. It is also just about as rare in this age of store-bought desserts and workaholism.

Last year, twenty-five percent of American workers got no paid vacation at all, while forty-three percent didn't even take a solid week off. A third fewer American families take vacations together today than they did in 1970. American workers receive the least vacation time among wealthy industrial nations. And it is no thanks to the US government—127 other countries in the world have a vacation law. We—the crackberry denizens and Protestant ethic superstars—do not.

A growing movement of nonprofits, citizen advocacy groups, and trade associations is trying to change all that. Take Back Your Time, a national organization with over ten thousand members, has declared getting a federal vacation law that guarantees Americans at least three week paid vacation a top priority issue in 2007. They are joined by Joe Robinson, author of the 2003 book *Work to Live* and a work/life balance coach, and the Adventure Travel Trade Association, among others.

This is not just a plea for more beach time. It is a movement that recognizes that Americans' lives are diminished by our work-above-all-else orientation. Dissatisfaction with work/life balance cuts across class boundaries, leaving too many Americans feeling estranged from the things they believe are most important—family, friends, well-being, spiritual practice. In what journalist Keith H. Hammonds calls our "postbalance world," most Americans live their lives in unsatisfying feast or famine. Unfortunately, there is more famine when it comes to relaxation, exploration, and rejuvenation these days—no thanks to federal policy. John Schmitt, senior economist and co-author of "No-Vacation Nation," a recent study by the Center for Economic Policy Research, says, "It's a national embarrassment that 28 million Americans don't get any paid vacation or paid holidays."

We don't get much time at home; and at work, we feel significantly unsupported. In the latest Pew Research Center survey on work, a near majority of workers (forty-five percent) now says benefits are worse than they had been twenty or thirty years ago. This includes a gamut of policies—health care, paternity leave, flextime—all of which America is pathetically behind other industrialized countries in legislating. There has certainly been a growing conversation about these issues, thanks to the mothers' movement led by groups like MomsRising, but legislated vacation time is often last on the list of demands. (Not so surprising when you consider how difficult it is for most mothers to believe they deserve a rest.)

Not only does less vacation time mean we have less time to develop our most critical and lasting relationships with family members and friends, but our physical health is in jeopardy when we refuse to unchain ourselves from the cubicle. Vacations cut down on stress, which any medical expert will tell you is at the center of so many of America's most pernicious health crises. Two researchers at the State University of New York at Oswego showed that an annual vacation can cut the risk of death from heart disease in women by fifty percent and in men by thirty-two percent. Taking time out, exploring new horizons, getting away from your desk and moving around, reconnecting with close friends and family are all safeguards against burnout and depression. But this kind of rejuvenation takes time—two weeks, most studies indicate. The average vacation in the United States is now only a long weekend, which just isn't long enough.

Cali Williams Yost, author of the 2005 book *Work+Life: Finding the Fit That's Right for You* and a coach on work/life balance, asserts that it is not just taking vacation that is important, but how we operate while on it that makes the big difference. She advises corporate clients on how to "avoid having technology become the Grinch that Stole Your Christmas (or Hanukkah, or Kwanzaa)" by setting personal goals around technology usage: "We all need to be much more conscious when we go on vacation."

But it's not all about self control; it's also about government control. Why does the government need to get involved? Because in this cutthroat economic environment, vacation—like parental leave—goes the way of the wimp. Even if workers are employed by companies that guarantee vacation time, many of them are afraid to take advantage because they might be seen as slackers. A culture of self-sacrifice has cropped up in so many careers, leaving those who take their full two weeks looking uncommitted and ineffective.

In truth, they are probably *better* employees for taking the time off. Three-week vacations have proven to be a boost to productivity and profits at enlightened American firms where the culture truly supports the practice. Especially in the knowledge economy, clear thinking and a fresh perspective are critical to best practice. How can anyone expect to get the newest ideas and most innovative approaches from workers who get only the occasional weekend getaway, cell phones still permanently attached to their ears?

Some companies are already reporting hard-and-fast evidence of the phenomenon, according to Robinson. Jancoa, a Cincinnati-based cleaning services company, extended its vacation benefits for its 468 employees to three weeks at a total cost of seven cents. Productivity and morale increased so much that the company was able to eliminate overtime and cut its retention and recruiting costs. The H Group, a management firm founded in 1990 and based in Salem, Oregon, has seen profits double since owner Ron Kelemen pushed his three-week vacation program.

The movement rallying around this issue hopes to get vacation law into the 2008 presidential conversation as well. They are framing it not only as a quality of life issue, but as an indispensable ingredient of global competition. The fastest growing economy in the world, China, offers three weeks off, which they call "Golden Weeks."

Robinson quips, "President Bush knows the value of vacation time. He enjoys his trips to his ranch. He ought to be the first to step up and say, 'Send me this bill and I'll sign it.'"

Discussion Questions

1. Compare the vacation time of American workers with that of workers in other wealthy nations. In terms of time off, was the percentage of American workers taking time to go on a family vacation what you expected it to be? Why or why not? Tell about the last time your family went on a vacation together.

2. How does the author feel the lack of sufficient "beach time" is harmful to Americans? Do you think the benefits of less time off outweigh the negatives she raises? Explain your answer.

3. Do you think workers at all jobs should get the same amount of vacation, or do you think the number of vacation days should be determined by seniority or the kind of work the person does? Justify your answer.

4. Do you think the Protestant work ethic Klemens discusses is responsible for creating a society of overworked Americans? Do you think, as Martin does, that Americans are unwilling to take time away from their jobs? Why? Consider the way many Japanese companies arrange group vacations for their workers. Do you think American companies should institute practices to encourage their employees to take a vacation?

5. Notice that, although this article is filled with assertions and statistics, Martin does not cite the outside references he has used as the basis for the information he provides. If you wanted to verify some of this information for your own research, would you be able to track down Martin's sources? How does this affect the credibility of his argument? If you were his editor, would you bring this to his attention? Explain your response.

THE IMPORTANCE OF WORK

BETTY FRIEDAN

Betty Friedan (1921–2006) was one of the founders of the National Organiza-
tion for Women. She attended Smith College, graduating with a degree in psy-
chology, and did graduate study at the University of California, Berkeley. Friedan
is a well-known feminist, public speaker, and writer whose essays have appeared
in numerous periodicals. Her books include It Changed My Life *(1976),* The
Second Stage *(1981), and* The Feminine Mystique *(1963), which many*
attribute to starting the "second wave" of the feminist movement and which is
excerpted below.

The question of how a person can most fully realize his own capacities and thus achieve
identity has become an important concern of the philosophers and the social and psychological thinkers of our time—and for good reason. Thinkers of other times put forth
the idea that people were, to a great extent, defined by the work they did. The work that
a man had to do to eat, to stay alive, to meet the physical necessities of his environment,
dictated his identity. And in this sense, while work was seen merely as a means of survival, human identity was dictated by biology.

But today the problem of human identity has changed. For the work that defined
man's place in society and his sense of himself has also changed man's world. Work,
and the advance of knowledge, has lessened man's dependence on his environment; his
biology and the work he must do for biological survival are no longer sufficient to define
his identity. This can be most clearly seen in our own abundant society; men no longer
need to work all day to eat. They have an unprecedented freedom to choose the kind
of work they will do; they also have an unprecedented amount of time apart from the
hours and days that must actually be spent in making a living. And suddenly one realizes
the significance of today's identity crisis—for women, and increasingly, for men. One
sees the human significance of work—not merely as the means of biological survival,
but as the giver of self and the transcender of self, as the creator of human identity and
human evolution.

For "self-realization" or "self-fulfillment" or "identity" does not come from looking into a mirror in rapt contemplation of one's own image. Those who have most fully
realized themselves, in a sense that can be recognized by the human mind even though
it cannot be clearly defined, have done so in the service of a human purpose larger than
themselves. Men from varying disciplines have used different words for this mysterious
process from which comes the sense of self. The religious mystics, the philosophers,
Marx, Freud—all had different names for it: Man finds himself by losing himself; man
is defined by his relation to the means of production; the ego, the self, grows through
understanding and mastering reality through work and love.

The identity crisis, which has been noted by Erik Erikson and others in recent years in the American man, seems to occur for lack of, and be cured by finding, the work, or cause, or purpose that evokes his own creativity. Some never find it, for it does not come from busy-work or punching a time clock. It does not come from just making a living, working by formula, finding a secure spot as an organization man. The very argument, by Riesman and others, that man no longer finds identity in the work defined as a paycheck job, assumes that identity for man comes through creative work of his own that contributes to the human community: The core of the self becomes aware, becomes real, and grows through work that carries forward human society.

Work, the shopworn staple of the economists, has become the new frontier of psychology. Psychiatrists have long used "occupational therapy" with patients in mental hospitals; they have recently discovered that to be of real psychological value, it must be not just "therapy," but real work, serving a real purpose in the community. And work can now be seen as the key to the problem that has no name. The identity crisis of American women began a century ago, as more and more of the work important to the world, more and more of the work that used their human abilities and through which they were able to find self-realization, was taken from them.

Until, and even into, the last century, strong, capable women were needed to pioneer our new land; with their husbands, they ran the farms and plantations and Western homesteads. These women were respected and self-respecting members of a society whose pioneering purpose centered in the home. Strength and independence, responsibility and self-confidence, self-discipline and courage, freedom and equality were part of the American character for both men and women, in all the first generations. The women who came by steerage from Ireland, Italy, Russia, and Poland worked beside their husbands in the sweatshops and the laundries, learned the new language, and saved to send their sons and daughters to college. Women were never quite as "feminine," or held in as much contempt, in America as they were in Europe. American women seemed to European travelers, long before our time, less passive, childlike, and feminine than their own wives in France or Germany or England. By an accident of history, American women shared in the work of society longer, and grew with the men. Grade- and high-school education for boys and girls alike was almost always the rule; and in the West, where women shared the pioneering work the longest, even the universities were coeducational from the beginning.

The identity crisis for women did not begin in America until the fire and strength and ability of the pioneer women were no longer needed, no longer used, in the middle-class homes of the Eastern and Midwestern cities, when the pioneering was done and men began to build the new society in industries and professions outside the home. But the daughters of the pioneer women had grown too used to freedom and work to be content with leisure and passive femininity.

It was not an American, but a South African woman, Mrs. Olive Schreiner, who warned at the turn of the century that the quality and quantity of women's functions in the social universe were decreasing as fast as civilization was advancing; that if women did not win back their right to a full share of honored and useful work, woman's mind and muscle would weaken in a parasitic state; her offspring, male and female, would weaken progressively, and civilization itself would deteriorate.

The feminists saw clearly that education and the right to participate in the more advanced work of society were women's greatest needs. They fought for and won the rights to new, fully human identity for women. But how very few of their daughters and granddaughters have chosen to use their education and their abilities for any large creative purpose, for responsible work in society? How many of them have been deceived, or have deceived themselves, into clinging to the outgrown, childlike femininity of "Occupation: housewife"?

It was not a minor matter, their mistaken choice. We now know that the same range of potential ability exists for women as for men. Women, as well as men, can find their identity only in work that uses their full capacities. A woman cannot find her identity through others—her husband, her children. She cannot find it in the dull routine of housework. As thinkers of every age have said, it is only when a human being faces squarely the fact that he can forfeit his own life, that he becomes truly aware of himself, and begins to take his existence seriously. Sometimes this awareness comes only at the moment of death. Sometimes it comes from a more subtle facing of death: the death of self in passive conformity, in meaningless work. The feminine mystique prescribes just such a living death for women. Faced with the slow death of self, the American woman must begin to take her life seriously.

"We measure ourselves by many standards," said the great American psychologist William James, nearly a century ago, in his great work *The Principles of Psychology* (1890). "Our strength and our intelligence, our wealth and even our good luck, are things which warm our heart and make us feel ourselves a match for life. But deeper than all such things, and able to suffice unto itself without them, is the sense of the amount of effort which we can put forth." If women do not put forth, finally, that effort to become all that they have it in them to become, they will forfeit their own humanity. A woman today who has no goal, no purpose, no ambition patterning her days into the future, making her stretch and grow beyond that small score of years in which her body can fill its biological function, is committing a kind of suicide. For that future half a century after the child-bearing years are over is a fact that an American woman cannot deny. Nor can she deny that as a housewife, the world is indeed rushing past her door while she just sits and watches. The terror she feels is real, if she has no place in that world.

The feminine mystique has succeeded in burying millions of American women alive. There is no way for these women to break out of their comfortable concentration camps except by finally putting forth an effort—that human effort that reaches beyond biology, beyond the narrow walls of home, to help shape the future. Only by such a personal commitment to the future can American women break out of the housewife trap and truly find fulfillment as wives and mothers—by fulfilling their own unique possibilities as separate human beings.

Discussion Questions

1. How does Friedan explain the change in the significance of work from the past to the present?

2. Does Friedan find all kinds of work to be equally satisfying? Where, according to Klemens, is job satisfaction found? Identify and discuss the points of disagreement in their positions.

3. Who, according to Friedan, were the early feminists, and in what ways did they succeed in reconstructing our ideas about women and work? How has the relationship between women and work changed in the history of America? How does Friedan feel about this change? Explain why you do or do not think her perspective has validity.

4. How does the relationship between work and identity that Friedan discusses correspond with Klemens's idea of the work ethic? Explain why you believe his idea to be either gender biased or gender neutral.

MEN AT WORK

ANNA QUINDLEN

Anna Quindlen graduated from Barnard College at Columbia University and has worked as a reporter and columnist for the New York Post, *the* New York Times, *and* Newsweek. *Her* New York Times *column, "Public and Private," received a Pulitzer Prize for Commentary in 1992. She is now a full-time best-selling novelist. The following essay is from a collection of her work titled* Thinking Out Loud: The Personal, the Political, the Public, and the Private *(1993).*

The five o'clock dads can be seen on cable television these days, just after that time in the evening the stay-at-home moms call the arsenic hours. They are sixties sitcom reruns, Ward and Steve and Alex, and fifties guys. They eat dinner with their television families and provide counsel afterward in the den. Someday soon, if things keep going the way they are, their likenesses will be enshrined in a diorama in the Museum of Natural History, frozen in their recliner chairs. The sign will say, "Here sit lifelike representations of family men who worked only eight hours a day."

The five o'clock dad has become an endangered species. A corporate culture that believes presence is productivity, in which people of ambition are afraid to be seen leaving the office, has lengthened his workday and shortened his home-life. So has an economy that makes it difficult for families to break even at the end of the month. For the man who is paid by the hour, that means never saying no to overtime. For the man whose loyalty to the organization is measured in time at his desk, it means goodbye to nine to five.

To lots of small children it means a visiting father. The standard joke in one large corporate office is that dads always say their children look like angels when they're sleeping because that's the only way they ever see them. A Gallup survey taken several years ago showed that roughly twelve percent of the men surveyed with children under the age of six worked more than sixty hours a week, and an additional twenty-five percent worked between fifty and sixty hours. (Less than eight percent of the working women surveyed who had children of that age worked those hours.)

No matter how you divide it up, those are twelve-hour days. When the talk-show host Jane Wallace adopted a baby recently, she said one reason she was not troubled by becoming a mother without becoming a wife was that many of her married female friends were "functionally single," given the hours their husbands worked. The evening commuter rush is getting longer. The 7:45 to West Backofbeyond is more crowded than ever before. The eight o'clock dad. The nine o'clock dad.

There's a horribly sad irony to this, and it is that the quality of fathering is better than it was when the dads left work at five o'clock and came home to café curtains and tuna casserole. The five o'clock dad was remote, a "Wait until your father gets home" kind of dad with a newspaper for a face. The roles he and his wife had were clear; she did nurture and home, he did discipline and money.

The role fathers have carved out for themselves today is a vast improvement, a muddling of those old boundaries. Those of us obliged to convert behavior into trends have probably been a little heavy-handed on the shared childbirth and egalitarian diaper-changing. But fathers today do seem to be more emotional with their children, more nurturing, more open. Many say, "My father never told me he loved me," and so they tell their own children all the time that they love them—when they're home.

There are people who think that this is changing even as we speak, that there is a kind of *perestroika* of home and work that we will look back on as beginning at the beginning of the 1990s. A nonprofit organization called the Families and Work Institute advises corporations on how to balance personal and professional obligations and concerns, and Ellen Galinsky, its cofounder, says she has noticed a change in the last year. "When we first started doing this the groups of men and women sounded very different," she says. "If the men complained at all about long hours, they complained about their wives' complaints. Now if the timbre of the voice was disguised I couldn't tell which is which. The men are saying: 'I don't want to live this way anymore. I want to be with my kids.' I think the corporate culture will have to begin to respond to that."

This change can only be to the good, not only for women but especially for men, and for kids, too. The stereotypical five o'clock dad belongs in a diorama, with his "Ask your mother" and his "Don't be a crybaby." The father who believes hugs and kisses are sex-blind and a dirty diaper requires a change, not a woman, is infinitely preferable. What a joy it would be if he were around more.

"This is the man's half of having it all," says Don Conway-Long, who teaches a course at Washington University in St. Louis about men's relationships that drew 135 students this year for thirty-five places. "We're trying to do what women want of us, what children want of us, but we're not willing to transform the workplace." In other words, the hearts and minds of today's fathers are definitely in the right place. If only their bodies could be there, too.

Discussion Questions

1. Why does Quindlen say that the "five o'clock dad" has become an endangered species?

2. What irony does Quindlen see in the relationship these new "visiting" fathers have with their children?

3. What change does Quindlen identify, and how does she explain this shift in men's attitude toward work versus time expectations? What do you think Klemens would say about the work ethic of these men? Why do you feel the change they desire either can, or cannot, be made without harming the economic future of America?

Assignment #7

"THE AMERICAN PARADOX"

This assignment focuses on the subject of food and its complex and significant impact on our world and on each of us individually. The lead reading selection that you will respond to is written by Michael Pollan, who has written widely on the subject. Read his essay carefully to determine the particular argument he is making in this relatively short essay. After reading Pollan's essay, look carefully at the writing topic that follows it; your assignment in this unit is to respond to this writing topic. As you have done in the previous assignments, be sure to make good use of the pages that follow Pollan's essay. They will help you to understand his ideas and develop your own argument in response to the writing topic.

The reading selections in "Extending the Discussion: Considering Other Viewpoints" may be especially important for this assignment because many of you probably know little about the issues that surround the topic of food. We think you will be interested to learn of some of the back stories on the food you eat. The propagation and distribution of food are determined by a host of priorities, necessities, vested interests, and traditions that most of us haven't given all that much thought to, but which make up a wide net of influence over our environment, our ethics, and our physical and mental health.

The prewriting exercises in this unit will take you through the writing process and help you work through some of these vital issues. Again, be sure to complete all of the pages, carefully following the directions and guidelines. But don't be afraid to move beyond them, too, now that you have become familiar with this book's strategies, so that your writing process is enriched as much as possible.

THE AMERICAN PARADOX

MICHAEL POLLAN

Michael Pollan is a professor of journalism at the University of California, Berkeley. He has written often about what he sees as mistakes in the way Americans think about, produce, and eat their food. He has won numerous awards from organizations such as the American Booksellers Association and the Humane Society of the United States. The following selection is adapted from his book In Defense of Food: An Eater's Manifesto *(2008).*

The scientists haven't tested the hypothesis yet, but I'm willing to bet that when they do, they'll find an inverse correlation between the amount of time people spend worrying about nutrition and their overall health and happiness. This is, after all, the implicit lesson of the French paradox, so called not by the French but by American nutritionists, who can't fathom how a people who enjoy their food as much as the French do—who blithely eat beef and cheese and drink red wine—can have substantially lower rates of heart disease than we do on our elaborately engineered low-fat diets. Maybe it's time we confronted the American paradox: a notably unhealthy population preoccupied with nutrition and the idea of eating healthily.

True, as omnivores—creatures that can eat just about anything nature has to offer and that in fact need to eat a wide variety of different things in order to be healthy—the "What to eat" question is somewhat more complicated for us than it is for, say, cows. Yet for most of our history, humans have navigated the question without expert advice. To guide us we had, instead, culture, which, at least when it comes to food, is really just a fancy word for your mother. What to eat, how much of it to eat, what order in which to eat it, with what and when and with whom have for most of human history been a set of questions long settled and passed down from parents to children without a lot of controversy or fuss. But over the last several decades, moms have lost much of their authority over the dinner menu, ceding it to scientists and food marketers—often an unhealthy alliance of the two—and, to a lesser extent, to the government, with its ever-shifting dietary guidelines, food-labeling rules, and perplexing pyramids. Think about it: Most of us no longer eat what our mothers ate as children or, for that matter, what our mothers fed us as children. This is, historically speaking, an unusual state of affairs.

What is driving such relentless change in the American diet? One force is a thirty-two-billion-dollar food-marketing machine that thrives on change for its own sake. Another is the constantly shifting ground of nutrition science that, depending on your point of view, is steadily advancing the frontiers of our knowledge about diet and health or is just changing its mind a lot because it is a flawed science that knows much less than it cares to admit. Part of what drove my grandparents' food culture from the American table was official scientific opinion, which, beginning in the 1960s, decided that animal fat was a deadly substance. And then there were the food manufacturers, who stood to make very little money from my grandmother's cooking, because she was doing so much from scratch—up to and including rendering her own cooking fats. Drawing on then-current science, they managed to sell her daughter on the virtues of hydrogenated vegetable oils, the trans fats that we're now learning may be, well, deadly substances.

Sooner or later, everything solid we've been told about the links between our diet and our health seems to get blown away in the gust of the most recent study. Consider the latest findings. In 2006 came news that a low-fat diet, long believed to protect against cancer, may do no such thing—this from the massive, federally funded Women's Health Initiative, which has also failed to find a link between a low-fat diet and the risk of coronary heart disease. Indeed, the whole nutritional orthodoxy around dietary fat appears to be crumbling. In 2005, we learned that dietary fiber might not, as we'd been confidently told for years, help prevent cancers and heart disease. And then, in the fall of 2006, two prestigious studies on omega-3 fats published at the same time came to strikingly different conclusions. While the Institute of Medicine at the National Academy of Sciences found little conclusive evidence that eating fish would do your heart much good, a Harvard study brought the hopeful piece of news that simply by eating a couple of servings of fish each week you could cut your risk of dying from a heart attack by more than a third.

The story of how the most basic questions about what to eat ever got so complicated reveals a great deal about the institutional imperatives of the food industry, nutrition science, and—ahem—journalism, three parties that stand to gain much from widespread confusion surrounding the most elemental question an omnivore confronts. But humans deciding what to eat without professional guidance—something they have been doing with notable success since coming down out of the trees—is seriously unprofitable if you're a food company, a definite career loser if you're a nutritionist, and just plain boring if you're a newspaper editor or reporter. And so, like a large, gray cloud, a great Conspiracy of Scientific Complexity has gathered around the simplest questions of nutrition, much to the advantage of everyone involved—except, perhaps, the supposed beneficiary of all this advice: us, and our health and happiness as eaters. For the most important thing to know about the campaign to professionalize dietary advice is that it has not made us any healthier. To the contrary: Most of the nutritional advice we've received over the last half century has actually made us less healthy and considerably fatter.

Nutrition science on one side and the food industry on the other have fostered needless complications around eating. Because in their view food is foremost a matter of biology, they preach that we must try to eat "scientifically"—by the nutrient and the number and under the guidance of experts. If such an approach to food doesn't strike you as the least bit strange, that is probably because nutritionists' thinking has become so pervasive as to be invisible. We forget that, historically, people have eaten for a great many reasons other than biological necessity. Food is also about pleasure, about community, about family and spirituality, about our relationship to the natural world, and about expressing our identity. As long as humans have been taking meals together, eating has been as much about culture as it has been about biology.

That eating should be foremost about bodily health is a relatively new and, I think, destructive idea—destructive not just of the pleasure of eating, which would be bad enough, but paradoxically of our health as well. Indeed, no people on earth worry more about the health consequences of their food choices than we Americans do—and no people suffer from as many diet-related health problems. We are becoming a nation of people with an unhealthy obsession with healthy eating.

Writing Topic

According to Pollan, what is wrong with the way Americans think about eating today? Do you agree with him? As you develop your argument, be sure to support your position with specific examples from your own experience, your observation of others, or your reading.

Vocabulary Check

Good writers choose their words carefully so that their ideas will be clear. In order for you to understand any reading selection, it is important to think about its key vocabulary terms and the way they are used by the author. Words can have a variety of meanings, or they can have specialized meanings in certain contexts. Look up the definitions of the following words or phrases from the essay. Find each word in "The American Paradox," and then choose the meaning that you think Pollan intended when he selected that particular word for use in his essay. Then, explain the way that the meaning or concept behind the definition is key to understanding his argument.

1. *inverse*

    definition: _____

    _____

    explanation: _____

    _____

    _____

    _____

2. *correlation*

    definition: _____

    _____

    explanation: _____

    _____

    _____

    _____

3. *implicit*

    definition: _____

    _____

    explanation: _____

    _____

    _____

    _____

4. *blithe*

definition: _____

_____

explanation: _____

_____

_____

_____

5. *elaborate*

definition: _____

_____

explanation: _____

_____

_____

_____

6. *paradox*

definition: _____

_____

explanation: _____

_____

_____

_____

7. *perplexing*

definition: _____

_____

explanation: _____

_____

_____

_____

8. *relentless*

definition: _____

_____

explanation: _____

_____

_____

_____

9. *orthodoxy*

definition: _____

_____

explanation: _____

_____

_____

_____

10. *foster*

definition: _____

_____

explanation: _____

_____

_____

_____

11. *pervasive*

definition: _____

_____

explanation: _____

_____

_____

_____

Questions to Guide Your Reading

Answer the following questions to gain a thorough understanding of "The American Paradox."

Paragraph 1

What relationship does Pollan believe exists between general well-being and a focus on nutrition?

Paragraph 2

According to Pollan, in the past, who and/or what governed what we ate? How does he think the entities that governed what we ate have changed?

Paragraph 3

What are the two main factors responsible for this change, according to Pollan?

Paragraphs 4 and 5

How does the dietary controversy example highlight the problematic relationship Pollan sees between nutritional science and good nutrition?

Paragraphs 6 and 7

a. What are some of the historic reasons for what and how we eat, according to Pollan? Explain the correlation Pollan finds between the historic reasons and the biological ones.

b. How can privileging science become harmful, in Pollan's view?

Prewriting for a Directed Summary

Now that you have used the questions above to understand "The American Paradox" as a whole, use the following questions as a guide to focus your attention on a particular perspective in the essay. This perspective will be important when you are working on your own essay in response to the writing topic for this assignment. Be sure to use the answers you give below when it is time to write a clear and coherent directed summary in response to the writing topic's first question.

first question in the writing topic:

According to Pollan, what is wrong with the way Americans think about eating today?

Although this question asks you to explain Pollan's views, it doesn't ask you to summarize the entire reading selection. Be sure to keep the question in mind as you present his ideas.

Hint

Be sure to look back to Part 1 and reread "A Review of the Guidelines for Writing a Directed Summary."

Focus Questions

1. When Pollan talks about the past, how does he think Americans decided the type and amount of food they ate, and the time and place to eat it?

2. What is responsible for the changes in the way Americans think about food, according to Pollan?

3. How can focusing on the nutritional value of foods be harmful to the health of Americans, in Pollan's view?

Developing an Opinion and Working Thesis Statement

The second question in the writing topic for "The American Paradox" asks you to take a position of your own. Your response to this part of the writing topic will become the thesis statement of your essay, so it is important to spend some time ensuring that it is fully developed and that it accurately reflects your position on the issue Pollan addresses. Use the framework below to develop your working thesis, but keep an open mind as you complete the prewriting pages that follow this one, and as you read and discuss the positions other writers take in the "Extending the Discussion" section of this chapter. You may find that, after giving more thought to the issue of food, you want to modify your position.

second part of the writing topic:

Do you agree with him?

Now that you have spent some time with "The American Paradox," you should have some idea about whether or not you are convinced by his argument. Remember that, at this stage of the writing process, you will develop only a working thesis statement. It will capture your position now, early in the thought process, and it may very well change as you do more exploration of the issue. Do you agree with Pollan?

Hint

It is a good idea to go back and review your answers to the "Questions to Guide Your Reading" to remind yourself of Pollan's central claim and his supporting evidence.

1. Use the following thesis frame to identify the basic elements of your working thesis statement:
   a. What is the issue of "The American Paradox" that the writing topic asks you to consider?

   _____

   b. What is Pollan's position on that issue?

   _____

   c. What is your position on the issue, and will you agree or disagree with Pollan's opinion?

   _____

   _____

   _____

2. Now use the elements you isolated in 1a, b, and c to write a thesis statement. You may have to revise it several times until it captures your idea clearly.

_____

_____

Prewriting to Find Support for Your Thesis

The last part of the writing topic asks you to support the position you put forward in your thesis statement. Well-developed ideas are crucial when you are making an argument because you will have to be clear, logical, and thorough if you are to be convincing. As you work through the exercises below, you will generate much of the 4Cs material you will need when you draft your essay's body paragraphs.

the writing topic's last part:

As you develop your argument, be sure to support your position with specific examples from your own experience, your observation of others, or your reading.

1. As you begin to develop your own examples, consider the ways in which you, your family, and your friends make choices about the food you eat. In the space below, list or freewrite about personal experiences that involved you, your friends, or your family in making decisions about food and diet. For example:

   List your favorite places to eat, favorite meals, or favorite food-related TV shows, movies, or books. What characteristics do they have that make them a favorite for you?

   Do you and your friends and family discuss food—for example, what to have for dinner, or what to prepare for a holiday or family celebration? Are decisions made solely on the basis of taste, or do other factors weigh into the discussions and ultimate decisions?

   Do you see any health factors in your friends and family that are related to the decisions they make about eating?

   Keep in mind Pollan's idea that Americans have an "unhealthy obsession with healthy eating." Feel free to include any experience, however minor or incidental.

   Once you've written your ideas, look them over carefully. Try to group your ideas into categories. Then, give each category a label. In other words, cluster ideas that seem to have something in common and, for each cluster, identify that shared quality by giving it a title.

2. Now broaden your focus; list or freewrite about examples from your studies, your readings, and your general knowledge of current events. For example:

> What are some of the food-related presentations commonly found in the media, say, in commercials, TV movies, talk shows, etc.? What is the overall message of these presentations?

> List any of the popular food trends that you've noticed over the past several years, such as the promotion of low-fat, low-carb, or high-protein diets. What is the effect of these trends, and what is the basis for your evaluation?

> Consider the food for sale in a local mall or downtown area where you live. Sit on a bench and observe how many of the people who walk by appear to have food-related health issues. Does the way that food is promoted and sold in these busy centers seem to support or contradict Pollan's view that Americans have an "unhealthy obsession with healthy eating"?

Once you've written your ideas, look them over carefully. Try to group your ideas into categories. Then, give each category a label. In other words, cluster ideas that seem to have something in common and, for each cluster, identify that shared quality by giving it a title.

Once you've created topics by clustering your ideas into categories, go through them and pick two or three specific ones to develop in your essay. Make sure that they are relevant to your thesis and that they have enough substance to be compelling to your reader. Then, in the space below, briefly summarize each item.

Hint

Once you've decided which categories and items you will use in your essay, take some time to explain below how each category and its items connect to your thesis statement. You will use these details for the next stage.

Revising Your Thesis Statement

Now that you have spent some time working out your ideas more systematically and developing some supporting evidence for the position you want to take, look again at the working thesis statement you crafted earlier to see if it is still accurate. As your first step, look again at the writing topic, and then write your original working thesis on the lines that follow it:

writing topic:

According to Pollan, what is wrong with the way Americans think about eating today? Do you agree with him? As you develop your argument, be sure to support your position with specific examples from your own experience, your observation of others, or your reading.

working thesis statement:

_____

_____

Remember that your thesis statement must answer the second question in the writing topic while taking into consideration the writing topic as a whole. The first question in the topic identifies the issue that is up for debate, and the last question reminds you that, whatever position you take on the issue, you must be able to support it with specific examples.

Often, after extensive prewriting and focused thought, you will find that the working thesis statement is no longer an accurate reflection of what you plan to say in your essay. Sometimes, only a word or phrase must be added or deleted; other times, the thesis statement must be significantly rewritten. The subject or the claim portion may be unclear, vague, or even inaccurate. When we draft, we work out our thoughts as we write them down; consequently, draft writing is almost always wordy, unclear, or vague. Look at your working thesis statement through the eyes of your readers and see if it actually says what you want it to say.

After examining it and completing any necessary revisions, check it one more time by asking yourself the following questions:

a. Does the thesis statement directly identify Pollan's argument?

b. Does your thesis state your position on the issue?

c. Is your thesis well punctuated, grammatically correct, and precisely worded?

Write your polished thesis on the lines below and look at it again. Is it strong and interesting?

_____

_____

Planning and Drafting Your Essay

Getting started on the draft is often the hardest part of the writing process because this is where you move from exploring and planning to getting your ideas down in a unified, coherent shape. Creating an outline will give you a basic structure for incorporating all the ideas you have developed in the preceding pages. An outline will also give you a bird's-eye view of your essay and help you spot problems in development or logic.

This outline doesn't have to contain polished writing. You may want to fill in only the basic ideas in phrases or terms.

Creating an Outline for Your Draft

I. Introductory Paragraph:
   A. An opening sentence that gives the reading selection's title and the author's full name, and that begins to answer the first question in the writing topic:

   _____

   B. Main points to include in the directed summary:
      1.

      2.

      3.

      4.

   C. Write out your thesis statement. (Look back to "Revising Your Thesis State-ment," where you reexamined and improved your working thesis statement.) It should clearly agree or disagree with "The American Paradox" and state a clear position using your own words.

   _____

II. Body Paragraphs
   A. The paragraph's one main point that supports the thesis statement:

   _____

      1. Controlling idea sentence:

      _____

      _____

    2. Corroborating details:

_____

_____

_____

_____

    3. Careful description of why the details are significant:

_____

_____

_____

_____

    4. Connection to the thesis statement:

_____

_____

_____

_____

B. The paragraph's one main point that supports the thesis statement:

_____

    1. Controlling idea sentence:

_____

_____

    2. Corroborating details:

_____

_____

_____

_____

    3. Careful description of why the details are significant:

_____

_____

_____

_____

4. Connection to the thesis statement:

_____

_____

_____

_____

C. The paragraph's one main point that supports the thesis statement:

_____

1. Controlling idea sentence:

_____

_____

2. Corroborating details:

_____

_____

_____

_____

3. Careful description of why the details are significant:

_____

_____

_____

_____

4. Connection to the thesis statement:

_____

_____

_____

_____

D. The paragraph's one main point that supports the thesis statement:

_____

1. Controlling idea sentence:

_____

_____

2. Corroborating details:

_____

_____

_____

_____

3. Careful description of why the details are significant:

_____

_____

_____

_____

4. Connection to the thesis statement:

_____

_____

_____

_____

III. Conclusion

A. Type of conclusion to be used:

_____

B. Key words or phrases to include:

_____

Getting Feedback on Your Draft

Use the following guidelines to give a classmate feedback on his or her draft. Read the draft through first, and then answer each of the items below as specifically as you can.

Name of draft's author: _____

Name of draft's reader: _____

The Introduction

1. Within the opening sentences,
   a. Pollan is correctly identified by first and last name.   yes   no
   b. the writing selection's title is included and
      placed within quotation marks.   yes   no
2. The opening contains a summary that
   a. explains what Pollan means by the term
      "the American paradox"   yes   no
   b. explains why he thinks Americans have an
      "unhealthy obsession with healthy eating"   yes   no
3. The opening provides a thesis that
   a. makes Pollan's conclusions clear.   yes   no
   b. gives the draft writer's opinion about those conclusions.   yes   no

If the answers to #3 above are yes, state the thesis below as it is written. If the answer to one or both of these questions is no, explain to the writer what information is needed to make the thesis complete.

_____

_____

_____

The Body

1. How many paragraphs are in the body of this essay? _____

2. To support the thesis, this number is   sufficient   not enough

3. Do paragraphs contain the 4Cs?

   Paragraph 1   Controlling idea sentence   yes   no
                   Corroborating details   yes   no
                   Careful description of why the
                        details are significant   yes   no
                   Connection to the thesis statement   yes   no

459

Paragraph 2	Controlling idea sentence	yes	no
	Corroborating details	yes	no
	Careful description of why the details are significant	yes	no
	Connection to the thesis statement	yes	no
Paragraph 3	Controlling idea sentence	yes	no
	Corroborating details	yes	no
	Careful description of why the details are significant	yes	no
	Connection to the thesis statement	yes	no
Paragraph 4	Controlling idea sentence	yes	no
	Corroborating details	yes	no
	Careful description of why the details are significant	yes	no
	Connection to the thesis statement	yes	no
Paragraph 5	Controlling idea sentence	yes	no
	Corroborating details	yes	no
	Careful description of why the details are significant	yes	no
	Connection to the thesis statement	yes	no

(Continue as needed.)

4. Identify any of the above paragraphs that are underdeveloped (too short). _____

5. Identify any of the above paragraphs that fail to support the thesis. _____

6. Identify any of the above paragraphs that are redundant or repetitive. _____

7. Suggest any ideas for additional paragraphs that might improve this essay.

_____

_____

_____

The Conclusion

1. Does the final paragraph avoid introducing new ideas and examples that really belong in the body of the essay?   yes   no
2. Does the conclusion provide closure (let readers know that the end of the essay has been reached)?   yes   no
3. Does the conclusion leave readers with an understanding of the significance of the argument?   yes   no

4. State in your own words what the draft writer considers to be important about his or her argument.

_____

_____

_____

5. Identify the type of conclusion used (see the guidelines for conclusions in Part 1).

_____

Editing

1. During the editing process, the writer should pay attention to the following problems in sentence structure, punctuation, and mechanics:
   - fragments
   - misplaced and dangling modifiers
   - fused (run-on) sentences
   - comma splices
   - misplaced, missing, and unnecessary commas
   - misplaced, missing, and unnecessary apostrophes
   - incorrect quotation mark use
   - capitalization errors
   - spelling errors

2. While editing, the writer should pay attention to the following areas of grammar:
   - verb tense
   - subject-verb agreement
   - irregular verbs
   - pronoun type
   - pronoun reference
   - pronoun agreement
   - noun plurals
   - prepositions

Content

_____ My essay has an appropriate title.

_____ I provide an accurate summary of Pollan's position on the issue presented in "The American Paradox."

_____ My thesis states a clear position that can be supported by evidence.

_____ I have enough paragraphs and argument points to support my thesis statement.

_____ Each body paragraph is relevant to my thesis.

_____ Each body paragraph contains the 4Cs.

_____ I use transitions whenever necessary to connect ideas to each other.

_____ The final paragraph of my essay (the conclusion) provides readers with a sense of closure.

Grammar, Punctuation, and Mechanics

_____ I use the present tense to discuss Pollan's argument and examples.

_____ I use verb tenses correctly to show the chronology of events.

_____ I have verb tense consistency throughout my sentences.

_____ I have checked for subject-verb agreement in all of my sentences.

_____ I have revised all fragments and mixed or garbled sentences.

_____ I have repaired all fused (run-on) sentences and comma splices.

_____ I have placed a comma after introductory elements (transitions and phrases) and all dependent clauses that open a sentence.

_____ If I present items in a series (nouns, verbs, prepositional phrases), they are parallel in form.

_____ If I include material spoken or written by someone other than myself, I have correctly punctuated it with quotation marks, using the MLA style guide's rules for citation.

Reviewing Your Graded Essay

After your instructor has returned your essay, you may have the opportunity to revise your paper and raise your grade. Many students, especially those whose essays receive nonpassing grades, feel that their instructors should be less "picky" about grammar and should pass the work on content alone. However, most students at this level have not yet acquired the ability to recognize quality writing, and they do not realize that content and writing actually cannot be separated in this way. Experienced instructors know that errors in sentence structure, grammar, punctuation, and word choice either interfere with content or distract readers so much that they lose track of content. In short, good ideas badly presented are no longer good ideas; to pass, an essay must have passable writing. So even if you are not submitting a revised version of this essay to your instructor, it is important that you review your work carefully in order to understand its strengths and weaknesses. This sheet will guide you through the evaluation process.

You will want to continue to use the techniques that worked well for you and to find strategies to overcome the problems that you identify in this sample of your writing. To recognize areas that might have been problematic for you, look back at the scoring rubric in this book. Match the numerical/verbal/letter grade received on your essay to the appropriate category. Study the explanation given on the rubric for your grade.

Write a few sentences below in which you identify your problems in each of the following areas. Then, suggest specific changes you could make that would improve your paper. Don't forget to use your handbook as a resource.

1. Grammar/punctuation/mechanics
   My problem:

   My strategy for change:

2. Thesis/response to assignment
   My problem:

   My strategy for change:

3. Organization
    My problem:

    My strategy for change:

4. Paragraph development/examples/reasoning
    My problem:

    My strategy for change:

5. Assessment
In the space below, assign a grade to your paper using a rubric other than the one used by your instructor. In other words, if your instructor assigned your essay a grade of *High Fail*, you might give it the letter grade you now feel the paper warrants. If your instructor used the traditional letter grade to evaluate the essay, choose a category from the rubric in this book, or any other grading scale that you are familiar with, to show your evaluation of your work. Then, write a short narrative explaining your evaluation of the essay and the reasons it received the grade you gave it.

    Grade: _____

    Narrative: _____

    _____

    _____

    _____

    _____

Extending the Discussion:
Considering Other Viewpoints

Readings

"Why Study Food?" by Warren Belasco

"Science Says There's No Such Thing as 'Comfort Food.' We All Beg to Differ." by Emma Brockes

"Eat Up. You'll Be Happier." by Pamela Druckerman

"A Seismic Shift in How People Eat" by Hans Taparia and Pamela Koch

"Rethinking Eating" by Kate Murphy

"The Impact That Cultural Food Security Has on Identity and Well-Being in the Second Generation U.S. American Minority College Students" by Kathrine E. Wright et al

"The Fine Line Between Culinary Appropriation and Appreciation: Don't Appropriate, Appreciate." by Kinsey Long

WHY STUDY FOOD?

WARREN BELASCO

Warren Belasco is a professor of American studies at the University of Maryland, Baltimore County, and editor of the journal Food, Culture & Society. *His books on American food production and consumption, and the relation of these to history, culture, and the environment, have contributed to the recent emergence of food studies as an academic subject for study at American colleges and universities. The following reading selection is from his book* Food: The Key Concepts *(2008).*

Food is the first of the essentials of life, the world's largest industry, our most frequently indulged pleasure, the core of our most intimate social relationships. It's very hard to imagine a positive social experience that does not involve the sharing of food—whether a simple cup of tea with an acquaintance, a lunchtime "bite" with colleagues, or a sumptuous lobster dinner with a lover. On a broader level, civilization itself is impossible without food: With the invention of agriculture some ten thousand years ago came city states and empires, art, music, and organized warfare. Agriculture remade the world, both physically and culturally, transforming landscapes and geography, subsidizing soldiers and poets, politicians and priests (Diamond 1999: 236).

For French epicure Brillat-Savarin, we are what we eat—and for Lucretius, we are what we won't eat. Our tastes are as telling as our distastes. To be a member of the Parakana people of the Amazon rain forest is to relish roasted tapir and to despise monkey meat, while the neighboring Arara feel quite the reverse (Rensberger 1991: A3). Food identifies who we are, where we come from, and what we want to be. "Food reveals our souls," sociologist Gary Alan Fine writes. "Like Marcel Proust reminiscing about a madeleine or Calvin Trillin astonished at a plate of ribs, we are entangled in our meals" (1996:1). Food is "a highly condensed social fact," anthropologist Arjun Appadurai observes, "and a marvelously plastic kind of collective representation" (1981: 494).

Food is also the object of major anxiety, for what and how we eat may be the single most important cause of disease and death. We can't live without food, but food also kills us. As psychologist Paul Rozin puts it, "Food is fundamental, fun, frightening, and far-reaching" (1999: 9-30). And probably nothing is more frightening or far-reaching than the prospect of running out of food. "A hungry stomach will not allow its owner to forget it, whatever his cares and sorrows," Homer wrote almost three thousand years ago. Even in good times, we are not allowed to forget our deeply rooted heritage of food insecurity. "When thou hast enough," Ecclesiasticus warned, *c.*180 BCE, "remember the time of hunger." As if to take advantage of the brief break from habitual scarcity, our bodies store up fat for the next famine—hence the current obesity crisis—while our prophets warn us against complacency. For much of history, the search for sufficient food drove the conquest and colonization of continents—and the enslavement or eradication of entire populations. Food matters. It has weight, and it weighs us down.

And yet, until recently, scholars were amazingly reluctant to study food, especially the aspect closest to our hearts (and arteries): food consumption. To be sure, food *production* has received considerable attention in established disciplines such as economics, chemistry, agronomy, engineering, marketing, and labor relations. Scientists have long explored the negative pathologies of malnutrition, hunger, and adulteration. But when it comes to analyzing the more positive and intimate features of what, how, and why we eat, academics have been considerably more reticent. Even now, with the rising interest in food studies, a serious analysis of family dinner rituals, cookbooks, or the appeal of fast food may still evoke surprise and even scorn. "Do professors really study *that!*" your friends and family ask. "If you're going to go around telling your colleagues you are a philosopher of food," philosopher Lisa Heldke writes, "you [had] better be prepared to develop a thick skin—and start a wisecrack collection" (2006: 202). Why this reluctance to address the wider meaning of our food behaviors? Why is food taken for granted, at least in academia?

For one thing, intellectuals are heirs to a classical dualism that prizes mind over body. In *Cooking, Eating, Thinking,* Heldke and her colleague Deane Curtin write, "Our tradition has tended to privilege questions about the rational, the unchanging, and the eternal, and the abstract and the mental; and to denigrate questions about embodied, concrete, practical experience" (Curtin and Heldke 1992: xiv). Philosopher Carolyn Korsmeyer agrees that "Taste and eating [are] tied to the necessities of existence and are thus classified as lower functions . . . operating on a primitive, near instinctual level" (1999: 1). There may indeed be some archetypal, dualistic disdain for something as mundane, corporeal, even "animalistic" as eating. "Put a knife to thy throat," urges Proverbs 23:2, "if thou be a man given to appetite." "Reason should direct and appetite obey," Cicero counseled in 44 BCE (Egerton 1994: 17). "Govern thy appetite well," advised Puritan poet John Milton, "lest Sin Surprise thee, and her black attendant Death" (Egerton 1994: 18). To some extent, we may still live with the prejudices of the nineteenth century, which gave birth to so many modern institutions, ranging from research universities to dinner parties. Genteel Victorians constructed such elaborate dining rituals partly because they harbored a deep suspicion of eating, which—like sex—they viewed as basically uncivilized. The novelist Joyce Carol Oates characterizes that attitude nicely: "Civilization is a multiplicity of strategies, dazzling as precious gems inlaid in a golden crown, to obscure from human beings the sound of, the terrible meaning of, their jaws grinding—the meaning of man's place in the food cycle that, by way of our imaginations, we had imagined might not apply to us" (1993: 25). In other words, food is gross.

Food scholarship has also been hindered by another Victorian relic, the "separate spheres"—the idealized bourgeois division between the private female sphere of *consumption* and the more public male sphere of *production.* While the concept did not reflect the daily realities for most women—to this day, women are major food producers across the globe—the ideological polarization certainly influenced the development of middle-class academia, for it effectively segregated women professionals in less valued "domestic" disciplines, particularly dietetics, home economics, social work, and nutrition education (along with elementary school teaching, nursing, and library science). Conversely, the male-dominated realms of industrial agriculture, food technology, mass retailing, and corporate management *have* generally received more public respect and academic prestige.

This institutionalized bias delayed serious attention to food even after the women's movement obliterated the separate spheres. While more women began to enter all fields of academia in the 1960s, it took several decades before scholars could begin to consider the traditional female ghetto of domesticity without Victorian-era blinders and prejudices, and even today, feminists who do treasure their cooking heritage and skills may risk the hostility of colleagues who feel that women should move on to more "serious" pursuits. In recent years, there have been significant and largely sympathetic reappraisals of women's food work (e.g., Strasser 1982, Cowan 1983, Shapiro 1986, 2004, DeVault 1991, Mennell et al. 1992, Avakian 1997), but the identification of food with oppression still slants the scholarship—as evidenced, perhaps, by the fact that there may be more research devoted to women's eating disorders than to women's positive connections to food.

The association of cooking with women's enslavement leads to another major reason for food's relative invisibility: technological utopianism. For millennia, food *has* meant unrelenting drudgery, not just for cooks, but also for all food workers—farmers, field laborers, butchers, grocers, clerks, servers, and so on. Since at least the nineteenth century, many reformers have attempted, in a sense, to "disappear" food, to make it less visible and less central as a burden or concern. Progressives applauded the modern economic shift from messy food production to automated manufacturing and white collar office jobs. Feminist utopians embraced almost any idea that would get food out of the home and thus free up women: the meal in a pill, foods synthesized from coal, centralized kitchens, and "self-service" electric appliances and convenience foods. For example, in 1870, novelist Annie Denton Cridge dreamed of a large, mechanized cooking establishment that, by feeding an eighth of Philadelphia's population at one seating, would give housewives time to read, think, and discuss big ideas—and all at a cost lower "than when every house had its little, selfish, dirty kitchen" (Belasco 2006a: 110). Similarly, farmer-utopians dreamed of push-button, fully automated factory farms as a way to save their children from back-breaking labor and rural isolation. Today we can recognize that those dreams came true; sort of. Whereas once most people were farmers, now a relative handful of highly mechanized farmers grows almost all our food, and in providing over fifty million meals a day, McDonald's comes very close to Cridge's "one big kitchen" vision. But the result has been further distancing from the traditional rituals, sensibilities, and practices of food production—as well as some negative consequences for our health and environment.

Even more important in distancing us from nature and tradition have been the efforts of the food industry to obscure and mystify the links between the farm and the dinner table. While these efforts were stepped up in the mid-nineteenth century (reflected in the above-mentioned, gendered separation of production from consumption), they date at least as far back as the first global food conglomerate, the East India

Company, which was dedicated to bringing exotic foodstuffs to European dining rooms and whose annual report in 1701 observed, "We taste the spices of Arabia yet never feel the scorching sun which brings them forth." In other words, this food company was rather proud that thanks to its noble service in distant lands, affluent consumers did not have to experience the strenuous and often violent production processes by which their sausage got peppered or their tea sweetened. Perhaps the most vivid recent example of how we no longer have to feel the "scorching sun" of food production is the meat-packing industry, whose main thrust over 150 years has been to insulate consumers from any contact with the disassembly of warm-blooded mammals into refrigerated, plastic-wrapped chops and patties. "Forget the pig as an animal," a modern livestock management journal advises. "Treat him just like a machine in a factory" (Byrnes 1976: 30). In his environmental history of Chicago, *Nature's Metropolis*, William Cronon writes that the meat-packing industry of the late nineteenth century actively encouraged such "forgetfulness." "In the packers' world it was easy not to remember that eating was a moral act inexorably bound to killing" (Cronon 1991: 256).

By the 1920s, the relationship between supplier and customer, plow and plate, was largely anonymous, as noted by agricultural geneticist Edward East: "Today [1924] one sits down to breakfast, spreads out a napkin of Irish linen, opens the meal with a banana from Central America, follows with a cereal of Minnesota sweetened with the product of Cuban cane, and ends with a Montana lamb chop and cup of Brazilian coffee. Our daily life is a trip around the world, yet the wonder of it gives us not a single thrill. We are oblivious" (East 1924: 64). If consumers in the 1920s were already complacent about what East called the "globe-girdling" food supply system, they are even more "oblivious" now, when the "forgetfulness" applies not just to spices, sugar, or meat, but to virtually everything we consume: tomatoes, bread, pasta, shrimp, apple juice, grapes, cornflakes, and so on. Food is so vague in our culture in part because, thanks to processing, packaging, and marketing, it *is* an abstraction—an almost infinite set of variations on a theme of corn, which, Michael Pollan demonstrates, is the basis of so many modern foodstuffs, from Big Macs to Twinkies (Pollan 2006: 15–31). According to farmer-poet Wendell Berry, the ideal corporate customer today is the "industrial eater . . . who does not know that eating is an agricultural act, who no longer knows or imagines the connections between eating and the land, and who is therefore necessarily passive and uncritical" (1989: 126). And furthering the critical challenges to those attempting to uncover the complex commodity chains connecting field and fork is the fact that people may not eat as regularly or as socially as they used to. Given that modern meals themselves are so ephemeral, it is not surprising that it takes some effort to see food as a subject worthy of serious social analysis.

Yet, despite these difficulties and delays, there is no question that more people are studying food than ever before. While it may be premature to announce the birth of a new discipline of food studies, signs of increased activity are everywhere. In addition to the food-related papers now presented regularly at mainstream academic conventions, there have been a number of major international conferences devoted entirely to food, and these have, in turn, resulted in published collections (e.g., Lentz 1999, Grew 1999, Mack 1999, Dietler and Hayden 2001, Belasco and Scranton 2002, Jacobs and

Scholliers 2003). New academic journals are appearing, culinary history societies are mushrooming, and publishers are announcing food series. There is also a lively market for food-related memoirs, essays, and annotated historical recipes. Serious analyses of the food system by Michael Pollan, Eric Schlosser, Laura Shapiro, and Marion Nestle straddle both "trade" (general) and textbook audiences. There are dozens of excellent websites devoted to the disciplined exploration of foodways, not to mention the thousands of sites dedicated to cooking, gastronomy, nutrition, and restaurant reviews. As hundreds of professors offer undergraduate food-related courses, several universities have established food studies concentrations and degrees, while other students seek to "do food" within conventional disciplines such as history, anthropology, and literary studies.

Trend-watchers might ask, why now? In part, scholarship is following wider urban middle-class culture, which, since the 1970s, has become much more interested in food-related matters of taste, craft, authenticity, status, and health. Food scholars belong to the same affluent social class that has fueled an unprecedented expansion and elaboration of restaurant and supermarket options, and this well-educated, trend-conscious public is literally hungry for analysis and perspective. Enthusiastic journalists and documentary filmmakers popularize the new work of food scholars. Socially conscious food professionals—chefs, managers, cookbook writers, etc.—also mingle and exchange ideas with food professors. Furthermore, as the world seems to spin helplessly from one major political crisis to another, large segments of the public look for ways to assert some control over their lives—and watching what you eat may be one such way to feel in charge of your destiny. Along these lines, the academic left has found food studies to be a fertile base for activist analysis of hunger, inequality, neo-colonialism, corporate accountability, biotechnology, globalization, and ecological sustainability. These concerns underlie much of the food scholarship today and animate many new food studies courses, in which students often attempt to recover and illuminate the invisible links in the global food chain. Finding out where our food comes from is an important step toward taking responsibility for our food's true *cost,* which Henry David Thoreau defined as "the amount of life exchanged for it, immediately or in the long run" (Orr 1994: 172).

So while food studies is now "respectable," it is also inherently subversive. To study food often requires us to cross disciplinary boundaries and to ask inconvenient questions. The food supply belongs to us all, yet in the past one hundred years or so, we have delegated the responsibility for understanding and controlling just about every step of the metabolic process to highly credentialed experts. These specialists have managed to mystify food so thoroughly that many people simply throw up their hands in justifiable confusion when it comes to understanding essential issues of health, agriculture, and business, not to mention cooking and taste. Michael Pollan writes, "Somehow this most elemental of activities—figuring out what to eat—has come to require a remarkable amount of expert help." Decrying "our national eating disorder," Pollan asks, "How did we ever get to a point where we need investigative journalists to tell us where our food comes from and nutritionists to determine the dinner menu?" (Pollan 2006: 1). Yet all too often the experts have led us astray—as for example the period after the Second World War, when specialists with endowed chairs at elite universities assured us that the first modern pesticide, DDT, was perfectly safe, that the Basic Four Food Groups constituted the best diet, and that in the near future, we'd be defeating world hunger with steaks made from algae, yeast, and coal dust. Specialists are useful to have around, of course, since modern life is far too complex for us to understand everything. But the problem with relying entirely on specialists is that sometimes they're wrong. Or worse, they tend to disagree. So to help us sort out the issues and gain some needed perspective, we need generalists—people with a decent grounding in science *and* poetry, agriculture *and* philosophy, who are not afraid to question assumptions, values, and methods. True, we may not understand all the biochemistry involved in nutrition, but we can speculate about why certain foods "taste good" at particular times and to particular people. We may not be able to explain why one pesticide works better on mites than another, but we can still ask why farm workers' children seem especially cancer-prone. We may not fully understand how genetic engineering works, but we still can wonder whether it is necessary in the first place. Such issues require that we think about matters political, historical, economic, sociocultural, and scientific *all at once*. As generalists, we study food as a *system*. Such holistic thinking actually restores our sense of power and humanity, for when it comes to eating, humans *are* generalists, i.e., omnivores.

While interdisciplinary study may entail a freewheeling crossing of disciplinary boundaries, it also requires a careful integration of themes or models on which to hang all these disparate ideas and insights. One needs to avoid the smorgasbord approach to learning—a little of this, a little of that. Or, to use another food metaphor, you can't leave a supermarket without bags to put all the groceries in; otherwise, you have a big mess on the floor. The inquiry needs sturdy containers in which to carry all that stuff away. To organize our inquiry, this book begins with the single question, "So what's for dinner?" Deciding what to eat may not be as simple as it sounds, for "Since Eve ate apples," Byron quipped, "much depends on dinner." Eating entails a host of personal, social, and even global factors that, in their entirety, add up to a complex *food system*. To sort out these variables, imagine a triangle with one point at the top and two on the bottom. Focus first on the baseline: Call the left point "Identity;" the right "Convenience." And call the apex "Responsibility."

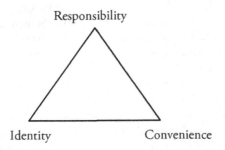

For the most part, people decide what to eat based on a rough negotiation—a pushing and tugging—between the dictates of identity and convenience, with somewhat lesser guidance from the considerations of responsibility. (The triangle is thus not quite equilateral, though the moralist might wish it were so.)

"Identity" involves considerations of personal preference, pleasure, creativity, the sense of who and where you are. Identity includes factors such as taste, family and ethnic background, personal memories (the association between particular foods and past events, both good and bad). The cultural aspects of identity include widely shared values and ideas, extravagant notions about the good life, as well as a community's special food preferences and practices that distinguish it from other communities—for example, those tapir-relishing Parakana versus the tapir-hating Arara. Gender also matters considerably in many cultures, as foods are often grouped as "male" and female"—for example, steaks versus salads. Deeply rooted in childhood, tradition, and group membership, the culinary dictates of identity are hard to change because they raise questions such as "How do I eat it?," "Should I like it?," "Is this *authentic*?," and "Is this what people like me eat?" At the identity point, food choices are expressed through rituals, etiquette, symbols, and arts. In studying food and identity, we look at what, where, and how people eat—and *don't* eat. And we examine how they represent, play with, and think about their food.

"Convenience" encompasses variables such as price, availability, and ease of preparation, which are all related to the requirements of energy, time, labor, and skill. In other words, convenience involves concerns such as "Can I get it?," "Can I afford it?," and "Can I make it?" Accounting for these all-important factors of convenience will lead us to look at the global food chain—the series of steps and processes by which food gets from farm to fork. Hence, we should examine the role of the people and institutions that make food accessible to us—e.g., farmers, migrant workers, processors, supermarkets, and restaurants. By smoothing food's flow from field to plate, for a price, the food industry sells us convenience. To be sure, there are enormous differences in the degree of convenience afforded different consumers. Some of us in the world have almost instant access to an unprecedented array of meal options, while other people's choices are severely restricted by economics, environment, and social structure. Such differences are starkly presented in *Hungry Planet,* where thirty families from all over the world are lined up separately behind a week's worth of food. Families from North America, Europe, Australia, and Kuwait are almost hidden by immense piles of plastic-wrapped "convenience foods," while people from Mali, Ecuador, and India seem much larger than the baskets of unprocessed grains and produce they consume. Somewhere in between, representing the world's "middle class," families from the Philippines, China, and Egypt stand around tables covered with raw fruits and grains as well as bottled soft drinks and bags of snacks (Menzel and D'Aluisio 2005).

And then, there's the matter of responsibility, which I put at the apex of the triangle not because it is the strongest factor but because maybe it *should* be. Responsibility entails being aware of the consequences of one's actions—both personal and social, physiological and political. It can involve short-term, acute consequences: Will this meal make me sick tomorrow? And it can involve long-term effects: Will it make me sick thirty years from now? Being responsible means being aware of one's place in the food chain—of the enormous impact we have on nature, animals, other people, and the distribution of power and resources all over the globe. It means feeling that "scorching sun" of the East India Company's Arabian enterprises; or appreciating Thoreau's "amount of life exchanged" to get your meal from farm to fork; or calculating, as the

Great Law of the Iroquois Confederacy once attempted, "the impact of our decisions on the next seven generations." In eating even the simplest dish, we join a chain of events linking people and places across the world and across time, too—past and future. "We are paying for the foolishness of yesterday while we shape our own tomorrow," environmentalist William Vogt wrote in 1948. "Today's white bread may force a break in the levees and flood New Orleans next spring. This year's wheat from Australia's eroding slopes may flare into a Japanese war three decades hence." Having a sense of responsibility entails both remembering how the food got to you (the past) and anticipating the consequences down the line (the future). "We must develop our sense of time and think of the availability of beefsteaks not only for this Saturday but for the Saturdays of our old age, and of our children" (Vogt 1948: 285, 63). Ultimately, assigning responsibility is a political process, for it entails sorting out the separate duties of individual consumers, food providers, and government. The poet-farmer Wendell Berry writes that "To eat responsibly is to understand and enact, as far as one can, the complex relationship" between the individual and the food system (Berry 1989: 129).

Although I have placed responsibility at the apex of my triangle, it is often the weakest of the three forces pulling at the individual food consumer. Still, many of us do want to be "conscientious consumers." "The unexamined life is not worth living," Socrates argued on behalf of acute self-consciousness. Also, knowing that "there's no free lunch," few of us want to be considered "deadbeats"—irresponsible people who skip out on the check, or worse, let our children pay our debts and then leave them worse off. "We're committing grand larceny against our children," was the charge put by environmental moralist David Brower when describing our reliance on wasteful, unsustainable resources and technologies. "Ours is a chain-letter economy, in which we pick up early handsome dividends and our children find their mailboxes empty" (as cited in McPhee 1971: 82). We must consider some of the consequences—personal and political, immediate and distant—of our food choices and practices.

To illustrate the complexities and rewards of taking this type of comprehensive, multidisciplinary approach to food, let's think about the simple act of toasting a piece of sliced white bread. Start with identity: Where does toast fit in the morning meal rituals of certain peoples? Why have so many cultures traditionally valued processed white grains over more nutritious whole grains, while wholegrain bread is now an elite marker? Why do we like the crunchy texture ("mouth feel") of toasted foods, and is the fondness for toasted *bread* widespread or, as one encyclopedia suggests, "Anglo-bred"? (Tobias 2004: 122). Why is wheat bread the "staff" of life in some cultures, while others put rice or corn tortillas in that central position? "No foodstuff bears greater moral and philosophical burden" than bread, food writer Tom Jaine observes (1999: 97). Who invented the sandwich, and what social function does it serve? Why do some cultures prefer wraps to sandwiches?

Then there are the convenience factors: Who grew, gathered, milled, and packaged the wheat? Who baked the bread? How did bread get so cheap? To turn the wheat into inexpensive sliced bread required the coordinated efforts of numerous companies specializing in food transportation, storage, processing, and marketing, as well as many others involved in manufacturing and selling tractors, trucks, slicers, and so on. Who invented sliced bread, anyway? When did store-bought white bread replace homemade whole wheat? When did they start putting vitamins back in white bread, and why? And who invented the pop-up toaster, and why?

And as for responsibility, think of toast's enormous "ecological footprint" (Wackernagel and Rees 1996). Growing that wheat helped some farmers pay their bills while also polluting their water supply with fertilizers and pesticides, eroding their soil, and, if they used irrigation, lowering their region's water table. The land used to grow the wheat had been acquired—or seized—long ago from other living creatures, human and otherwise, and converted to growing a grass that had originated as a weed in the Middle East and had been gradually domesticated and improved by five hundred generations of gatherers, peasants, farmers, and, only just recently, scientists. By extending the bread's shelf life, the plastic wrapping lowered costs, raised consumer convenience, and increased profits for corporate processors, distributors, and supermarkets. That packaging also helped to put thousands of neighborhood bakers out of business. Making the plastic from petrochemicals may have helped to foul Cancer Alley in Louisiana, and if the oil came from the Middle East, may have helped to pay for the restoration of royalty in Kuwait, which was destroyed several years ago by an Iraqi army *also* financed by petrochemical bread wrappers. (Or perhaps the oil came from Venezuela, where it paid for Hugo Chavez's left-leaning reorganization of the oligarchy.) The copper in the toaster and electrical wiring may have been mined during the dictatorships of Pinochet in Chile, Mobutu in Zaire, or Chiluba in Zambia. The electricity itself probably came from a power plant burning coal, a source of black lung, acid rain, and global warming. And so on. All of this—and much more—involved in making toast. And we have not even mentioned the butter and jam!

While the variables affecting our decision to toast bread are complex, they are relatively uncontroversial compared with the triangle of tense contradictions surrounding the decision to eat another central staple, meat. Identity: The ability to afford meat has long served as a badge of success, health, and power, especially for men. Throughout the world, economic mobility has almost invariably meant an increase in meat consumption—a process called a "nutrition transition" (Sobal 1999: 178). Given the prestige accorded beef, particularly in the West, it is not surprising that the "cowboy"—a Spanish invention *(vaquero)*—has achieved mythical status. While some cultures accord culinary primacy to cattle, others prize pigs, sheep, poultry, fish, and rodents, and some eat no meat at all. Westerners have long denigrated vegetarian cuisines, and such prejudices have even been reflected in medical texts, as in a 1909 text: "White bread, red meat, and blue blood make the tricolor flag of conquest." "The rice-eating Hindoo and Chinese, and the potato-eating Irish are kept in subjection by the well-fed English," influential Victorian physician George Beard agreed. Conversely, vegetarians may frame meat-eaters as less "civilized," as in George Bernard Shaw's famous prediction, "A hundred years hence a cultivated man will no more dream of eating flesh or smoking than he now does of living, as [Samuel] Pepys's [seventeenth century] contemporaries did, in a house with a cesspool under it." Whether staple or taboo, animal foods carry significant cultural meaning throughout the world (Belasco 2006a: 8, 10). Convenience: Biologically, meat may be prized because it offers a compact package of nutrients.

It can be relatively easy to cook, especially if it is of the well-fatted, grain-fed variety produced by the modern livestock industry. Meat production has long been the focus of many laborsaving innovations—hence the early rise of the slaughterhouse "disassembly" line, which in turn became the model for so many other mass production industries. A significant proportion—perhaps even most—of modern agricultural science is devoted to devising ever more efficient ways to grow cheap corn and soy for livestock, especially fat-marbled beef. And making this meat convenient—cheap, easy, and accessible—is also a primary goal and achievement of the fast food industry.

But the responsibility considerations are enormous: acute poisoning from "dirty beef"; chronic heart disease from animal fats; the possible mistreatment of animals and workers in animal factories; the immediate and long-term impact on the environment in terms of energy, groundwater pollution, soil loss, and even climate change. The resource-intensive nature of animal production has been known for centuries. William Paley's 1785 *Principles of Moral and Political Philosophy* observes: "A piece of ground capable of supplying animal food sufficient for the subsistence of ten persons would sustain, at least, the double of that number with grain, roots, and milk." In 1811, radical publisher Richard Phillips argued that British farmers could potentially feed 47,000,000 vegetarians "in abundance," "but they sustain only twelve millions *scantily*" on animal products (Belasco 2006a: 5).

In addition, there are the conflicts ensuing from differences in diet, especially meat-eaters vs. vegetarians. In Plato's *Republic*, written over 2,400 years ago, Socrates argued that because domesticated meat production required so much land, it inevitably led to territorial expansion and war with vegetarian neighbors (Adams 1992: 115). *In Guns, Germs, and Steel*, Jared Diamond suggests that Eurasia—Plato's home region—was the origin of many expansionist empires precisely because it harbored such an abundance of domesticated mammals (1999: 157-175). According to medievalist Massimo Montanari, invasion of the declining, and still largely vegetarian, Roman Empire by northern, meat-eating "barbarians" brought widespread deforestation and consolidated landholding to accommodate larger herds of livestock (1999: 77-78). Following the adoption of this Germanic model, environmental historian William Cronon observes, "domesticated grazing animals—and the tool which they made possible, the plow—were arguably the single most distinguishing characteristic of European agricultural practices." And after 1492, European livestock may have done more to destroy Native American ecosystems than all the invading armies combined (1983: 128). "The introduction of livestock proved to be the greatest success story in the culinary conquest of America," Jeffrey Pilcher observes in his history of Mexican foodways. "Herds [of cattle] overran the countryside, driving Indians from their fields" (1998: 30).

Differences in gender attitudes toward meat also have had important consequences. Men have long invoked their power over women as a rationalization for having the best cuts of scarce meat, and such differences in nutrition may indeed have made men more powerful than women deprived of iron, protein, and calcium. In short, with so much at stake in our steaks, there is an almost classic conflict between the rich rewards and stark consequences of an animal-based diet. Such conflicts make for exciting drama—and interesting study. . . .

But perhaps the best place for the individual consumer to begin to reconcile the contradictory tugs of identity, convenience, and responsibility is in the kitchen. As I tell my students at the end of my food course, if you want to create a better future, start by learning to cook. In our quick-and-easy age, it's one of the more subversive things you can do, for when you cook you take control of a piece of the food chain. Moreover, you may start to wonder how the food got to your kitchen—and that's a really good question.

Works Cited

Adams, Carol J. (1992), *The Sexual Politics of Meat: A Feminist-Vegetarian Critical Theory*, New York: Continuum.

Appadurai, Arjun (1981), "GastroPolitics in Hindu South Asia," *American Ethnologist* 8(3): 494–511.

Avakian, Arlene Voski (ed.) (1997), *Through the Kitchen Window: Women Writers Explore the Intimate Meanings of Food and Cooking*, Boston: Beacon Press.

Belasco, Warren, and Scranton, Philip (eds), (2002), *Food Nations: Selling Taste in Consumer Societies*, New York: Routledge.

Belasco, Warren, (2006), *Meals to Come: A History of the Future of Food*, Berkeley: University of California Press.

Berry, Wendell (1989), "The Pleasures of Eating," *Journal of Gastronomy* 5(2): 125–31.

Byrnes, J. (1976), "Raising Pigs by the Calendar at Maplewood Farm," *Hog Farm Management* (September): 30.

Cowan, Ruth Schwartz (1983), *More Work for Mother: The Ironies of Household Technology from the Open Hearth to the Microwave*, New York: Basic Books.

Cronon, William (1983), *Changes in the Land: Indians, Colonists, and the Ecology of New England*, New York: Hill and Wang.

Cronon, William (1991), *Nature's Metropolis: Chicago and the Great West*, New York: Norton.

Curtin, Deane, and Heldke, Lisa M. (eds) (1992), *Cooking, Eating, and Thinking: Transformative Philosophies of Food*, Bloomington, IN: Indiana University Press.

DeVault, Marjorie L. (1991), *Feeding the Family: The Social Organization of Caring as Gendered Work*, Chicago: University of Chicago Press.

Diamond, Jared (1999), *Guns, Germs, and Steel: The Fates of Human Societies*, New York: Norton.

Dietler, Michael, and Hayden, Brian (eds) (2001), *Feasts: Archaeological and Ethnographic Perspectives on Food, Politics, and Power*, Washington, DC: Smithsonian Institution Press.

East, Edward M. (1924), *Mankind at the Crossroads*, New York: Charles Scribner's Sons.

Egerton, March (ed.) (1994), *Since Eve Ate Apples*, Portland, OR: Tsunami Press.

Fine, Gary Alan (1996), *Kitchens: The Culture of Restaurant Work*, Berkeley: University of California Press.

Grew, Raymond (ed.) (1999), *Food and Global History*, Boulder: Westview Press.

Heldke, Lisa (2006), "The Unexamined Meal Is Not Worth Eating, or Why and How Philosophers (Might/Could/Do) Study Food," *Food, Culture, and Society: An International Journal of Multidisciplinary Research* 9(2): 201–19.

Jacobs, Marc, and Scholliers, Peter (eds), (2003), *Eating Out in Europe*, Oxford: Berg.

Jaine, Tom (1999), "Bread," in Alan Davidson (ed.), *Oxford Companion to Food*, New York: Oxford University Press, pp. 95–8.

Korsmeyer, Carolyn (1999), *Making Sense of Taste: Food and Philosophy*, Ithaca, NY: Cornell University Press.

Lentz, Carola (ed.) (1999), *Changing Food Habits: Case Studies from Africa, South America, and Europe*, Amsterdam: Harwood.

Mack, Arien (ed.) (1999), "Food: Nature and Culture," *Social Research* 66(1).

McPhee, John (1971), *Encounters with the Archdruid: Narratives about a Conservationist and Three of His Natural Enemies*, New York: Farrar, Straus & Giroux.

Mennell, Stephen, Murcott, Anne, and van Otterloo, Anneke (1992), *The Sociology of Food: Eating, Diet, and Culture*, London: Sage.

Menzel, Peter, and D'Aluisio, Faith (2005), *Hungry Planet*, Berkeley: Ten Speed Press.

Montanari, Massimo (1999), "Food Systems and Models of Civilization," in Jean-Louis Flandrin and Massimo Montanari (eds), *Food: A Culinary History from Antiquity to the Present*, New York: Columbia University Press, pp. 69–78.

Oates, Joyce Carol (1993), "Food Mysteries," in Daniel Halpern (ed.), *Not for Bread Alone*, Hopewell, NJ: Ecco Press, pp. 25–37.

Orr, David (1994), *Earth in Mind: On Education, Environment, and the Human Prospect*, Washington, DC: Island Press.

Pilcher, Jeffrey M. (1998), *Que Vivan los Tamales! Food and the Making of Mexican Identity*, Albuquerque, NM: University of New Mexico Press.

Pollan, Michael (2006), *The Omnivore's Dilemma: A Natural History of Four Meals*, New York: Penguin.

Rensberger, Boyce (1991), "Anthropology: Diets that Define Amazon Tribes," *Washington Post*, December 30, p. A3.

Rozin, Paul (1999), "Food is Fundamental, Fun, Frightening, and Far-Reaching," in Mack, Arien (ed.), "Food: Nature and Culture," *Social Research* 66(1), pp. 9–30.

Shapiro, Laura (1986), *Perfection Salad: Women and Cooking at the Turn of the Century*, New York: Farrar, Straus & Giroux.

Shapiro, Laura (2004), *Something from the Oven: Reinventing Dinner in 1950s America*, New York: Viking.

Sobal, Jeffrey (1999), "Food System Globalization, Eating Transformations, and Nutrition Transitions," in Raymond Grew (ed.), *Food in Global History*, Boulder, CO: Westview, pp. 171–93.

Strasser, Susan (1982), *Never Done: A History of American Housework*, New York: Pantheon Books.

Tobias, Ruth (2004), "Toast," in Andrew Smith (ed.), *Oxford Encyclopedia of Food and Drink in America*, New York: Oxford University Press, p. 122.

Vogt, William (1948), *The Road to Survival*, New York: William Sloane Associates.

Wackernagel, Mathis, and Rees, William (1996), *Our Ecological Footprint: Reducing Human Impact on the Earth*, Gabriola Island, BC: New Society Publishers.

Discussion Questions

1. Explain Warren Belasco's statement that "civilization is impossible without food." Imagine a world without any industry or cultural traditions related to food. Describe the changes in daily living that would result. After doing this mental exercise, why do you think that Belasco's statement is or is not basically correct?

2. What reasons does Belasco give to explain the previous lack of any serious study of food? Why do you think that currently there is an increase in food studies? What would Pollan say?

3. Reproduce Belasco's food pyramid. Explain each point on the triangle in relation to the *food system*. Now discuss these labels in relation to your own diet. Consider which point most often governs your food choices, and tell why you do or do not feel physically, emotionally, and intellectually satisfied with your diet.

4. Belasco refers, in "Why Study Food," to Pollan, and summarizes some of what Pollan argues in "The American Paradox." Go back and review what Belasco says about Pollan's view. Make two lists, one itemizing Pollan's basic assertions, and the other itemizing Belasco's. Compare the two lists. What ideas do these two writers share? Do you find any areas of disagreement? Explain.

SCIENCE SAYS THERE'S NO SUCH THING AS "COMFORT FOOD." WE ALL BEG TO DIFFER.

Emma Brockes

Emma Brockes graduated from Oxford University and is a writer and a journal-ist. She writes on a number of subjects. Her first book, What Would Barbra Do? *(2007), explores her great affection for, and interest in, stage musicals. Her most recent book,* She Left Me the Gun: My Mother's Life before Me *(2014), is a memoir that traces Brockes's journey to South Africa after her mother's death to find out what drove her mother to emigrate from Johannesburg to London. The following reading is from her blog, which is published by the* Guardian, *an online weekly newspaper.*

Most of us know this intuitively—that comfort and junk foods are subtly distinct. The former is an emotional as well as a nutritional unit, and the latter is merely a sugar rush. Besides which, no cookbook would dare put the word "junk" in its title, but whole shelves are devoted to the art of the comfort food. If, after a hard day, you make yourself mashed potatoes with gravy, or mac and cheese with brown sauce, or scram-bled eggs with the consistency of an Ultimate Frisbee, it is probably because someone once made it for you exactly that way. And while no two people's comfort foods are alike, the terrain is broadly the same: sloppy food you can spoon-feed yourself, with at least one element everyone else finds revolting.

For this reason, other people's comfort food has an editorial interest. It has a story, as Mark Bittman reflected recently in the *New York Times* in a charming piece about bagels and lox. Or it adds a certain humanity to high office. Madeleine Albright, in an interview I did with her many years ago, volunteered that after a rough day, "I come home, put on a flannel nightgown, [and] make myself the most disgusting thing, which is cottage cheese with ketchup." If one needs further evi-dence for how fascinating other people's food choices are, one need only look at all the websites devoted to death row inmates' last meals.

So it is with some surprise, then, that we greet research coming out of the Univer-sity of Minnesota this month suggesting that our faith in certain foods to lift our spirits and soothe our feelings is entirely without cause. In a study presented at a meeting of the Association for Psychological Science, subjects were asked to come up with two foods—one they thought of as a "comfort" food—which is to say a food which they said had the power to change their moods—and one that they liked but which had no emotional resonance. As in a scene from *A Clockwork Orange*, subjects were then shown a video designed to disturb them in some way and, after it was over, asked how they felt (which was always unhappy). They were then given either their self-identified comfort food, the other food, a granola bar (as a kind of kill-joy control), or nothing at all—and again asked how they were feeling. The results surprised even the researchers. Irrespective of which food they ate, three minutes after the test, all participants in the study had cheered up. "People can develop these very unhealthy habits, where they just immediately reach for these yummy foods when they feel sad," said researcher Hather Scherschel Wagner. It makes no sense, she said, because "whether it's your comfort food, or it's a granola bar, or if you eat nothing at all, you will eventually feel better. Basically, comfort food can't speed up that healing process."

I have several problems with the methodology of this study, chief among them what happens when you ask people to self-report feelings. As we know from the way we ourselves might lie or exaggerate in a private journal, the very fact of studying one's own reaction to something changes its nature. Secondly, an artificially-induced feeling of crappiness is, one would think, completely different to the multi-layered and highly personal reasons one might turn to comfort food in regular life—a specific response to a specific and complicated psychological state that it is almost impossible to recreate in lab conditions.

Then again, the phenomenon of comfort food is barely complicated enough to merit study. When you are threatened, you retreat in your mind to places of happiness. Comfort food is merely an *aide-mémoire* that uses more than one of your senses.

None of this undermines the fact that most comfort foods are very bad for you and are only supposed to be a once-in-a-while measure. (Michelle Obama, writing in the *New York Times* on Thursday, reminded us of this by castigating the food lobbies for undermining efforts to promote healthy eating among children: "Remember a few years ago when Congress declared that the sauce on a slice of pizza should count as a vegetable in school lunches?")

But since comfort food really is just a route back into memory, it seems odd to reject it as meaningless—even if it is a placebo. As unfashionable cuisines come back into style—artisanal gefilte fish, anyone? —promoted by the grandchildren of their original enthusiasts, the overlap between food, family, and feeling is as strong as it ever was. Bread sauce the consistency of glue, fish finger sandwiches, shepherd's pie with meat and potato that can be mashed into a brown paste and other people at the table shout at you—it might not present well in research, but most of us know that happiness is made of exactly this.

Discussion Questions

1. Discuss the difference between comfort food and junk food. Give examples of things you have seen other people eat while under emotional stress. Describe your reaction to their choices.

2. What were the findings of the University of Minnesota's study on comfort foods? Why does Emma Brockes question the validity of this study? If you were conducting your own study on this topic, describe the changes you would make. Would Pollan agree with Brockes, or would he agree with the findings of the study?

3. What is an *aide-mémoire*? How can food serve as an *aide-mémoire*? Identify a food and explain the reason that it functions as your *aide-mémoire*. Tell about a recent time when you enjoyed this particular food. How did eating it make you feel at that time?

4. Review Michael Pollan's essay and then list the points from his essay that you think Brockes would agree with. Compare the tone and development of the two readings. Do you think Brockes and Pollan are writing with the same readership in mind? Explain.

5. If Brockes decided to rewrite her essay for submission to a scholarly journal, what might her thesis statement look like? Draft one possible version.

EAT UP. YOU'LL BE HAPPIER.

PAMELA DRUCKERMAN

Pamela Druckerman is an American author and journalist. She received a BA in philosophy from Colgate University and an MA in international affairs from Columbia University's School of International and Public Affairs. She has been a staff reporter for The Wall Street Journal, *and her articles have appeared in prestigious publications such as* The New York Times *and* The Washington Post. *Her book,* Lust In Translation: Infidelity from Tokyo to Tennessee *(2007), examines various cultures's attitudes towards adultery. She has also written* Bringing Up Bebe: One American Mother Discovers the Wisdom of French Parenting *(2012).*

My father-in-law, an anthropologist, likes to talk about the time he ate dog penis. He was visiting a remote town in South Korea, and the mayor invited him to lunch. Once they'd finished the dog soup (not a big deal), a waitress carried out the boiled penis on a silver plate. The mayor cut it lengthwise with scissors, then served half to each of them.

"It tasted exactly like tripe—intestine," my father-in-law recalls. "You're always supposed to say, 'like chicken,' but it didn't taste at all like chicken."

Anthropologists are at the extreme end of what used to be a universal rule of hospitality: When a host offers you food, you eat it. It's a show of trust, and a sign of belonging. Refuse his meal and you're effectively rejecting him.

But as anyone who has recently tried to host a birthday party or a dinner in the English-speaking world knows, this rule no longer matters. Forget about dog penis; try offering visitors lasagna (it's not vegan, not gluten-free, and it couldn't have been cooked by a caveman).

Our increasingly choosy food habits are the subject of a French collection of academic essays, *Selective Eating: The Rise, Meaning and Sense of Personal Dietary Requirements,* which will be published in English next week. The editor, Claude Fischler, a social anthropologist, chose the topic after discovering that even anthropologists aren't exempt: An Australian colleague said she had asked her Aboriginal subjects to accommodate her gluten-free diet, followed by choice, not by medical necessity.

Having lived in America and France, I've been on both sides of the picky-eating divide. I know it's tiresome to hear about the paradoxically fabulous French eating habits. But it's no accident that UNESCO made the French gastronomic meal part of the "Intangible Cultural Heritage of Humanity." It's worth looking at how they cope with picky eaters.

When I arrived in Paris about a decade ago, I was a vegetarian (out of squeamishness) and on a low-carbohydrate diet. This had seemed reasonable in New York, but it baffled Parisians. Restaurants balked at making substitutions. Hostesses didn't ask for my dietary requirements.

In one study, 68 percent of French adults said they force themselves to eat some of everything when they're invited to someone's house. A Parisian academic told me she became incensed when an American dinner guest requested a vegetarian meal. "Although she was extremely friendly and pleasant—never again!"

There are French vegetarians, too, of course. Lots of people here go on diets, including low-carbohydrate ones. Gluten-free pasta has appeared in the supermarket. But people are low-key about their by-choice eating schemes. The overarching conventional wisdom—what everyone from government experts to my French girlfriends take as articles of faith—is that restrictive diets generally don't make you healthier or slimmer. Instead, it's best to eat a variety of high-quality foods in moderation and pay attention to whether you're hungry.

In "Selective Eating," Jean-Denis Vigne, of France's National Museum of Natural History, concludes that the Paleolithic diet is "more inspired by the myth of the noble savage than by the realities revealed by science," and that humans are adaptable omnivores.

Choosy eating interferes with another key aspect of French mealtimes: the shared experience of food. In France, "eating does not have the sole purpose of nourishing the biological body but also and above all of nourishing the social bond," writes the social psychologist Estelle Masson in *Selective Eating*.

This can seem excessively formal. When I invited some French families over to eat pizza and watch a soccer match on TV, they automatically assembled at my dining-room table for a sit-down meal. (I had foolishly envisioned eating pizza on the couch.)

We Anglophones have reasons for adopting strange diets. Increasingly, we live alone. We have an unprecedented choice of foods, and we're not sure what's in them, or whether they're good for us. And we expect to customize practically everything: parenting, news, medicines, even our own faces.

Anyway, we're not trying to have a shared experience of food. Mr. Fischler says that in his focus groups, Americans often described eating as part of an individual journey of self-discovery, in which each person tries to "find out over time and experience what my true nutritional self is, and satisfy it."

But selective eating may not lead us to our best selves. Since I've lived in France, there's been a march of studies pointing to the wisdom of what the French have been doing all along. Apparently, it's fine to eat some cheese, butter, chocolate, and red meat; diets rarely work; and to lose weight, you should exercise more and eat less. Mr. Fischler is currently studying the health impact of eating together by looking at buffet tables at Club Med and the American "freshman 15."

Eating among the French certainly affected me. After a few years here, I gave up most of my selective food habits. I still wouldn't eat a dog's penis, but I have tried oysters. It turns out that the best part of going with the food flow isn't the health benefits or the cuisine, it's the conversation. You can finally talk about something else.

Discussion Questions

1. What has historically been the universal rule of hospitality? What is signified by eating the host's food? How is rejection of the food perceived by the host? Tell about a time you ate something you would have preferred not to eat in order to be polite.

2. Discuss the French approach to food and eating. In what ways is it similar to and/or different from your own?

3. What are some of the reasons, according to Druckerman, that account for our eating habits? Do all or some of these reasons apply to your own diet? Explain.

4. Do you think Michael Pollan would approve of the effect that living in France had on Pamela Druckerman's eating habits? Explain.

A SEISMIC SHIFT IN HOW PEOPLE EAT

Hans Taparia And Pamela Koch

> *Hans Taparia is an American food activist and teacher. He earned his BS in management science from the Massachusetts Institute of Technology. He is a clinical assistant professor of business and society at New York University Stern School of Business, where he teaches courses in marketing, professional responsibility, and leadership. Pamela Koch earned an EdD from Teachers College Columbia University and is a professor at Teachers College Columbia University. She has written* ten Farm to Table and Beyond *(2008) and* Choice, Control: Using Science to Make Food *(2010).*

It's easy to make fun of people in big cities for their obsession with gluten, or chia seeds, or cleanses.

But urbanites are not the only ones turning away from the products created by big food companies. Eating habits are changing across the country and food companies are struggling to keep up.

General Mills will drop all artificial colors and flavors from its cereals. Perdue, Tyson, and Foster Farm have begun to limit the use of antibiotics in their chicken. Kraft declared it was dropping artificial dyes from its macaroni and cheese. Hershey's will begin to move away from ingredients such as the emulsifier polyglycerol polyricinoleate to "simple and easy-to-understand ingredients" like "fresh milk from local farms, roasted California almonds, cocoa beans, and sugar."

Those announcements reflect a new reality: Consumers are walking away from America's most iconic food brands. Big food manufacturers are reacting by cleaning up their ingredient labels, acquiring healthier brands and coming out with a prodigious array of new products. Last year, General Mills purchased the organic pasta maker Annie's Homegrown for $820 million—a price that was over four times the company's revenues, likening it to valuations more often seen in Silicon Valley. The company also introduced more than 200 new products, ranging from Cheerios Protein to Betty Crocker gluten-free cookie mix, to capitalize on the latest consumer fads.

Food companies are moving in the right direction, but it won't be enough to save them. If they are to survive changes in eating habits, they need a fundamental shift in their approach.

The food movement over the past couple of decades has substantially altered consumer behavior and reshaped the competitive landscape. Chains like Sweetgreen, a salad purveyor, are grabbing market share from traditional fast food companies. Brands such as Amy's Kitchen, with its organic products, and Kind bars are taking some of the space on shelves once consumed by Nestlé's Lean Cuisine and Mars.

For the large established food companies, this is having disastrous consequences. Per capita soda sales are down 25 percent since 1998, mostly replaced by water. Orange juice, a drink once seen as an important part of a healthy breakfast, has seen per capita consumption drop 45 percent in the same period. It is now more correctly considered a serious carrier of free sugar, stripped of its natural fibers. Sales of packaged cereals, also heavily sugar-laden, are down over 25 percent since 2000, with yogurt and granola taking their place. Frozen dinner sales are down nearly 12 percent from 2007 to 2013. Sales per outlet at McDonald's have been on a downward spiral for nearly three years, with no end in sight.

To survive, the food industry will need more than its current bag of tricks. There is a consumer shift at play that calls into question the reason packaged foods exist. There was a time when consumers used to walk through every aisle of the grocery store, but today much of their time is being spent in the perimeter of the store with its vast collection of fresh products—raw produce, meats, bakery items and fresh prepared foods. Sales of fresh prepared foods have grown nearly 30 percent since 2009, while sales of center-of-store packaged goods have started to fall. Sales of raw fruits and vegetables are also growing—among children and young adults, per capita consumption of vegetables is up 10 percent over the past five years.

The outlook for the center of the store is so glum that industry insiders have begun to refer to that space as the morgue. For consumers today, packaged goods conjure up the image of foods stripped of their nutrition and loaded with sugar. Also, decades of deceptive marketing, corporate-sponsored research, and government lobbying have left large food companies with brands that are fast becoming liabilities. According to one recent survey, 42 percent of millennial consumers, ages 20 to 37, don't trust large food companies, compared with 18 percent of non-millennial consumers who feel that way.

Food companies can't merely tinker. Nor will acquisition-driven strategies prove sufficient, because most acquisitions are too small to shift fortunes quickly. Acquired brands such as Annie's Homegrown, Happy Baby, and Honest Tea account for 1 percent or less of their buyers' revenues. Moreover, these brands, along with their missions and culture, tend to get quickly lost in the sales and marketing machine of big food companies. It is easy for them to get orphaned.

For legacy food companies to have any hope of survival, they will have to make bold changes in their core product offerings. Companies will have to drastically cut sugar; process less; go local and organic; use more fruits, vegetables and other whole foods; and develop fresh offerings. General Mills needs to do more than just drop the artificial ingredients from Trix. It needs to drop the sugar substantially, move to 100 percent whole grains, and increase ingredient diversity by expanding to other grains besides corn.

Instead of throwing good money after bad for its lagging frozen products, Nestlé, which is investing in a new $50 million frozen research and development facility, should introduce a range of healthy, fresh prepared meals for deli counters across the country.

McDonald's needs to do more than use antibiotic-free chicken. The back of the house for its 36,000 restaurants currently looks like a mini-factory serving fried frozen patties and french fries. It needs to look more like a kitchen serving freshly prepared meals with locally sourced vegetables and grains—and it still needs to taste great and be affordable.

These changes would require a complete overhaul of their supply chains, major organizational restructuring and billions of dollars of investment, but these corporations have the resources. It may be their last chance.

Discussion Questions

1. Describe the "new reality" facing big food manufacturers. Explain your own reasons for purchasing or avoiding food packaged under major brand names.

2. Discuss beverage consumption today. What types of drinks are losing sales? What are their most likely replacements? Are all of the replacements healthier than the originally popular drinks? How has branding been involved in the sale of these now-popular beverages?

3. What area of the grocery store has come to be known as "the morgue"? Describe the route you follow when you enter a food market. Do you go up and down the aisles? Circle the perimeter? Only search out particular items? How does your method compare to that of your parents or grandparents?

4. How does the information in this article support or contradict Michael Pollan's argument about our current food obsession?

RETHINKING EATING

Kate Murphy

Having radically changed the way we communicate, do research, buy books, listen to music, hire a car, and get a date, Silicon Valley now aims to transform the way we eat. Just as text messages have replaced more lengthy discourse and digital vetting has diminished the slow and awkward evolution of intimacy, tech entrepreneurs hope to get us hooked on more efficient, algorithmically derived food.

Call It Food 2.0.

Following Steve Jobs's credo that "people don't know what they want until you show it to them," a handful of high-tech start-ups are out to revolutionize the food system by engineering "meat" and "eggs" from pulverized plant compounds or cultured snippets of animal tissue. One company imagines doing away with grocery shopping, cooking, and even chewing, with a liquid meal made from algae byproducts.

This, of course, flies in the face of an entrenched local and artisanal food movement that has restaurant servers waxing romantic about where items on the menu come from and how they are prepared—the more natural and less processed, the better. And yet, despite their radically different approaches, the high- and low-tech culinary camps share a common desire to create a more sustainable food supply and, less loftily, to capitalize on people's appetites.

"Ever since Sylvester Graham invented the graham cracker, people have been trying to materialize their ethical position into morally or ideological pure foods," says Heather Paxson, an anthropologist at the Massachusetts Institute of Technology. "The graham cracker was supposed to increase the moral fiber of humans by filling them up so they wouldn't be lascivious from eating meat and other rich foods."

Whether for moral reasons or because of a Jobsian belief in the superiority of their vision, high-tech food entrepreneurs are focusing primarily on providing alternatives to animal protein. The demand is certainly there. Worldwide consumption of pork, beef, poultry, and other livestock products is expected to double by 2020. Animal protein is also the most vulnerable and resource-intensive part of the food supply. In addition to livestock production's runoff pollution, antibiotic abuse, and immense use of land and water, it is responsible for 14.5 percent of greenhouse gases, according to the United Nations.

Venture capital firms like Kleiner Perkins Caufield & Byers, Closed Loop Capital, Khosla Ventures, and Collaborative Fund have poured money into Food 2.0 projects. Backing has also come from a hit parade of tech-world notables including, Sergey Brin of Google, Biz Stone of Twitter, Peter Thiel of PayPal, and Bill Gates of Microsoft, as well as Li Ka-shing, Asia's wealthiest man, who bought early stakes in Facebook and Spotify.

"We're looking for wholesale reinvention of this crazy, perverse food system that makes people do the wrong thing," says Josh Tetrick, the vegan chief executive of San Francisco-based Hampton Creek. His company has created an egg substitute using protein extracted from the Canadian yellow pea, incorporating it into Just Scramble, Just Mayo, and Just Cookie Dough, which are starting to find their way onto grocery store shelves nationwide.

While current egg replacers (Ener-G, the Vegg, etc.) and meat alternatives (Tofurky, Soyrizo, etc.) have not achieved a high degree of household penetration, Hampton Creek and its rivals say they can come up with better products by relying more on computational science than food science.

Instead of the go-to ingredients previously used in animal protein substitutes—soy, wheat gluten, vegetable starches—Food 2.0 companies are using computer algorithms to analyze hundreds of thousands of plant species to find out what compounds can be stripped out and recombined to create what they say are more delicious and sustainable sources of protein.

"Our vice president of data was head of data analytics for Google Maps and You-Tube, and our last seven hires have been data scientists," Mr. Tetrick says. "We can run our experiments in the cloud rather than always having to grind ingredients up and trying them out in a recipe."

Meanwhile, in vitro meat producers such as Brooklyn- and California-based Modern Meadow and researchers in Europe are using tissue engineering technology developed for medical purposes like growing skin and organs.

"Most of the time, I make blood vessels," says Mark Post, a professor of vascular physiology at Maastricht University in the Netherlands. He led the team that made the first test tube burger, grown from cattle stem cells, which was eaten in front of reporters at a news conference in London last year. "We showed it can be done," Dr. Post said, acknowledging that at $332,000 for that single patty there's still a long way to go to make the product feasible.

But there's a significant ick factor when it comes to so-called Frankenfoods. Public health experts also point out that there's much we don't know about how foods nourish us. Stripping out and recombining a food's constituent parts or growing it in a PETRI dish is unlikely to replicate all the benefits. Critics also question whether the resources and emissions required to make these products are less harmful to the environment than more traditional production methods.

Instead of centrifuging out plant proteins, "Why not just eat the vegetables?" asks Marion Nestle, author of *Food Politics* and professor of nutrition, food studies, and public health at New York University.

High-tech food entrepreneurs, mostly white, well-educated young men who have spent much of their lives fueling up on fast food, say they want to provide more convenience and better taste.

"Being forced to take time from my day and having my train of thought interrupted by hunger was really bothersome to me," says Rob Rhinehart of San Francisco, the inventor of Soylent, a liquid meal replacement now being delivered to some 60,000 customers who preordered it during a yearlong crowdfunding campaign that ended in May and raised $3 million. "Trying to eat a balanced diet looked like I was leaping into a sea of complexity, of biochemistry and cooking, sourcing and cleaning."

To which Dr. Nestle says, "Sex is messy and a lot of trouble, too."

And like sex, food is fraught with emotional, psychological, social, cultural, gender, and religious associations. Sharing a meal is how we establish and maintain relationships. It is how we celebrate and mourn. Some attach their identity to the food they eat. Others use it to exert or lose control. These unpredictable and perhaps intransigent views and expectations may be Food 2.0's most daunting challenge.

"The cultural significance of meat is the biggest obstacle we face," says Ethan Brown, a vegan and the chief executive of Beyond Meat, which has developed a proprietary process of isolating and realigning the molecules of plant proteins to mimic the taste and texture of meat. "We need to make it clear you're not choosing between shooting a buck on the range and our product, but a highly manufactured Tyson product and our product."

So expect some rather intensive and slick social and mass media marketing. Advertising got us to accept and even crave Cheetos, Oreos, and Coca-Cola even though nature might have argued against it. Why not these high-tech iterations of meat and eggs? Or, in the end, will it all be like Tofurky, no matter how many algorithms you use to slice it?

Discussion Questions

1. Explain the way "high- and low-tech culinary camps" approach food. What things do they have in common? What things distinguish them from each other? According to your own recent eating habits, are you more of a "low-tech" or a "high-tech" consumer? Given enough time and money, how would your eating habits change?

2. Discuss some of the moral and ethical positions, as well as the health concerns, that affect people's food choices. How do you think Michael Pollan would respond to each of them? How do you think most people living in Third World countries would react to our recent cultural obsession with food choices?

3. Explain some of the Food 2.0 projects. How are Food 2.0 supporters trying to teach these goals? In your opinion, why will they or won't they ultimately be successful in changing the way we eat?

4. Marion Nestle is quoted twice in this article. From these two quoted passages, why do you surmise that her book, *Food Politics*, would more likely support or contradict Michael Pollan's argument about our attitude toward food? Why do you think it would or would not agree with your own attitude toward food?

THE IMPACT THAT CULTURAL FOOD SECURITY HAS ON IDENTITY AND WELL-BEING IN THE SECOND GENERATION U.S. AMERICAN MINORITY COLLEGE STUDENTS

Kathrine E. Wright, Julie E. Lucero, Jenanne K. Ferguson, Michelle L. Granner, Paul G. Devereux, Jennifer L. Pearson, Eric Crosbie

The following article is an excerpt from a more extensive and well-documented research project written by the above authors and published by The National Center for Biotechnology, International Society for Plant Pathology.

Food contributes to an individual's physical and mental well-being and expresses one's cultural identity through preparation, sharing, and consumption (i.e., foodways). Inadequate access to cultural foods can create cultural stress and affect one's identity and well-being. In particular, second-generation U.S. American student populations may have a higher risk for cultural stress due to academic stress, environmental changes, being away from family, and diminished financial stability to purchase cultural foods.

College populations continue to grow and become more diverse, and with the increasing second-generation American students, it is essential to improve the access and availability of cultural foods to improve their overall well-being.

First[1] and second-generation[2] Americans have been among the fastest-growing populations in the United States due to the Immigration and Nationality Act of 1965, which abolished race and ethnicity-based quotas and created an immigration boom (Kammer 2015). The immigration boom in the United States has also led to an increase in second-generation American university students. The proportion of second-generation American undergraduate students increased by 60% (6 percentage points) between the academic year 1999-2000 and the academic year 2011-2012, increasing the university student population's cultural and ethnic diversity across the United States (Arbeit et al.2016). Among these second-generation American undergraduates, 46% identified as Hispanic or Latino, 23% identified as White, 14% identified as Asian, 10% identified as Black, and 7% identified as another race or ethnicity (Arbeit et al. 2016

From *Food Security*, Volume 13 by Katherine E. Wright, Julie E. Lucero, Jenanne K. Ferguson, Michelle L. Granner, Paul G. Devereux, Jennifer L. Pearson, Eric Crosbie. Copyright © 2021 by International Society for Plant Pathology and Springer Nature B.V. Reprinted by permission.

[1]First-generation American immigrants are individuals who were born outside the United States (Arbeit et al. 2016).

[2]Individuals who were born in the United States to at least one parent who was foreign-born. The term "first-generation American" is also sometimes used in the literature to describe this same population (Arbeit et al. 2016).

The drastic environmental change that occurs with collegial transition often creates stressors for incoming college students (Fisher 1994). In addition to these stressors, second-generation Americans face additional barriers while attending colleges, such as acculturation stress, cultural barriers, and discrimination, which have been associated with poorer physical and mental health outcomes (Finch et al. 2001); Finch and Vega 2003; Flores et al. 2008; Lee et al. 2004. Second-generation Americans often play a balancing act between their cultural and ethnic identity and their American identity, creating additional stress for students (Schwartz et al. 2010). Having a powerful sense of ethnic identity is positively associated with well-being in various ethnic groups (Burnett-Zeigler et al. 2013; Daponte and Bade 2000; Phinney et al. 1997; Roberts et al. 1999). Thus, identity maintenance in second-generation American students could improve well-being outcomes, especially when navigating collegial transition stress (Outten et al. 2008; Ruiz 1990).

Consuming cultural foods is one method students may use to improve to maintain identity and well-being. The foods one consumes, and the transmission of meal-based rituals passed from one generation to the next, are markers of one's cultural and ethnic identity (Noriza et al. 2012; Steinberg 2012). Preparing, sharing, and consuming cultural foods, otherwise known as foodways, are physical and symbolic acts that bind with an individual's cultural identity, which act as "performative pedagogies of remembering" (Herakova and Cooks 2017, p. 241; Parraga 1990; Peñaloza 1994). Additionally, cultural food consumption is associated with nostalgia, familial memories, and feelings of pleasure, belonging, comfort, and well-being (Coveney and Bunton 2003; Locher et al. 2005; Osella and Osella 2008). Thus, many individuals try to safeguard their culture through foodways, particularly when transplanted to a culturally different location (Beoku-Betts 1995).

Unfamiliar cultural environments challenge one's traditional foodways and diminish the ability to prepare, share, and consume traditional foods, leading to cultural food insecurity. Power (2008) defined cultural food insecurity as having unreliable access to traditional/country food obtained through traditional harvesting practices. Expanding upon Power's definition, cultural food security exists when there is the availability, access, utilization (i.e., food preparation, sharing, and consumption; foodways), and stability of cultural foods (Alonso et al. 2018). Without these vital identity components, acculturative stress (i.e., losing part of one's culture; Gabaccia 2009) and food shock can occur, which can negatively affect the students' identity and well-being (Kim 2001; Lum and de Ferrière le Vayer 2016), by creating feelings of social isolation (Vallianatos and Raine 2008) and the loss of their cultural heritage and identity (Gabaccia 1998). Therefore, second-generation American university students must maintain their cultural and ethnic identity, as it has positive effects on well-being and health-related quality of life outcomes (Gray-Little and Hafdahl 2000; Ryff et al. 2003; Tsai et al. 2001; Umaña-Taylor et al. 2002; Utsey et al. 2002).

Unfortunately, food insecurity has become a growing concern in higher education. Students who self-identify as a racial or ethnic minority experience food insecurity at higher rates than their peers (El Zein et al. 2017; Gaines et al. 2014

Payne-Sturges et al. 2018). Data collected from 2007 to 2009 indicated that 26% of college and university students surveyed had foreign-born parents (Schwartz et al. 2011). In 2012, 16% of college students were second-generation Americans (Arbeit et al. 2016). While data on cultural food security is not available, second-generation American students who have traditional and cultural needs may be more likely to experience food insecurity than other college students. This is because they are more likely to be negatively affected by diminished access and availability to food that meets their food needs due to structural barriers.

Among students in the study, cultural food preparation, sharing, and consumption practices were deeply rooted in their [second-generation Americans'] cultural history, which had been generationally passed down. Through these food practices, second-generation American students learned about cultural norms, cultural traditions, and cultural history, and they connected with and understood their family and ancestors. These students often tied foodways to memories of family. This is critical when second-generation Americans are at college away from their families, as students mentioned that these memories were often the only thing tying them back to their cultural and ethnic identity. In our interviews, one student stated:

> A lot of my older elders and other relatives, a lot of them still reside in my parents' home countries, Taiwan and Thailand, so whenever I did visit them when I was young, you know, the food is very different and also the typical eating habits are also quite different. So perhaps then I didn't realize, but now that I've grown up, I do appreciate, and I do, think back to just all the love and all the wonderful times and care spent and care given to us from those times.

Furthermore, preparing, sharing, and consuming cultural foods embedded students into their social networks that allowed for creating bonds with others through commonalities such as food, music, dance, and language (i.e., culture). Carrying out these practices created a sense of belonging and helped maintain the second-generation Americans' identity, primarily when carried out with other students who shared similar cultural backgrounds. Not only was it essential to have foods that connected students to their family, but it was also essential to connect to others who share similar food memories and food associations among their peers. Other students mentioned that sharing their culture with friends from other cultures helped strengthen their identity and their bond with their friends. As one student put it:

> I think [sharing cultural foods] definitely makes [my identity] stronger. Whenever I, in general, get to talk about being Eritrean or the history or like the different types of food and how it's prepared and stuff, I feel like it provides my friends with a better understanding of who I am and how I grew up. And like, what my culture looks like. And I think [sharing food] provides us with a stronger bond because it makes them know me much better because they know me that way.

Unfortunately, students mentioned that the lack of diversity in [the surrounding city's] food and population often prevented them from preparing, sharing, consuming their cultural foods, bonding with like identities, and speaking their traditional language with others. Students indicated that losing these experiences made them feel like a significant component of themselves was missing.

When second-generation Americans go off to college and disperse from their families, it is up to them to find a way to uphold these cultural practices. On top of this pressure, students are also struggling with their self-identity as they move from late adolescence into young adulthood, while also becoming disoriented in an unfamiliar environment without their foodways and cultural ties. Thus, this tumultuous time causes second-generation Americans to experience a significant amount of stress. Universities may thwart access and availability stressors by developing campus organizations to identify their cultural food needs and secure food and monetary donors to supplement the food pantry with cultural food staples. These organizations could further develop a grocer and restaurant directory with transportation information for each. Cultural foods are potentially a remedial solution to alleviate cultural shock and acculturative stress in second-generation Americans.

Works Cited

Alonso EB, Cockx L, Swinnen J. Culture and food security. Global Food Security. 2018;17:113–127. doi: 10.1016/j.gfs.2018.02.002.

Arbeit, C. A., Staklis, S., & RTI International. (2016). New American undergraduates: Enrollment trends and age at arrival of immigrant and second-generation students. (statistics in brief NCES 2017-414). Institute of Education Sciences.

Beoku-Betts JA. We got our way of cooking things: Women, food, and preservation of cultural identity among the Gullah. Gender & Society. 1995;9(5):535–555.

Burnett-Zeigler I, Bohnert KM, Ilgen MA. Ethnic identity, acculturation and the prevalence of lifetime psychiatric disorders among black, Hispanic, and Asian adults in the US. Journal of Psychiatric Research. 2013;47(1):56–63.

Coveney J, Bunton R. In pursuit of the study of pleasure: Implications for health research and practice. Health. 2003;7(2):161–179. doi: 10.1177/1363459303007002873.

Daponte, B. O., & Bade, S. L. (2000). The evolution, cost, and operation of the private food assistance network. Institute for Research on Poverty, University of Wisconsin-Madison.

El Zein A, Shelnutt K, Colby S, Olfert M, Kattelmann K, Brown O, Kidd T, Horacek T, White A, Zhou W. Socio-demographic correlates and predictors of food insecurity among first year college students. Journal of the Academy of Nutrition and Dietetics. 2017;117(10):A146.

Finch BK, Hummer RA, Kol B, Vega WA. The role of discrimination and acculturative stress in the physical health of Mexican-origin adults. Hispanic Journal of Behavioral Sciences. 2001;23(4):399–429.

Finch BK, Vega WA. Acculturation stress, social support, and self-rated health among Latinos in California. Journal of Immigrant Health. 2003;5(3):109–117.

Fisher, S. (1994). Stress in academic life: The mental assembly line. Open University Press.

Flores E, Tschann JM, Dimas JM, Bachen EA, Pasch LA, de Groat CL. Perceived discrimination, perceived stress, and mental and physical health among Mexican-origin adults. Hispanic Journal of Behavioral Sciences. 2008;30(4):401–424.

Gabaccia, D. R. (1998). Immigration, isolation, and industry. In *We Are What We Eat* (p. 54). Harvard University press.

Gabaccia, D. R. (2009). *We are what we eat: Ethnic food and the making of Americans.* Harvard University Press.

Gaines A, Robb CA, Knol LL, Sickler S. Examining the role of financial factors, resources and skills in predicting food security status among college students. International Journal of Consumer Studies. 2014;38(4):374–384. doi: 10.1111/ijcs.12110.

Gray-Little B, Hafdahl AR. Factors influencing racial comparisons of self-esteem: A quantitative review. Psychological Bulletin. 2000;126(1):26–54.

Herakova L, Cooks L. Hands in the dough: Bread and/as a pedagogy of performative remembering. Text and Performance Quarterly. 2017;37(3–4):239–256.

Kammer, J. (2015). The hart-Celler immigration act of 1965. Center for Immigration Studies.

Kim, Y. Y. (2001). *Becoming intercultural: An integrative theory of communication and cross-cultural adaptation.* Sage.

Lee J-S, Koeske GF, Sales E. Social support buffering of acculturative stress: A study of mental health symptoms among Korean international students. International Journal of Intercultural Relations. 2004;28(5):399–414.

Locher JL, Yoels WC, Maurer D, Van Ells J. Comfort foods: An exploratory journey into the social and emotional significance of food. Food & Foodways. 2005;13(4):273–297.

Lum, C. M. K., & de Ferrière le Vayer, M. (2016). *Urban foodways and communication: ethnographic studies in intangible cultural food heritages around the world.* Rowman & Littlefield Publishers.

Noriza, I., Zahari, M. M., Shazali, M., Rosmaliza, M., & Hannita, S. (2012). Acculturation, foodways and Malaysian food identity. Current Issues in Hospitality and Tourism Research and Innovations, 359–363.

Osella C, Osella F. Food, memory, community: Kerala as both 'Indian Ocean'zone and as agricultural homeland. South Asia: Journal of South Asian Studies. 2008;31(1):170–198.

Outten HR, Schmitt MT, Garcia DM, Branscombe NR. Coping options: Missing links between minority group identification and psychological well-being. Applied Psychology. 2008;58(1):146–170.

Parraga IM. Determinants of food consumption. Journal of the American Dietetic Association. 1990;90(5):661–663.

Payne-Sturges DC, Tjaden A, Caldeira KM, Vincent KB, Arria AM. Student hunger on campus: Food insecurity among college students and implications for academic institutions. American Journal of Health Promotion. 2018;32(2):349–354.

Peñaloza L. Atravesando fronteras/border crossings: A critical ethnographic exploration of the consumer acculturation of Mexican immigrants. Journal of Consumer Research. 1994;21(1):32–54.

Phinney JS, Cantu CL, Kurtz DA. Ethnic and American identity as predictors of self-esteem among African American, Latino, and White adolescents. Journal of Youth and Adolescence. 1997;26(2):165–185.

Power EM. Conceptualizing food security for aboriginal people in Canada. Canadian Journal of Public Health. 2008;99(2):95–97.

Roberts RE, Phinney JS, Masse LC, Chen YR, Roberts CR, Romero A. The structure of ethnic identity of young adolescents from diverse ethnocultural groups. The Journal of Early Adolescence. 1999;19(3):301–322.

Ruiz AS. Ethnic identity: Crisis and resolution. Journal of Multicultural Counseling and Development. 1990;18(1):29–40.

Ryff, C. D., Keyes, C. L., & Hughes, D. L. (2003). Status inequalities, perceived discrimination, and eudaimonic well-being: Do the challenges of minority life hone purpose and growth? *Journal of Health and Social Behavior*, 275–291.

Schwartz SJ, Unger JB, Zamboanga BL, Szapocznik J. Rethinking the concept of acculturation: Implications for theory and research. American Psychologist. 2010;65(4):237–251

Schwartz SJ, Weisskirch RS, Zamboanga BL, Castillo LG, Ham LS, Huynh Q-L, Park IJ, Donovan R, Kim SY, Vernon M. Dimensions of acculturation: Associations with health risk behaviors among college students from immigrant families. Journal of Counseling Psychology. 2011;58(1):27–41.

Steinberg A. What we talk about when we talk about food: Using food to teach history at the tenement museum. The Public Historian. 2012;34(2):79–89.

Tsai JL, Ying Y-W, Lee PA. Cultural predictors of self-esteem: A study of Chinese American female and male young adults. Cultural Diversity and Ethnic Minority Psychology. 2001;7(3):284–297.

Umaña-Taylor AJ, Diversi M, Fine MA. Ethnic identity and self-esteem of Latino adolescents: Distinctions among the Latino populations. Journal of Adolescent Research. 2002;17(3):303–327.

Utsey SO, Chae MH, Brown CF, Kelly D. Effect of ethnic group membership on ethnic identity, race-related stress, and quality of life. Cultural Diversity and Ethnic Minority Psychology. 2002;8(4):366–377.

Vallianatos H, Raine K. Consuming food and constructing identities among Arabic and south Asian immigrant women. Food, Culture & Society. 2008;11(3):355–373. doi: 10.2752/175174408X347900.

Discussion Questions

1. Explain the way obtaining familiar food has become problematic for American minority college students? How does this lack of cultural food cause insecurity and identity issues?

2. What is the main point of difference between the scientific studies of comfort food and Emma Brockes' discussion of the way they function? How would her idea support the importance of access to ethnic foods on campus?

3. Discuss the similarities and differences between Pamela Druckerman's experience with French food while living in France with minority college students experience with the type of mainstream American food available while living on a college campus. Why do or do you not think there were times during her years living abroad that she experienced insecurity about her identity because of the change in her eating habits?

4. What are some of the solutions offered by this article to mitigate the food-related stress experienced by minority college students? What ways, if any, does your college address the issue? Brainstorm some other ideas that could be implemented at your school.

THE FINE LINE BETWEEN CULINARY APPROPRIATION AND APPRECIATION DON'T APPROPRIATE, APPRECIATE.

KINSEY LONG

Kinsey Long is a student at the University of California, Berkeley. She loves Japanese food and old Taylor Swift songs. The following article was written for Spoon University, an international site for connecting with students to form communities at their college campuses in order to exchange information and to share their interest in and love of food.

In this day and age, everyone has heard of political correctness. It's defined as the act of avoiding certain behavior or language that could insult or exclude discriminated groups of people. An example of being politically correct, or "PC," would be when the city of Berkeley changed the language in their municipal code to use only gender-neutral terms. A category of political *incorrectness* is cultural appropriation—defined as the inappropriate adoption of a minority culture by people of a different culture. The cultural appropriation of foods is defined as culinary appropriation, a common phenomenon in America.

There are clear reasons why one should avoid cultural appropriation. Oftentimes, it trivializes a history of violent oppression, for example dressing up in "black face" for Halloween. It could also pander to a racist stereotype, like the portrayal of subservient Asian women in film. Or it allows privileged people to exploit an oppressed race financially or culturally, as seen by whitewashing in Hollywood. Generally speaking, cultural appropriation prioritizes the entertainment or enjoyment of privileged people at the expense of a marginalized population.

Of course, there is a lot of controversy regarding political correctness and cultural appropriation, largely revolving around freedom of expression and determining what is appropriate or not. Is it okay for non-black celebrities to wear cornrows or dread-locks? Is it acceptable to say the m-word while singing a song? Should the Washington Redskins football team change its name?

People often talk about what cultural appropriation looks like in art, fashion, and sports, but rarely do we discuss how it manifests in food. The line between appropriation and appreciation is particularly thin when it comes to cultural foods, and this article hopes to draw a clearer line between the two.

Exploring other culinary cultures through eating or cooking is, in most cases, a sign of culinary appreciation. Of course, it is acceptable to eat pasta if you aren't Italian, or make pho if you aren't Vietnamese. As long as a person is open-minded to different cuisines, it's completely justifiable and beneficial for someone to try unfamiliar foods. Oftentimes, this can lead to the creation of incredible fusion dishes like the "sushiritto" and Korean barbecue rice burger.

However, it is critical to be mindful of how we react to different cuisines. It's okay to have a preference between cuisines, but not okay to automatically wrinkle your nose at an unfamiliar dish. "Lunchbox racism" is an example of when culinary distaste becomes politically unacceptable. The term comes from a common scenario where children of immigrants bring their home-cooked lunches to school and are faced by a chorus of "your lunch smells bad" and "that looks disgusting" from their peers. "Lunchbox racism" may seem like something that only occurs in primary schools, but it also can occur when adults travel abroad and react in horror at local food that they are offered. This is not to say that picky eaters are politically incorrect by any means. The difference between being a picky eater versus "lunchbox racism" is that the latter makes people feel ashamed about their culinary culture, and that is unacceptable.

On the other hand, appreciating a traditional meal by turning it into a food trend could also be seen as a trivialization of a culture. In her comic *Just Eat It*, writer Shin Yin Khor explains how food adventurers turn food cultures into medals of their own worldliness: "Eat, but don't expect a gold star for your gastronomical bravery. Eat, but don't pretend that the food lends you cultural insight into our 'exotic' ways. Eat, but recognize that we've been eating, too, and what is our sustenance isn't your adventure story. Just—eat."

Poorly made cultural dishes can be offensive, but are they culinary appropriation? As mentioned before, it is acceptable for people of one culture to experiment with another culture's cuisine, and to cook it poorly by accident is understandable. However, there can be much more controversy if the dish is inauthentic and misrepresents the cuisine.

A major debate regarding food authenticity is whether Americanized Chinese food is considered culinary appropriation. Since Chinese people frequently criticize such food for inaccurately reflecting the cuisine, it could be considered an "inappropriate adoption of a minority culture." A significant issue with the redesigned cuisine is that it creates many misconceptions about Chinese food. Representing an ancient culinary culture with takeout boxes, fortune cookies, and rice drowning in soy sauce is simply inaccurate. The frequent mispronunciation of dishes like "chow mein" and renaming of other dishes like "orange chicken" or "Kung Pao chicken" could also be considered an offensive mischaracterization of traditional Chinese delicacies. As a counterargument, one could claim that Americanized Chinese food has evolved into a separate cuisine, intending to represent a new Chinese-American immigrant culture rather than traditional Chinese culture. Perhaps if Americanized Chinese food actively relabeled itself as such, then it would be less controversial.

While people may be offended by culinary appropriation, few will actively condemn the act and demand change. However, the public has retaliated against a few cases of culinary appropriation, most of which involve the monetary exploitation of a traditional cultural recipe by someone of a different culture.

A controversial example of this is a case in Portland, where two non-Hispanic women traveled to Mexico, learned to make burritos from reluctant locals, and then opened a food truck. They were accused of starting a business based on stolen recipes and eventually had to shut down their food truck. Cultural cuisines are meant to be shared, but profiting from and taking credit for the cooking techniques of marginalized cultures is inappropriate. There is no such thing as copyright for recipes, so there is only a subjective moral line between respectfully adapting a recipe and stealing it.

What everyone should always consider is that food is a part of people's identities and should be treated with respect. You don't have to love a dish, but you also don't need to disrespect it along with the culture it belongs to. You can and should add your own twist to a dish, but recognize its differences from the traditional version. You can definitely recreate other people's cultural recipes, but don't claim it as your own for money. Don't appropriate food; appreciate it.

Discussion Questions

1. Explain in your own words the difference between appreciation and appropriation of cultural foods. Give some personal or hypothetical examples of each.

2. What is "lunchbox racism"? How can it be practiced by adults as well as children? If more ethnic foods were made available on college campuses in the dining halls and food courts in response to student requests, could a form of "lunchbox racism" be the result? Explain. Do you think a kind of reverse "lunchbox racism" might be occurring at American tourist attractions, such as Disneyland, that are frequently visited by foreigners? Why?

3. What are the two positions on ethnic foods, such as Chinese or Mexican food, served in American restaurants, particularly chain restaurants? Which argument do you find most convincing? Do you think the author's suggestion to resolve the controversy has merit? Why or why not?

4. How does money enter into the discussion of food appropriation? Do you think people should be allowed to copyright recipes? Explain.

Assignment #8

ARGUMENTS IN LITERATURE: "THE NIGHTINGALE AND THE ROSE"

This assignment asks you to write an essay that identifies and responds to an argument in Oscar Wilde's "The Nightingale and the Rose." Before you begin reading the story, we recommend that you turn to Part 1's "Finding and Using Arguments in Literature." It presents an explanation of how arguments are made through literature, some strategies to help you identify them, and an extended example that locates an argument in an excerpt from Charles Dickens's *A Christmas Carol*. After you study this extended example, return to this unit and read Oscar Wilde's short story "The Nightingale and the Rose." You will then write an essay that responds to the writing topic that immediately follows the story. As in previous assignments in *Write It Review*, you will find prewriting and drafting activities following Wilde's story that will help you to respond to the topic in an effective way. We encourage you to take full advantage of these prewriting and drafting activities because they will ensure that you develop your thoughts and organize them within an effective essay format. And, as in previous units, at the end of this unit you will find extended reading that offers a range of ideas on love--the topic of this unit. Read and discuss them carefully with classmates. The various perspectives in these reading selections will generate some useful ideas of your as you work to develop your thesis statement and support for "The Nightingale and the Rose."

THE NIGHTINGALE AND THE ROSE

Oscar Wilde

"She said that she would dance with me if I brought her red roses," cried the young Student; "but in all my garden there is no red rose."

From her nest in the holm-oak tree the Nightingale heard him, and she looked out through the leaves, and wondered.

"No red rose in all my garden!" he cried, and his beautiful eyes filled with tears. "Ah, on what little things does happiness depend! I have read all that the wise men have written, and all the secrets of philosophy are mine, yet for want of a red rose is my life made wretched."

"Here at last is a true lover," said the Nightingale. "Night after night have I sung of him, though I knew him not: Night after night have I told his story to the stars, and now I see him. His hair is dark as the hyacinth-blossom, and his lips are red as the rose of his desire; but passion has made his face like pale ivory, and sorrow has set her seal upon his brow."

"The Prince gives a ball tomorrow night," murmured the young Student, "and my love will be of the company. If I bring her a red rose, she will dance with me till dawn. If I bring her a red rose, I shall hold her in my arms, and she will lean her head upon my shoulder, and her hand will be clasped in mine. But there is no red rose in my garden, so I shall sit lonely, and she will pass me by. She will have no heed of me, and my heart will break."

"Here indeed is the true lover," said the Nightingale. "What I sing of, he suffers— what is joy to me, to him is pain. Surely Love is a wonderful thing. It is more precious than emeralds, and dearer than fine opals. Pearls and pomegranates cannot buy it, nor is it set forth in the marketplace. It may not be purchased of the merchants, nor can it be weighed out in the balance for gold."

"The musicians will sit in their gallery," said the young Student, "and play upon their stringed instruments, and my love will dance to the sound of the harp and the violin. She will dance so lightly that her feet will not touch the floor, and the courtiers in their gay dresses will throng around her. But with me she will not dance, for I have no red rose to give her"; and he flung himself down on the grass, and buried his face in his hands, and wept.

"Why is he weeping?" asked a little Green Lizard, as he ran past him with his tail in the air.

"Why, indeed?" said a Butterfly, who was fluttering about after a sunbeam.

"Why, indeed?" whispered a Daisy to his neighbor, in a soft, low voice.

"He is weeping for a red rose," said the Nightingale.

"For a red rose?" they cried; "how very ridiculous!" and the little Lizard, who was something of a cynic, laughed outright.

From The Happy Prince and Other Tales by Oscar Wilde, 1888.

But the Nightingale understood the secret of the Student's sorrow, and she sat silent in the oak tree, and thought about the mystery of Love.

Suddenly, she spread her brown wings for flight, and soared into the air. She passed through the grove like a shadow, and like a shadow she sailed across the garden.

In the center of the grass-plot was standing a beautiful Rose-tree, and when she saw it, she flew over to it, and lit upon a spray.

"Give me a red rose," she cried, "and I will sing you my sweetest song."

But the Tree shook its head.

"My roses are white," it answered; "as white as the foam of the sea, and whiter than the snow upon the mountain. But go to my brother who grows round the old sundial, and perhaps he will give you what you want."

So the Nightingale flew over to the Rose-tree that was growing round the old sundial.

"Give me a red rose," she cried, "and I will sing you my sweetest song."

But the Tree shook its head.

"My roses are yellow," it answered; "as yellow as the hair of the mermaiden who sits upon an amber throne, and yellower than the daffodil that blooms in the meadow before the mower comes with his scythe. But go to my brother who grows beneath the Student's window, and perhaps he will give you what you want."

So the Nightingale flew over to the Rose-tree that was growing beneath the Student's window.

"Give me a red rose," she cried, "and I will sing you my sweetest song."

But the Tree shook its head.

"My roses are red," it answered, "as red as the feet of the dove, and redder than the great fans of coral that wave and wave in the ocean cavern. But the winter has chilled my veins, and the frost has nipped my buds, and the storm has broken my branches, and I shall have no roses at all this year."

"One red rose is all I want," cried the Nightingale, "only one red rose! Is there no way by which I can get it?"

"There is a way," answered the Tree; "but it is so terrible that I dare not tell it to you."

"Tell it to me," said the Nightingale, "I am not afraid."

"If you want a red rose," said the Tree, "you must build it out of music by moonlight, and stain it with your own heart's-blood. You must sing to me with your breast against a thorn. All night long you must sing to me, and the thorn must pierce your heart, and your life-blood must flow into my veins, and become mine."

"Death is a great price to pay for a red rose," cried the Nightingale, "and Life is very dear to all. It is pleasant to sit in the green wood, and to watch the Sun in his chariot of gold, and the Moon in her chariot of pearl. Sweet is the scent of the hawthorn, and sweet are the bluebells that hide in the valley, and the heather that blows on the hill. Yet Love is better than Life, and what is the heart of a bird compared to the heart of a man?"

So she spread her brown wings for flight, and soared into the air. She swept over the garden like a shadow, and like a shadow she sailed through the grove.

The young Student was still lying on the grass, where she had left him, and the tears were not yet dry in his beautiful eyes.

"Be happy," cried the Nightingale, "be happy; you shall have your red rose. I will build it out of music by moonlight, and stain it with my own heart's-blood. All that I ask of you in return is that you will be a true lover, for Love is wiser than Philosophy, though she is wise, and mightier than Power, though he is mighty. Flame-colored are his wings, and colored like flame is his body. His lips are sweet as honey, and his breath is like frankincense."

The Student looked up from the grass, and listened, but he could not understand what the Nightingale was saying to him, for he only knew the things that are written down in books.

But the Oak-tree understood, and felt sad, for he was very fond of the little Nightingale who had built her nest in his branches.

"Sing me one last song," he whispered; "I shall feel very lonely when you are gone."

So the Nightingale sang to the Oak-tree, and her voice was like water bubbling from a silver jar.

When she had finished her song the Student got up and pulled a notebook and a lead pencil out of his pocket.

"She has form," he said to himself, as he walked away through the grove, "That cannot be denied to her; but has she got feeling? I am afraid not. In fact, she is like most artists; she is all style, without any sincerity. She would not sacrifice herself for others. She thinks merely of music, and everybody knows that the arts are selfish. Still, it must be admitted that she has some beautiful notes in her voice. What a pity it is that they do not mean anything, or do any practical good." And he went into his room, and lay down on his little pallet-bed, and began to think of his love; and, after a time, he fell asleep.

And when the Moon shone in the heavens, the Nightingale flew to the Rose-tree, and set her breast against the thorn. All night long she sang with her breast against the thorn, and the cold crystal Moon leaned down and listened. All night long she sang, and the thorn went deeper and deeper into her breast, and her life-blood ebbed away from her.

She sang first of the birth of love in the heart of a boy and a girl. And on the topmost spray of the Rose-tree, there blossomed a marvelous rose, petal following petal, as song followed song. Pale was it, at first, as the mist that hangs over the river—pale as the feet of the morning, and silver as the wings of the dawn. As the shadow of a rose in a mirror of silver, as the shadow of a rose in a water-pool, so was the rose that blossomed on the topmost spray of the Tree.

But the Tree cried to the Nightingale to press closer against the thorn. "Press closer, little Nightingale," cried the Tree, "or the Day will come before the rose is finished."

So the Nightingale pressed closer against the thorn, and louder and louder grew her song, for she sang of the birth of passion in the soul of a man and a maid.

And a delicate flush of pink came into the leaves of the rose, like the flush in the face of the bridegroom when he kisses the lips of the bride. But the thorn had not yet reached her heart, so the rose's heart remained white, for only a Nightingale's heart's-blood can crimson the heart of a rose.

And the Tree cried to the Nightingale to press closer against the thorn. "Press closer, little Nightingale," cried the Tree, "or the Day will come before the rose is finished."

So the Nightingale pressed closer against the thorn, and the thorn touched her heart, and a fierce pang of pain shot through her. Bitter, bitter was the pain, and wilder and wilder grew her song, for she sang of the Love that is perfected by Death, of the Love that dies not in the tomb.

And the marvelous rose became crimson, like the rose of the eastern sky. Crimson was the girdle of petals, and crimson as a ruby was the heart.

But the Nightingale's voice grew fainter, and her little wings began to beat, and a film came over her eyes. Fainter and fainter grew her song, and she felt something choking her in her throat.

Then she gave one last burst of music. The white Moon heard it, and she forgot the dawn, and lingered on in the sky. The red rose heard it, and it trembled all over with ecstasy, and opened its petals to the cold morning air. Echo bore it to her purple cavern in the hills, and woke the sleeping shepherds from their dreams. It floated through the reeds of the river, and they carried its message to the sea.

"Look, look!" cried the Tree, "the rose is finished now"; but the Nightingale made no answer, for she was lying dead in the long grass, with the thorn in her heart.

And at noon the Student opened his window and looked out.

"Why, what a wonderful piece of luck!" he cried; "here is a red rose! I have never seen any rose like it in all my life. It is so beautiful that I am sure it has a long Latin name"; and he leaned down and plucked it.

Then he put on his hat, and ran up to the Professor's house with the rose in his hand.

The daughter of the Professor was sitting in the doorway winding blue silk on a reel, and her little dog was lying at her feet.

"You said that you would dance with me if I brought you a red rose," cried the Student. "Here is the reddest rose in all the world. You will wear it tonight next your heart, and as we dance together, it will tell you how I love you."

But the girl frowned.

"I am afraid it will not go with my dress," she answered; "and, besides, the Chamberlain's nephew has sent me some real jewels, and everybody knows that jewels cost far more than flowers."

"Well, upon my word, you are very ungrateful," said the Student angrily; and he threw the rose into the street, where it fell into the gutter, and a cart-wheel went over it.

"Ungrateful!" said the girl. "I tell you what, you are very rude; and, after all, who are you? Only a Student. Why, I don't believe you have even got silver buckles to your shoes as the Chamberlain's nephew has"; and she got up from her chair and went into the house.

"What a silly thing Love is," said the Student as he walked away. "It is not half as useful as Logic, for it does not prove anything, and it is always telling one of things that are not going to happen, and making one believe things that are not true. In fact, it is quite unpractical, and, as in this age to be practical is everything, I shall go back to Philosophy and study Metaphysics."

So he returned to his room and pulled out a great dusty book, and began to read.

Writing Topic

According to the story, why does the Nightingale, an ideal representation of love, have to die? Do you agree with the story's point of view on love? Be sure to support your position with specific examples drawn from your own experience; your observation of others; your reading of literature; your viewings of movies, television, or other media; and your understanding? gained from the larger society and culture to which you belong.

To respond to this topic, consider the way the other readings in this unit work with literature as argument, either to analyze literature to identify an argument, such as in "Shakespeare Flirts with the Sadistic: *The Taming of the Shrew* as a Redefinition of Love," or to use arguments in literature to support an essay writer's own argument, such as in "The Honeymoon's Just Beginning" and "The Importance of Being Married." How do the views of love in any or all of these readings support or counter your own view of love?

Vocabulary Check

Use a dictionary to define the following words from Oscar Wilde's "The Nightingale and the Rose." Write all meanings that are relevant to the ideas in the passage. Then find each word in his story and underline the sentence that contains it.

1. *wretched*

2. *seal (not the animal)*

3. *clasp (verb)*

4. *gallery*

5. *courtier*

6. *throng (verb)*

_____

_____

_____

_____

7. *cynic*

_____

_____

_____

_____

8. *soar*

_____

_____

_____

_____

9. *sundial*

_____

_____

_____

_____

10. *scythe*

_____

_____

_____

_____

11. *chariot*

_____

_____

_____

_____

12. *frankincense*

_____

_____

_____

_____

13. *pallet*

_____

_____

_____

_____

Questions to Guide Your Reading

Paragraphs 1-2

What is the Student looking for in the garden? Why does he need it? Who overhears the Student in the garden?

Paragraph 3

Does the Student think that his studies have helped him find happiness in life? Why or why not?

Paragraph 4

Why is the Nightingale predisposed to have sympathy for the Student's situation?

Paragraph 5

What is the occasion the Student anticipates, and what are the two alternative experiences he foresees for himself at that time?

Paragraph 6

How does the Nightingale define true love?

Paragraph 7

What are the details of the negative alternative that the Student pictures in his mind, and what is his response to them?

Paragraphs 8-13

How do the other characters in nature feel about the Student's emotional response to the situation? Why does the Nightingale not share their reaction?

Paragraphs 14-26

Why is each of the trees the Nightingale visits unable to give her what she wants?

Paragraphs 27-30

Why does the third tree hesitate to tell the Nightingale about a way to obtain the object the bird seeks?

Paragraph 31

How does the Nightingale reason that it is important to pay the ultimate price for the prize it desires? Is her decision an easy one?

Paragraphs 32-34

What message does the Nightingale sing to the Student? What does the Nightingale ask in return for her sacrifice?

Paragraph 35

How does the Student respond to the Nightingale? Why is that the nature of his response?

Paragraphs 36-40

How does the Oak-tree feel about the Nightingale's plan? What favor does the tree ask of the Nightingale? How does the Student respond to the favor the Nightingale grants the tree?

Paragraphs 41-51

What are the stages that lead to the conclusion of the Nightingale's plan?

Paragraphs 52-54

When does the Student discover the result of the Nightingale's sacrifice? To what does he attribute this result? What action does the Student then take?

Paragraphs 55-60

What does the Student say to the girl? How does she respond? What is his reaction to her response?

Paragraphs 61-62

What conclusion does the Student come to about love? How does this conclusion change his life?

Prewriting for a Directed Summary

Don't forget to look carefully at the writing topic that follows Wilde's story. Notice its three parts. The first part asks you about a central idea in the story—ideal love. Because you are working with literature, you will have to interpret the elements from the story to identify its messages. Remember that you will want to write a *directed* summary, meaning one that responds specifically to the first question in the writing topic. Your answers to the questions below will guide you to discover the story's thesis statement—its position—on the first question regarding ideal love.

> first part of the writing topic:
>
> *According to the story, why does the Nightingale, an ideal representation of love, have to die?*

To answer this question, you must do more than simply retell the plot of the story. Before you can explain the necessity of the Nightingale's death, you must also consider the difference between the Nightingale's definition of love and the love experienced by the Student.

Focus Questions

1. What is the reason that the Student weeps at the beginning of the story? What is it he wants, and what is stopping him from obtaining his heart's desire? Does the Nightingale have the same understanding as the Student of that desire? What general issue is the story representing with this conflict?

2. Why is the Nightingale predisposed to help the Student? Did the Nightingale know the Student before the evening the story takes place?

3. How does the Nightingale provide the Student with the object he seeks? What reasons does the bird give for making the ultimate sacrifice? What characteristics of love does this sacrifice represent?

4. What is the basis of the Student's love for the girl? When he contemplates the character of the object of his love, what qualities does he see in her? In what important way is she different from the Nightingale?

5. Identify the Student's, the Nightingale's, and the girl's view of love in the story. These different views form the terms of the argument. How is each of the main characters aligned in relation to the conflict? That is, examine the words and actions of each character to determine the understanding of love each seems to have, and how these views differ.

6. In the end, what happens to both the token of the Student's love and the love itself?

Before drafting your working thesis statement, spend some time with the "5 Strategies to Identify Arguments in Fiction" that are presented earlier in this unit. They will help you to focus your ideas as you plan your directed summary, and, because they are designed to help you to interpret a work of literature, they will get you thinking about the position you want to take in your thesis statement. Here they are:

5 Strategies to Identify Arguments in Fiction

1. List the main characters in the story. Briefly summarize their words and actions. What do these things suggest about their personalities and relationships with each other?

2. Identify the main conflict in the story. What is the subject or issue of the conflict? What more general issue is the story *representing* with this conflict?

3. Identify the two or more sides of the conflict. Looking back at the characters you listed in #1, what does each character contribute to the conflict through his or her words or actions? Look carefully at the evidence that each character (including the narrator) presents, and try to determine how the evidence is being linked to support a position.

4. Look over what you wrote for #2 and #3, and then try to state the argument that the story and its characters are representing. This time, try to state the argument in general terms that readers can apply to their own lives.

5. Identify how the story resolves the conflict. This resolution leads directly to the thesis statement, or the story's position in the argument.

Developing an Opinion and Working Thesis Statement

The second question in the writing topic asks you to consider the story's position, think about the reasons it presents for taking that position, and decide if you are convinced that the story is right.

second question in the writing topic:

Do you agree with the story's point of view on love?

Make sure you answer this part of the question directly; it is your thesis statement. It is very important that you write a clear thesis statement, one that focuses on the story as a whole.

1. Use the following thesis frame to formulate the basic elements of your thesis statement:

   a. What is the issue of the story that the question asks you to consider?

   _____

   b. What is the story's point of view on that issue?

   _____

   c. What is your position on the issue, and will you agree or disagree with the story's perspective?

   _____

   _____

   _____

2. Now use the elements you isolated in the thesis frame to write a thesis statement. You likely will have to revise it several times until it captures your idea clearly.

   _____

   _____

Prewriting to Find Support for Your Thesis Statement

The last part of the writing topic asks you to develop and support the position you took in your thesis statement by drawing on your own experience and readings.

third part of the writing topic:

Be sure to support your position with specific examples drawn from your own experience, your observations of others, and your observations drawn from the media and the larger society and culture to which you belong.

Use the guiding questions below to develop your ideas and find concrete support for them. The proof or evidence you present is an important element in supporting your argument and a significant aspect of making your ideas persuasive for your readers.

1. As you begin to develop your own examples, think about how important love is in your life and in the lives of those you know. How do you and others imagine ideal love? Does gender affect one's idea of love? Is ideal love found in the relationships you and others have had? Any experience you have had that says something about this central idea can provide you with an example to support your thesis. List as many ideas as you can and freewrite about the significance of each. Is your point of view on love like or unlike that of the story?

   Once you've written your ideas, look them over carefully. Try to group the ideas you've listed or developed in your freewriting into categories. Then, give each category a label. That is, cluster ideas that seem to have something in common and, for each cluster, identify that shared quality by giving it a name.

2. Now make another list, but this time focus on examples from the media and your knowledge of contemporary society. Which of these examples affirm the ideas in Wilde's story, and which ones challenge them? List and/or freewrite about all the relevant ideas you can think of, even those about which you are hesitant.

Once you've written your ideas, look them over carefully. Try to group the ideas you've listed, or developed in your freewriting, into categories. Then, give each category a label. That is, cluster ideas that seem to have something in common and, for each cluster, identify that shared quality by giving it a name.

3. Now that you've developed categories, look through them and select two or three to develop in your essay. Make sure they are relevant to your thesis and are important enough to persuade your readers. Then, in the space below, briefly summarize each item in your categories and explain how it supports your thesis statement.

The information and ideas you develop in this exercise will become useful when you turn to planning and drafting your essay.

Revising Your Thesis Statement

Now that you have spent some time working out your ideas more systematically and developing some supporting evidence for the position you want to take, look again at the working thesis statement you crafted earlier to see if it is still accurate. As your first step, look again at the writing topic, and then write your original working thesis on the lines that follow it.

writing topic:

According to the story, why does the Nightingale, an ideal representation of love, have to die? Do you agree with the story's point of view on love? Be sure to support your position with specific examples drawn from your own experience, your observations of others, and your observations drawn from the media and the larger society and culture to which you belong.

working thesis statement:

_____

_____

Remember that your thesis statement must answer the second question in the writing topic while taking into consideration the writing topic as a whole. The first question in the topic identifies the issue that is up for debate, and the last question reminds you that, whatever position you take on the issue, you must be able to support it with examples.

Now, you should decide whether the working thesis statement that you drafted earlier in this unit should change. Does it still accurately reflect what you plan to say in your essay? Perhaps you will want to change only a word or phrase, but be open to a decision to significantly rewrite it. Draft writing is almost always wordy, unclear, or vague. Look at your working thesis statement through the eyes of your readers and see if it actually says what you want it to say.

After examining it and completing any necessary revisions, check it one more time by asking yourself the following questions:

a. Does the thesis directly identify the story's overall message about love?

b. Does your thesis state your position on love and whether your position agrees or disagrees with the story's?

c. Is your thesis well punctuated, grammatically correct, and precisely worded?

Write your polished thesis on the lines below and look at it again. Is it strong and interesting?

_____

_____

Planning and Drafting Your Essay

Now that you have examined the view of love in "The Nightingale and the Rose" and thought at length about your own view, draft an essay that responds to all parts of the writing topic. Use the material you developed in this section to compose your draft. Don't forget to turn back to Part 1, especially "The Conventional Argument Essay Structure," for further guidance on the essay's conventional structure.

Do take the time to develop an outline because it will give you a basic structure for incorporating all the ideas you have developed in the preceding pages. An outline will also give you a bird's-eye view of your essay and help you spot problems in development or logic. The form below is modeled on "The Conventional Argument Essay Structure" in Part 1, and it can guide you as you plan your essay.

This outline doesn't have to contain polished writing. You may want to fill in only the basic ideas in phrases or terms.

Creating an Outline for Your Draft

I. Introductory Paragraph
    A. An opening sentence that gives the reading selection's title and author and begins to answer the writing topic:

_____

    B. Main points to include in the directed summary:
       1.

       2.

       3.

       4.

    C. Write out your thesis statement. (Look back to "Revising Your Thesis Statement," where you reexamined and improved your working thesis statement.) It should clearly agree or disagree with the argument in Wilde's story and state a clear position using your own words.

_____

II. Body Paragraphs

A. The paragraph's one main point that supports the thesis statement:

_____

1. Controlling idea sentence:

_____

_____

2. Corroborating details:

_____

_____

_____

_____

3. Careful explanation of why the details are significant:

_____

_____

_____

_____

4. Connection to the thesis statement:

_____

_____

_____

_____

B. The paragraph's one main point that supports the thesis statement:

_____

1. Controlling idea sentence:

_____

_____

2. Corroborating details:

_____

_____

_____

_____

3. Careful explanation of why the details are significant:

_____

_____

_____

_____

4. Connection to the thesis statement:

_____

_____

_____

_____

C. The paragraph's one main point that supports the thesis statement:

_____

1. Controlling idea sentence:

_____

_____

2. Corroborating details:

_____

_____

_____

_____

3. Careful explanation of why the details are significant:

_____

_____

_____

_____

4. Connection to the thesis statement:

_____

_____

_____

_____

D. The paragraph's one main point that supports the thesis statement:

_____

1. Controlling idea sentence:

_____

_____

2. Corroborating details:

_____

_____

_____

_____

3. Careful explanation of why the details are significant:

_____

_____

_____

_____

4. Connection to the thesis statement:

_____

_____

_____

_____

Repeat this form for any remaining body paragraphs.

III. Conclusion (Look back to "Conclusions" in Part 1. It will help you make some decisions here about what type of conclusion you will use.)

A. Type of conclusion to be used:

_____

B. Key words or phrases to include:

_____

Getting Feedback On Your Draft

Use the following guidelines to give a classmate feedback on his or her draft. Read the draft through first, and then answer each of the items below as specifically as you can.

Name of draft's author: _____

Name of draft's reader: _____

The Introduction

1. Within the opening sentences,
   a. the author's first and last name are given.   yes   no
   b. the story's title is given and placed within quotation marks.   yes   no
2. The opening contains a summary that
   a. summarizes the Nightingale's death in the story.   yes   no
   b. interprets the Nightingale's death in terms of what
      it says about ideal love.   yes   no
3. The opening provides a thesis that makes clear the draft
   writer's opinion regarding the view of love in the story.   yes   no

If the answer to #3 above is yes, state the thesis below as it is written. If the answer is no, explain to the writer what information is needed to make the thesis complete.

_____

_____

_____

The Body

1. How many paragraphs are in the body of this essay? _____
2. To support the thesis, this number is   sufficient   not enough
3. Do paragraphs contain the 4Cs?

Paragraph 1	Controlling idea sentence	yes	no
	Corroborating details	yes	no
	Careful explanation of why the details are significant	yes	no
	Connection to the thesis statement	yes	no
Paragraph 2	Controlling idea sentence	yes	no
	Corroborating details	yes	no
	Careful explanation of why the details are significant	yes	no
	Connection to the thesis statement	yes	no

Paragraph 3	Controlling idea sentence	yes	no
	Corroborating details	yes	no
	Careful explanation of why the details are significant	yes	no
	Connection to the thesis statement	yes	no
Paragraph 4	Controlling idea sentence	yes	no
	Corroborating details	yes	no
	Careful explanation of why the details are significant	yes	no
	Connection to the thesis statement	yes	no
Paragraph 5	Controlling idea sentence	yes	no
	Corroborating details	yes	no
	Careful explanation of why the details are significant	yes	no
	Connection to the thesis statement	yes	no

(Continue as needed.)

4. Identify any of the above paragraphs that are underdeveloped (too short). _____

5. Identify any of the above paragraphs that fail to support the thesis. _____

6. Identify any of the above paragraphs that are redundant or repetitive. _____

7. Suggest any ideas for additional paragraphs that might improve this essay.

_____

_____

_____

The Conclusion

1. Does the final paragraph avoid introducing new ideas
   and examples that really belong in the body of the essay?   yes   no
2. Does the conclusion provide closure (let readers know
   that the end of the essay has been reached)?   yes   no
3. Does the conclusion leave readers with an understanding
   of the significance of the argument?   yes   no

4. State in your own words what the draft writer considers to be important about his
   or her argument.

_____

_____

_____

5. Identify the type of conclusion used (see the guidelines for conclusions in Part 1).

Editing

1. During the editing process, the writer should pay attention to the following problems in sentence structure, punctuation, and mechanics:
    fragments
    misplaced and dangling modifiers
    fused (run-on) sentences
    comma splices
    misplaced, missing, and unnecessary commas
    misplaced, missing, and unnecessary apostrophes
    incorrect quotation mark use
    capitalization errors
    spelling errors

2. While editing, the writer should pay attention to the following areas of grammar:
    verb tense
    subject-verb agreement
    irregular verbs
    pronoun type
    pronoun reference
    pronoun agreement
    noun plurals
    prepositions

Final Draft Checklist

Content

_____ My essay has an appropriate title.

_____ I provide an accurate summary of the position on love that the "The Nightingale and the Rose" takes.

_____ My thesis states a clear position that can be supported by evidence.

_____ I have enough paragraphs and argument points to support my thesis.

_____ Each body paragraph is relevant to my thesis.

_____ Each body paragraph contains the 4Cs.

_____ I use transitions whenever necessary to connect ideas to each other.

_____ The final paragraph of my essay (the conclusion) provides readers with a sense of closure.

Grammar, Punctuation, and Mechanics

_____ I use the present tense to discuss the story's argument and examples.

_____ I use verb tenses correctly to show the chronology of events.

_____ I have verb tense consistency throughout my sentences.

_____ I have checked for subject-verb agreement in all of my sentences.

_____ I have revised all fragments and mixed or garbled sentences.

_____ I have repaired all fused (run-on) sentences and comma splices.

_____ I have placed a comma after introductory elements (transitions and phrases) and all dependent clauses that open a sentence.

_____ If I present items in a series (nouns, verbs, prepositional phrases), they are parallel in form.

_____ If I include material spoken or written by someone other than myself, I have correctly punctuated it with quotation marks, using the MLA style guide's rules for citation.

Reviewing Your Graded Essay

After your instructor has returned your essay, you may have the opportunity to revise your paper and raise your grade. Many students, especially those whose essays receive nonpassing grades, feel that their instructors should be less "picky" about grammar and should pass the work on content alone. However, most students at this level have not yet acquired the ability to recognize quality writing, and they do not realize that content and writing actually cannot be separated in this way. Experienced instructors know that errors in sentence structure, grammar, punctuation, and word choice either interfere with content or distract readers so much that they lose track of content. In short, good ideas badly presented are no longer good ideas; to pass, an essay must have passable writing. So even if you are not submitting a revised version of this essay to your instructor, it is important that you review your work carefully in order to understand its strengths and weaknesses. This sheet will guide you through the evaluation process.

You will want to continue to use the techniques that worked well for you and to find strategies to overcome the problems that you identify in this sample of your writing. To recognize areas that might have been problematic for you, look back at the scoring rubric in this book. Match the numerical/verbal/letter grade received on your essay to the appropriate category. Study the explanation given on the rubric for your grade.

Write a few sentences below in which you identify your problems in each of the following areas. Then, suggest specific changes you could make that would improve your paper. Don't forget to use your handbook as a resource.

1. **Grammar/punctuation/mechanics**
   My problem:

   My strategy for change:

2. **Thesis/response to assignment**
   My problem:

   My strategy for change:

3. Organization
My problem:

My strategy for change:

4. Paragraph development/examples/reasoning
My problem:

My strategy for change:

5. Assessment

In the space below, assign a grade to your paper using a rubric other than the one used by your instructor. In other words, if your instructor assigned your essay a grade of *High Fail*, you might give it the letter grade you now feel the paper warrants. If your instructor used the traditional letter grade to evaluate the essay, choose a category from the rubric in this book, or any other grading scale that you are familiar with, to show your evaluation of your work. Then, write a short narrative explaining your evaluation of the essay and the reasons it received the grade you gave it.

Grade: _____

Narrative: _____

_____

_____

_____

_____

Extending the Discussion: Considering Other Viewpoints

Reading Selections

"The Importance of Being Married" by Ninetta Papadomichelaki and
    Keith Vance
"The Honeymoon's Just Beginning" by Bobby Lazar

THE IMPORTANCE OF BEING MARRIED

NINETTA PAPADOMICHELAKI AND KEITH VANCE

Keith Vance and Ninetta Papadomichelaki are faculty members in the University Writing Program at the University of California, Riverside. They have published Compass: Paths to Effective Reading *and* Compass: Guidebook to English Grammar.

The debate over gay marriage, many believe, is one of the most divisive factors in American society today, and a plethora of essays has been written either decrying such marriages as abominations or supporting them as the evolution of human relationships and communities. Here follow some of the most pertinent arguments of both sides. On the one side, marriage conservatives feel that 1) marriage is rooted in male/female sexuality and is thus meant to exist between a man and a woman; 2) marriage between a man and a woman is a religious sacrament; 3) marriage serves as a stabilizing institution in society; 4) also for some, most homosexuals cannot handle the responsibilities of marriage. On the other side of the debate, proponents of same sex marriages vehemently refute these claims. They argue that for significant portions of the population, same sex sexuality is equally as strong as the heterosexual one. They believe that equality before the law mandates that the state broaden its legislation to include same sex unions while they promote the expansion of the same idea for religious ceremonies. They scorn the argument that homosexuals lack responsibility by pointing out that same sex partnerships can be equally as durable and strong as heterosexual unions. Besides, if homosexuals are considered competent enough to hold posts of responsibility at all levels of society, why would they be less capable within marriage?

The problem, however, with this debate is that it is asking the wrong question. Instead of "why should homosexuals marry," one should ask, "why should anyone get married?" What is it that makes marriage such an important or even mandatory institution today? To begin to answer these questions, one should look for the essence of marriage in the origins of its modern conceptualization. While people have been "marrying" even before the Romans controlled the world, the formulation of the modern institution of marriage derived from the tradition of Western romantic love in the Middle Ages. In the thirteenth and fourteenth centuries, medieval authors produced an array of what were called "romance" manuscripts that included new notions of romantic love. Indeed, Chrétien de Troyes and other figures created numerous such stories—about knights and their damsels falling in love despite social forces that might be aligned to stop them—whose *dénouement* is a hoped-for marriage. Undoubtedly, the most famous story of Western romantic love is Shakespeare's *Romeo and Juliet*, in which the two title characters, despite the warring family history, secretly marry and thereafter consummate their love. It is mainly through these romances that marriage became figured as the conclusion of romantic love whereby partners choose each other for life. One need only look at modern romantic comedies churned out by Hollywood by the score to find this prevalent notion that love is inextricably connected to marriage. Love is still supposed to bring couples together, and its suitable social culmination is marriage.

Despite, however, the literary efforts of poets from the past, marriage for much of its history was not about love at all. Marriage was primarily about economics and alliances. When two people married, their families were combined, and property changed hands. Even in the Middle Ages, despite the literature of the period, marriage was typically arranged by the parents as more of a combination of the resources of the two families than anything remotely relevant to love. So, while many people focus on Romeo and Juliet's undying love for each other, what is so often missed about *Romeo and Juliet* is the underlying premise of the play: the massive traditional social forces of tradition and economics aligned against love. Contributing to this traditional idea of marriage as an economic transaction was also the institution of dowry, the ceremonial gift of goods and money along with the bride. Even today, in some countries, dowries still constitute an important part of the ritual of marriage, providing the contractual backbone to the rite.

Of course, today and for most of the US, marriage has changed quite a bit from its roots as a fundamentally economic institution. Today, a dowry has become an outdated custom or a joke rather than a necessary component of marriage; only few parents arrange the marriages of their sons or daughters; and certainly neither women nor their property is any longer relegated as the legal property of the father or of the husband. Since women have the same rights as men, it is entirely possible for single women to exist outside the structure of marriage; they can be financially independent, and they can have fulfilling careers and access to their own funds. Marriage doesn't even provide a tax break because in many cases couples pay the so-called "marriage penalty" by being charged more taxes than if they filed as individuals. So marriage is no longer the bulwark of economic security that it once was reputed to be.

However, one can argue that the significance of marriage as a predominant social institution remains intact. True, besides its economic significance, one other major reason for marriage has been its role in cementing social relationships and providing the only acceptable path towards creating a family. In tighter communities, everyone knows what they are supposed to do, the road they are supposed to follow, and the social roles they have been assigned; in these societies, marriage is one of the stepping stones into adult life, and the family unit is the primary organizing feature of society. However, any society, including the American one, could be organized on the principle of a commune with groups of ten or fifteen people sharing finances, property, and workload duties, but it is not. Instead, the most prevalent institution in our society is the "nuclear" family whose symbol is marriage. Indeed, statistics from the Census Bureau show that 96.7% of Americans will marry at least one time during their lives.

Even the social dimension of marriage might be on the wane. Divorce statistics hover around 50%, and there has been a 40% rise since 1990 in the number of couples who live together but are not married in the US. In Europe, this trend is even more pronounced. In a 2006 survey conducted by the German Federal Statistics Office, only 38% of German women and 30% of German men thought marriage was necessary for creating a union. Even having children out of wedlock, which has been one of the primary reasons for marrying, is no longer socially stigmatized but rather legally facilitated and socially more accepted. Across Europe, for instance, one in three children is born to unwed parents, which reflects the sixfold increase in the number of unwed parents since the 1970s; at the same time, most of these births take place in unmarried households by choice.

So why would anyone get married nowadays if it is no longer about fusing two families economically, if women have the economic power to live on their own, if no social stigma attaches to having children outside of marriage? The practical significance of marriage as an institution has definitely waned and will continue to do so once legislation awards unwedded unions of both heterosexual and homosexual couples and single parent families with the same legal privileges that it awards families of married heterosexuals. Indeed, it is mostly these privileges and perhaps a remainder of the medieval notion of romantic love, as well as religious convictions that still grant the institution of marriage such importance. However, if there were no legal differentiation, couldn't two people "love" each other without the ritual and the paper? So why should anyone, including same-sex partners, desire to participate in a social institution that is slowly becoming obsolete?

Discussion Questions

1. Why do the authors claim that the debate about same-sex marriage is focusing on the wrong question? What, in their opinion, is the right question? Do you think that a discussion of this "right question" might change the way people on both sides of the debate view legislation legalizing same sex marriage? Why or why not?

2. Discuss the concept of "Western romantic love" and its origins. What role did literature play in the spread of this idea?

3. What things, other than love, had previously been the main considerations for marriage? Why do you think marriages arranged with these factors in mind would or would not be a good idea today?

4. How do the authors use literature to illustrate the conflict between love and other considerations as a basis for marriage? Why do you or don't you think the characters in that play should have put familial considerations before love? Explain why you would or would not marry someone you loved without your family's approval.

5. Referring back to "The Nightingale and the Rose," discuss a character's representation of "the notion of romantic love" and a character's representation of the practical side of a couple's union. In what way is the Nightingale's death a commentary of both the notion of love and love itself? Why do you think the Nightingale is either noble or foolish?

THE HONEYMOON'S JUST BEGINNING

Bobby Lazar

Bobby Lazar, MA, is an author, teacher, and world traveler. A lifelong science fiction aficionado, he enjoys nothing more than reading, discussing, and writing about the great classics of the genre, from H. G. Wells to Robert A. Heinlein and beyond.

If you're a fan of the now-defunct drama *Mad Men*, which is set in 1960s America, you might remember an episode called "At the Codfish Ball," in which Peggy Olson, an advertising copywriter, has reason to believe that her boyfriend, Abe, is about to pop the question over dinner in an upscale restaurant. She wedges a makeover and a new frock into her work day, only to receive Abe's proposal not to marry but to move in together. Although somewhat taken aback, Peggy soon recovers and accepts. A female coworker declares her brave and romantic, but Peggy never receives the blessing of her conservative Catholic mother, who sneers and tells her that if she is lonely, she should content herself with a sequence of feline companions until she finally ascends to the great advertising agency in the sky.

Times have changed a good deal since the mid-sixties. Anyone living in the United States knows that cohabitation has conclusively entered the mainstream and is more popular than ever. Shacking up is no longer shocking. In fact, cohabitation supporters say that the practice has definite advantages, among them an opportunity for couples to take their relationship for a "test drive" before entering into a more binding commitment that is more difficult and expensive to dissolve than a simple shared living arrangement. Arguments against cohabitation are numerous, including religious objections, the fact that many such arrangements end quickly, and the perception that cohabitors are not sufficiently committed. But the most damning objection is the statistical claim that cohabiting couples face a higher rate of relationship failure if they later decide to marry; quite a number of studies have shown that indirect marriages (in which a legal marriage is preceded by cohabitation) have a higher divorce rate than direct marriages (in which couples marry without first living together). Premarital cohabitation is thus seen as causing many indirect marriages to fail.

Much speculation (and often much hand-wringing) attends this higher divorce statistic: Among various explanations, interested parties theorize that unmarried couples who live together may be destroying the magic of marriage, that the casual way that many couples drift into living together must somehow be to blame, or that cohabiting couples marry because of pressure from families or society, and thus doom their relationships. Whatever the explanation, a common view is that cohabitation causes future marriages to break down and that surely, if we want to reduce the divorce rate, we ought to discourage cohabitation altogether. But such arguments depressingly elevate the "sanctity" of direct marriage over the legitimacy of indirect marriage and nonmarital cohabitation, and they tend to favor statistics (which, after all, can rarely account for all the variables) over the personal choices of individuals with different needs and desires. Furthermore, emerging research indicates that the higher divorce rate—a key element in the array of negative outcomes called "the cohabitation effect"—is little more than a failure of statistics to consider key variables that, once accounted for, level the playing field between direct and indirect marriage.

Cohabitation can be the best alternative for people who do not believe in conventional marriage. My own experience attests to this reality. Influenced by an adolescent literary diet of the giants of science fiction, I grew up with unconventional ideas about marriage despite my conservative parents. I lost myself in Heinleinian universes, in which three or more partners join in extended marriage arrangements that are otherwise fairly conventional. I also favored an odd little pair of Tanith Lee dystopias, in which the Jang (essentially ageless teenagers) marry for only a short, predetermined time frame, mainly for the purpose of copulation; adults, who often enter into stable long-term relationships, have no provision for marriage. Theodore Sturgeon and Robert Silverberg offered food for thought as well, always forcing me to consider the complex terrain formed by sex, love, and social and legal conventions. Consequently, I entered into my first cohabitation arrangement when I was barely twenty-one. The relationship lasted for eight years, six of them in shared living quarters, and I have never felt more married than I did during the last two years, despite the absence of a marriage certificate. Neither I nor my partner believed in the sanctity of marriage or had any intention of marrying, so cohabitation was the only reasonable option for us. Other unconventional couples who do not want to marry in the first place are doubtless a minority among cohabitors, but their choices should be respected without dire predictions of future relationship failure and a recommendation that the couples simply live apart. People express love and build relationships in different ways; living together outside of marriage should remain a personal choice unfettered by other people's unsolicited judgment.

In my twenties, I was relatively unconcerned about what other people might think of my cohabitation arrangement. But the judgment of others is a potent force in most people's lives and relationships, and, as I discovered, science fiction is particularly good at teasing out the inanity of tautologies, such as a critic's insisting that people should do what they've always done just because they've always done it that way. Our self-imposed blinders impel us to dictate how other people should live their lives. Ted Sturgeon's pioneering short novel *Venus plus X*, first published in 1960, demonstrates the hypocrisy of judging other people's choices. Charlie Johns, a fairly typical human male from the twentieth century, wakes up in Ledom, a utopia of the far future. The Ledom, who outwardly resemble human males, are essentially neuter, but they fall in love, marry, and have children, just as twentieth-century denizens do. Johns accepts their way of life because he assumes that they have simply evolved that way and have no choice in the matter. But as time goes by, the Ledom want to know what he thinks of them; he becomes irrational and hate-filled when he finds out that they are not "natural" mutations but a self-engineered people who do not reproduce naturally. At this point, once he realizes that the Ledom are "queer" by choice, he sees them as perversions of nature: men who couple with other men and enter into immoral relationships. He does not see that they are kind and thoughtful, that they form affectionate bonds, or that they love their children. All he knows is what he has been raised to believe: that deviations from certain norms are disgusting aberrations. The whole scenario turns out to be merely an elaborate thought experiment, but Johns's perceptions are well entrenched and his revulsion all too real.

The first time I read this book, I immediately saw the connection with my own living situation; even in the 1980s, I routinely encountered people's open disapproval of my coresidence, their opinion that my partner and I were not serious, and their assumption that a cohabiting woman must ultimately have marriage on her mind, whereas the man in the relationship must be unwilling to commit. *Venus plus X* questions our perceptions of sex and gender, especially outside of heteronormative relationships, but also offers insight into our tendency to judge any kind of atypical loving or living arrangement. Nowadays, I make a different connection, this time between Charlie Johns and those who argue against cohabitation. I am not saying that pundits who deplore cohabitation are automatically hateful or irrational like Charlie Johns, but they do share a common feature: a fatal American flaw, the attitude that anything less than "marriage" is somehow inferior. I am convinced that this hidden judgment is largely responsible for a whole host of problematic attitudes and actions. I do not mean just the negative perceptions of cohabitation or even the tendency to impose general statistics on cohabiting individuals who want to make their own choices. I am also referring to the absurd length of time that supposedly unbiased family scholars and researchers took to realize that their hidden assumptions were preventing them from fairly accounting for the supposedly higher divorce rate in indirect marriages. Collectively, these experts have been the Charlie Johns of relationship research, so entrenched in the supposed superiority of conventional marriage that they could not look outside their own narrow view and perform fair and insightful research.

The hidden assumption that marriage is superior to cohabitation is stitched into the very fabric of decades of research that measures the lifespan of direct and indirect marriages. Research in the last decade and a half indicates two major issues with the indirect marriage divorce statistics: that they are heavily predicated on obsolete data from the 1970s, and that they do not "compar[e] like with like," so the numbers are misleading (de Vaus et al. 39). The passage of time takes care of the obsolete figures, but researcher bias was largely responsible for the second oversight. In 2003, a team of researchers in Australia noted a disparity in the "*measurement explanation*" for the "survival gap" between direct and indirect marriages (de Vaus et al. 35, original italics) and found the gap considerably lessened when the "*same length of the live-in relationship*" was accounted for (de Vaus et al. 35, original italics). In other words, "In the case of indirect marriages this would mean adding the period spent together before the registered marriage to the period of marriage" (de Vaus et al. 35). The total duration of an indirect marriage would thus include both the years of cohabitation and the years of legal marriage. Zooming in on the rate at which women left their marriages, the authors found that accounting for the premarital cohabitation resulted in a dramatic shift in the numbers. Although the indirect marriages still had a somewhat lower survival rate after the duration adjustment, the authors considered the difference in their particular data set to be "a statistically non-significant 4.9 per cent" (de Vaus et al. 38). While a disparity of nearly five percent seems anything but insignificant, it is certainly a vast improvement over more than twenty-five percent, which the authors report as the rate at which women left their indirect marriages in 1980s Australia (de Vaus et al. 38). American figures are doubtless similar. Simply ignoring all of the premarital years of a relationship is not only disrespectful but inaccurate, clearly resulting in skewed statistics. If scholars had respected cohabitation and conventional marriage in equal measure, this oversight would have been corrected long before—and this study would be better known in scholarly circles.

Again, one of my own relationship experiences is relevant here. After my first coresidence ended, I entered into a long-term relationship with another partner when I was in my late twenties. Over the years, our situation was protean enough to confound the usual statistics on indirect marriage. We began living together part-time, mostly on the weekends, about a year into the relationship, and we continued in this vein for several years. We then lived together full time for a long stretch before finally succumbing to the tempting array of legal and financial inducements offered by conventional marriage. Our legal union lasted for less than five years, implying a short-lived failure. Yet we had been together for two decades, cohabiting part time for seven years and full time for twelve. Researchers using conventional measures would label my marriage as a five-year disappointment because of its short duration. In contrast, David de Vaus and his colleagues would understand the value of considering the length of the whole relationship and determining its stability in those terms; in their eyes, my marriage was at least a twelve-year venture and, if numbers can tell the whole story, a moderately stable one. Of course, my partner and I felt that we had enjoyed a fulfilling twenty-year success. Although I do not believe that we all get one (and only one) true love, my ex-partner was the love of my life, and I deeply resent any implication that the relationship was a dismal failure; only the participants get to decide how successful their relationships are.

The most damning condemnation of the cohabitation effect's higher divorce rate has come to light only in the last few years. Recent research from the Council on Contemporary Families demonstrates that a hidden variable can make all the difference. The study's principal author, Arielle Kuperberg of the University of North Carolina, Greensboro, used fairly recent American data from the mid-1990s on and accounted for the age of the participants. In a 2014 journal article, Kuperberg states that the most accurate predictor of marriage duration is actually the initial age at which the couple begins living together, regardless of whether the marriage is preceded by cohabitation; once age is factored into the equation, divorce statistics for indirect marriage are "remarkably similar" to those for direct marriage (362). In fact, premarital cohabitors, on average, began coresiding two years *earlier* than conventional married couples did (Kuperberg 358). The higher incidence of relationship dissolution among the very youngest couples makes sense; these people have limited experience in selecting and living with a mate, so they are more likely to face a break-up even in a conventional direct marriage. Younger people are also more open to impulsive actions and risk-taking; more experience in life and in love results in greater stability. Ultimately, we should not be surprised that very young couples are more likely than older ones to break up, period, at least until a point of stability is reached in their middle to late twenties (Kuperberg 362). Kuperberg's article explores other variables in a complex system of human relationships, so age is not the only factor. And cohabitation critics will likely still find something to complain about. But the data do show that the supposedly higher risk of indirect marriage dissolution is largely a myth.

The United States is slowly shifting toward an attitude of greater acceptance of differences. With rising cohabitation rates, declining divorce rates, and the recent legalization of same-sex unions in America, the future of marriage should prove interesting. But regardless of how long a relationship lasts, we should accept the validity of a couple's years of premarital cohabitation and resist the urge to inflict general statistics on individuals who have their own experiences and standards. Cohabitation is no longer the ugly stepsister of marriage. Perhaps it never really was.

Works Cited

"At the Codfish Ball." *Mad Men*. Dir. Michael Uppendahl. Perf. Jon Hamm and Elisabeth Moss. AMC, New York. 29 Apr. 2012. Television.

de Vaus, David, et al. "Premarital Cohabitation and Subsequent Marital Stability." *Family Matters* 65 (Winter 2003): 34-39. Print.

Kuperberg, Arielle. "Age at Coresidence, Premarital Cohabitation, and Marriage Dissolution: 1985-2009." *Journal of Marriage and Family* 76.2 (2014): 352-369. Print.

Sturgeon, Theodore. *Venus plus X*. 1960. London: Sphere, 1978. Print.

Discussion Questions

1. What do you think Bobby Lazar means by "the magic of marriage"? In what ways is it similar to and/or different from the "mystery of love" of which the Nightingale sings and the notion of "Western romantic love" discussed by Vance and Papadomichelaki?

2. Discuss Lazar's use of science fiction to encourage his audience to consider love and marriage from unconventional perspectives. Why do you find these examples more or less successful than the author's statistical arguments?

3. When you learn that a couple's relationship is cohabitational rather than marital, do you see their union as "somehow inferior?" Why or why not? How might the couple be treated differently than a married couple by their family, friends, and society?

4. Lazar claims that his ex-partner was "the love of my life"; yet the two are no longer together. Do you think it is possible for a relationship with one's true love not to work out? Why? Explain your reasons for agreeing or disagreeing with the author's claim that it is possible to have more than one "true love."

Part 3 contains two case studies made up of reading selections and some sample essays written in response to their writing topics. These essay responses were written by students like you, taking a college-level writing class and using *Write It Review* as their text.

For each case study you are assigned, read the main selection carefully and then annotate each so that you understand its argument and supporting evidence. Then, examine the student essays that follow it. Score each of them, using the scoring rubric in Part 1. Then, discuss each of these student essays with your classmates and identify each essay's strengths and weaknesses. For practice, your instructor may ask you to write a detailed plan identifying the specific steps you would take if you were going to revise one of the essays.

Case Studies

Case Study #1: "The Benefits of 'Negative Visualization'" by Oliver Burkeman

The following case study references the Burkeman essay in Assignment 2, followed by six timed-writing essays written by students like you. You should read the essay and student responses for each, and examine them over for their strengths and weaknesses. A set of study questions follows each student essay to help you evaluate its success.

THE BENEFITS OF "NEGATIVE VISUALIZATION"

Oliver Burkeman

Oliver Burkeman is a British journalist who was educated at the University of Cambridge. He writes for the Guardian, *a British newspaper based in New York. His weekly column is titled* This Column Will Change Your Life, *and it focuses on issues related to social psychology, the self-help culture, and what he calls the science of happiness. His books to date are* HELP! How to Become Slightly Happier and Get a Bit More Done *(2011) and* The Antidote: Happiness for People Who Can't Stand Positive Thinking *(2012). The following reading is an excerpt from that book.*

Behind many of the most popular approaches to happiness is the simple philosophy of focusing on things going right. In the world of self-help, the most overt expression of this outlook is the technique known as "positive visualization": if you mentally picture things turning out well, the reasoning goes, they're far more likely to do so. "There is a deep tendency in human nature to become precisely what you visualize yourself as being," said Norman Vincent Peale, the author of *The Power of Positive Thinking*, in a speech he gave to executives of the investment bank Merrill Lynch in the mid-1980s. Even most people who scoff at Peale's homilies, however, might find it hard to argue with the underlying outlook: that being optimistic about the future, when you can manage it, is generally for the best.

Yet there are problems with this outlook, aside from just feeling disappointed when things don't turn out well. These problems are particularly acute in the case of positive visualization. Over the last few years, the German-born psychologist Gabriele Oettingen and her colleagues have constructed a series of experiments designed to unearth the truth about "positive fantasies about the future." The results are striking: Spending time and energy thinking about how well things could go, it has emerged, actually reduces most people's motivation to achieve them. Experimental subjects who were encouraged to think about how they were going to have a particularly high-achieving week at work, for example, ended up achieving less than those who were invited to reflect on the coming week, but given no further guidelines on how to do so.

It doesn't necessarily follow, of course, that it would be a better idea to switch to "negative visualization" instead, and to start focusing on all the ways in which things could go wrong. Yet that is precisely one of the conclusions that emerges from Stoicism, a school of philosophy that originated in Athens a few years after the death of Aristotle and that came to dominate Western thinking about happiness for nearly five centuries. For the Stoics, the ideal state of mind was tranquility—not the excitable cheer that positive thinkers usually seem to mean when they use the word "happiness." And tranquility was to be achieved not by strenuously chasing after enjoyable experiences, but by cultivating a kind of calm indifference towards one's circumstances. One way to do this, the

Stoics argued, is by turning towards negative emotions and experiences—not shunning them, but examining them closely instead.

When it comes to beliefs about the future, the evangelists of optimism argue that you should cultivate as many positive expectations about the future as you can. But this is not the good idea that it may at first appear to be. For a start, as Gabriele Oettingen's experiments demonstrate, focusing on the outcome you desire may actually sabotage your efforts to achieve it. More generally, a Stoic would point out, it just isn't a particularly good technique for feeling happier. Ceaseless optimism about the future only makes for a greater shock when things go wrong; by fighting to maintain only positive beliefs about the future, the positive thinker ends up being *less* prepared, and *more* acutely distressed, when things eventually happen that he can't persuade himself to believe are good. (And such things will happen.) This is a problem underlying all approaches to happiness that set too great a store by optimism. Trying to see things in an exclusively positive light is an attitude that requires constant, effortful replenishment. Should your efforts falter or prove insufficient when confronted by some unexpected shock, you'll sink back down into—possibly deeper—gloom.

The Stoics propose a more elegant, sustainable, and calming way to deal with the possibility of things going wrong: Rather than struggling to avoid all thought of these worst-case scenarios, they counsel actively dwelling on them, staring them in the face. The first benefit of dwelling on how bad things might get is a straightforward one. Psychologists have long agreed that one of the greatest enemies of human happiness is "hedonic adaptation"—the predictable and frustrating way in which any new source of pleasure we obtain, whether it's as minor as a new piece of electronic gadgetry or as major as a marriage, swiftly gets relegated to the backdrop of our lives. We grow accustomed to it, and so it ceases to deliver so much joy. It follows, then, that regularly reminding yourself that you might lose any of the things you currently enjoy—indeed, that you will definitely lose them all, in the end, when death catches up with you— would reverse the adaptation effect. Thinking about the possibility of losing something you value shifts it from the backdrop of your life back to center stage, where it can deliver pleasure once more. The second subtler and arguably even more powerful benefit of the premeditation of evils is as an antidote to anxiety. Consider how we normally seek to assuage worries about the future: We seek reassurance, looking to persuade ourselves that everything will be all right. But reassurance is a double-edged sword. In the short term, it can be wonderful, but like all forms of optimism, it requires constant mainte- nance: If you offer reassurance to a friend who is in the grip of anxiety, you'll often find that a few days later, he'll be back for more. Worse, reassurance can actually exacerbate anxiety. When you reassure your friend that the worst-case scenario he fears probably won't occur, you inadvertently reinforce his belief that it would be catastrophic if it did. You are tightening the coil of his anxiety, not loosening it.

All too often, the Stoics point out, things will not turn out for the best. But it is also true that, when they do go wrong, they'll almost certainly go less wrong than you were fearing. Losing your job won't condemn you to starvation and death; losing a boyfriend or girlfriend won't condemn you to a life of unrelenting misery. Those fears are based on irrational judgments about the future. The premeditation of evils is the way to replace these irrational notions with more rational judgments; spend time vividly imagining exactly how wrong things could go in reality, and you will usually find that your fears were exaggerated. If you lost your job, there are specific steps you could take to find a new one; if you lost your relationship, you would probably manage to find some happiness in life despite being single. Confronting the worst-case scenario saps it of much of its anxiety-inducing power. Happiness reached via positive thinking can be fleeting and brittle; negative visualization generates a vastly more dependable calm.

Writing Topic

According to Burkeman, in what ways is "negative visualization" more likely to make people happier than "positive visualization"? What do you think of his views? To develop your own position, be sure to discuss specific examples; these examples can be drawn from anything you've read, as well as from your observations and experiences.

First Student Response

In the essay "*The Benefits of Negative Visualization*," Oliver Burkeman discusses the ways "negative visualization" is more likely to make people happier than "positive visualization". Burkeman starts off the essay by explaining negative visualization and positive visualization. "Negative visualization" is when we think about the worst possible outcome or how something can go wrong, while "positive visualization" is when we see our outcome to be very successful. One of the ways "negative visualization" is more likely to make people happier than "positive visualization", is when people visualize the worst possible outcome, which will motivate them to do better. Picturing the worst outcome can motivate us to do better because it pushes us to make our outcome successful. Another way "negative visualization" is likely to make people happier is that, it can reduce anxiety and fear. People would not need other people to reassure and tell them that everything will turn out fine. The last way "negative visualization" can make people happier is by picturing how things can go wrong which can help them accept their result rather than feeling shock. Based on my experiences, I agree with Burkeman's claim that "negative visualization" is more likely to make people happier than "positive visualization."

Anxiety and fear are the two emotions most felt in a situation or problem. Throughout my first year of high school, "positive visualization" caused me great fear and anxiety. When I had a test coming up, I would always think that I would receive an A on the test. I would study last minute thinking that I would ace the test. When I took the test, I struggled on some of the questions; however, I still thought I would do great. After a couple of days, the teacher would pass back the test and I was shocked that my score was no what I expected. I did not learn my lesson there because it happened many times before I realized I should not have picture a successful result. When I received those scores, I feared that I would not pass the class and I was always stressed out when I looked at my scores. Before every test, I would tell my friends that I feared not passing the test and they would always have to reassure me. Thinking that my situation would turn out successful caused me anxiety and fear. I was shocked from the outcome of my test because I thought I was going to receive a good score. If I had, had a "negative visualization" of how I was going to do on those test, I wouldn't have been shocked by the scores that I received. 1 would have accepted my results because I knew I was going to get those scores. I would not have needed reassurance from other people telling me that I would do fine on the test, and it wouldn't have led me to feel anxiety and fear. Ultimately, my experience concurs with Burkeman's claim that "positive visualization" will make people less happy than "negative visualization."

Positive visualization can cause a negative impact on a person: however, "negative visualization" can create a better outcome for a person's success. An example of a "negative visualization" was when I was a senior in high school, it was my last year on the track and field team. I wanted to get invited to the Arcadia Invitational, which is, an annual track and field meet, that is held at a high school in my district. At the beginning of the season I was not doing that well on my personal record (PR) time. My unsuccessful PR time made me realized that I would not be invited the Arcadia Invitational. I asked my coach train me harder so that I could be invited to the Invitational. I trained daily for at least three hours and changed my eating habits. It was hard to change my eating habits because I used to eat whatever I felt like indulging. By the middle of the season, I had gotten faster and my PR record went up, but I still was not qualified for the Invitational. I started to put more time into my trainings. I would run in the morning before school and afterschool. My hard work had paid off because I got invited to the Arcadia Invitational. I was so happy and excited to compete in the meet. [Sadly, after the second track meet, I felt a great pain on my right leg, which turned out to be a hairline fracture on my right knee. I had to stop my track and field practices because of the pressure I put myself in caused me to have a hairline fracture.] Negative visualization of how I was not going to be invited to the Arcadia Invitational, motivated me to train harder. From my experience of achieving my goal to be invited to the Arcadia Invitational, my "negative visualization" motivates me to do better in my practices. Therefore, "negative visualization" can motivate people to change their attitude practices to achieve a positive outcome.

Burkeman also discusses how shock is a factor when having a positive visualization. This factor of shock relates to one of my experience during a volleyball game against Mountain View High School, in my junior year. Mountain View high school was known to be the easiest school to win against. My teammates and I were confident that this was going to be an easy game. We thought that there was no real competition so there was nothing to worry about. Knowing that we would win was a defeating outcome because unfortunately, we were wrong about the other team. We could not believe that we had lost. My teammates and I visualize the outcome of the game to be successful so we did not try as hard as we were supposed to. Ultimately, my experience concurs with Burkeman's claim on how "negative visualization" makes people happier than "positive visualization because if my teammates and I had though negatively about the outcome of the game we could have won the game or at least known what to expected. We would not have felt shocked and accepted out outcome.

In the essay "*The Benefits of Negative Visualization,*" Oliver Burkeman, argues about how "negative visualization" is more likely to make people happier than "positive visualization". I agree with the author's claim because of my own experiences. From my experience of thinking positively about the outcome of my scores on tests and winning the game. I would not have felt anxiety and fear of not passing my class and shocked that I didn't win the game. When I thought negatively about not being able to get invited to the Arcadia Invitational it motivated me to try harder. Overall, from my experiences, I believe that people need to negatively visualize a bad outcome to their problem or situation because it can motivate them to do better, reduce anxiety and fear, and help them to accept their outcome.

Assessment Questions

1. Does this essay have a directed summary that answers the first question in the writing topic?

2. Does this essay have a thesis statement that answers the second question in the writing topic?

3. Does this essay develop and support its thesis through strong body paragraphs that open with a topic sentence, and present specific examples that support that topic and tie back to the thesis? Evaluate the effectiveness of these examples: is each one detailed, easy to follow, and clearly relevant to the thesis and topic sentence?

4. Is the essay grammatically correct, well punctuated, and precisely worded, or do significant errors limit the essay's effectiveness?

5. Using the conventional standards presented in the scoring rubric in Part 1 of this book, what score does this essay deserve? Explain.

Second Student Response

The Law of Attraction claims that the energy sent into the world, whether good or bad, directly results in the events that will take place. Positive energy attracts positive outcomes and vice versa. Oliver Burkeman disagrees with this claim in "The Benefits of 'Negative Visualization'." According to Burkeman, negative visualization does not bring bad events to someone, rather it prepares someone if failure were to occur. As a result, there is a reduction of the anxiety that one would have had if they used positive visualization and received constant reassurance. As Burkeman mentions, the Stoics believe that tranquility is obtained by investigating negative emotions and experiences rather than running away from these thoughts and towards the more enjoyable scenario. Disregarding the fact that negative events can occur in a lifetime leads to a greater and more devastating shock if it actually were to occur. Negative visualization creates an open window to see all circumstances and allows us to be better prepared for the worst-case scenarios and be able to attain tranquility and less anxiety.

To strengthen his claim, Burkeman includes the state of mind of the Stoics. "For the Stoics the ideal state of mind is tranquility." (Burkeman 4). A way to get this feeling of calmness is by refusing to avoid negative situations. It is easy to ignore when something looks as if it will not turn out in one's favor, but it is the act of investigating these experiences rather than ducking away from them that brings less anxiety and more feelings of readiness and tranquility. I agree with the Stoics' advice because I believe that taking on negative emotions head on will relieve the pain that may come by having a feeling of acceptance of bad situations that are bound to occur. In James Clear's article "How to Be Happy When Everything Goes Wrong," Clear involves the devastating story of Rachelle Friedman, a woman who became paralyzed from the chest down after hitting her head in the shallow end of a pool. Rachelle's life changed dramatically due to her losing the ability to move, but she did not give up. Instead, she searched for a job, although there was difficulties finding one that would accommodate her new disability, she got married as planned, and had the mindset that it could have been a lot worse. She used negative visualization to see that her situation could have ended worse than it did and that allowed her to continue through life and have the feeling of peace with her condition. Accepting these bitter events and emotions guarantees a mat to soften the blow when you fall.

Another way to deal with emotions that come from a negative event is to imagine the loss of something you once adored because, strangely, it leaves you with more pleasure. Burkeman brings up the negative effect of getting used to things that once made us happy, which, through hedonic adaptation, is that these items begin to shift out of our main focus as any new valuables we obtain take a hold of the gears. Picture this: your family surprises you on your sixth birthday with a brand new puppy named Cheerio. As you take in all the glory and beauty of your new beloved pet, your older dog Honey Nut watches from inside of his cage. Your appreciation for Honey Nut transfers onto Cheerio as you rub the belly of your new pet that now overshadow Honey Nut, who used to get all your attention. In order to reverse this effect, Burkeman suggests, "Thinking about the possibility of losing something of value shifts it from the backdrop of our lives back to center stage, where it can deliver pleasure once more." (Burkeman 6). The idea that something could happen to Honey Nut allows you to realize the value of your older pup.

Positive reassurance creates more anxiety than negative visualization does. This is caused by the constant relief of the possibilities of anything bad ever happening, even though it is part of life to experience some negative events. A problem with positive visualization is that we confuse "imagining success with having already achieved it." (Burkeman 3). In my sophomore year of high school, my basketball team was warming up before our big game against one of our biggest competitors at Cresenta Valley High School. Apparently, according to multiple outside sources, CV had been playing horribly and were on a losing streak for some odd reason. We considered this a huge advantage and began playing the game as if their losing streak was supposed to continue, no matter how horribly my team would play. Our reassurance quickly ran around and kicked us in the butt when our two point lead was killed by a three-pointer they made at the buzzer. We lost the game by one point, but it took us a while to realize that we had just imagined that we already won the game and the reality was that we lost. We got positive reassurance from outside sources that clouded our playing ability because we were told that "we got this." This proves that positive reassurance doesn't allow for any possibilities of negative things to even be thought about. More disappointment comes if the reassurance was made up merely of false hope. Negatively viewing the situation would have made us play harder if we had only thought that there was a slight possibility that we could've lost the game we originally thought we had in the bag.

It is fine to think of the worst-case scenario when going into a risky situation because when something happens, it most likely will never be as bad as it was thought to turn out. "Confronting the worst-case scenario saps it of much of its anxiety-inducing power." (Burkeman 7). In the movie, "10 Things I Hate About You," the protagonist Kat only thought about the negative outcomes of her getting together with bad boy Patrick. This acknowledgement of negative possibilities allowed her to put her guard up and save herself from having a lot more hurt when she found out the truth about his intentions. Negative visualization created paths for her to see every direction that a certain scenario can lean towards.

Negative visualization creates an open window to see all circumstances and allows us to be better prepared for the worst-case scenarios and be able to attain tranquility. We must see the endless possibilities that may come from life and we have to learn to accept the fact that bad things may happen. This acceptance will reduce the shock and hurt we experience when we face these unwanted circumstances. "Ceaseless optimism about the future only makes for a greater shock when things go wrong." (Burkeman 5). Positive visualization creates temporary happiness, but creates even more disappointment if the situation does not gravitate towards the wanted end goal. Our society should imagine the possible ways in which situations will not go in our favor in order to gain peace with undesirable moments that are inevitable in this life full of ups and downs.

Works Cited

Burkeman, Oliver. "The Benefits of Negative Visualization." *The Antidote: Happiness for People Who Can't Stand Positive Thinking*, Canongate, 2013.

Clear, James. "The Impact Bias: How to Be Happy When Everything Goes Wrong." *James Clear*, 18 Sept. 2017, jamesclear.com/impact-bias.

Junger, Gil, director. *10 Things I Hate about You*. 1999.

Assessment Questions

1. Does this essay have a directed summary that answers the first question in the writing topic?

2. Does this essay have a thesis statement that answers the second question in the writing topic?

3. Does this essay develop and support its thesis through strong body paragraphs that open with a topic sentence, and present specific examples that support that topic and tie back to the thesis? Evaluate the effectiveness of these examples: is each one detailed, easy to follow, and clearly relevant to the thesis and topic sentence?

4. Is the essay grammatically correct, well punctuated, and precisely worded, or do significant errors limit the essay's effectiveness?

5. Using the conventional standards presented in the scoring rubric in Part 1 of this book, what score does this essay deserve? Explain.

Third Student Response

In the essay *The Benefits of "Negative Visualization"* the author Oliver Burkeman writes about the ways that negative visualization is more likely to make people happier than positive visualization. Some of the ways that negative visualization is more likely to make someone happier is that it helps reduce anxiety, another way is that it is great when you are trying to avoid the shock when things don't go according to plan. According to Burkeman's views it is better to have negative visualization because negative visualization helps create a more realistic view on things. When thinking about positive visualization it has been proven to make a less determined person, and according to Burkeman negative visualization makes someone more motivated to achieve their goal.

The first argument that Burkeman makes is that positive visualization can make people less likely to achieve their goal. In the essay Burkeman states, ". . . focusing on how well things can go . . . actually reduces most peoples motivation to achieve them." (1). What it means is that when someone visualizes themselves getting the perfect grade in an assignment they do not put in as much hard work as someone that knows that they are going to probably get a low grade or possibly fail the assignment. For a person to actually achieve success they must put in a lot of work so that they can get the score they worked for. In the other hand that one person who believe that they know what they are doing and put in less work and try less are going to get the lower grade because they visualize themselves getting the perfect grade. The negative visualization is going to work in the favor of the person with negative visualization because they are going to put in more effort for the better grade than the one that they visualize themselves actually getting, which is the lower grade. Having negative visualization helps that student have a more realistic view on the grade that they are going to get.

Another argument that Burkeman make about negative visualization is that it is better because it helps avoid the shock when things don't go the way that you visualize them. In the essay Burkeman sates, "Ceaseless optimism about the future only makes for a greater shock when things go wrong . . ." (2). This indicates is that when someone visualizes a bright and happy future where they have everything the makes a perfect life will be in shock when things don't go as they visualize. In the month of march when all the colleges are sending their acceptance letters to all the seniors many get those rejection letters from schools such as Harvard and Stanford to some it might not have been a shock because they were already knew but to other students they already visualize getting the acceptance letter so when they get denied they get the biggest shock of their life. That one person has put themselves so up the scale that they look down at others and when things don't go as they plan the fall hurts the most. In this type of situation there is a difference between positive visualization and determination that determine person would go through all the ins and outs to get in the other person is just seeing themselves getting the good grade so they get lazy and don't try at all. Another example would be the "American Dream" which in the 1960 it consisted of the job, the house, and the family. Many immigrated to America visualizing that they were going to automatically get that, not realizing the hard work that it consisted of. Those with negative visualization it helped because they knew that coming was going to be hard and they all ready visualize being in a small house fitting for a job that many also came to get. The reason why negative visualization is better because the future is unpredictable so visualizing the worse could possibly lead to having a more realistic future.

Reassurance can be a good thing or a bad thing. In a the good part of the reassurance is that if someone has cancer a good thing that the person can is to be there for them and keep on reassuring that if they fight that they will get through it. It could also create anxiety and as Burkeman states ". . . reassurance is a double-edge sword." (2). Many can come back and back just to feel as though they know that everything is going to be all right and. ". . . it requires constant maintenance . . ." (2) In a situation in which a close friends witnesses the separation of parents they go to you for reassurance and they will keep coming back for more because they know that you are going to be there for them. When there is no more reassurance by you because you are tired of constantly saying the same thing they can have anxiety. Sometime not giving a friend or love one can help them heal faster because they can help themselves have a more realistic view on what happened. That can happen because they are able to be happy that the worst case did not happened.

Many can ask what the true meaning of happiness is and what it means to actually be happy. Burkeman argues that, ". . . the ideal state of mind is tranquility . . . positive thinkers usually seem to mean when they use the word "happiness."" (2) I would categorize myself as a positive thinker personally because I know that every day I push myself to think positive so that I won't feel stress or sad. The way that Burkeman has categorized happiness made me think about the way that I want to always have my mind and to not have a cluttered mind. To be truly happy does not mean that you need to have positive visualization, it is to be in a state of mind that tranquil. Even having negative visualization can lead to happiness because visualizing the worst case scenario can lead someone to appreciate the little things more. An example would *be How to be happy when everything goes wrong* by James Clear states, ". . . extreme inescapable situations often trigger a response from our brain that increases positivity and happiness." (Clear 1) The way that the brain works is unique because having positive visualization is not what actually the worst cases scenario in their mind did not happened but that they have a calm mind because their good. Negative visualization creates a more realistic view on in this situation because imagining the worst scenario can have a person be calm because they could have been in a worst situation and have lost even more.

In conclusion Burkeman states that negative visualization is better because it helps create a more realistic point of view. If there is positive realization it makes someone less determined, it helps lessen the shock in it also may create anxiety. The difference between positive visualization ad positive thoughts is that with positive visualization you see good thing happen and positive thoughts you think about the good things and that may help people just go on. Negative visualization is better for a person because it helps create a more tranquil mind and that is what most would consider a happy person.

Assessment Questions

1. Does this essay have a directed summary that answers the first question in the writing topic?

2. Does this essay have a thesis statement that answers the second question in the writing topic?

3. Does this essay develop and support its thesis through strong body paragraphs that open with a topic sentence, and present specific examples that support that topic and tie back to the thesis? Evaluate the effectiveness of these examples: is each one detailed, easy to follow, and clearly relevant to the thesis and topic sentence?

4. Is the essay grammatically correct, well punctuated, and precisely worded, or do significant errors limit the essay's effectiveness?

5. Using the conventional standards presented in the scoring rubric in Part 1 of this book, what score does this essay deserve? Explain.

Fourth Student Response

"The Benefits of Negative Visualization" by Oliver Burkeman embraces a topic that is often overlooked. It elaborates on the theory that negative visualization in the daily life may provide more benefits than one might think. Contrary to popular belief, Burkeman argues that focusing on positive thoughts and hoping for the best case scenario of any situation may not be of much assistance. He uses Stoic philosophy and social experiments to support the idea that humans must accept negative thoughts and feelings to achieve the worldwide goal of true fulfillment and happiness. Overall, the author's views are properly defended and can prove to be useful when put into practice. However, Burkeman's advice also fails to analyze and warn about the negative reaction that a good portion of the population may face if they incorrectly tested this theory.

Authors such as Norman Vincent Peale who wrote an entire book on *The Power of Positive Visualization*, claim that being happy is as simple as becoming what you visualize yourself as. On the contrary, Oliver Burkeman makes an interesting and contradicting point. It is "that it's our relentless effort to feel happy, or to achieve certain goals, that is precisely what makes us miserable." (Burkeman 1) The author uses this as the first glimpse of his perspective on the topic which begins to attack the idea of positive visualization. To justify his dissenting opinion, Burkeman consults the school of philosophy of Stoicism. Stoics argue that "tranquility is to be achieved not by chasing enjoyable experiences but by cultivating a kind of calm indifference towards one's circumstances." (Burkeman 2) In other words, we must not push away our negative experiences but instead ruminate on them. The author then contemplates an experiment directed by psychologist Gabriele Oettingen as evidence towards this claim. The experiment consisted of workers who were instructed to positively visualize and achieve a successful week at work in contrast to the control group who was just told to reflect on that week. The group that was influenced by the positive visualization accomplished less than the control group. Burkeman concludes that "Spending time and energy focusing on how well things go, actually reduces most people's motivation to achieve them." (Burkeman 1) This meaning that once a person visualizes what it is like to succeed, they get caught up in this idea and forget to act upon it. An example of this sort of situation could be its effect on an athlete's performance. There are occasions where a high ranking athlete might rely on memories of past victories and imagine these same results on future events. They will recreate the image in their minds of them scoring the final point or being the first to cross the finish line and distort it so that it applies to an upcoming competition. This mentality will not advocate for the necessary motivation to work hard enough to create the same if not better results. Consequently, this athlete's overconfidence that is regularly considered as arrogance by society, will lead to their defeat.

The New Year's holiday is a time of cheerfulness and anticipation towards the oncoming year. 'Tis the season of the New Year's Resolution that is fun to participate in This popular tradition might be one of the most distinguishable cases where positive visualization ends in failure which is why many see it as a joke. During the festivities, individuals are so caught up in the joyous atmosphere that promotes pleasant thoughts and feelings that people want to conserve. A common New Year's resolution is planning to lose weight. Therefore, when a woman declares that she will lose a few pounds in the forthcoming year, her goal will be tied up to the ambiance of the holidays where she will imagine nothing but positive images of herself achieving this objective. She will visualize herself in her new and improved body and forget the obstacles that are attached to accomplishing it. The amount and strength of these visuals in her mind will make the brain carry this out as if she has already physically executed her goal and will fail to act upon it. Alternatively, this example will not convey such a huge impact on the woman's life because her realization of loss will be prolonged through out that year. Burkeman alerts us about an issue that will instantly affect the individual. "Ceaseless optimism about the future only makes for a greater shock when things go wrong. . . the positive thinker ends up being less prepared, and more acutely distressed, when things eventually happen that he or she can't persuade himself or herself to believe are good." (Burkeman 2) What he means by this is that when one visualizes only the most convenient situations, there is a greater disturbance to the individual when circumstances don't play out in their favor. For instance, when one loses a large sum of money, they will most likely face a great deal of mental trauma. This is why the author suggests "hedonic adaptation." This is when individuals place "sources of pleasure to the backdrop of our lives" and "regularly remind ourselves that we might lose any of the things we currently enjoy." (Burkeman 2) This will not only help reduce the stress and anxiety that comes with losing any of these goods but also compel us to appreciate them.

Though all the arguments made by the author have met more than exceptional standards, there is one concept Burkeman does not include in this excerpt from his book. He forgets about those who may not be raised to mentally sustain these ideas. There are people who will take negative visualization to an extreme measure which will completely undermine the motivation that it is supposed to produce. In a case such as that of college applications, Burkeman might argue that negatively visualizing the admissions process and imagining that you will not be accepted into any colleges, will bring greater joy once you are accepted into any of them and maybe even make you feel the gratitude that will motivate you into working hard on your studies. Unfortunately, based on personal experiences, there has been an occurrence where a friend did not apply to any universities because he believed that he would not be admitted in any of them. His fear of rejection did not even let him open an application because all he could visualize was these future-altering letters that would turn him down. This negative visualization most definitely did not benefit him.

All in all, negative visualization may change people's lives for the better. Burkeman reporting this undiscussed topic will allow us to appreciate what we have and aid us to prepare for our worst possible life situations through "hedonic adaptation" and the tranquil state of mind proposed by the Stoics. However, it must also be kept in mind that it does not apply to the entire population because everyone's brains work and develop completely differently and to others, it may produce the opposite effect and cause more harm.

Works Cited

Burkeman, Oliver. *The antidote: happiness of people who can't stand positive thinking.* Canongate, 2013.

Assessment Questions

1. Does this essay have a directed summary that answers the first question in the writing topic?

2. Does this essay have a thesis statement that answers the second question in the writing topic?

3. Does this essay develop and support its thesis through strong body paragraphs that open with a topic sentence, and present specific examples that support that topic and tie back to the thesis? Evaluate the effectiveness of these examples: is each one detailed, easy to follow, and clearly relevant to the thesis and topic sentence?

4. Is the essay grammatically correct, well punctuated, and precisely worded, or do significant errors limit the essay's effectiveness?

5. Using the conventional standards presented in the scoring rubric in Part 1 of this book, what score does this essay deserve? Explain.

Fifth Student Response

In Oliver Burkeman's essay, "The Benefits of Negative Visualization", he talks about the benefits of negative visualization. He describes this idea as a way to vision a negative scenario in order to recapture the contentment we seek. Negative visualization allows us to focus on all the things that could go wrong in order to appreciate things more. It allows us to think about the worst scenario and be able to over come that situation. This ideology allows us to enter this stage where we have inner peace with ourselves, since we have already imagined the feeling behind the negative outcome. Unlike positive visualization is a state of mind that sees everything positive and hopes to achieve what is reaching for. I agree with Burkeman's idea of negative visualization because thinking about the negative outcomes of a situation can help you focus you on the situation you are trying to achieve, instead of distracting you.

Everyone expects that if you visualize positive things then it will be positive outcomes will result. However, the fact is that at times it doesn't turn out like that. Negative visualization allows us to regain focus on the situation. It allows us to really to focus on the importance of it and makes us appreciate what we have. It was winter quarter when I was going through some personal problem. At some point I realize that I was going to not pass that quarter. I saw that I was not doing good in my Sociology class. It was that moment when I began to negative visualize. Our final was coming up and I knew that I wasn't trying my best to study for the exam. I knew that this was going to result in an F in that class. I began to negative visualize before the day of my midterm. I began to visualize my self not doing good in the exam. I saw myself going on I learn and checking my grade seeing the fail in the course. Then I visualize myself getting an email that I was on probation. At that moment I started getting really sad but I knew that If I already gone through the feelings then I wasn't going to be sad when I actually get the grade. I in fact did end up failing my class, which made me go on probation. I went on Winter break and as I visualized I went to check my grade and indeed I got the F and also an email saying that I was on probation. Since I had already visualized negatively I wasn't affected because that sad feeling I already had gone through it. I knew that was going to be the consequences of my actions. As you can see I didn't choose positive visualization because that would gotten me in a comfortable position, which is what I tried to avoid. If I think positive and it comes out negative then I would be very sad and not be happy like I have hoped. I would have ended very comfortable and not would have tried my best and would be disappointed in myself.

Using negative visualization actually did help me. Since I knew what was going to be the feeling of being on probation and getting an F it turns out it had a positive effect on me. I discovered that I was actually grateful for being able to have an opportunity to do better. My main focused that year was to do good because I didn't want to get kicked out. It actually changed me an impacted me in a beneficial way. I started going to my professor's office hours or ask my TA's questions. I did all these possible things to get good grades. At the end of spring quarter I raised my grade and passed all my classes with a passing grade. I finally received the grade I wanted. Negative visualization helps us understand the emotions before we make our own decisions.

Throughout life I always have thought that positive visualization was very beneficial. However, that not the case having that mentality actually makes you very comfortable with the situation. When this happens you start moving away from your set goal. You actually don't appreciate what you have. When I was small I knew my dad had a problem with alcohol. I grew up and I always knew he has this problem but it got to a point that it was getting out of control. I knew I had to do something for my emotional and mental health. I never wanted to think positive because the truth is that people like that don't actually turn to something positive, on the contrary turns out negative.

I knew that one day my dad was gong to die or get an illness. I began to use negative visualization. One day my dad didn't come back home. We were very worried and didn't know what had happened to him. I started visualizing him that he was in the hospital for some reason and that he was okay. That he was taken there because he had an epilepsy attack. I visualized that I was there and that he got a head surgery again for safety reason. It made me feel better because I actually visualized where he was and it made me feel calm that he was not dead. Days later the police came to tell us where my dad was hospitalized. I enter his room and saw him filled with tubes and that he was sleeping. I was in shocked at first but I just knew that this day was going to come sooner. or later. I was in peace because it could have been worse but thankfully he survived his stroke. Negative visualization helped me to be strong and in peace with myself because I already knew something like this incident was going to happen. I had to prepare myself. Although I already had negative visualization I couldn't hold it no more so I began to cry I didn't want to accept the fact that he was in this position. The nurse told us that he had suffered a big stroke. My heart dropped because I knew he was never going to be the same. Burkeman's idea showed us that negative visualization can reduce our anxiety to the max. In this case this it reduced my anxiety and it didn't make me paranoid. Think about like this we already have a piece of the cake before actually trying it.

Whether it's visualizing someone's death, losing a job, or failing a grade that should not be an excuse to not make it into positive. The ideology of negative visualization is for you have to realize what you got before its too late. Another way I use negative visualization to my benefit is when I see my grandpa. My grandpa is in an old age where he is not how he used to be. I grew up with him, so I'm very close to my grandpa. I always visualize what would happen if he were to die and not be able to see him anymore. I see myself without being able to ask him for advice or anything else. It gets me sad at some point but it actually worth thinking like that because it makes me value him more. It makes me feel for a second what would life be without him. Negative visualization makes me realize what I have and that every moment I am with my grandpa is. Who knows how long I will have my grandpa but just knowing to always spend time with him makes it more meaningful for him. Even though it seems a little harsh but it can happen it just reality.

Negative visualization actually makes us appreciate something or in some case reduce anxiety. We must realize that positive visualization doesn't help us achieve something but helps us feel satisfaction. You tend to feel that you are going to accomplish something and turn out like how you want it but if it doesn't turn out how you want it will have an effect on you. Therefore negative visualization will make you enter reality and see things how they are. Next time you analyze or encounter a situation what visualization will you pick?

Assessment Questions

1. Does this essay have a directed summary that answers the first question in the writing topic?

2. Does this essay have a thesis statement that answers the second question in the writing topic?

3. Does this essay develop and support its thesis through strong body paragraphs that open with a topic sentence, and present specific examples that support that topic and tie back to the thesis? Evaluate the effectiveness of these examples: is each one detailed, easy to follow, and clearly relevant to the thesis and topic sentence?

4. Is the essay grammatically correct, well punctuated, and precisely worded, or do significant errors limit the essay's effectiveness?

5. Using the conventional standards presented in the scoring rubric in Part 1 of this book, what score does this essay deserve? Explain.

Sixth Student Response

Throughout generations, people believed that having positive visualizations can make situations better, however when you are in a situation that gives you a negative outcome you become devastated. Oliver Burkeman in his essay, "The Benefits of "Negative Visualization'" discusses how negative visualization is more likely to make people happier than positive visualization. Burkeman supported that negative visualization makes an individual happier rather than positive visualization; he supported this claim by describing how spending time and focusing on how well things would go reduces one's motivation to achieve their goal. Tranquility gives individuals the opportunity to focus on negative emotions, positive thinkers are less prepared and more acutely distressed, "negative visualization" causes less stress, and being prepared for the worst-case scenario helps establish what to expect. When using negative visualization, it would be beneficial to use it to prepare oneself for the worst-case scenarios and to reduce both fear and anxiety. In regards to Burkeman's position, I can relate to the information he is presenting and apply it to my personal life. Therefore, I can strongly agree with his point of view that negative visualization is more likely to make an individual happier than positive visualization.

Before I tried out for Track and Field, I imagined myself getting a bad time running my mile, imagining how half way into the mile I would be puffing for air, my sides beginning to burn, and I would be struggling to breathe. This was something that was unnecessary for me to think about considering I would do the mile twice a week for regular physical education. When it came to throwing both the shot put and the discus I imagined myself struggling to pick up the eight-pound shot put and having it roll out of my hand because my fingers were not able to stand the weight of it. How I'd go pick up the discus and I'd be unable to hold on to it right, even if it was similar to a Frisbee. This then led me to visualize something even more severe than not being able to throw which was throwing it backwards and making a total fool of myself. When it came to jumps, I replayed in my head over and over again falling into the large sand pit, that looked as if I had the sand of the beach right on the school's track. I visualized myself landing on my feet, but landing so strong onto the sand pit that my feet would sink too low that gravity would drag me down. Replaying negative outcomes helped me minimize my anxiety by telling myself that not everything is negative, how many experiences can be taken as a learning lesson.

Burkeman did not mention that having negative visualization would help a person improve, but in my opinion it is helpful. Having the negative visual would allow the individual to fixate on the negative outcome which then would help them find various ways in improving themselves. Having the visualization that something negative would occur would allow people to concentrate on how to avoid a negative outcome. When try outs came around I did decent on my mile by learning techniques that would help with my breathing. I was able to throw both the shot put and discus forward, without either object falling from my hands, by watching videos on the technique necessary for each event. In jumps I did fall into the sand, but I was also the girl that did the best, and was approved by the coach. I was able to accomplish this because I would practice long jump on my front porch. In my scenario, I began with anxiety because I had the mentality that I would end up choking and doing bad, but having myself think of the anxiety actually reduced it. My anxiety was able to come down because I went to the try outs not thinking how well I was going to do, instead I chose to wing it and accept the outcomes that will come after. Thinking in this direction actually made me only believe that the worst-case scenario can happen, but as Burkeman mentioned that our idea in our mind is less likely to occur. Burkeman believed that thinking about the worst-case scenario would decrease individuals' stress.

Burkeman mentions in his essay reassurance can actually bring individuals more anxiety because a handful of individuals have the tendency to hold onto anxiety when it comes to the idea of reassurance. As mentioned in the essay, " . . . reassurance can actually exacerbate anxiety" (2). While many believe that reassurance may take some weight off of peoples' shoulders it would actually "tightening the coil of his anxiety" (3) as Burkeman mentioned. This would then lead to giving an individual advice and mentioning to them how the awful outcomes they are imaging would not happen. This would then make the individual receiving the reassurance believe if the most damaging result does happen then their life would be "ruined" in their eyes. A personal example would be when I had my first boyfriend. I was so caught up with young love that I would visualize myself being the best girlfriend material. Imagine myself picking him up from every downfall, helping him keep up with school work, and give him advice when he feels like he's falling short on something. When having this visualization, I had my mind set that everything would work out and that I had the perfect presentation of the person I wanted to be with him. He had the tendency of reassuring me that I was doing great and I was the one that encouraged him to improve every day.

One day when we had an argument about his actions and we tried to figure out a way to work it out, which I positively visualized as civil and calm. Sadly, I was in for a shock, when the argument escalated, we began to argue and everything we once ignored and sealed was brought up. After a few months of the same arguments we officially broke up, in my mind I knew that just because I believed everything would come out the perfect does not mean the outcome would be as imagined. Receiving his reassurance gave me warmth and the satisfaction that I was doing my part as a girlfriend. In my situation, having the positive visualization only gave me the mentality that everything would end up as I wish it would have, but I was short. When individuals lack the reassurance, they have the likelihood to start thinking about the worst-case scenario possible.

As human beings, we have a tendency of thinking about the most damaging outcome. As Burkeman mentioned, "But it is also true that, when they go wrong, they'll almost certainly go less wrong than we feared." (3). I myself have always had the mentality of believing the worst case scenario is going to happen, by doing this I give my emotions the time to adjust for something devastating. When my sister, Eufelia, and I got a phone call from my other sister, Liz, telling US that we need to go to the hospital she's been in a car accident. Hearing that I became so shocked that I began to visualize the worst. The main reason I expected the worst-case scenario was because both of my nieces were with her, a four-month-old and a two-year-old. I imagined my nieces extremely injured, with bruises and broken arms and needing surgery. When we arrived, my nieces were okay, they had gone through x-rays and they came out unharmed. One of my nieces did have an injury to her nose, but it was minor and only bruised. My smallest niece had no type of injury on her, since she was in a protective car seat. Liz on the other hand cracked her skull she was the one that had to go through extreme x-rays, but everything was alright. She only needed to get a few stitches that were going to be taken off within a week. Liz and my nieces only had a few injuries, nothing severe happened which relieved my emotions. Having the worst-case scenario on my mind made me over think the situation, when knowing that the worst didn't actually happened lifted the weight off my shoulders. Knowing that my mentality was ready for the worst actually made my anxiety go down. I knew if I had a positive visualization and the worst actually happened I would feel as if my life was ready to crumble and coming to an end.

Burkeman discussed how negative visualization can bring an individual more happiness rather than positive visualization. The reasons in which Burkeman agreed with this is because he believed that having a negative visualization would help individuals minimize their anxiety and also prepare them for the worst-case scenario. Looking back to Burkeman's point of view of negative visualization I can heavily say I agree. Since I was small I grew the mentality to always expect the worst because the best in never guaranteed. In many situations, it has worked in my advantage, so with this on my mind I have been able to adjust my emotions and handle what life has thrown in my direction.

Assessment Questions

1. Does this essay have a directed summary that answers the first question in the writing topic?

2. Does this essay have a thesis statement that answers the second question in the writing topic?

3. Does this essay develop and support its thesis through strong body paragraphs that open with a topic sentence, and present specific examples that support that topic and tie back to the thesis? Evaluate the effectiveness of these examples: is each one detailed, easy to follow, and clearly relevant to the thesis and topic sentence?

4. Is the essay grammatically correct, well punctuated, and precisely worded, or do significant errors limit the essay's effectiveness?

5. Using the conventional standards presented in the scoring rubric in Part 1 of this book, what score does this essay deserve? Explain.

Case Study #2: "What Management Doesn't Know"

The following case study is based on Devon Hackelton's "What Management Doesn't Know." Read the Hackelton essay and the student responses that follow. Evaluate the strengths and weaknesses of those responses using the scoring rubric that is in Part 1. A set of study questions follows each student essay to help you in evaluating its success.

WHAT MANAGEMENT DOESN'T KNOW

Devon Hackelton

Devon Hackelton graduated from California Polytechnic University, Pomona (1997) with an MA in rhetoric and composition. He has taught at UCR since 2001, most recently in the University Writing Program. Before his teaching career, he worked a variety of blue-collar jobs for eighteen years, from serving chicken to cleaning medical clinics to repairing industrial air conditioners while attending high school and college, and later while teaching college level classes part-time. In his spare time, he enjoys online gaming and writing poetry. His most recent poems, "A Reflection" and "Common Threads," have appeared in Spring 2012 issue of the Pomona Valley Review.

I worked as an "engineer" for a retail mall for fourteen years, painting and repairing the infrastructure of a one million square foot complex and the surrounding forty-three acres. During my employment, twelve different mall managers came and went. None of these managers had ever worked as a security guard, janitor or repair technician: all of them had college degrees, mostly in business, but even then, only a few had ever worked as a retail salesperson. They knew about compliance issues, bottom lines, and revenue enhancements, but they didn't know the first thing about operating a floor buffer, apprehending a shoplifter, replacing an air conditioner motor or selling culottes. They learned about customer service at training seminars and paraded the employees into the office once a month to remind us we should look neat and presentable, and we should stop whatever we were doing if a customer needed assistance.

One day, my boss sent me to the food court to fix a leaky hydraulic line in the trash compactor. Now this compactor was about the size of a semi trailer and it was full of discarded pizza, burgers, ice cream, chow mein, soda, napkins, paper towels from the restroom, and countless other bits of rotten refuse. And to get to the leaky hose, I had to enter the back of the machine where all of the grease and sludge had accumulated over the years. Every time I leaned in to disconnect or connect the hoses, some part of my body or clothing would come into contact with that feral slime until, by the time the hose was changed, I was a walking, stinking mess. As soon as I finished, my manager called me over the two-way radio to help a customer who had dropped his keys in an elevator shaft. I told my boss that I was dirty, but he said it was an emergency and questioned how dirty could I get by working on the compactor. After all, he said, the outside of the compactor was hosed down daily. So I went to help the customer, who was already upset and even more upset when he caught a whiff of me. Within an hour, the very same manager who ordered me to fix the compactor and then ordered me to help the customer threatened to fire me for my appearance. The next day I called in sick; in reality, I had stayed awake all night visualizing different methods of revenge.

Sadly, disconnects like the one between my boss and I occur regularly in the business world, sometimes with deadly results. In unrelated incidents between July 2nd and 9th, 2003, three Midwestern employees killed a total of ten coworkers, injured thirteen others, and took their own lives. All three were targeting bosses or supervisors. The U.S. Bureau of Labor Statistics reports that 709 people were murdered on the job in 1998 and 106 of those people were killed by employees or former employees. While most employee-employer conflicts are not this severe, immeasurable working hours are lost annually due to a lack of understanding and communication between workers and managers.

Communication breakdowns occur, in part, because managers do not understand their employees' jobs and associated stresses. In the last thirty years, most businesses have ended hiring management internally; gone are the hopes of starting in the mailroom and one day being the CEO of a corporation. Fast food restaurants, interestingly, are an exception. Most fast food managers have cooked and cleaned and taken customer orders and unloaded trucks. They know what concerns their employees face in any given task, and the managers are able to offer suggestions and better assign certain employees to certain tasks based on the managers' prior experiences, undoubtedly saving their companies money and allowing for a more smoothly operating workplace.

The only other industry that trains its workforce similarly is education. Teachers know what it means to be a student and know the particular hardships and stresses students face. Students are more likely to complete assignments because they know that their teachers have been assigned and have completed similar tasks in the past. This shared understanding creates a level of respect between student and instructor.

Unfortunately, this respect is seldom found in other professions. Currently, there is a cyclic trend of employees not being promoted to management because they lack some requisite educational degree. Managers and supervisors are hired straight out of college and have little or no understanding of the workings of a company. Strangers make decisions without input from the employees and the employees begin to be suspicious or resentful of management. Then, when there is an opportunity for an employee to advance into management, the employee often refuses to take it in fear of being seen as one of *them*. For instance, one of my relatives has worked for a large railroad for over thirty years. He started as a brakeman, and is now a conductor. His next step should have been engineer and then a possible move into management; however, he chose not to be promoted. Management to him is a dirty word: he says supervisors are book-learned idiots who have no idea about the physical work or dangers involved with operating a two hundred ton locomotive hauling fifty freight cars at seventy miles per hour. He and his co-workers take pleasure in stretching a three-hour job into twelve hours because they are "following the asinine rules of management." He has a plan to increase productivity and cut costs, but when asked why he doesn't present his plan to his bosses, my father-in-law argues that nobody would listen to an uneducated conductor. Instead, he and his cohorts stay bitter, freight moves slowly, business costs increase, and top railroad executives hire new college graduates who have never worked on a train to create cost cutting plans.

It is time for a change. Businesses and corporations should strive to look internally when filling management positions. Bosses should possess some hands-on experience in a variety of jobs that are a part of the business, maybe by working in different departments, even for a short time, before assuming their supervisor role. Workers deserve the reassurance that comes with knowing their bosses understand and have experienced the workers' duties. It just makes ethical and financial sense.

Writing Topic

Why does the author believe managers should have hands-on experience in a variety of jobs that are part of the business before holding supervisor positions? Do you feel that his argument is valid? Support your response using examples from your own experience, observations, and readings.

First Student Response

In the essay "What Management Doesn't Know," the author explains his opinion on the management position. The author explains that managers should get chosen based on experience. Many people may have a great education, but without experience the manager may not understand his/her employees. Another reason for experienced managers is, because they know how to deal with many situations because they themselves have gone through them. The author also states that managers with higher education intimidate those with less education. The authors point of view is valid. If these were managers who could understand their employers communication would be higher. They would also know not to pressure their employers because that can cause a lot of stress in the working environment.

My father works in the Post Office as an electronic technician. He has applied for the supervisors position many times. Every time someone else with less experience get the position because he/she has a higher degree. They may be more educated but they do not know how things work. In order to fix a machine a person needs as much time, depending on how big or small the machine may be, in order to fix it. The person in the higher position may not understand and request something else to be done, yet he/she will want it done quickly. My dad says that he was working on a machine and that his supervisor asked him to work on another machine. My dad went to work on the other machine like an hour later because the machine he was fixing prior to that is much larger. His supervisor got mad and said that he was messing around with the other machine. The supervisor made this big problem that could have been avoide if he/she knew what was going on.

Assessment Questions

1. Does this essay have a directed summary that answers the first question in the writing topic?

2. Does this essay have a thesis statement that answers the second question in the writing topic?

3. Does this essay develop and support its thesis through strong body paragraphs that open with a topic sentence, and present specific examples that support that topic and tie back to the thesis? Evaluate the effectiveness of these examples: is each one detailed, easy to follow, and clearly relevant to the thesis and topic sentence?

4. Is the essay grammatically correct, well punctuated, and precisely worded, or do significant errors limit the essay's effectiveness?

5. Using the conventional standards presented in the scoring rubric in Part 1 of this book, what score does this essay deserve? Explain.

Second Student Response

In "What Management Doesn't Know", Devun Hackleton writes about the communication breakdowns that occur because management doesn't understand their employee's jobs and associated stresses. The author believes that managers should have hands-on experience in a variety of jobs that are part of the business before holding supervisor positions. Managers need hands-on experience so they make correct judgements and decisions, because college degrees can't be substituted for years of experience.

An example of management having experience amounting to a successful business is my father. My father has been in the tire business for 35 years. He started as a mechanic for a large company and through experience, worked his way to the top. After working for many different companies, he gained the experience and opened his own shop. He is an example of effective management because he can do every operation his employees are capable of, and he is always aware of what goes on in his shop. He is capable of overseeing and understanding everything that is done in the shop and is always there to troubleshoot.

Today, companies who are hiring, are making too much emphasis on the education that their future employees hold. For management positions, experience is far more important than the level of education one holds. For management that lacks experience in the field, the basis of the decisions are blind because they are unaware of the circumstances. The management doesn't understand what goes on and shouldn't be able to make decisions that can affect others. For example, in the essay, the mall manager had no idea of the cleanliness of the trash compactor but still sent the author to aid another customer while he was filthy. This shows the lack of knowledge or absent mind of the management because they really don't know what is going on.

The author is correct where he states that companies should fill management jobs internally. Not only does this allow employees to earn higher positions that they have worked hard for, but also allows for effective management. An example of an efficient and lucrative business is the world of fast food. People need to start at the bottom of the chain and work their way up to become apart of management. This situation allows the management to understand and have experienced the worker's duties. If management understands and respects the other employees, there will be a mutual respect which allows for a more efficient workplace.

Managers who have never been in a certain business have no idea what is going on and how to deal with problems. No wonder why employees either hate or plot to kill their bosses due to their ignorance of situations. In order for their to be a safe, lucrative, and efficient business there needs to be management with experience.

Assessment Questions

1. Does this essay have a directed summary that answers the first question in the writing topic?

2. Does this essay have a thesis statement that answers the second question in the writing topic?

3. Does this essay develop and support its thesis through strong body paragraphs that open with a topic sentence, and present specific examples that support that topic and tie back to the thesis? Evaluate the effectiveness of these examples: is each one detailed, easy to follow, and clearly relevant to the thesis and topic sentence?

4. Is the essay grammatically correct, well punctuated, and precisely worded, or do significant errors limit the essay's effectiveness?

5. Using the conventional standards presented in the scoring rubric in Part 1 of this book, what score does this essay deserve? Explain.

Third Student Response

In the essay "What Management Doesn't Know," the author describes the lack of communication between employers and employees and the lack of hands-on experience of many employers. He writes that if employers don't have any experience in the fields they're managing, there is a lack of communication with the employees. Managers do not know the kind of stress and dangers their employees go through every day. This problem occurs because managers and supervisors are hired straight out of college and do not know the workings of a company. Many are also hired straight out of college to create cost-cutting plans. They have no idea how the field works and do not create the most cost effective plans. Employees who have been in the field for a long time are the best for management because of the experience and the knowledge of the tasks involved in the field. Manager should understand and experience the work of their employees before taking the role of a supervisor. I agree with the author's argument because I have been employed in a case where the manager had no hands-on experience and in a case where he did.

Employers should have experience in the jobs of a business before becoming supervisors. I have been employed in a flower distributing company as a filing clerk and the jobs that were given to me were just ridiculous. My manager had no experience in the jobs that I did and was actually hired out of college. There was one task he gave me that really showed he did not understand the difficulties involved in the job. I was told to organize a large file cabinet that was so ridiculously unorganized that not even my manager knew what to do. The files were thrown everywhere with no labels whatsoever. I wasn't familiar with the documents in the cabinet, and my manager didn't realize that the files were impossible to organize. He kept hurrying me and telling me he needed the files organized in a short amount of time. After a few days, my co worker talked to the manager and I was relieved of the job. I saw that the manager wasnt happy but I also knew he had no idea what the difficulties were in the task. I continued to work there and began to realize that the managers did not communicate with their employees and many people were not happy with the way they were treated. This experience definitely shows I agree with the author's position that higher positions should have experience in the field before handling the job as supervisor.

Managers with experience are more communicative and understanding than those without. My second job involved a lot of lifting and moving of heavy boxes. Not only was it strenuous but the warehouse was extremely hot. My manager always told me to take breaks and drink water. He understood the difficulties of the tasks I was doing because he was doing the same tasks before he hired employees. He knew that it was impossible to work in the heat and offered to help me when I needed help. It made the job much easier for me because I had no problems or difficulties with the job. There was a lot of communication between me and my manager. My manager also knew a lot about the business and the most beneficial ways for the company. He knew exactly what to do to keep the employees happy and did his best to keep the company strong. The people with handson experience are better for high positions than those highered straight out of college.

I was much happier at my second job and I agree that managers should have some experience in the field they are supervising. It is essential to the company and for the wellbeing of the employees. The author's argument is definitely valid because I have personally experienced his position on the issue.

Assessment Questions

1. Does this essay have a directed summary that answers the first question in the writing topic?

2. Does this essay have a thesis statement that answers the second question in the writing topic?

3. Does this essay develop and support its thesis through strong body paragraphs that open with a topic sentence, and present specific examples that support that topic and tie back to the thesis? Evaluate the effectiveness of these examples: is each one detailed, easy to follow, and clearly relevant to the thesis and topic sentence?

4. Is the essay grammatically correct, well punctuated, and precisely worded, or do significant errors limit the essay's effectiveness?

5. Using the conventional standards presented in the scoring rubric in Part 1 of this book, what score does this essay deserve? Explain.

Fourth Student Response

In "What Management Doesn't Know", Devin Hackleton explains how managers should have experiences within the particular business before becoming a manager or supervisor. It is not fair for the employees to take orders from a manager that do not even know what to do. A lot of times, managers or supervisors are hire due to the amount of education they have. They may not be experienced and definitely lack skills on the smaller jobs of the company. Even if the managers hold a high position, it does not mean they are well experience or train for the job. What makes these managers different from employees is that managers receive much more education then employees. I believe that Hackelton's argument on managers having more experience within the business before having them promote to higher positions is valid because managers are suppose to know more then the employees.

If managers are hire immediately after they graduate from college, they lack experience and also skills regarding the job. For example, when I was working in a dentist office last summer, my manager was a girl that just graduated from college. She was hired a couple of months after the office hired me. My new manager have no idea on how to manage an office. Therefore, I had to teach her and assisted her on what to do. It did not make any sense to me that I have to listen to someone that knew less then me on what to do in the office. Hackleton states in his essay, "Managers and supervisors are hired straight out of college and have little or no understanding of the workings of a company." It is not reasonable that a complete stranger can become a manager immediately. Where employees do not even get promoted or received a higher raise. Being a manager does not mean they need more education then the employees in the company, but it means that these managers need to have more experiences then the employees. I felt that I had the role of a manager instead, yet I still get pay minimum wage. Also, a lot of times, I had to worked overtime in order to help my so-called manager finish her work.

Managers or supervisors should always start off at the company as employees, and then get promote to a higher position. For example, I used to worked at the doctor's office. My manager was a mid-thirties woman who is extremely intelligent within the company. She knows everything regarding the company. When I was hired, she helped me and assisted me on everything possible. I was amazed on how much information she knew and she was able to train me into a good assistant. Since she used to be an assistant in the office, she knew all the stress I was going through. There was a lot of paperwork and other office-related things to do. Hackleton states, "Communication breakdowns occur because managers do not understand their employee's jobs and associated stresses." Since my manager been through what I was currently going through, she guided me throughout the time I was working there. I am glad that my manager was experienced in the business, because otherwise no one else could had assisted me in the office.

Managers or supervisors should be well-trained and experienced in the company before they get a promotion. The job system in the company should be rank from employees to managers. I do not think it is fair for employees to listen to a complete stranger at work, where the employees will not feel secure. Most of the time, managers will lack skills regarding the business they may be working for. It will make much better sense if an employee is promoted to a manager position because this former employee have experience and been through a long period of training.

Assessment Questions

1. Does this essay have a directed summary that answers the first question in the writing topic?

2. Does this essay have a thesis statement that answers the second question in the writing topic?

3. Does this essay develop and support its thesis through strong body paragraphs that open with a topic sentence, and present specific examples that support that topic and tie back to the thesis? Evaluate the effectiveness of these examples: is each one detailed, easy to follow, and clearly relevant to the thesis and topic sentence?

4. Is the essay grammatically correct, well punctuated, and precisely worded, or do significant errors limit the essay's effectiveness?

5. Using the conventional standards presented in the scoring rubric in Part 1 of this book, what score does this essay deserve? Explain.

Index